Ex Parte Milligan Reconsidered

Ex Parte Milligan Reconsidered

RACE AND CIVIL LIBERTIES FROM THE LINCOLN ADMINISTRATION TO THE WAR ON TERROR

Edited by
Stewart L. Winger and Jonathan W. White

University Press of Kansas

Published by the University Press of Kansas (Lawrence, Kansas 66045), which was organized by the Kansas Board of Regents and is operated and funded by Emporia State University, Fort Hays State University, Kansas State University, Pittsburg State University, the University of Kansas, and Wichita State University.

Library of Congress Cataloging-in-Publication Data

Title: Ex parte Milligan reconsidered : race and civil liberties from the Lincoln administration to the war on terror / Stewart L. Winger, Jonathan W. White.
Description: Lawrence : University Press of Kansas, 2020. | Includes index.
Identifiers: LCCN 2019045951 ISBN 9780700629367 (cloth) ISBN 9780700629374 (epub)
Subjects: LCSH: War and emergency powers—United States—Congresses. | Civil rights—United States—History—Congresses. | Executive power—United States—History—Congresses. | Civil supremacy over the military—United States—History—Congresses. | Courts-martial and courts of inquiry—United States—History—Congresses. | War on Terrorism, 2001–2009—Congresses. | Milligan, Lambdin P.—Trials, litigation, etc.
Classification: LCC KF5060 .A75 2016 | DDC 343.73/0143—dc23
LC record available at https://lccn.loc.gov/2019045951.

British Library Cataloguing-in-Publication Data is available.

Printed in the United States of America

10 9 8 7 6 5 4 3 2 1

The paper used in this publication is recycled and contains 30 percent postconsumer waste. It is acid free and meets the minimum requirements of the American National Standard for Permanence of Paper for Printed Library Materials Z39.48–1992.

Contents

Illustrations

Foreword

This elegant volume transforms current debates over civil liberties by listening carefully to the past. The focal point is *Ex parte Milligan,* a landmark decision involving a conspiracy against the US government in 1864, at the very end of the Civil War. The accused men, including Lambdin P. Milligan, for whom the case is named, supported the Confederacy, although they lived within the United States, in Indiana, where the events also unfolded. During the war, President Abraham Lincoln used war powers to deal with dissent to the war effort, which allowed federal authorities to step in and bypass the usual procedures in civilian courts. So Milligan and his compatriots wound up in a military court, where they were convicted. On appeal, the US Supreme Court sided with the convicted conspirators, ruling that it was unconstitutional to try US citizens in military tribunals when civilian courts were still in operation, as they were in Indiana. The military's jurisdiction only applied in areas that were actually at war with the United States: Indiana was not one of those places. After the war, critics of Reconstruction pointed to the case as an example of the Republican Party's abuse of federal power. In the realm of law, though, *Ex parte Milligan* quietly faded away—until recently, when legal scholars reached for it as a precursor to debates over the expansion of federal authority in the country's never-ending war on terror after the attack on the World Trade Center on September 11, 2001. To those unschooled in history, the questions in the case seem timeless. In 1864, as in the current context, they involved the relationship between the individual liberties outlined in the Bill of Rights and the authority of the federal government to check them in the name of protecting the safety and well-being of the larger community. *Ex Parte Milligan Reconsidered* disrupts that assumption, revealing the connections between the past and present to be far less linear and far more revealing,

In fact, to say that *Ex Parte Milligan Reconsidered* is just about that one case vastly understates the book's scope. The editors, Stewart L. Winger and Jonathan W. White, have brought together a group of original, wide-ranging chapters that reach beyond the four corners of the case as decided by the US Supreme Court and lay out the broader historical context that produced it and shaped its implications. The results reframe our understanding of the Civil War and the institutional history of the legal system as well as the trajectory of civil liberties. As the chapters in this volume suggest, *Ex parte Milligan* says as much about enduring political conflicts within the United States as it does about the endless war on terror.

Ex parte Milligan seems prescient now—as if the past was speaking directly to issues in our own time. The chapters in *Ex Parte Milligan Reconsidered* hold up a cautionary hand. As they show, the *text* of *Ex parte Milligan* misconstrues the legal *context* of the time. The civil liberties that now mean so much to us were not really at stake in the Civil War era, because they did not yet exist in the form that they do today.

The editors begin by reminding us that the case was an anomaly in its own time. In general terms, people in the nineteenth century could not reach for the Bill of Rights to protect their civil liberties, because those amendments were more narrowly construed, as was the reach of federal authority. To the extent that the things we now call civil liberties were protected at all in the decades before the Civil War, it was by states, which listed out protected rights in their constitutions and which took the lead in defining the legal status of the people who lived within their borders. Those powers were why some states permitted slavery and others did not. As this volume shows, neither *Ex parte Milligan* nor the wartime restrictions put in place by President Lincoln did much to change that situation. Change came after the war, with the Reconstruction amendments—the Thirteenth, Fourteenth, and Fifteenth—and related legislation, which did place limits on states' ability to withhold rights from US citizens, particularly people of African descent. Even then, federal oversight applied to states' application of rights. States still retained the authority to define what those rights were and to limit their distribution, if it was in the public interest or if the people whose rights they were restricting—such as women—were not protected by the Reconstruction amendments. It was not until the twentieth century that the amendments we now call the Bill of Rights were reinterpreted to establish freedom of speech and other civil liberties.

As the chapters in the volume show, *Ex parte Milligan* was less about civil liberties as we now define them and more about other kinds of liberties that we now take for granted, namely basic rights. The Civil War promised to transform the legal order through the abolition of slavery, which transferred property rights from their masters to enslaved people. Abolition necessarily involved the extension of other basic rights deemed necessary to operate in American society: to marry, to claim one's own children, to move freely, to own property, to enter into contracts, to access the courts, and even to vote. If anything, those liberties were far more contentious than the ones decided in *Ex parte Milligan.* They not only drove secession but also inspired dissent within the United States during the Civil War. Milligan and his compatriots, like other Confederate sympathizers in the United States, did not just oppose the war effort or the Republican Party; they also opposed abolition. More to the point, they saw the recognition of African Americans' rights as an infringement of their own liberties, which flowed from a legal order that sanctioned white supremacy and gave all white people authority over all African Americans, even in states that had abolished slavery. Many white people in the United States as well as the Confederacy experienced the recognition of African Americans' rights as a denial of their rights.

This point, which the volume makes with compelling clarity, is profound. The civil liberties that mattered to Milligan and his co-conspirators were the rights that they sought to withhold from African Americans. That was why they opposed the war effort, as led by the Republican Party. Histories of the Civil War have long downplayed opposition within the United States to the war effort as inconsequential, partisan bickering. *Ex Parte Milligan Reconsidered,* by contrast, suggests that such opposition was a clear and present danger. Both popular and academic histories have sidestepped that issue, locating opposition to abolition and racial equality among white people within the states of the former Confederacy. But, as the chapters in this volume indicate, white supremacy was a national phenomenon, not a regional one.

This perspective of the legal terrain changes our understanding of the history and trajectory of civil liberties. When the focus is inward, on the legal issues debated within cases like *Ex parte Milligan,* the questions center on the relationship between individuals and the federal government. Civil liberties become not only a given but also an obvious good, on which everyone agreed. The identity of those individuals is irrelevant, because they are interchangeable: civil liberties apply to them all. The main point of conflict is with the federal government, which is the entity that intervenes to place limits on those liberties. The legal question, then, is how far the federal government can go with those limitations, without crossing over into unconstitutional territory.

By broadening the focus to take in the legal order that gave rise to the case, *Ex Parte Milligan Reconsidered* reveals how artificial that construction of civil liberties is. For Milligan and others like him, the federal government was the problem. But for African Americans at the time, it was the solution, because people like Milligan were the problem. Military officials not only disciplined those, like Milligan, who opposed the war effort but also intervened on behalf of African Americans in the states of the former Confederacy, both during and immediately after the war. During Reconstruction, federal authority was extended in an effort to safeguard African Americans' rights. The meaning of those rights, moreover, was never a given. Milligan and other whites like him saw a legal order that included expansive rights *over* African Americans. That was a definition of rights and liberties that African Americans and Reconstruction-era Republicans sought to end.

The volume then follows the implications into the present, using *Ex parte Milligan* to consider the changes in civil liberties and conflicts over them. As the authors show, the case did point to the future: one where the Bill of Rights would play a larger role in defining the civil rights of all Americans and where those rights would expand in new areas. But that path was long, steep, and rocky. To get where we are today—a place where we can talk about civil liberties as if they always existed—required determination, struggle, and bloodshed. *Ex Parte Milligan Reconsidered* reveals that difficult history, one that makes us appreciate the liberties that we have. That history also goes a long way in explaining why the extension of rights to previously marginalized groups has been—and still is—so contentious. Civil liberties were never a "thing" that people could simply pick up and claim. They were created by people, with the necessary backing of government authority—authority that was actually exercised at the behest of the people. No wonder civil liberties have been so contested. The legal issues are part and parcel of the ongoing debate about what liberty is about, who should have it, and what America stands for.

Laura F. Edwards

Acknowledgments

This book was the result of an academic conference at Illinois State University in September 2016 entitled "*Ex Parte Milligan* at 150: The Constitution & Military Commissions in American Wars on Terror." We especially wish to acknowledge Dr. Meghan Leonard of the Illinois State University Department of Politics and Government for her unswerving dedication, hard work, and wise counsel. Without her the conference would not have been possible. It is a pleasure also to acknowledge the conference participants who enlivened the conversation during, between, and after the sessions, and to thank the individuals and organizations who made the conference possible through their financial support: Robert J. Lenz, the Illinois State University History Department, the David Davis Mansion Foundation, the Abraham Lincoln Association, the Illinois State University Foundation, the Fell Trust, the Sage Foundation, the We the People Program, the Illinois Center for Civic Education, and the Constitutional Rights Foundation Chicago. Special thanks go to the Illinois State University Provost's Research and Graduate Studies, the Colleges of Arts and Sciences, and the History Department for their generous book subvention.

Special thanks as well go to our editor at the University Press of Kansas, David Congdon, for his enthusiastic support of the book project. We are also extraordinarily grateful to Thomas Mackey of the University of Louisville and Howard Ball of the University of Vermont for their kind and generous reading of the manuscript.

Introduction

Ex Parte Milligan at 150—The Constitution and Military Commissions in American Wars on Terror

Stewart L. Winger

This volume originated with a conference held at Illinois State University in 2016 titled "*Ex parte Milligan* at 150: The Constitution and Military Commissions in American Wars on Terror." The title of course presumed we contextualize the Civil War and especially Reconstruction as a "war on terror." Though one might reasonably contest the analogy, it seems fair to assert that before and especially after Appomattox, terrorist insurgencies rose to halt the assertion of black freedom by the Republican Party, the Union Army, and African Americans themselves.

For some, particularly in the George W. Bush administration, the war on terror of the early twenty-first century seemed unprecedented, calling for a rethinking of international law and American constitutionalism from top to bottom, from *jus ad bellum* to *jus in bello,* from an acceptance of "preemptive war" to a redefinition of torture. But in our reigning interpretation of Reconstruction, Eric Foner long ago attributed the failure to establish adequate freedom for African Americans during Reconstruction in good part to terrorism. No other factor "would have proved decisive, without the campaign of violence that turned the electoral tide in many parts of the South, and the weakening of Northern resolve, itself a consequence of social and political changes that undermined the free labor and egalitarian precepts at the heart of reconstruction policy."[1] Terrorist insurgencies rose after Appomattox to halt the imposition of black freedom by the Republican Party and by African Americans themselves. Like the Taliban in Afghanistan, they waited out the resolve of the Republican Party and the Union Army. Indeed, the renewed use by the Supreme Court of *Ex parte Milligan* as a precedent in our current war on terror suggests that, rather than facing entirely unprecedented circumstances, in fact we have been here before.

In his Pulitzer Prize–winning book *The Fate of Liberty,* Mark E. Neely Jr. in 1991 argued that *Milligan* was "irrelevant."[2] In *Ex parte McCardle* the Supreme Court declined the opportunity to strike down the use of military commission trials, thus *seeming* to open the way for their further use in the South during Reconstruction. (In fact, as John Lupton's chapter in this book explains, precisely the opposite happened.) Then in the late nineteenth century, prevailing legal opinion sided with the Chase opinion and even the Lincoln administration: the amendments granting trial by jury had to be construed in light of the rest of the Constitution, which vested the war power with Congress.[3]

Fittingly holding the Lieber Chair of Political Science at Columbia University, John W. Burgess remarked in 1890 that if *Milligan* were ever subjected to the strain of actual war, it would necessarily be disregarded. In 1891 Sydney George Fisher, later author of *The Evolution of the Constitution of the United States* (1897), said it was

> generally admitted that when a government is attacked by rebellion it is impossible for it to protect itself from conspirators and assassins if every one of them has to be taken before a court of law and proved guilty beyond a reasonable doubt. In such a crisis some arbitrary power must be given. . . . To preserve the balance between liberty of the citizen and the safety of the government is one of the great problems of political science.[4]

As Chief Justice Chase had reminded the Court in *Milligan,* Lincoln himself had been a victim of precisely such a conspiracy.[5] *Ex parte Milligan,* argued Neely, was in eclipse.

The reputation of *Milligan* rebounded somewhat in the 1920s. In response to the actions of the Wilson administration, what we now think of as First Amendment free speech rights were slowly carved out, essentially for the first time. In 1923 the concurrent development of civil libertarianism more generally led Charles Warren to describe *Milligan* as "one of the bulwarks of American Liberty." Nevertheless, Warren himself suggested that classifying civilian defendants as "war spies" would allow the use of trial by military commission.[6]

When the chips were down, Neely argued, *Milligan* remained irrelevant. In *Milligan,* Justice Davis had held that military commission trials could not replace civilian trials when courts were open and where there was no war. In his sweeping opinion, threatened invasion was not sufficient. The invasion had to be actual. Neely cited a case involving the Roosevelt administration policy, in the wake of the surprise attack on Pearl Harbor, of interning Japanese immigrants and Japanese-American citizens on the West Coast during World War II. The argument on behalf of the government given by Colonel Charles Fairman of the judge advocate general's staff seems to have persuaded the judge in the case. "When one considers certain characteristics of modern war—mobility on land, surprise from the air, sabotage, and the preparation of fifth columns—it must be apparent that the dictum that 'martial law cannot arise from a threatened invasion' is not an adequate definition of the extent of the war power of the United States."[7]

Neely might also have cited *Ex parte Quirin,* a case involving Nazi saboteurs during World War II in which the Roosevelt administration used a military commission to try, convict, and sentence to death eight conspirators, two of whom were US citizens.[8] (Two of the sentences were commuted.) The courts were open and there was "no war" in the sense that Davis had meant it, because there was no actual invasion. Yet because the defendants were unlawful enemy combatants, the *Quirin* Court sanctioned the use of military commissions.

Davis's grounds for denying Milligan's belligerent status were questionable, leading to considerable confusion in later case law.[9] Conveniently enough, the Court in *Quirin* simply accepted at face value Davis's characterization of Milligan as a nonbelligerent and then distinguished Quirin's situation, holding that in contrast to Milligan, Quirin and his fellow conspirators were "unlawful combatants" who had offended against the laws of war.[10] The Court upheld the use of military commissions in *Quirin* and limited the *Milligan* requirement of a civilian trial to what we now call noncombatants. For combatants, the laws of war or international law prevailed rather than the US Constitution as construed in the Davis opinion. (Since the 1916 Articles of War had authorized military commissions to try violations of the laws of war, the *Quirin* decision did not speak to the question of naked presidential authority versus congressional power raised by the Chase concurrence.) Historian Curtis Bradley concluded, "The Supreme Court largely disregarded *Milligan* in *Quirin, Korematsu,* and *Hamdi.*"[11] Neely might well have added that in these cases too, *Milligan* had been rendered "irrelevant."

Since Neely's *The Fate of Liberty* of 1991, however, and particularly since the War on Terror and the invasions of Afghanistan and Iraq, two related developments, one in constitutional law itself and another in the field of history, made a reconsideration of *Ex parte Milligan* imperative. Along with the fortuitous 150th anniversary of the writing of the opinion in Bloomington, Illinois, these developments prompted reexamination.

Because of 9/11, the War on Terror, and the War in Iraq, it is now more difficult to dismiss *Ex parte Milligan* as irrelevant to our constitutional debates. Citing *Quirin* and two other World War II–era cases, the administration of George W. Bush exercised and defended sweeping executive discretion in prosecuting the War on Terror, including the use of military commissions, an assertion seemingly counter to Davis's majority opinion as well as the Chase concurrence.[12] This reopened questions of both US constitutional law and international law that stretched back past *Quirin* to the Davis opinion in *Milligan.* Rejecting the Bush administration's arguments, *Ex parte Milligan* was cited in four Supreme Court decisions arising from the wars in Afghanistan and Iraq, and in the War on Terror: *Rasul v. Bush* (2004), *Hamdi v. Rumsfeld* (2004), *Hamdan v. Rumsfeld* (2006), and *Boumediene v. Bush* (2008).[13]

Notorious for authoring memos sustaining the Bush administration's use of enhanced interrogation techniques—the so-called torture memos—John Yoo in 2009 used Neely's analysis of *Milligan*'s "irrelevance"—particularly the stripping of habeas jurisdiction in response to *McCardle*—to argue that "some believe that the courts should still decide cases challenging government authority without taking account of wartime conditions. This approach ignores the costs of judicial intervention, not only to the war effort but to the court."[14] In setting himself against the Davis opinion, Yoo drew to the Bush administration the precedent of Lincoln's suspension of the privilege of the writ of habeas corpus and his use of military commissions during the Civil War.[15]

In response to this seemingly innocuous call for judicial restraint, Jonathan Hafetz replied in the same journal issue that Bush's efforts to deny habeas protections could be distinguished from Lincoln in at least three ways. First, Bush sought permanent detention, whereas Lincoln in both word and deed sought only temporary suspension of habeas privileges.[16] Second, Hafetz pointed out that unlike Lincoln, the Bush administration sought changes in the law to deny habeas to foreign nationals, contrary to constitutional guarantees of equal protection of the law. Scholars have only recently turned their attention to the treatment of foreign nationals under Lincoln, which is not central to our inquiry here.[17]

Third and most importantly for our purposes, Hafetz argued that

> at bottom, Lincoln's suspension rested on the notion that in a time of crisis and public danger, habeas corpus might have to be sacrificed temporarily to preserve the public safety and the larger framework of government—a situation expressly contemplated by the Suspension Clause and consistent with the writ's history. . . . But, as time has made clear, the Bush administration's efforts to eliminate habeas corpus had little, if anything, to do with security, and everything to do with covering up [the] embarrassment, if not illegality [of its use of torture.][18]

The question here is whether the suspension of habeas corpus and the use of military commissions under the Lincoln administration were qualitatively different from the attempt to suspend by the Bush administration and Republicans in Congress. Hafetz here contends that the purpose of the Bush administration in keeping detainees out of civilian court was to prevent evidentiary challenges to coerced testimony. Hafetz is essentially correct in assuming here that the Lincoln administration resorted to military commissions not for the purpose of using coerced testimony by and against unlawful combatants, but for a series of less nefarious reasons.[19] Sometimes local civilian juries were biased, and sometimes the nature of the charges precluded the use of civil courts—for instance, when considering violations of the laws of war or of nations rather than violations of civilian law, or violations of general orders under martial law. Conversely, it is also true that military commissions often did not provide defendants with the full suite of procedural protections customary in the mid-nineteenth century, leaving open a struggle over claims to Lincoln's mantle of legitimacy.

Yoo further characterized the Supreme Court rulings in *Hamdi* and *Hamdan* as demonstrating the irrelevance of *Milligan*. "In *Hamdi v. Rumsfeld*, a four-Justice plurality upheld the detention of an alleged terrorist who was a U.S. citizen captured in Afghanistan but required judicial review of the detention to protect due process standards. Nevertheless, the *Hamdi* plurality concluded that *Milligan* did not require a civilian trial [for Hamdi] because *Milligan* did not apply to prisoners who had joined or associated themselves with enemy forces."[20] As in *Quirin*, the sweeping guarantees of due process from *Milligan* did not apply to combatants. Yoo attempted here to wave off *Milligan* as the Lincoln administration had waved off habeas corpus challenges during the Civil War.

To this, Justice Breyer rejoined that in *Quirin* itself the Court had taken cognizance of a habeas petition from an unlawful combatant. In *Rasul* the Court held that the executive could detain enemy combatants including American citizens. This would seem to run counter to Davis's resounding dictum that "the Constitution of the United States is a law for rulers and people, equally in war and in peace, and covers with the shield of its protection all classes of men, at all times and under all circumstances."[21] But within that, in both *Rasul* and *Hamdi,* the Court also ruled that combatants held to be unlawful must be able to challenge their detention status and be accorded the basic elements of due process. As in *Hamdi,* the Court had not released Quirin, but neither the *Quirin* nor *Hamdi* decisions in fact represented a full repudiation of *Milligan.*

Following *Hamdi,* the Court in *Hamdan* held that Hamdan's military commission lacked authority because its procedures violated both the Uniform Code of Military Justice and the Geneva Conventions. Finally, in *Boumediene v. Bush,* the Supreme Court held that a congressional statute could not restrict habeas petition rights beyond the limits of the suspension clause: "The privilege of the writ of *habeas corpus* shall not be suspended, unless when in cases of rebellion or invasion the public safety may require it."[22] Ironically, this was precisely the ground Lincoln seized without hesitation in the earliest moments of the Civil War—ground he never abandoned.[23] For a narrow majority of the Court, *Milligan* was not dead as a precedent, and the Lincoln administration did not serve as an authority for the Bush administration's actions. The meaning of *Ex parte Milligan* had reached a crisis of interpretation.

At the same time that this controversy was working its way through the courts, Civil War historians found themselves in a related crisis of interpretation. The wars in Iraq, Afghanistan, and on terror accelerated existing trends toward rethinking the meaning of the Civil War and the teleological narrative of American freedom. After Vietnam, the sense was that something somewhere had gone wrong, but the assumption coming out of World War II generally persisted: wars could and should end in clean moral victories, and in the triumph of right. After the civil rights movement, the destruction of slavery quite naturally came to be seen as a good. James M.

McPherson's *Battle Cry of Freedom* (1988), most prominently, ended with a sad but triumphant signing ceremony at Appomattox Court House.[24] Without kicking the white South and Copperheads entirely to the curb, Civil War history was once again a story of progress toward the fulfillment of the American promise, as it had been for abolitionists and nationalists of the late nineteenth century. In spite of Vietnam, this so-called neo-abolitionist scholarship of the Civil War generally stayed within a World War II frame of unconditional surrender and unambiguously total victory.[25]

But the seemingly endless wars in Iraq and Afghanistan prompted Civil War historians to reexamine how wars end—or rather do not really end. These more recent experiences suggested that wars continue to smolder long after the mission-accomplished banner has gone up and one side's forces have melted back into the civilian population.[26] Far from being minor skirmishes, wars on terror and insurgencies, with all their problems for civil liberties, often present battles at least as significant and decisive as those on the "conventional" battlefield.

This "new revisionism" started slightly earlier;[27] nevertheless, it was not by accident that historical narratives of the triumph of American values faced increased challenges at the close of America's "unipolar moment," when American values seemed to face tougher than expected challenges abroad and even at home.

The lesson in these more pessimistic, neo-revisionist histories has been similar. Reconstruction was really a war on terror; and in *this* war on terror, the terrorists won. The success of the Ku Klux Klan in reestablishing white supremacy by suppressing the vote through lynch law called into question the "mission accomplished" grand narrative of Appomattox. In addition, the sheer carnage, terrorism, and curtailment of civil liberties in the Civil War led some historians to question the entire Union war effort. For neo-revisionists on the more extreme end of the spectrum, the Civil War now seemed to have been not a *Battle Cry of Freedom* but *This Terrible War*, a war just as futile as the wars in Iraq and Afghanistan had become.[28]

By no means have all Civil War historians embraced the new revisionism.[29] Nevertheless, these same forces that gave rise to neo-revisionism prompted even historians sympathetic to the Union war effort and thus fairly characterized as at least somewhat "neo-abolitionist" or "neo-nationalist" to explore ambiguities, ironies, and moral complexities.[30] Both neo-abolitionist and neo-revisionist historians now routinely point out that the

Civil War included guerrilla warfare, violent domestic dissent, and terrorism, which provoked limits on civil liberties both justified and unjustified. In these tellings, the war continued long after Appomattox Court House, some dating it to 1871, some to 1877, and some even to *Plessy v. Ferguson* in 1896.[31] Even for neo-abolitionists, the Civil War now raises profound questions about the relationship of terror, the state, and civil liberties. Almost unavoidably, both neo-revisionists and neo-abolitionists now view the Civil War less through the lens of World War II and more through the lenses of Iraq, Afghanistan, and the War on Terror. Having broken with lingering consensus-era assumptions about the American past, historians now see the Lincoln administration's use of military law in the context of intense domestic conflict within the North and within the South.

As in constitutional law, historians are at odds about the meaning of the Civil War and Reconstruction and, in particular, its legacy for civil liberties. In light of these rapid developments both in constitutional law and in historical scholarship born of the wars in Afghanistan, Iraq, and the War on Terror, a reevaluation of *Ex parte Milligan* has become imperative.

PART 1: THE MEANING OF MARTIAL LAW

The first set of chapters in this volume grapples with the significance of military rule for African Americans during and following the Civil War, raising a set of questions oddly overlooked in historical treatments of civil liberties during the period. *Ex parte Milligan* held that Lincoln had overstepped his authority under the Habeas Corpus Act in failing to charge Milligan in civil court, but as historian K. Luci Petlack argues, "this verdict concerned itself only with the civil liberties of free, white Americans and not those of free, black Americans. Understanding the livelihood provided to black men and women under strong military presence as existed during wartime, one might reconsider the stance that military rule equated to a loss of American freedom."[32]

In the wake of pro-Southern riots seeking to prevent the passage of Union troops through Baltimore on the way to relieve Washington, DC, in 1861, Lincoln suspended the privilege of the writ of habeas corpus while Union troops moved into the contested region and occupied Baltimore for the rest of the war. This occupation provided the template for other occupations, such as those of Cincinnati and New Orleans. Upon taking over the city of Baltimore, General Benjamin F. Butler, who later argued for the government in *Milligan,* prohibited displays of Confederate emblems, including flags, photographs, socks, and badges. By the end of the war, at least nine newspapers were closed. Butler deemed a zero-tolerance attitude toward Confederate activity necessary to establish order and effect reconstruction in the face of an implacable enemy.

Resistance to the Union war effort and concomitant violence against African Americans was endemic, requiring the occupation of an ostensibly "Northern" city like Cincinnati. The New York draft riots were also race riots,[33] and they were but the largest in a locally led but nationwide terror campaign against black freedom during the Civil War and Reconstruction. Violence tore apart many cities, including New York, Cincinnati, Baltimore, Memphis, and New Orleans, and, as Christopher Phillips adds, Chicago, Toledo, Indianapolis, Evansville, and a host of smaller cities as well. Such circumstances required federal military intervention to forestall organized desertion and draft resistance, to protect African Americans, and to restore order.

Once the federal government became fully committed to the destruction of slavery, black liberty began to expand in these occupied areas. In Baltimore, the black community founded a newspaper, opened new houses of worship, and established schools for black women and children. The response and the results in New Orleans under Butler and in Cincinnati under General Ambrose Burnside were similar. After all, the military crackdown came in part as a response to barbarous and racist assaults on African Americans unleashed by the Emancipation Proclamation and the draft, which taken together forced white men into a fight for black freedom against their own deeply held understanding that the United States was to be a white man's republic.[34] It had been Burnside's orders that resulted in the arrest of Clement Vallandigham, signaling, once again, the way racial attitudes often dictated attitudes toward civil liberties defined negatively as freedom from specifically federal government coercion.[35]

General Butler has endured in the American imagination as a caricature—a vulgar, self-interested scoundrel and cross-eyed battlefield incompetent who blundered his way from assignment to assignment. Yet beneath the effrontery of Butler's pronouncements was a brooding, contemplative man—one whose cunning legal mind worked overtime, and one who developed a remarkably sophisticated understanding of the cause and consequences of the Civil War. In chapter 1, "Benjamin F. Butler, *Ex Parte Milligan*, and the Unending Civil War," Brian Matthew Jordan argues that in his generally dismissed argument before the Court, Butler brought wartime experience with Southern intransigence and racism to a remarkable argument on the government's behalf in *Milligan*.

In chapter 2, "Martial Law and the Expansion of Civil Liberties during the Civil War," Jonathan W. White explores the effect of military rule on the black community, concentrating on the real-world effect of military commissions and extending the analysis to the Reconstruction period. Ironically, military rule can have positive effects in addition to the well-noted negative effects on civil liberties. Not always a diminution of due process, in fact military commission trials actually proved a lesson in civics for African Americans because for the first time they could testify against whites, cross-examine white witnesses, and appeal convictions through the military chain of command. During Reconstruction as well as in wartime occupations, the need for military commission trials became even more acute. The more important meaning of the military commissions may not have been the denial of process to whites, but the opening of process to blacks.[36] This is why Copperheads and the white South so hated them.[37] (The prewar denial of privileges and immunities to blacks accused of being fugitive slaves, or postwar re-enslavement and disfranchisement of freedmen, rarely if ever troubled them.) Judge Advocate General Joseph Holt, long a bête noire for neo-Confederates,[38] looms heroic here in his insistence on the use of military commissions to secure meaningful black freedom.

In chapter 3, Mark S. Schantz explores one particular case of the use of military commissions, and the clear denial by Lincoln himself of regular due process rights to a doctor, David M. Wright, who had assassinated Lieutenant Alanson Sanborn, the white officer of the First US Colored Infantry in occupied Norfolk, Virginia. Lincoln intervened personally and decisively to make sure the defendant was hanged. So far, so draconian. But Lincoln took it to be a military necessity that an example be set for those who would take aim at black soldiers or their officers. Histories of civil liberties in the period have too often obscured the chief bone of contention in many of these Civil War civil liberties cases: race, racism, and the fate of white supremacy. Emotionally charged racist rhetoric almost always accompanied Copperhead complaints about civil liberties. Conversely, the one unpardonable sin for the generally compassionate Lincoln was not support for secession but failure to treat black troops as prisoners of war.[39] The arguments advanced by the judge advocate were strong enough to send Wright to the gallows. Despite three petitions signed by the best of Norfolk's citizens, one hysterical escape attempt, the possibility of an insanity plea, and Wright's wife's last-ditch attempt to meet Lincoln in person, the president dug in his heels. There would be no pardon, no last-minute reprieve, no weeping, no regret.

The case raises important questions about the character of Abraham Lincoln and race. There are two main anti-Lincoln traditions—one holding that Lincoln did not really care about the fate of African Americans and the other holding that Lincoln cavalierly traduced upon white civil liberties. The Wright-Sanborn case demonstrates that these two traditions are in fact mutually exclusive. Lincoln ran roughshod over the civil liberties of some white men—in the case of Dr. Wright, quite self-consciously. But all the more gallingly to the Copperheads, he did so on behalf of black freedom. The persistent Copperhead complaint that "Black Republicans" and Lincoln put the rights of African Americans (to use the polite usage) above the rights of white men, was not without merit.

In pressing his case against Wright, the judge advocate relied heavily on Lincoln's General Orders No. 100, otherwise known as the Lieber Code, a document put in place to govern martial law and protect emancipation. Charting new territory, Schantz shows us the code in action at the trial level.

When it came to emancipation, and to the cause of protecting white officers and black troops, Lincoln understood what was at stake: either the Union would stand with its efforts to free black men and let them fight, or it would capitulate to waves of assassination and reprisals. That Lincoln handled the case so deftly has helped obscure the racial politics of Civil War military commission trials. Curtailment of white civil liberties was often in the service of black freedom.

PART 2: THE COPPERHEADS OF THE MIDDLE WEST

The chapters in part 2 set the immediate historical context for the *Milligan* case, analyzing the anti-war Copperhead dissent in the Midwest and the Republican response to it. They describe the proceedings in Lambdin Milligan's military commission trial as well as the disposition of his case in the US Supreme Court. Earlier historians reduced to insignificance the "Copperhead" threat to the Union war effort, but recent scholarship moves Copperheads to center stage as Lincoln's most troubling political opponents, with important consequences for overarching Civil War narratives. If the Copperhead threat was real, then Lincoln administration efforts to thwart its membership seem less hysterical and highhanded. And if the Copperheads replace the abolitionists or radicals as Lincoln's chief adversaries, Lincoln's genuine racial egalitarianism becomes more apparent.

Paradoxically, however, Davis's opinion in *Ex parte Milligan* nevertheless remains a landmark in the history of civil liberties. How is this paradox to be explained? The Civil War was not merely between the Blue and the Gray, clearly defined and equally honorable, and it was not merely between a clearly defined "North" and an equally solid "South." Christopher Phillips, one of the leading social historians of the Middle West in this period, dismisses this as "the familiar binary between free and slave states." After the Preliminary Emancipation Proclamation and the Enrollment Act, opposition to the Union war effort was extensive in the border states and in what used to be called "the lower North."[40] Phillips calls this "the middle border," a region that contained "slave states" like Kentucky and Missouri and also large parts of the "free states" of Ohio, Indiana, and Illinois.[41]

In chapter 4, "Race, Class, and Copperheadism: The Localist Foundations of Dissent in the Civil War's Middle Border," Phillips describes the social context of the "middle border" that gave rise to the *Milligan* case in the first place. On the ground, the American Civil War, even in "the North," was a seething cauldron of local animosities, including political and class divides that predated the war. Phillips writes that daily conflicts were fought "in the streets, schools, churches, courthouses, and other public and private spaces of individual communities." With the other authors in this section of the book, Phillips agrees that "local resistance efforts proved acutely disruptive to the war effort."

But while he explores the often-vicious racism of Copperheads, Phillips also portrays that racism as part of a broader resistance to "modernization" and Yankee imperialism. In this, he revives in modified form the revisionist narrative lines of historian Frank L. Klement.[42] Phillips also uncovers the local boards of trade that were established to prevent trade in contraband goods with the Confederacy. Republicans used their dominance of these boards to aid themselves, their families, and their friends to the detriment of

Peace Democrats and Unionist slaveholders. In addition to Democrat vigilante groups protecting deserters and draft avoiders, Phillips reminds us that Republicans had their vigilante groups as well, often consisting of former or furloughed Union soldiers. Phillips thus nudges us back a bit toward the neo-revisionist side of the spectrum, cautioning against too sanguine a view of the Republicans and giving a more empathetic view of anti-war Democrats. Consonant with neo-revisionism, what emerges is a world of ironies and moral complexities that fit only uncomfortably with Republican demands for all-or-nothing patriotism. This was the world that spawned Milligan's discontent.

In chapter 5, "'The State Was Honeycombed with Secret Societies': Governor Oliver P. Morton and the Copperheads in Indiana," A. James Fuller picks up the story, describing how Milligan came to be arrested, charged, and put before a military commission. Fuller concedes that the Copperhead threat was real, or, in what amounts to the same thing, that Indiana governor Oliver P. Morton was sincerely convinced and had good reason to believe the threat was real. That Morton on occasion put the brakes on military overzealousness testified to his willingness to be guided by the evidence. But Fuller finds that Morton *also* used the case opportunistically and for political effect, and though there was also a problem with gaining convictions in civilian court, this political calculus does help explain why Morton opted to push for a military commission trial during the 1864 elections rather than wait for a civilian trial.

Fuller thus synthesizes neo-abolitionist and neo-revisionist approaches. Along the way, he provides a clear chronological history of developments and decisions regarding civil liberties and the war in Indiana that resulted in Milligan's prosecution. Fuller includes relatively little-known instances of violent resistance to Republican rule in Indiana. Morton's rule was at best quasi-legal, since with Lincoln's support Morton chose to run the state on borrowed money rather than call a Democratic legislature back into session to acquire the requisite appropriation. (Those keeping score should note that this flew in the face of Lincoln's stated reasons for the war in his First Inaugural, that elections have consequences and that resorting to illegality upon losing an election was "the essence of anarchy."[43]) But once Lincoln decided the fight for a Union dedicated to the ultimate extinction of slavery was a just war, it seems he never noticed this inconsistency.

In chapter 6, "'These Scoundrels Stand in No Fear of the Civil Courts; They Do, of the Military': The Decision to Use Military Commissions to Try the Indiana Conspirators in 1864," Stephen E. Towne zeros in specifically on the decision to use military commissions rather than the federal courts as provided for by the Habeas Corpus Act of 1863. He then brings his unique understanding of the inner workings of Union counterintelligence to the story. Towne argues that although the chief Union spymaster Henry B. Carrington preferred using federal courts to try Milligan and the other Indianapolis conspirators, Governor Morton, and ultimately, Abraham Lincoln, decided that the federal courts were failing to convict or were otherwise too lenient. Lincoln made the determination that international law and "public safety" (language borrowed and extended from the suspension clause of the US Constitution) warranted the use of military commissions. Like Fuller, Towne sees the decision to use military commissions as motivated both by genuine concerns for the public safety (what we now call national security) *and* by a principled political opportunism.

The upshot of the work of Phillips, Fuller, and Towne is clear. The threat from disloyal operatives in the North was real. The North was riven with potentially violent disagreement about the legitimate ends of republican government.[44] The Lincoln administration faced plots to enable a Confederate invasion, disrupt the draft, shield deserters, assassinate recruitment officers, liberate Confederate prisoners, and even to create an independent Northwest Confederacy, all of which came on top of opposition to emancipation and assaults on African Americans. If these threats were real, then the actions of the Lincoln administration (as well as Davis's characterization of Milligan as a noncombatant) appear in a much different light. Rather than part of an attempt to destroy civil liberties and establish a despotism, as Davis and Milligan's counsel feared (and as historian Klement asserted), the use of military commissions in the North in fact came as a response to widespread disloyal activity.

PART 3: THE MILLIGAN *DECISION*

In chapter 7, "*Ex Parte Milligan* in Context and History: David Davis and the Constitutional Politics and Law of Civil Liberty," Michael Les Benedict examines of the roots of David Davis's opinion. Andrew Jackson and his followers had embraced a form of "popular constitutionalism," which held that in a republic, the Constitution meant what the people said it meant. In response, the young Lincoln and David Davis both took the Whig line that this made a mockery of the rule of law and was in effect a form of lawlessness. General Jackson's behavior in New Orleans, regarding Indian removal in *Worcester v. Georgia* (1832), or against the Bank, and Democratic mob activity—for instance, against Mormons in Illinois—evidenced the same "mobocratic" spirit. This was later confirmed in Whig thinking by the lawless behavior of the Polk administration in provoking a war against the sister republic of Mexico. But this high judicial supremacy worked less well for Republicans after *Dred Scott,* even as, in an ironic reversal, Democrats began to find it more attractive. Lincoln and most Republicans came to accept the ineluctability of popular constitutionalism.[45]

Nevertheless, several influential old Whigs, including Davis, adhered to old Whig notions of high judicial supremacy rooted in mistrust of "the virtue and intelligence of the people," as well as distaste for black people in particular. Benedict details Davis's constitutional politics. Davis hoped to convince the American people that he was right about the meaning of a written constitution and the threat posed by congressional radicals. This explains why he actively worked to get *Milligan* before the Supreme Court. Benedict reprises the arguments before the Court, pointing out, for instance, that Benjamin Butler did not thoroughly present the Lincoln administration's views of the commander-in-chief clause and international law and that he also failed to argue for Milligan's belligerent status. This allowed Davis to write an opinion almost entirely consonant with the Copperhead view that the Lincoln administration had acted beyond the law and the Constitution. Davis's opinion left a lasting imprint on historical understandings of the Lincoln administration regarding civil liberties, but it did not, argues Benedict, provide the firm precedent in American constitutional law Davis expected.

In chapter 8, Michael Haggerty explores the way Chief Justice Salmon P. Chase's experience with fugitive slave case law shaped his view of federalism prior to *Ex parte Milligan.* Chase was a former Democrat who in the 1830s and 1840s used the logic of states' rights, individual rights, and state-level habeas corpus to combat the kidnapping of freemen and -women. An early adopter of the tactic of legal activism, Chase became known as the "Attorney General of Fugitive Slaves," developing his position that the Constitution was antislavery.

But in the postwar period when federal power was no longer the enemy of the freed men and women, Chase was in a bind. The perceived "lawlessness" in the South, particularly the 1866 massacres in New Orleans and Memphis, exposed the divide between Andrew Johnson and Chase. Johnson felt the need to remove the army so that black people would stop asserting themselves. Chase was frustrated with the failures of local law enforcement and local officials who would not enforce the law if it meant protecting a newly emancipated population. Prior to the war, Chase utilized writs of habeas corpus to try to free fugitive slaves from law enforcement officers enforcing federal fugitive slave laws. In the postwar period, he faced the opposite problem. He *wanted* local law enforcement and local courts to enforce federal law. This was particularly true when it came to his support for the extension of suffrage, which he saw as the best guarantee that black people would be protected by the law.

As it applied to Milligan, the only solution appeared to be congressionally authorized military courts that could preempt the local tribunals dominated by white supremacist judges and juries. Thus, while the old Whig Davis moved into line with a liberal Democrat like David Dudley Field, the former Democrat Chase moved in the opposite direction, toward the old Whig willingness to accept a federal police power. It lies close to hand that the transformation of both men's constitutional jurisprudence was motivated primarily by their underlying attitudes toward blacks.

In chapter 9, "The Least Naive Position: The Lincoln Administration and International Law in American Wars on Terror," I compare the arguments in *Ex parte Milligan* of Benjamin Butler, Salmon Chase, David Field, David Davis, and the Lincoln administration. As heirs of the twentieth century's battles against totalitarianism, we tend to find the Davis opinion more attractive than Lincoln's. Yet his ringing endorsement of what we have since come to call the Bill of Rights was the more anomalous opinion at the time. And though seemingly dismissive of basic Bill of Rights protections to us, in fact Lincoln's position made a good deal of sense in the mid-nineteenth century. The situation is further complicated because Davis and Lincoln both innovated, and yet in different ways each remained within a mid-nineteenth century constitutional paradigm alien to modern understandings of civil liberties.

Drawing on insights from the other chapters in this volume, I argue for a revision of our largely negative judgment regarding Lincoln's handling of wartime civil liberties. Rather than the Bill of Rights, which was only in its nascence as a guardian of individual rights, Lincoln relied on the law of nations, which for him were not a foreign imposition but constitutive of the US constitutional order itself. Lincoln, no less than Davis, contributed to the most recent Supreme Court rulings regarding the scope of civil liberties during wars on terror. I further propose that in situations when the civil order is threatened by terror, a reliance on international law rather than the Bill of Rights makes eminent sense. We might actually learn from the Lincoln administration and from Radical Reconstruction something important about the relationship of freedom and power. The wisdom of historical experience seems to indicate that the Lincoln administration and the Radicals were eventually forced to adopt the least naive position regarding civil liberties, the Bill of Rights, and the laws of war.

PART 4: THE PRECEDENTIAL POWER OF MILLIGAN

The chapters in Part 4 explore the enduring significance of the *Milligan* decision, including its immediate impact on Reconstruction in the South as well as in World War I, World War II, and the modern War on Terror. While the *Milligan* decision had limited influence on American jurisprudence in the twentieth century, the War on Terror has brought *Milligan* back to the fore as one of the greatest articulations of the American commitment to individual liberty.

In chapter 10, John A. Lupton reminds us just how different the legal and administrative order was in the nineteenth century. He examines at the state level Mark E. Neely's contention that *Ex parte Milligan* was "irrelevant," finding that the particularities of nineteenth-century law meant that detainees could and did recover damages for false imprisonment in lawsuits against federal officials. Along the way, Lupton notes that Davis's contention in *Milligan* was rooted in previous state-level decisions. The Lincoln administration held that it was the nature of the act that decided whether a given action posed a threat to the public safety and the war effort. Even prior to *Milligan,* Davis and many state courts held that it was the location (whether in the immediate area of hostilities and whether civil courts were open) that determined whether the actor was a belligerent who could be legitimately tried by military commission.

Milligan had a surprising effect. After *Milligan,* state courts cited the Davis opinion as a precedent for holding officials liable for damages for false imprisonment. Congress attempted to grant indemnity from these lawsuits to federal officials, but state courts regarded such attempts to be unconstitutionally ex post facto. Even after *Ex parte McCardle* would seem to have forestalled the further application of *Milligan* to military tribunals in the South, it remained precarious for federal officials to use military commissions in the presence of an often-hostile state judiciary. Military commission trials soon stopped. Far from irrelevant, *Milligan* had teeth even in retreat.

As a leading authority not only of the legal history of Reconstruction but of US constitutional history as a whole, it is only fitting that Michael Les Benedict weigh in again on the lasting importance of *Milligan.* In chapter 11, "*Ex parte Milligan* in Context and History: From Reconstruction to the War on Terror," he revises Neely's case that *Milligan* has been "irrelevant." To the contrary, though confined by subsequent courts, *Milligan* expressed arguably for the first time certain "American" commitments to constitutionally protecting individual liberty. Benedict adduces numerous examples in which *Milligan* continued to have limited but profound operative effects in law. When it comes to American citizens, in some sense the Chase opinion has carried the day, while in the case of foreign nationals, international law (and therewith the views of the Lincoln administration) have come to the fore. Nevertheless, against all attempts of the Bush administration, Benedict argues, *Milligan* has not been entirely disregarded by the Court in the War on Terror.

Finally, in chapter 12, "*Ex Parte Milligan* and the War on Terrorism: Testing the Constitutional Bedrock of a Civilian Criminal Trial," Jonathan Hafetz brings the perspective of a practicing defense lawyer in the Guantanamo Bay cases. Hafetz extends Benedict's case that, in spite of *Milligan's* flaws and notwithstanding *Ex parte Quirin, Milligan* remains both a moral beacon and good law. Davis in *Milligan* expressed the moral sense of the community and the commitment of the judiciary to fair trial, the rights of the accused, and high professional standards of due process.

In contrast to the Reconstruction period, where courts remained openly hostile to Unionists, soldiers, and newly freed blacks, in the War on Terror, recent civilian courts have done a better job than military commissions at reaching verdicts and meting out punishments. Hafetz finds that in *Hamdan v. Rumsfeld,* the Court actually relied on Chase's *Milligan* opinion rather than Davis's when it demanded congressional authorization for military commission trials. (It is also possible to argue that in insisting on Common Article Three procedural protections the Court in *Hamdan* approaches Lincoln's position on international law prescribing limits on US action.) In *United States v. Al Bahlul,* the DC Circuit has upheld the use of conspiracy as a charge before a military commission because, though not a valid charge under international law, historically conspiracy has been tried by military commission in the United States. But it remains to be seen whether other charges, such as engaging in cyberattacks, will be allowed under military jurisdiction. In this sense, then, the tensions between *Milligan* and *Quirin* remain in play. Thus, in addition to its aspirational quality as a beacon of due process, Hafetz argues, *Milligan* remains an essential part of the existing constitutional order.

Viewing the struggles over racial reconstruction in the United States during and after the Civil War as a "war on terror" elucidates constitutional issues in our current War on Terror and vice versa, and this has led to a number of startling conclusions.

Perhaps most strikingly, civil liberties for whites and blacks in this period were often inversely related. The question of how African Americans faired under military occupation has seldom, if ever, been brought into the conversation about the Lincoln's administration's civil liberties record. Lincoln's emancipation record, suspect for many on other grounds, has been handled separately from the issue of civil liberties, leaving civil libertarians free to chastise the Lincoln administration. But in so doing, they have implicitly identified with the supposed victims of Lincoln's overreach—defendants like John Merryman, Clement Vallandigham, Lambdin P. Milligan, or later William McCardle, all virulently antiblack and pro-Union only on the fantastic assumption that the South would accept Union were slavery restored.[46]

But putting African Americans back into the center of the picture where they surely belong has potentially profound consequences for our understanding of the history of civil liberties during the Civil War and Reconstruction.[47] Rather than an unambiguous story of the deprivation of white civil liberties, Lincoln and the Republicans often restricted white civil liberties in order to defend the civil liberties of African Americans. (Considering the overall purpose of the war, dooming slavery to its "ultimate extinction," one might argue they restricted white civil liberties *primarily* in order to expand and defend the civil liberties of African Americans.) A judicial warning shot against the use of the military to secure black freedom, *Milligan* had profound implications for the postwar fate of African Americans that need to be considered in any assessment of the significance of the decision.

Second, several of the historians writing here have been part of an effort to revise our understandings of the Copperheads, or Peace Democrats, in the Civil War era. Significant numbers of white Northerners refused to become a part of a war on behalf of black freedom. While traditionally taken to be a mostly imaginary threat, recent research has revealed a violent and even revolutionary domestic threat in the North during the Civil War. This poses significant and perhaps insurmountable challenges to the standard view that Lincoln was overreaching in *Milligan.*

Third, Justice David Davis was breaking new constitutional ground in *Ex parte Milligan,* bringing to the Court a view of the judiciary as the guardian of individual constitutional rights. Lincoln has frequently been seen as an insufficient constitutional reasoner when it comes to civil liberties. But in fact, his views may have been closer to the nineteenth-century consensus than those of Davis. Writing for a five-member majority, Davis contended that trying civilians before military tribunals violated several of the rights enumerated in the Bill of Rights. This was a remarkable holding. In upholding the rights of an alleged traitor, the Court here *for the first time* used the Bill of Rights to expand civil liberty. Moreover, this case represented only the third time that the Supreme Court exercised the power of judicial review to strike down a federal law or action, the first two being *Marbury v. Madison* (1803) and *Dred Scott v. Sandford* (1857). After *Dred Scott,* it was only the second use of the Bill of Rights to create an individual right. *Ex parte Milligan* was the big bang of the Bill of Rights—the arrival to the Supreme Court of liberal constitutionalism as we know it. Justice Davis's opinion brought this line of thinking into an opinion of the Supreme Court, arguably for the first time.

Fourth, a reconsideration of *Ex parte Milligan* raises questions about the place of international law in the use of war powers. Recent scholarship has emphasized the reliance of the Lincoln administration on the laws of war. And in light of the Supreme Court's reliance on international law in its recent jurisprudence, Lincoln may in the end prove to have been at least as farsighted a constitutional thinker as Davis.

Fifth, our reexamination of *Milligan* leads to reflections on the validity or invalidity of the use of military commissions (and other controversial uses of executive power) in our current war on terror. Contrary to assertions by the Bush administration, *Ex parte Milligan* remains relevant and good law, though its scope has been restricted.

Finally, the implications of *Ex parte Milligan* have to be reassessed in light of recent scholarship that extends the war beyond Lee's surrender at Appomattox. At the deepest level of political theory, the campaign of terror that arose in post-invasion Iraq again forces basic questions about the role of force in establishing domestic tranquility—something, tragically, thinkers on both the right and the left may have taken for granted. The Lincoln administration and subsequent Republican responses to our earlier "war on terror" may prove profoundly instructive.

In sum, the chapters in this volume illustrate a number of potentially startling recent scholarly conclusions about the Civil War period as well as about the Constitution in our current war on terror—conclusions about the actions of Civil War–era Republicans regarding racial resettlement and white racist terrorism and about the persistent relevance of the *Milligan* decision. The chapters here raise profound questions about the role of the judiciary and the Bill of Rights in wartime, and about the place of the laws of war or international law in our constitutional order. In the end, a reevaluation of *Ex parte Milligan* may force us to rethink the fundamental nature of liberal constitutionalism itself.

NOTES

1. Eric Foner, *Reconstruction: America's Unfinished Revolution, 1863–1877* (New York: Harper & Row, 1988), 603.

2. Mark E. Neely Jr., *The Fate of Liberty: Abraham Lincoln and Civil Liberties* (New York: Oxford University Press, 1991), 176–177.

3. Neely cites John W. Clampitt, "Military Commissions," in John Joseph Lalor, *Cyclopaedia of Political Science, Political Economy, and of the Political History of the United States* (Chicago: Melbert B. Cary, 1884), 838. Clampitt copies William Winthrop, *Digest of Opinions of the Judge Advocate General of the Army: Containing a Selection of Official Opinions Furnished to the President, the Secretary of War, the Adjutant General, Heads of Bureaus of the War Department, Commanding Officers, Judge Advocates and Members of Military Courts, and Other Officers of the Army and Soldiers, between September, 1862, and July, 1868* (Washington, DC: Government

Printing Office, 1868), 229–230. Winthrop copies Major General Halleck's General Orders No. 1.

4. Peter J. Barry, "*Ex parte Milligan:* History and Historians," *Indiana Magazine of History* 109, no. 4 (2013): 362–363. Barry gives a less pointed, but more comprehensive, survey of the same history that Neely surveys.

5. *Ex parte Milligan,* 132.

6. Neely, *Fate of Liberty,* 179–181, 175, 182–183.

7. Neely, 183.

8. *Ex parte Quirin,* 317 US 1.

9. In this volume, John Lupton suggests that Davis's reasoning in this regard reflected a preexisting general understanding of common law among state jurists.

10. 317 US at 45–46; Curtis A. Bradley, "The Story of *Ex parte Milligan:* Military Trials, Enemy Combatants, and Congressional Authorization," 122, and Dawn E. Johnson, "The Story of *Hamdan v. Rumsfeld:* Trying Enemy Combatants by Military Commission," in Christopher H. Schroeder and Curtis A. Bradley, *Presidential Power Stories* (New York: Foundation Press, 2009), 465.

11. Bradley, "The Story of *Ex parte Milligan,*" 121.

12. Barry, "*Ex parte Milligan:* History and Historians," 376; John Yoo, "Lincoln and Habeas: Or Merryman and Milligan and McCardle," *Chapman Law Review* (2008): 509; *Hamdi v. Rumsfeld,* 542 US 519 (2004). For further analysis, see Jonathan Hafetz, "Stretching Precedent beyond Recognition: The Misplaced Reliance on World War II Cases in the War on Terror," *Review of Litigation* (2008): 365.

13. *Rasul v. Bush,* 542 US 466 (2004); *Hamdi v. Rumsfeld* 542 US 507 (2004), *Hamdan v. Rumsfeld* 548 US 557 (2006), and *Boumediene v. Bush* 128 S. Ct. 2329 (2008). See Johnson, "The Story of *Hamdan v. Rumsfeld*"

14. John Yoo, "Merryman and Milligan (and McCardle)," *Journal of Supreme Court History* 34, no. 3 (2009): 258; Yoo, "Lincoln and Habeas," 533.

15. Jonathan W. White, *Abraham Lincoln and Treason in the Civil War: The Trials of John Merryman* (Baton Rouge: Louisiana State University Press, 2011), 120.

16. One could argue that by ignoring or letting pass the reporting and time limit provisions of the Habeas Corpus Act of 1863, which he had signed, Lincoln too had sought indefinite suspension of habeas corpus. Hafetz is right about this, but his point is not immediately obvious.

17. For a more complete treatment of this topic, see Robert O. Faith, "'This Despotic and Arbitrary Power': British Diplomacy and Resistance in the Habeas Corpus Controversy of the American Civil War" (PhD diss., University of Akron, 2018).

18. Jonathan Hafetz, "A Different View of the Law: Habeas Corpus during the Lincoln and Bush Presidencies," *Chapman Law Review* (2008): 446–447. See also Johnson, "The Story of *Hamdan v. Rumsfeld,*" 453, 455, 462, 466.

19. White, *Abraham Lincoln and Treason,* 118.

20. Yoo, "Merryman and Milligan (and McCardle)," 245; Yoo, "Lincoln and Habeas," 509.

21. *Ex parte Milligan,* 120–121.

22. Stephen G. Breyer, *The Court and the World: American Law and the New Global Realities* (New York: Alfred A. Knopf, 2015), 77–78. *Rasul v. Bush,* 542 US 466 (2004); *Hamdi v. Rumsfeld* 542 US 507 (2004), *Hamdan v. Rumsfeld* 548 US 557 (2006), and *Boumediene v. Bush* 128 S. Ct. 2329 (2008). See also Johnson, "The Story of *Hamdan v. Rumsfeld.*"

23. If one goes to the *Collected Works of Abraham Lincoln* online at https://quod.lib.umich.edu/1/lincoln/ and executes a basic search of the term "public safety," one gets a clear indication that this is so.

24. James M. McPherson, *Battle Cry of Freedom: The Civil War Era* (New York: Oxford University Press, 1988).

25. Yael A. Sternhell, "Revisionism Reinvented?: The Antiwar Turn in Civil War Scholarship," *Journal of the Civil War Era* 3, no. 2 (2013): 239.

26. Edward Ayers, "The First Occupation," *New York Times Magazine,* May 29, 2005.

27. Edward L. Ayers, "What Caused the Civil War," in *What Caused the Civil War?: Reflections on the South and Southern History* (New York: W. W. Norton, 2005). For earlier emphasis on the role of terrorism and the need for coercion to control it, see Michael Perman, *Reunion without Compromise; the South and Reconstruction: 1865–1868* (Cambridge: Cambridge University Press, 1973); George C. Rable, *But There Was No Peace: The Role of Violence in the Politics of Reconstruction* (Athens: University of Georgia Press, 1984).

28. Harry S. Stout, *Upon the Altar of the Nation: A Moral History of the American Civil War* (New York: Viking, 2006); Michael Fellman, Lesley J. Gordon, and Daniel E. Sutherland, *This Terrible War: The Civil War and Its Aftermath* (New York: Longman, 2003).

29. See, most especially, James Oakes, *Freedom National: The Destruction of Slavery in the United States, 1861–1865* (New York: W. W. Norton, 2013).

30. I have particularly in mind William Alan Blair, *With Malice toward Some: Treason and Loyalty in the Civil War Era* (Chapel Hill: University of North Carolina Press, 2014); John Fabian Witt, *Lincoln's Code: The Laws of War in American History* (New York: Free Press, 2012); and Gregory P. Downs, *After Appomattox: Military Occupation and the Ends of War* (Cambridge, MA: Harvard University Press, 2015).

31. Fellman, Gordon, and Sutherland, *This Terrible War;* Downs, *After Appomattox.*

32. K. Luci Petlack, "A Dilemma of Civil Liberties," *Ohio History* 120 (2013): 47–69; Karin Leann Petlack, "A Dilemma of Civil Liberties: Blacks under Union Military Control, 1861–1866" (PhD diss., University of California Davis, 2013).

33. Iver Bernstein, *The New York City Draft Riots: Their Significance in American Society and Politics in the Age of the Civil War* (New York: Oxford University Press, 1990).

34. Mark Neely contests this interpretation. See Mark E. Neely Jr., *Lincoln and the Democrats: The Politics of Opposition in the Civil War* (New York: Cambridge University Press, 2017), 85–135.

35. An important example of an exception to this rule would be David Davis's cousin Henry Winter Davis, who was both a radical on African American freedom and sympathetic to Democratic complaints about the Lincoln administration's treatment of dissent.

36. Detlev F. Vagts, "Military Commissions: The Forgotten Reconstruction Chapter," *American University International Law Review* 23, no. 2 (2008): 231–274.

37. Again, Neely contests this. See note 34 *supra.*

38. Elizabeth D. Leonard, *Lincoln's Forgotten Ally: Judge Advocate General Joseph Holt of Kentucky* (Chapel Hill: University of North Carolina Press, 2011), 319–322.

39. Witt, *Lincoln's Code,* 288. This is not to say that as commander in chief, Lincoln did not feel he *had* to support this new supply of highly motivated fighting men.

40. Stephen E. Towne, *Surveillance and Spies in the Civil War: Exposing Confederate Conspiracies in America's Heartland* (Athens: Ohio University Press, 2015).

41. Christopher Phillips, *The Rivers Ran Backward: The Civil War and the Remaking of the American Middle Border* (New York: Oxford University Press, 2016).

42. Frank L. Klement, *Lincoln's Critics: The Copperheads of the North* (Shippensburg, PA: White Mane, 1999).

43. Roy P. Basler, et al., eds., *The Collected Works of Abraham Lincoln,* 9 vols. (New Brunswick, NJ: Rutgers University Press, 1953), 4: 268.

44. Towne, *Surveillance and Spies in the Civil War*; Jennifer L. Weber, *Copperheads: The Rise and Fall of Lincoln's Opponents in the North* (Oxford: Oxford University Press, 2006).

45. Basler et al., *Collected Works of Abraham Lincoln,* 2: 398–410.

46. Wendy Swanberg, "*Ex parte McCardle* and the First Amendment during Reconstruction," in David B. Sachsman, ed., *A Press Divided: Newspaper Coverage of the Civil War* (New Brunswick, NJ: Transaction Publishers, 2014). For Klement, see *The Limits of Dissent: Clement L. Vallandigham and the Civil War* (Lexington: University Press of Kentucky, 1970); *Dark Lanterns: Secret Political Societies, Conspiracies, and Treason Trials in the Civil War* (Baton Rouge: Louisiana State University Press, 1984); and *Lincoln's Critics.*

47. Laura F. Edwards has recently demonstrated the importance of connecting race, emancipation, and legal history in *A Legal History of the Civil War and Reconstruction: A Nation of Rights* (New York: Cambridge University Press, 2015).

Part One

The Meaning of Martial Law

CHAPTER 1

Benjamin F. Butler, *Ex Parte Milligan*, and the Unending Civil War

Brian Matthew Jordan

"No graver question," associate justice David Davis insisted, "was ever considered" by the US Supreme Court than the one it took up "out of order" the second week of March 1866.[1] The case concerned Lambdin Purdy Milligan, a shrill Hoosier Copperhead who made no secret of his opposition to the Lincoln administration and the Union war effort. "Hardheaded, dogmatic, and often imprudent," the reedy Milligan joined with the Sons of Liberty, a treasonous cadre that endeavored to empty Northern prison camps and incite "insurrection" in the Midwest.[2] In October 1864, Union general Alvin P. Hovey arrested Milligan for "affording aid and comfort to rebels against the authority of the United States." Along with four of his fellow conspirators, Milligan was tried by a military commission in Indianapolis and sentenced to hang "by the neck." The judgment, however, "aroused great excitement in Indiana and in the Northwest," and some civilians began "questioning why there had not been a civil trial." Nine days before Milligan was to be fitted with a government noose, his attorney sought for him a writ of habeas corpus, asking the federal circuit court to either take up the matter or "discharge" Milligan "from custody altogether." While the judges on the Indiana court agreed that Milligan's military trial was illegal, they nonetheless resolved to send the matter to the Supreme Court. In doing so, they posed for the justices a stubborn query: did military commissions have "jurisdiction legally to try and sentence" a citizen in those places where judges still gaveled functioning civilian courts to order?[3]

It was burly and balding Benjamin Franklin Butler, obliged to squint from a lazy eye, who took the lead in arguing the government's case, preparing (with Attorney General James Speed) a strident, sweeping defense of military law. Butler defined "martial law" as "the will of the commanding officer" as "expressed in time of war, within the limits of his military jurisdiction, as necessity demands, and prudence dictates, restrained or enlarged by the orders of his military or supreme executive chief." Martial law was not, he insisted, "unregulated, arbitrary," or subject to the "unjust caprice of a commanding and despotic officer." Instead, Butler demanded, "when the law is silent" and "when the traitor within plots to bring into its peaceful communities the braver rebel who fights without," civil law was inadequate. The same "military necessity" that supplied the logic for emancipation necessarily underwrote the work of the Indianapolis tribunal that condemned Lambdin Milligan to death.[4]

As the prize-winning legal historian John Fabian Witt has pointed out, Butler and Speed "made a broad argument where a narrow one would have sufficed to sustain Milligan's conviction." "They contended that the laws of war afforded the president and the Army the power to declare martial law even outside active war zones and to prosecute U.S. citizens and others before military tribunals, so long as the 'quality of the acts' charged made them the 'proper subject of restraint by martial law.'"[5] While the cantankerous Illinois Republican Orville Hickman Browning panned Butler's efforts before the court, deeming his "manner pompous, and his matter paltry," the general truly believed that his arguments were strong and deserving of a broad audience. Significantly, he engaged the services of his brother-in-law, the Massachusetts publisher Fisher Ames Hildreth, who reproduced his labors in the form of a handsome pamphlet for public dissemination. Decades later, he crowed about his achievement in the pages of his garrulous memoir, *Butler's Book*.[6]

In his history of civil liberties during wartime, William H. Rehnquist insisted that it is "difficult to explain why" Speed tapped Butler to argue the *Milligan* case. While an "able lawyer and advocate," Rehnquist pointed out that General Butler was hardly a stranger to "controversy." "Perhaps," the late chief justice reckoned, "it was because until very recently [Butler] had been a Democrat, and might be thought to appeal to the Democratic appointees." But this suggestion makes little sense, for the general who refused to return to bondage freedom-seeking slaves at Fortress Monroe, who tamed the secessionist mobs of New Orleans, and who celebrated the daring martial feats of the all-black division he commanded in the Army of the James lost whatever influence he once brandished in the Democrat Party long before the end of the war. Indeed, dyspeptic Democratic newspaper editors liberally heaped opprobrium on Butler throughout the Civil War,

Figure 1.1. Major General Benjamin F. Butler. Courtesy of the Library of Congress.

Figure 1.2. Benjamin F. Butler arguing a case in court in Massachusetts just before the war. From Benjamin F. Butler, *Butler's Book: Autobiographical and Personal Reminiscences* (Boston: A. M. Thayer, 1892).

mocking him as "the tool and apologist of the administration in its extreme abolition policy." A luckless Confederate freely confided to Butler after the war that his "assassination was proposed to me" by "at least two persons of the Wilkes Booth order." Without hyperbole, one contemporary newspaper declared Butler "the best hated man who ever lived."[7]

But upon closer inspection, perhaps it is not so difficult to explain Speed's decision to engage Butler in arguing the government's case. After all, converts make zealots,[8] and no other general had done more to sensationalize the problem of treason and loyalty during the war. And no other potential government counsel approximated either Butler's shrewd language or clever stagecraft. The historian Michael D. Pierson has persuasively argued that Butler "turned New Orleans into a theater," reserving for himself the "starring role" in a drama about the "superiority of the Union." According to Pierson, Sarah Jones Hildreth, a talented tragedienne who dazzled prewar audiences on stages from Cincinnati to Charleston, aided her husband in staging his big "show." But New Orleans was only one act in the "ongoing public performance" of Butler's life. The carefully scripted drama began when Ben Butler confronted hostile mobs in Maryland in April 1861; it continued deep into the wearisome years of Reconstruction, during which he literally and metaphorically brandished the "bloody shirt."[9]

Butler first honed the style that his enemies came to fear—and combined to defuse—as a New England lawyer, deft party operative, and labor reform advocate. In the 1840s he built a legal practice in the humming mill town of Lowell, Massachusetts; the firm quickly outgrew its space in the Wyman's Exchange Building on Merrimack Street and soon boasted a second office in downtown Boston. Those who underestimated Butler as a simple "country lawyer" did so at their peril.[10] To prepare for a trial, he not only mastered even the most recondite details of his case; he also sought an education in relevant fields. When representing a plaintiff who contracted scurvy on a ship whose captain had "not taken any sufficient supplies of fresh provisions and vegetables," Butler indefatigably "rummaged libraries, pored over encyclopedias and gazetteers, ferreted out old sailors," then intently "studied five treatises on scurvy," among them "one very old German one printed in Latin" that he was certain the defendant's expert witnesses had not read. Butler prepared just as earnestly for *Milligan,* mining the congressional speeches of John Quincy Adams and even the debates of the British Parliament as he prepared his case. Still, he conducted most of the "research" for *Milligan* during his service in the Civil War. That Butler's unique wartime experiences informed his arguments was made evident when he conceded to the court that "there is a dearth of precedents bearing on the exact point raised here."[11]

Oddly, Butler biographers have either neglected the general's argument in *Milligan* or attributed to pure "self-interest" the vehemence with which he argued the government's case. "Butler did not shrink from using the Supreme Court as a forum in which to justify his own wartime actions," his biographer Richard West contends in *Lincoln's Scapegoat General,* who likewise notes that Butler's "effectiveness was sometimes enhanced by his finding an angle of his client's case that was highly personal to himself."[12] While the polemical general was aware that the impending decision would, in part, function as a "referendum" on his generalship, Butler's argument was principally indebted to his gnawing conviction that the results of the war were both incomplete and in peril. Union victory demanded eternal vigilance. Much more than any unseemly legacy shaping, what Butler sought from the court in *Milligan* was what he sought throughout the war: a frank acknowledgment of the scope and stubbornness of the rebellion, the dimensions of which he came to appreciate while confronting perfidy and treason firsthand throughout the war. Dubious about so-called expressions of loyalty from former rebels, he urged the Court to concede that military law would remain a vital remedy until the spirit of secession was dead and the civil rights of black Americans assured. "Why," he asked, was there no sound precedent for the case? "It is because the facts are unprecedented," he contended, and "because the war out of which they grew is unprecedented also."[13]

Throughout the war, by distinguishing between treason and loyalty, Butler reached for and demanded frank acknowledgment of the realities of the rebellion.[14] In this quest, military law—together with rhetoric—became his weapons. The essence of secession revealed itself in a most shocking way to Butler the very first week of his war, when a regiment of the Massachusetts militiamen under his command attempted to pass through Baltimore, en route to their "camp of rendezvous" at Washington. On April 19, 1861, a secessionist throng greeted the men of the Sixth Massachusetts with stones; the rioters likewise twisted "pieces of iron" from a nearby foundry into deadly missiles, killing four soldiers (among them Privates Luther Ladd and Addison Whitney, two sons of Lowell). Butler was in Philadelphia with the balance of his men as violence gripped the streets. Although the rioters encumbered his most direct path to the nation's capital, they fortified the general's "determination to do his duty." Floating down the jagged Chesapeake in an extemporaneous detour, the general unmoored his troops at Annapolis, a point from which he could freight them into Washington. In doing so, he snubbed the advice of Maryland governor Thomas Holliday Hicks, who "most earnestly" advised the Massachusetts general to unload his troops "elsewhere." Indeed, the bizarre admonition merely invited Butler's suspicions of Hicks's true allegiances.[15]

It seemed that threats to the Union could lurk behind the mask of loyalty. Everywhere he turned in the Old Line State, Butler confronted telling evidence of treachery. At the United States Naval Academy, Superintendent

George S. Blake was "considerably alarmed for the safety of the frigate 'Constitution,'" which prompted Butler to secure the wooden-hulled War of 1812 relic. Baltimoreans who sympathized with the rebels smuggled material goods south and conducted a campaign of misinformation among Butler's men. "Under the guise of bearer of dispatches and reporters of newspapers," the general protested, "we are overrun by the meanest and most despicable kind of Spies, who add impudence and brazen effrontery to traitorous and lying reports with which to injure us."[16] As though Butler required further evidence of Maryland's precarious Unionism, the Annapolis & Elk Ridge Railroad Company "had taken up the rails upon their roads for the purpose of preventing the passage of [federal] troops to Washington," obliging his men to seize the railroad and repair miles of sabotaged track before pushing on to Washington.[17]

Butler tarried but a few days in the capital before planting a headquarters flag at Relay House in Maryland. From this rail depot, he was to await instructions for a drive on Baltimore. But as Union General in Chief Winfield Scott toiled on a cumbrous, multipronged plan to capture the city, the Lowell lawyer, especially eager to avenge the blood of Ladd and Whitney, spurred into action on his own accord; by May 13, he had parked his troops atop Federal Hill. "I had the courage," Butler famously insisted years later, "to rely on my convictions." The next day, in a proclamation addressed to the citizens of Baltimore, Butler reassured that "no loyal and well-disposed citizen will be disturbed." Although "the ordinary operations of the corporate government of the city of Baltimore" would continue, the general earnestly "invited" municipal authorities to "co-operate with the general in command," so as to demonstrate that Baltimore "is in fact, patriotic and loyal to the Union, the Constitution, and the laws." Butler outlawed the display of rebel ensigns and pledged to confiscate "articles fitted to aid and support" the "so-called Confederate States."[18] As if to set the tone of the occupation, the Eighth Massachusetts detained a civilian named "Spencer," who applauded the April 19 rioters.[19]

Butler's desire to dramatize the consequences of disloyalty for Baltimoreans, however, became most evident in his treatment of the millionaire machinist and Maryland state legislator Ross Winans, "a gray-haired old man of more than three score and ten" who the general defamed as "a bitter rebel."[20] Allegedly, Winans's foundry was "constantly turning out cannon, shot and shells for the South" and had produced the John Brown–style pikes wielded "by the mob which attacked the Sixth Regiment." Almost immediately, Butler sized up Winans as a prominent foil who could illustrate the folly of treason. "If such a man, worth $15,000,000, were hanged for treason," the general later explained, "it would convince the people of Maryland, at least, that the expedition we were upon was no picnic excursion, and would show those disposed to join the rebel army . . . that we were engaged in suppressing a treasonable rebellion." Butler's troops arrested the millionaire and packed him off to a holding cell at Fort McHenry, inviting an imbroglio that ended with the prisoner's release just days later.[21]

Though General Scott upbraided Butler for his "hazardous occupation of Baltimore," Northerners feted the intrepid commander as a "hero." "Butler has performed real service," the Massachusetts Republican George Boutwell wrote. "His actions in Md. were wise and vigorous. We have a hard contest before us, but the rebels cannot escape." Lincoln apparently agreed, pinning a second star on Butler's shoulder boards.[22] Believing that he was spiriting Butler to the war's margins, Scott ordered the newly minted major general to take command of the Military Department of Virginia and North Carolina. Yet before leaving the nation's capital, Butler responded to a "serenade" of several thousand gathered outside of the National Hotel. In his remarks, he defied those who doubted the necessity or wisdom of the war. This "unholy, fratricidal war," Butler insisted, has been "forced upon us." Now, there could be only one response. "Woe, woe to them who have made the necessity," he declared. "Our hands are clean, our hearts are pure, but the Union must be preserved. . . . The day of compromise is passed." The general confirmed for the crowd what his actions in Maryland had already demonstrated to the nation: he would mince no words and spare no remedy in suppressing the rebellion. The lessons of Maryland would not go unlearned.[23]

As it turned out, of course, Winfield Scott had merely shown his new nemesis the way to his next and much larger stage: Fortress Monroe, the sturdy military installation that commanded the historic Virginia Peninsula bounded by the York and James Rivers. Just one day after Butler arrived (as legislators in Richmond were ratifying the Old Dominion's secession ordinance), three freedom-seeking slaves—each of whom had been pressed into manual labor on a nearby Confederate battery—slipped within the federal lines and sought sanctuary. After harvesting much valuable information about the enemy, the general agreed to harbor the men; he immediately set them to work. They were "human beings wrecked upon a civilized coast," Butler reflected a year later.[24]

The following day, Confederate major John Baytop Cary, the memorably whiskered delegate of the slaves' owner, met Butler and sought to recapture the fugitives. "What do you mean to do with those Negroes?" Cary demanded to know. Butler's response was characteristically swift and direct: "I intend to hold them."

"Do you mean, then, to set aside your constitutional obligation to return them?" the confounded Cary rejoined.

Butler replied that he intended "to take Virginia at her word, as declared in the ordinance of secession passed yesterday," for he was "under no constitutional obligations to a foreign country, which Virginia now claims to be." "I shall hold these negroes as contraband of war," the general continued, "since they are engaged in the construction of your battery and are claimed as your property. The question is simply whether they shall be used for or against the Government of the United States."[25]

What Butler achieved at Fortress Monroe was significant, but not for the reasons that many historians have rehearsed. For one, it is not especially useful to think of Butler's "contraband of war" declaration as somehow setting the nation down the "path" toward emancipation, for the work of pulling up the peculiar institution was so freighted with contingency and fraught with complexity that it fairly mocks our attempts to chart a logical evolution of policy and agency. For another, military emancipation was anything but "new" in May of 1861. As the historian James Oakes reminds, both the British forces and the Continental Army availed themselves of the remedy during the Revolution: "freeing slaves in wartime," Oakes writes, "was a mainstream idea whose origins lay well outside the abolitionist movement."[26] Butler reminded the court of this historical reality in *Milligan,* suggesting that a defense of military law was also a defense of emancipation.

Indeed, the real significance of what Butler accomplished at Fortress Monroe rests in how he "weaponized" language: reducing to "an epigram," in the words of his staff officer Theodore Winthrop, the complex legal niceties of military emancipation that had flummoxed diplomats and policy makers for decades in the early republic.[27] The Boston abolitionist Wendell Phillips cogently observed that "when the rebellion first broke forth no man dared speak out touching the negro. The South fought to sustain slavery, and the North fought not to have it hurt. But Butler pronounced that magic word, 'contraband,' and summoned the negro into the arena." Indeed, as historian Kate Masur has noted, the word *contraband* quickly became "culturally powerful."[28]

As abolitionists heaped accolades on Butler, however, the general inadvertently offered his critics an entering wedge. In June, as he remained behind at Fortress Monroe, his forces staggered into a foolhardy fight at Big Bethel. Two months later, as the Lincoln administration reeled from a defeat at Bull Run that fairly dwarfed Butler's debacle on the Peninsula, Winfield Scott appointed Major General John Wool to command of the Department of Virginia and North Carolina. Always persuaded that enemies conspired and plotted against him, Butler conjectured that Big Bethel and the angst-ridden atmosphere in Washington had provided rhetorical cover for his dismissal.[29]

Butler had a point. His "contraband" declaration, after all, invited many hundreds of freedom-seeking men, women, and children into his lines, raising the key questions that Butler would pose to federal policy makers in a prolix dispatch to Secretary of War Simon Cameron: "What shall be done with them?" the general asked. "What is their state and condition?"[30]

"We, their salvors, do not need and will not hold such property, and will assume no such ownership," Butler persisted. "Has not, therefore, all proprietary relation ceased? Have they not become, thereupon, men, women, and children? No longer under ownership of any kind, the fearful relics of fugitive masters, have they not by their master's acts, and the state of war, assumed the condition—which we hold to be the normal one—of those made in God's image?" "My duty as a humane man is very plain," he resolved. "I should take the same care of these men, women, and children, houseless, homeless, and un-provided for, as I would of the same number of men, women, and children, who, for their attachment to the Union, had been driven or allowed to flee from the Confederate states."[31]

Cameron supplied a "weak and weaseling" response, which all too predictably riled the forthright commander.[32] "The reply of the secretary," Butler informed his wife, "is too namby pamby, and shows these people are not up to the occasion." "The negro will be free. It is inevitable," he assured. "We may patch it as we please but the fact will work itself out."[33] In August 1861, the general revealed his emerging understanding of the link between the

Union and emancipation in a remarkable letter to his friend Edward Lillie Pierce:

> This nation bound by its constitutional ties and the obligations of brotherhood has refused to interfere with slavery, being content to bear the national sin rather than convulse the nation's peace, overthrow the form of government and break up the foundations of society by eradicating it. This was expediency if not sound—perhaps those who believe in an overruling Providence will say that our present troubles were brought upon us because of our winking at sin. But now in every state . . . our brothers have repudiated all constitutional obligations [and] have upheaved the very foundation of political moral social and even religious relations with us for this very cause. We as a country have passed through all the agony, the convulsions, the disturbance of relations in society and the political revolutions which we have endeavored heretofore to avoid about this matter and are now engaged in a devastating and desolating war of which this is the sole cause. Shall we now end the war and not eradicate the cause?[34]

If success is the best revenge, then Butler got his two weeks later at the head of the army in a combined operation aimed at Cape Hatteras. Starved for encouraging news, the bloodless victory along the North Carolina coast—according to at least one account—"seized" President Lincoln with delight. Butler took advantage of the moment and his command of the president's ear, securing a furlough and instructions to "study out another job." As it turned out, that job was the command of the 15,000 infantrymen—among them many New Englanders that he recruited that winter—in the Department of the Gulf. The men would soon ready a combined army-navy operation on New Orleans.[35]

Not unreasonably, Butler's antagonists believed they would hear little else from him—and their predictions might have come true, had all but three of Admiral David Glasgow Farragut's ships not passed Forts Jackson and St. Phillip during the wee morning hours of April 24, 1862. Farragut proceeded directly to New Orleans—now outlined in plumes of smoke from the burning bales of cotton frantically heaped on her levees—and received her surrender. On May 1, Farragut ceded to Butler the prized Crescent City, the largest in the Confederacy. That day, Butler issued a public proclamation to the citizens of New Orleans, demanding "utmost deference and respect" for the flag, renewed oaths of allegiance to the Union, and the suppression of traffic in Confederate bonds. Butler placed telegraphic communication under federal surveillance, prohibited assemblies in the streets, and demanded "all species of disorder quelled." "The armies of the United States came here not to destroy, but to restore order out of chaos," he counseled.[36]

Butler faced a prodigious challenge in New Orleans. Hungry, indigent, and unruly civilians choked the streets, stubbornly refusing to acknowledge their status as occupied subjects. The prospect of "full-scale urban warfare" hung like a pall over the city. At once, Butler needed to feed and pacify its denizens. He remedied hunger and listlessness by forming "broom brigades" that tended to the unhygienic city's mud-daubed streets for modest wages and rations. Then, hoping to tutor New Orleans civilians in loyalty, he contrasted his efforts with the cold apathy of Confederate officials in General Orders No. 25: "This hunger does not pinch the wealth and influential, the leaders of the rebellion, who have gotten up this war, and are now endeavoring to prosecute it without regard to the starving poor, the workingman, his wife and child," he began. "Lafayette Square, their home of affluence, was made the depot of stores and munitions of war for the rebel armies, and not of provisions for their poor neighbors." Indicting the Confederacy as an "oligarchy" whose conceited officials had selfishly betrayed their obligations to the Union and the working poor, Butler demanded to know "how long" the people of Louisiana would stomach their ubiquitous rhetoric about chivalry and sovereignty. "How long will you be made the serfs of these leaders?" he asked. He would underscore the point in August, when he assessed those who had "aided the rebellion with their means" more than one-third of a million dollars for his ambitious relief efforts.[37]

Once more, Ben Butler reached for the clarity of contrasts, "interpreting the Civil War," in the words of historian Harold Raymond, "as a conflict between aristocratic slave power and democracy."[38] This was the very logic that underlined his much more famous General Orders No. 28, which declared that any woman who displayed "contempt for any officer or soldier of the United States" would be "treated as a woman of the town plying her avocation." Just as he had relied on the power of words and availed himself of the secessionists' definition of slaves as "property" the year before at Fortress Monroe, Butler now appropriated the secessionists' most cherished constructions of "proper" gender roles. Women who elected to announce their political opinions were not "pious, pure, and submissive," as the much vaunted "cult of true womanhood" demanded; instead, they were no better than cheap harlots who stepped into the public sphere in defense of a wretched cause.[39]

Yet "public" women were hardly Butler's only concern. He eyed the foreign consuls domiciled in the Crescent City with the same guarded skepticism that he had perfected in Baltimore, persuaded (and mostly accurately, as it turned out) that they were abetting the rebellion. When Mayor John Monroe and other city officials proved allergic to Butler's policies, they were packed off to Fort Jackson as prisoners.[40] And to further underscore the utter necessity of loyalty, Butler refused to issue a stay of execution for William Mumford, the forty-one-year-old rebel sympathizer who not only "maliciously" removed the Stars and Stripes that Admiral Farragut posted above the US Mint but then "dragged it through the streets and spit on it . . . until it was torn to pieces."[41]

Butler's chief aim was to champion loyalty in Louisiana. But because loyal slaveholders in Louisiana dreaded slave rebellion, Butler—as historians like Murray M. Horowitz have pointed out—was unable to draw the "distinctions" he preferred. He intuited that the situation on the ground in Louisiana was complex; President Lincoln would come to realize this, too, when he attempted to model wartime reconstruction in the state. So it was that Butler bickered with his abolitionist subordinate John Phelps, a Vermonter who began mustering regiments of African American soldiers. It would be a tense summer as Butler and Phelps traded barbs.[42]

Butler's clash with Phelps may have reassured loyal slaveholders, but it prompted some among the radicals to join the band of voices heaping derision upon him. Ultimately, the president bowed to pressure from those critics and, on November 8—the day after the Republicans held on to their majorities in Congress by razor-thin margins—relieved Butler of command. In a "farewell message" to the citizens of Louisiana, Butler dispensed his wisdom: "Months of experience and of observation," he began, "have forced the conviction that the existence of slavery is incompatible with the safety either of yourselves or of the union. As the system has gradually grown to its present huge dimensions, it were best if it could be gradually removed; but it is better, far better, that it should be taken out at once, than that it should longer vitiate the social, political, and family relations of your country." Emancipation had become a military necessity.[43]

President Lincoln, however, refused to relieve Butler of command entirely. Instead, he was whisked north to mark time, which afforded him the opportunity to deliver a major New York City address on "how to prosecute and how to end the war." The *New York Times* nodded approvingly after the "full, clear, and eloquent speech," remarking that it was performed with the "frankness and earnestness [that] mark his character." Not surprisingly, Butler announced that there could be no "half way" measures in suppressing the rebellion. With secession, the rebels had "repudiated the Constitution of the United States by vote in solemn convention; and not only that, but they took arms in their hands, and undertook by force to rend from the Government what seemed to them the fairest portion of the heritage which my fathers had given to you and me as a rich legacy for our children," he thundered. "When they did that, they abrogated, abnegated, and forfeited every constitutional right, and released me from every constitutional obligation, so far as they were concerned." "It is the duty of every man to be loyal to the Government, to sustain it, to pardon its errors, and help it rectify them, and to do all he can to aid it in carrying the country on in the course of glory and grandeur in which it was started by our fathers."[44]

After a restless summer in exile ("I am sick at heart having to lie here idle while the great game of the life of country is playing and Lee incompetently rule[s] the hour," he confided to his friend Edward Pierce in July), Butler returned to Fortress Monroe and, on November 2, 1863, took command of the Military Department of Virginia and North Carolina. The general would not mark time. When Butler reprised his New Orleans performance in the city of Norfolk, he estranged Governor Francis Pierpont, the loyal Unionist who led the "restored" government that President Lincoln's administration fitfully attempted to midwife in the Old Dominion.[45]

"From the beginning," historian William C. Harris has written, "because of its Lilliputian size and its pretensions of authority," the restored government in Virginia "was subjected to severe ridicule." Butler counted himself among the project's most earnest skeptics, deeming the local government "useless, expensive, & inefficient" and most civilians "loyal with lip service only." "Nineteen twentieths" of the population was "disloyal," Butler alleged, with "more than one half" lending succor to the rebels. The "restored" government made a mockery of Unionism. Accordingly, Butler issued an order "threatening punishment to any person who used any disrespectful language to any officer or soldier in the Union army." To sustain the "large numbers of officers, soldiers, clerks, and messengers" necessary to short-circuit liquor smuggling in Norfolk, he imposed a tax, to be paid into the "provost marshal's fund," of "one per cent on all goods shipped into his military district." The general likewise demanded new oaths of allegiance for "former citizens asking any favor or privilege of the government" and specified a provost marshal's court as the venue for all civil disputes, criminal matters, and real estate transactions in Norfolk. "When they become loyal in heart as on lip," Butler wrote, "and speak of taking the oath of allegiance to their country, not as a requirement but as a duty, it will be time enough to discuss their constitutional rights."[46]

Governor Pierpont registered a litany of complaints in a mid-January 1864 missive to Butler. "The civil authorities will attend to administering the civil and criminal law," the exasperated governor maintained, and "the military attend to everything that has for its object the rendering of the army efficient and well-disciplined." Any other approach, Pierpont fretted, would depart from "that *due process* of law." But Butler had a tin ear for such worries, further vexing the governor. Refusing to back down, Pierpont pilloried Butler's "gross assumption of power" in a frantic dispatch to Edwin Stanton. "I don't intend to give up all the civil rights of the people without a struggle," he warned the war secretary.[47]

After his own review of Pierpont's grievances with Butler, Lincoln demanded a response from the general.[48] Butler was, of course, more than happy to oblige, describing a ham-fisted civil government that was powerless to protect its starving people and incapable of cleaning or illuminating its filthy streets. Just as it had been "necessary to keep a military guard in Norfolk . . . to prevent rebel sympathizers from murdering union officers in the street," Butler maintained, "so it is necessary in my judgment that there should be a wholesome fear of the Provost Court to prevent the same rebel sympathizers from oppressing true union men under the form of not too well established law." In the matter of the one-cent tax, the general simply argued that "there are special expenses to which the United States is put in occupying large towns." In short, the military could not be expected to assume the mundane costs of municipal government.[49]

If anything, Butler's paper war with Governor Pierpont—along with his defense of his actions for the president—only persuaded the general of his righteousness. In March 1864, for instance, he caught up with the

Reverend George Dodd Armstrong, a Washington College chemistry professor turned Presbyterian minister who, in 1857, lent his voice to the proslavery canon with his 148-page tract, *The Christian Doctrine of Slavery.*[50] Armstrong further invited attention as the author of a stirring Thanksgiving sermon, "The Good Hand of Our God Upon Us," preached after the Confederate victory at the first battle of Manassas and later serialized by a Norfolk publisher. Reverend Armstrong swore an oath of amnesty, but misgivings persisted about the depth of his loyalty. In a hard-hitting interview, the general alleged that Armstrong merely wished "to avoid confiscation of his property" by swearing the oath. "I wish the President of the United States were here to hear what his Oath of Amnesty is called by you, you unrepentant, wicked Rebel," Butler scowled before ordering his interviewee hauled off to a military prison.[51]

Three months later, citing views "represented" to him by "many loyal citizens of Norfolk," Butler called for a public referendum on the future of Norfolk's civil government. Butler crowed once the ballots had been tallied, conveniently overlooking the troublesome fact that most men of Norfolk refused to participate in the election. "With a unanimity almost unexampled," he explained, the citizens of Norfolk had opted "against the further trial of the experiment of a municipal government." Without hesitation, Butler gleefully ordered "all attempts to exercise civil office and power" in Norfolk to "cease" at once.[52]

Confounded, Pierpont hoped to find an ally in Attorney General Edward Bates, a "doctrinaire" conservative from Missouri who, throughout the war, had demonstrated a willingness to defy "aggressive military commanders."[53] Scorning both Butler's "mock election" and his "compendious order" suppressing civil government, Bates demanded action. Butler, the attorney general alleged, handled Pierpont "with studied insult and contempt," refusing to acknowledge the legitimacy of Virginia's restored government. "I will not trouble you," he added, "with any remarks upon the strange and dangerous anomaly of a mere military officer ordering an election by the people, upon any subject, and without any reference to the laws of the land . . . and I, designedly, abstain from making any observations upon the plain absurdity of appealing to a popular vote to determine the question whether the laws of the land shall prevail, or martial law be established in their stead."[54]

Lincoln brooded for days before broaching the subject at a meeting of his cabinet on July 19, which erupted in a feisty discussion. While no patron of Butler, Secretary of State William Seward (after tending to the gripes of foreign consuls that Butler affronted in New Orleans, the nation's chief diplomat was keenly aware of how tiresome and time-consuming a dispute with the general could be) thought that any assessment of Butler's actions depended on the "question of military necessity." With the federal armies swinging spades around Petersburg and invested in a stubborn campaign before Atlanta, with a dim view of his own prospects for reelection (and thus little desire to declare war on a general beloved by the Radicals, whose ballots he needed in November), and with an instinctive confidence in Butler that he made manifest throughout the war, Lincoln was—much to his attorney general's vexation—unwilling to engage the matter.[55]

As Butler's biographer Hans Trefousse has argued, Butler "may well have been encouraged by the President's silence."[56] When a wiry Norfolk circuit court judge named Edward K. Snead "advertised in the city papers" that he would spurn Butler and gavel a new term to order "on Tuesday, August 2," Butler sent for Snead, subjecting him to an "examination" at his headquarters on July 31.[57] Throughout the forceful grilling, Butler betrayed his views on martial law. "A military commander must exercise his duties and [powers] within his department in face of the enemy or he is unfit to be [e]ntrusted with the command," the general explained. "Martial law governs the section of country under military occupation whenever in the judgment of the Comdg. Officer it is necessary for the peace and well-being of that part of the country within his department."[58]

Snead was agnostic. Suppose Butler commanded him "to slay all the male infants in Norfolk." Would he be obliged to obey him? "You would, sir," Butler replied, "or take the consequences, I assure you."

> You see if it were not so, all military authority would come to an end in a moment. By the civil law it is murder to deliberately kill a human being; now I am ordering my soldiers to kill all of your fellow-citizens of Virginia over here in the trenches that they can. May I not do so? There is nothing in the constitution of Virginia which permits. It is possible that it might become necessary to slay all the male infants in Norfolk in retaliation for a like outrage, but hardly probable. . . . As military law is the supreme one here, you will take care to obey it. The law martial was well known to our constitution—the powers and rights given by it have been defined for 2000 years far better than the civil law. . . . You would be as much puzzled to find the exact limits of martial pow-

ers in the books as to find the British Constitution. It is like most of the law which governs us in fact—parts unwritten law.[59]

Although Butler intuited that "a trap" had been set for him, he was unwilling to "yield."[60] Adding Edward Snead to a daunting litany of foils—among them Ross Winans, Major Cary, and William Mumford—Butler ordered the judge "stayed and quieted," held as a prisoner "until he gives his parole that he will in no way oppose the military orders of the Commanding General of this Department." Distinguishing between those who risked all for the Union cause and those who impeded the war effort, Butler directed Snead "to be treated with tenderness and care, so that he may take no detriment in sharing, with the soldiers of the United States, the fatigues necessarily incident to camp life."[61]

The next day, Butler dispatched a discursive defense of his actions in Norfolk to the president. Echoing his interview with Judge Snead and anticipating his arguments in *Milligan,* Butler defended military law as "a well known, well settled & well defined part of the common law of this country, received by us from England" and enshrined in the Constitution.[62] A week later, in a reply to Butler, Lincoln lamented the "considerable trouble" the situation in Norfolk invited, as well as the "crimination and recrimination" that had become "mingled in it." "Nothing," the president wrote, "justifies the suspending of the civil by the military authority, but military necessity. And whatever is not within such necessity should be left undisturbed." A "popular vote," he admonished, could not decide the fate of civil law in an occupied zone. Yet even as he regretted his failure to intervene earlier that year, Lincoln opted not to send—or even conclude—his missive. Much like the letter he wrote scolding George G. Meade for his failure to aggressively pursue Lee after the battle of Gettysburg, this note remained tucked away in a desk drawer, unsent.[63] Four months later, after Butler called for another public referendum on civil law in Virginia, Lincoln finally forwarded the memo to Butler. Yet the general would have no chance to plead his case. After an embarrassingly unsuccessful attempt on Wilmington's Fort Fisher, Benjamin Butler was cashiered, and his growing chorus of detractors exhaled.[64]

Still, Butler refused to yield the larger struggle for the Union and emancipation. In January 1865 he warned an audience at Lowell's Huntington Hall that the struggle was far from over. "Do not be carried away by any delusive cry of peace," he admonished. "If all men had been perfect, this Rebellion had not existed. It was the imperfection of men that brought it upon us, and through imperfect men it must be brought to an end. Therefore, let every man gird himself for still greater efforts."[65]

Ever dutiful, Butler continued to register his concerns into the years of Reconstruction. He feared that the rebels would escape punishment for treason, and that this would inspire them to "renew the contest in which they [had] signally failed." Butler was not only "anxious to have Lee seized and tried for treason" but visited with Andrew Johnson in an attempt to persuade the new president that a military commission could prefer treason charges against Jefferson Davis. Still, if he had little confidence in Southern juries to mete out justice, he held Northern civilians no less accountable.[66] "Have we liberated the negro to hate him?" he pointedly asked one Ohioan in an August 1865 letter. "Fought for his emancipation for four years only to deepen our dislike to him? Called upon him to stand side by side with us in the shock of arms . . . only to intensify our pride of race? Have we broken up a social condition which at least he found tolerable, to put him in one, where his existence is an impossibility?"[67]

Butler keenly anticipated the trials that remained still ahead, together with the forces—the Northern drive for sectional reconciliation and a murderous Southern counterrevolution—that would conspire to overthrow Reconstruction. In *Milligan,* Butler invited the nation at large to subscribe to his view that the Civil War was not yet over. Until the great questions of the war had been settled, military law seemed necessary and relevant. "We do not desire to exalt the martial above the civil law," he cautioned the Court, "or to substitute the necessarily despotic rule of the one, for the mild and healthy restraints of the other." But when the "law is silent" and "justice is overthrown," when "the bayonet is called in as the final arbiter; when on its armed forces the government must rely for all it has of power, authority, and dignity; when the citizen has to look to the same source for everything he has of right in the present, or hope in the future, then we ask that martial law may prevail, so that the civil law may again live, to the end that this may be a 'government of laws and not of men.'"[68]

As John Fabian Witt has recently argued, Butler's argument was, above all else, "calculated . . . to defend the authority of military commissions and martial law during postwar Reconstruction." The threat of another rebellion exploding into life seemed all too real. Extraordinary times called for extraordinary measures. "Whenever we are thrown into a war again," Butler contended, "whenever, hereafter, we have to defend the life of the nation from dangers which invade it, we shall have set precedents for how a nation may preserve itself from self-destruction."[69] Owing in part to his reputation among historians as "a man without principle or consistency," the general's argument in *Milligan* has been too hastily dismissed. But recent work that has restored to view just how precarious Union victory was, together with an ongoing Butler revisionism, demands that we take his argument—however wanting in nuance—seriously. Butler's effort was of a piece with his Civil War. No less than at Baltimore and Fortress Monroe, New Orleans and Norfolk, in *Milligan* Butler endeavored to cast into sharp relief the real and urgent perils of treason, rebellion, and slavery. That so many of his contemporaries found Butler's argument blustery and self-serving should detract neither from its convictions nor its prescience.[70]

NOTES

1. David Davis as quoted in Charles Warren, *The Supreme Court in United States History* (Boston: Little, Brown, 1922), 3: 148; William H. Rehnquist, *All the Laws but One: Civil Liberties in Wartime* (New York: Knopf, 1998), 117.

2. Frank L. Klement, *Dark Lanterns: Secret Political Societies, Conspiracies, and Treason Trials in the Civil War* (Baton Rouge: Louisiana State University Press, 1984), 112.

3. Samuel Klaus, ed., *The Milligan Case* (London: George Routledge & Sons, 1929), 69, 38–40, 226.

4. John Fabian Witt, *Lincoln's Code: The Laws of War in American History* (New York: Free Press, 2012), 310, 311.

5. Witt, *Lincoln's Code*, 311.

6. Orville Hickman Browning as quoted in David Mayer Silver, *Lincoln's Supreme Court* (Urbana: University of Illinois Press, 1956), 230; *Argument of Benjamin F. Butler, In Behalf of the Government in the Cases of Lambdin P. Milligan and Others, Petitioners for a Writ of Habeas Corpus, Before the Supreme Court of the United States, at Washington, D.C., December Term, 1865* (Lowell, MA: Hildreth & Hunt, 1866), copy in Benjamin Franklin Butler Papers, Box 174, Folder 6, Manuscript Division, Library of Congress, Washington, DC; Benjamin F. Butler, *Butler's Book: Autobiography and Personal Reminiscences of Major General Benj. F. Butler* (Boston: A. M. Thayer, 1892), 1007–1009.

7. Rehnquist, *All the Laws But One*, x; James M. Folsom to Benjamin F. Butler,

September 22, 1873, in MS Am 1248.2, Houghton Library, Harvard University; *Wisconsin Daily Patriot* (Madison), September 5, 1863.

8. An outspoken Democrat before the war, Butler placed Jefferson Davis's name into contention at the Democratic National Convention in Charleston, South Carolina, in the spring of 1860. As a student at Waterville College, he penned essays sharply critical of abolitionists.

9. Michael D. Pierson, *Mutiny at Fort Jackson: The Untold Story of the Fall of New Orleans* (Chapel Hill: University of North Carolina Press, 2008), 168, 159. My argument here is indebted to Pierson's deft analysis. My argument likewise builds on Harold B. Raymond, "Ben Butler: A Reappraisal," *Colby Quarterly* 6, no. 11 (September 1964): 445–479, esp. 478–479. On Sarah Jones Hildreth, "Ben Butler's Wife: A Romance Which the Doughty General Has Not Put into His Autobiography," newspaper clipping in Ames Family Papers, Sophia Smith Collection, Box 13, Folder 14, Smith College; Butler, *Butler's Book,* 79; Cowley, *History of Lowell,* 86; undated reminiscence in Ames Family Papers, Sophia Smith Collection, Box 9, Folder 12, Smith College; Gamaliel Bradford, "Mrs. Benjamin F. Butler," *Atlantic Monthly* (April 1925): 518–527; "General Butler's Home," newspaper clipping in Butler Scrapbook, Butler Papers, Box 260; *Daily Constitution* (Middletown, CT), April 10, 1876; *Daily Inter Ocean* (Chicago, IL), April 15, 1876.

10. Butler, *Butler's Book,* 1018. For additional background on Butler's legal practice, see Butler Papers, Box 174, Folder 18.

11. Butler, *Butler's Book,* 1018–1020; "Reply of Benjamin F. Butler for the United States," in Klaus, *Milligan Case,* 209–223, quote at 211.

12. Richard Sedgwick West, *Lincoln's Scapegoat General: A Life of Benjamin F. Butler, 1818–1893* (Boston: Houghton Mifflin, 1965), 312–313. Howard P. Nash Jr.'s *Stormy Petrel: The Life and Times of General Benjamin F. Butler, 1818–1893* (Rutherford, NJ: Fairleigh Dickinson University Press, 1969) neglects Butler's argument in *Milligan* entirely, while both Robert Holzman, *Stormy Ben Butler* (New York: Collier Books, 1954) and Hans L. Trefousse, *Ben Butler: The South Called Him Beast!* (New York: Twayne Publishers, 1957) mention *Ex parte Milligan* only in passing.

13. John Fabian Witt argues, "Speed and Butler hoped to vindicate . . . the availability of the laws of war as a basis for federal authority moving forward into Reconstruction." Witt, *Lincoln's Code,* 311. This chapter builds on and lends context to Witt's argument. Butler as quoted in Klaus, *Milligan Case,* 211.

14. Raymond, "Ben Butler," 478–479; Pierson, *Mutiny at Fort Jackson.*

15. Benjamin F. Butler to John Andrew, April 19, 1861, and Benjamin F. Butler to the Eighth Regiment, August 2, 1869, both in Jessie Ames Marshall, ed., *Private and Official Correspondence of Gen. Benjamin F. Butler during the Period of the Civil War* (Norwood, MA: Plimpton Press, 1917), 1: 17, 1: 23 (hereafter cited as *POCBFB*); Thomas H. Hicks to Benjamin F. Butler, April 20, 1861, *POCBFB,* 1: 18; Raymond, "Ben Butler," 447–448; Holzman, *Stormy Ben Butler,* 42–44; West, *Scapegoat General,* 51–54; Trefousse, *Ben Butler,* 65–67.

16. *POCBFB,* 1: 33; 1: 60; see also Holzman, *Stormy Ben Butler,* 44; West, *Scapegoat General,* 55–63; Trefousse, *Ben Butler,* 65–67.

17. *POCBFB,* 1: 43 and 1: 33; see also Holzman, *Stormy Ben Butler,* 45-48; West, *Scapegoat General,* 61; Trefousse, *Ben Butler,* 65–67, 70.

18. *POCBFB,* 1: 83–85; Butler, *Butler's Book,* 227; Holzman, *Stormy Ben Butler,* 46–49; West, *Scapegoat General,* 65–73; Trefousse, *Ben Butler,* 72–76.

19. *POCBFB,* 1: 71.

20. Butler, *Butler's Book,* 227.

21. "Iron Foundries and Machine Shops of Baltimore," *New Hampshire Statesman* (Concord, NH), May 4, 1861; "Important from Maryland," *New York Herald,* May 16, 1861; Thomas A. Bland, *Life of Benjamin F. Butler* (Boston: Lee & Shepard, 1879), 46; J. Blakeslee Frost, *The Rebellion in the United States* (Hartford: Author, 1863), 2: 223; Butler, *Butler's Book,* 227–288; "The Release of Ross Winans," *New York Times,* May 18, 1861; Holzman, *Stormy Ben Butler,* 48; West, *Scapegoat General,* 68; Trefousse, *Ben Butler,* 74, 76.

22. *POCBFB,* 1: 85; Butler, *Butler's Book,* 227; George Boutwell to Whiting Griswold, September 1861, in Whiting Griswold Correspondence, Manuscript Division, Library of Congress; *The Life and Public Services of Major General Butler, the Hero of New Orleans* (Philadelphia: T. B. Peterson & Brothers, 1864), 46–47; West, *Scapegoat General,* 72–75; Trefousse, *Ben Butler,* 74–76; Raymond, "Ben Butler," 448.

23. Butler as quoted in *The Life and Public Services of Major General Butler, the Hero of New Orleans,* 47; Butler, *Butler's Book,* 225–242; Holzman, *Stormy Ben Butler,* 49–51; Raymond, "Ben Butler," 449.

24. Holzman, 54–55; West, *Scapegoat General,* 75, 78–79, 81–86; Trefousse, *Ben Butler,* 77–79; *POCBFB,* 1: 516–517.

25. Butler, *Butler's Book,* 257; West, 81–82; Adam Goodheart, *1861: A Civil War Awakening* (New York: Knopf, 2011), 312–314.

26. James Oakes, *The Scorpion's Sting: Antislavery and the Coming of the Civil War* (New York: W. W. Norton, 2014), 14; Raymond, "Ben Butler," 465–466. See also Chandra M. Manning, *Troubled Refuge: Struggling for Freedom in the Civil War* (New York: Knopf, 2016); Glenn David Brasher, *The Peninsula Campaign and the Necessity of Emancipation* (Chapel Hill: University of North Carolina Press, 2012); Goodheart, *1861,* 340–346.

27. "Theodore Winthrop," *Atlantic Monthly* 8 (August 1861): 248; Oakes, *Scorpion's Sting,* 104–165.

28. "The State of the Country," in *Speeches, Lectures, and Letters by Wendell Phillips* (Boston: James Redpath, 1863), 529; Kate Masur, "'A Rare Phenomenon of Philological Vegetation': The Word 'Contraband' and the Meanings of Emancipation in the United States," *Journal of American History* 93, no. 4 (March 2007): 1054; Goodheart, *1861,* 329–330.

29. Cornelius Parker to Butler, May 28, 1861, Benjamin F. Butler Papers, Box 5; West, *Lincoln's Scapegoat General,* 84–85, 95, 105–106; Holzman, *Stormy Ben Butler,* 58–61; Raymond, "Ben Butler," 449; Trefousse, *Ben Butler,* 84.

30. *POCBFB,* 1:186; Goodheart, *1861,* 330, 338–339; Murray M. Horowitz, "Ben Butler and the Negro: 'Miracles Are Occurring,'" *Louisiana History* 17, no. 2 (Spring 1976): 170–172. For recent work on the "contraband" problem as it intersected with the question of women and children, see Stephanie McCurry, *Women's War: Fighting and Surviving the American Civil War* (Cambridge, MA: Harvard University Press, 2019); and Amy Murrell Taylor, *Embattled Freedom: Journeys through the Civil War's Slave Refugee Camps* (Chapel Hill: University of North Carolina Press, 2018).

31. *POCBFB,* 1: 187.

32. West, *Scapegoat General,* 105.

33. *POCBFB,* 1: 215; West, 105–106.

34. Butler to Edward Lillie Pierce, August 15, 1861, in Edward Lillie Pierce Letters, MS Am 1495, Houghton Library, Harvard University, Cambridge, MA.

35. Holzman, *Stormy Ben Butler,* 62–65; West, *Scapegoat General,* 107, 110–118; Raymond, "Ben Butler," 450; Trefousse, *Ben Butler,* 85–86.

36. James M. McPherson, *War on the Waters: The Union and Confederate Navies, 1861–1865* (Chapel Hill: University of North Carolina Press, 2012), 60–66; Holzman, 73–78; Trefousse, 106–107; West, 125–130, 133–135; *POCBFB,* 1: 433–436. On Butler in New Orleans, see also Chester Hearn, *When the Devil Came Down to Dixie: Ben Butler in New Orleans* (Baton Rouge: Louisiana State University Press, 2000), 52–109; Pierson, *Mutiny at Fort Jackson,* chapter 6; and Terry L. Jones, "The Beast in the Big Easy," *New York Times,* May 18, 2012.

37. *POCBFB,* 1: 457–459; McPherson, *War on the Waters,* 66; Holzman, 81–83; Trefousse, 120; West, 145, 146–147; see also Raymond, "Ben Butler," which detects the general's use of contrasts.

38. Raymond, 464.

39. West, *Scapegoat General,* 139–140; Holzman, *Stormy Ben Butler,* 92; Raymond, 459.

40. Holzman, 92–95; West, 145–146.

41. Holzman, 79–80; West, 151; Robert P. Broadwater, "Personality," *America's Civil War* 18 (November 2005): 20, 60; Butler, *Butler's Book,* 439; Raymond, "Ben Butler," 458–459.

42. Horowitz, "Ben Butler and the Negro," 172–173, 175, 176–178; see also Dudley Taylor Cornish, *The Sable Arm: Negro Troops in the Union Army* (New York: W. W. Norton, 1966); and Howard C. Westwood, "Benjamin Butler's Enlistment of Black Troops in New Orleans in 1862," *Louisiana History* 26, no. 1 (Winter 1985): 5–22. On Lincoln and the complexities of Reconstruction in Louisiana, see especially LaWanda Cox, *Lincoln and Black Freedom: A Study in Presidential Leadership* (Columbia: University of South Carolina Press, 1981).

43. Horowitz, 177–178, 184; West, *Scapegoat General,* 200–204; *POCBFB,* 2: 554–557; Butler, *Butler's Book,* 539.

44. Horowitz, 184; "Gen. Butler in New York," *New York Times,* April 3, 1863; Benjamin F. Butler, *Character and Results of the War: How to Prosecute and How to End*

It: A Thrilling and Eloquent Speech (Philadelphia: Printed for Gratuitous Distribution, 1863), 10, 32; Holzman, *Stormy Ben Butler,* 110–111.

45. Benjamin F. Butler to Edward Lillie Pierce, July 20, 1863, in Edward Lillie Pierce Letters, MS Am 1495, Houghton Library, Harvard University, Cambridge, MA; Butler, *Butler's Book,* 617; West, *Scapegoat General,* 264; Raymond, "Ben Butler," 460.

46. William C. Harris, *With Charity for All: Lincoln and the Restoration of the Union* (Lexington: University Press of Kentucky, 1997), 164; Benjamin F. Butler to Abraham Lincoln, August 1, 1864, in Abraham Lincoln Papers, Manuscript Division, Library of Congress; *POCBFB,* 3: 451; Francis H. Pierpont, "Letter to His Excellency the President and the Honorable Congress of the United States, on the Subject of Abuse of Military Power in the Command of General Butler in Virginia and North Carolina," in Jon L. Wakelyn, ed., *Southern Unionist Pamphlets and the Civil War* (Columbia: University of Missouri Press, 1999), 279–280; West, *Lincoln's Scapegoat General,* 264; *Life and Public Services of Major General Butler* (Philadelphia: T. B. Peterson & Brothers, 1864), 104.

47. F. H. Pierpont to Edwin M. Stanton, January 20, 1864, in *POCBFB,* 3: 323–324.

48. Abraham Lincoln to Benjamin F. Butler, [January 18, 1864], in Roy P. Basler et al., eds., *The Collected Works of Abraham Lincoln* (New Brunswick, NJ: Rutgers University Press, 1953), 7: 135–136.

49. Benjamin F. Butler to Abraham Lincoln, February 23, 1864, Lincoln Papers; Thomas C. Parramore with Peter C. Stewart and Tommy L. Bogger, *Norfolk: The First Four Centuries* (Charlottesville: University of Virginia Press, 1994), 216.

50. George D. Armstrong, D.D., *The Christian Doctrine of Slavery* (New York: Charles Scribner, 1857); Sean Scott, "His Loyalty Was but Lip Service: Loyalty Oaths and the Military Arrests of Two Ministers in Occupied Virginia during the Civil War," *Virginia Magazine of History and Biography* 122, no. 4 (2014): 315, 316–317.

51. West, *Lincoln's Scapegoat General,* 266–268; Scott, "His Loyalty Was but Lip Service," 317; George D. Armstrong, *"The Good Hand of Our God Upon Us': A Thanksgiving Sermon, Preached on Occasion of the Victory of Manassas, July 21st, 1861, in the Presbyterian Church, Norfolk, Virginia* (Norfolk: J. D. Ghiselin, 1861).

52. *POCBFB,* 4: 587, 4: 588–589; Marvin R. Cain, *Lincoln's Attorney General: Edward Bates of Missouri* (Columbia: University of Missouri Press, 1965), 292–293; David Work, *Lincoln's Political Generals* (Urbana: University of Illinois Press, 2009), 167.

53. Cain, *Lincoln's Attorney General,* ix, 292; Francis Pierpont to Edward Bates, June 28, 1864, Lincoln Papers.

54. Edward Bates to Abraham Lincoln, July 11, 1864, Lincoln Papers.

55. Edward Bates, diary entries for July 20, 1864, and July 31, 1864, in *The Diary of Edward Bates, 1859–1866,* ed. Howard K. Beale (Washington, DC: Government Printing Office, 1933), 386–387; Trefousse, *Ben Butler,* 168; Francis H. Pierpont to Abraham Lincoln, July 14, 1864, Lincoln Papers; Harris, *With Charity for All,* 164–165, 167.

56. Trefousse, 168.

57. Charles A. Page, *Letters of a War Correspondent* (Boston: L. C. Page, 1899), 204; West, *Scapegoat General,* 271.

58. *POCBFB,* 4: 572, 4: 570.

59. *POCBFB,* 4: 573–574.

60. *POCBFB,* 4: 576.

61. *POCBFB,* 4: 574.

62. Benjamin F. Butler to Abraham Lincoln, August 1, 1864, Lincoln Papers.

63. Abraham Lincoln to Benjamin F. Butler, August 9, 1864, Lincoln Papers; West, *Lincoln's Scapegoat General,* 272, 278.

64. Abraham Lincoln to Benjamin F. Butler, December 21, 1864, Lincoln Papers; West, 278; Trefousse, *Ben Butler,* 169; Louis P. Masur, *Lincoln's Last Speech: Wartime Reconstruction and the Crisis of Reunion* (New York: Oxford University Press, 2015), 126–127; Harris, *With Charity for All,* 169–170.

65. "Major Gen. Butler at Home," speech at Huntington Hall, Lowell, Massachusetts, January 29, 1865, Benjamin Butler Papers, Box 180, Folder 5.

66. *Macon Telegraph,* February 3, 1866; *Hartford Daily Courant,* February 7, 1866.

67. Benjamin Butler to "W. M. Dixon" [William Martin Dickson], August 15, 1865, Benjamin F. Butler Papers, Box 208, Manuscript Division, Library of Congress; Butler, *Butler's Book,* 916.

68. Butler as quoted in Klaus, *Milligan Case,* 223; Benjamin F. Butler, *The Private Volunteer Soldier: What He Demands as the Results of the War: Address Given before the John A. Andrew Grand Army Post of Boston, at Music Hall, May 30, 1876* (Boston: Press of Rockwell and Churchill, 1876), 16–19; Nina Silber, *The Romance of Reunion: Northerners and the South, 1865–1900* (Chapel Hill: University of North Carolina Press, 1993); David W. Blight, *Race and Reunion: The Civil War in American Memory* (Cambridge, MA: Harvard University Press, 2001).

69. Butler as quoted in Klaus, 211–212. On fears of a "second" civil war, see especially Mark Summers, *A Dangerous Stir: Fear, Paranoia, and the Making of Reconstruction* (Chapel Hill: University of North Carolina Press, 2009).

70. Raymond, "Ben Butler," 464, 479; Butler as quoted in Klaus, 223; Witt, *Lincoln's Code,* 311.

CHAPTER 2

Martial Law and the Expansion of Civil Liberties during the Civil War

JONATHAN W. WHITE

As a slave in Maryland—or even as a free black woman in the North before the Civil War—Harriet Tubman would have never been able to testify in court against a white man. Now, in June 1863, in Beaufort, South Carolina, she found herself a witness against Private John E. Webster of the Forty-Seventh Pennsylvania Volunteers, who was charged with embezzling and misapplying military stores. Tubman's testimony in the case was unremarkable; what is noteworthy is that by the midpoint of the Civil War she and several contrabands were called to testify in the trial.[1] A sea change had taken place in American law in a very short time as African Americans were openly admitted to testify against whites in military courts.

The standard historical interpretation of "civil liberties in wartime" is that civil liberties diminish when a nation faces a national security threat. Instances abound in American history: the Alien and Sedition Acts of 1798, Andrew Jackson's declaration of martial law in New Orleans during the War of 1812, Abraham Lincoln's suspension of the privilege of the writ of habeas corpus during the Civil War, Woodrow Wilson's repressive internal security measures during World War I, Franklin D. Roosevelt's internment of 120,000 Japanese Americans during World War II, and the suppression of suspected Communists during the Cold War. Americans in the twenty-first century continue to debate these issues—from George W. Bush's indefinite detention of suspected terrorists at Guantanamo Bay, to Barack Obama's use of unmanned drones to kill enemy fighters (including noncombatants and American citizens), to Donald J. Trump's so-called Muslim ban.

During the Civil War, Lincoln faced stiff criticism from Democrats and conservative Republicans for trying civilians in military courts in violation of their Fifth and Sixth Amendment rights. In light of the holding in *Ex parte Milligan* after the war, historians, lawyers, and political scientists have focused intense scrutiny on the negative aspects of Lincoln's habeas corpus policies. But concentrating only on violations of civil liberties in wartime misses a very important component of the story. Indeed, the institution of martial law and the use of military courts to try civilians during the Civil War did not *only* diminish civil liberties—they also *expanded* citizens' rights in several important ways. Perhaps most obviously, the Emancipation Proclamation was an extraordinary use of presidential and military authority that expanded the rights of African Americans. But the Union's use of courts-martial and military tribunals to try white civilians also opened up new opportunities for African American men and women, giving them a voice—and legal personhood—in the criminal justice system in the United States. In these and other ways, the presence of Union armies in the border regions and the South created new legal, political, and social opportunities for African American men and women who had just a few years earlier been declared noncitizens in the infamous *Dred Scott* decision.

In recent years a few scholars have begun to recognize the ways that civil liberties expand in wartime. Alexander Keyssar's magisterial history of suffrage in America shows how the right to vote has expanded during or immediately following periods of wartime, while suffrage has routinely contracted during long stretches of peace. During the Civil War, for example, the right to vote was extended to Union soldiers and, immediately after the war, to African American men. Relying on Keyssar's analysis, Mark A. Graber points to other ways that civil liberties have expanded as a result of military action.[2]

Military occupation and martial law opened up a number of social, political, and legal opportunities for minority groups and women during the Civil War. Historian Chandra Manning calls this "a central paradox of war"—that "its chaos brought suffering and new possibilities not merely at the same time, but intimately connected to each other."[3] Manning explores these issues within the black community, but, in fact, they were also "intimately connected" to the experiences of whites during the war—especially Southerners and Southern-sympathizing Democrats. According to Luci Petlack, as anti-war, antiblack Democrats became subject to arrest or other forms of suppression by Union military authorities, black communities in various parts of the nation were able to establish newspapers, form community organizations, expand religious institutions, and increase educational opportunities "with little fear of assault." Indeed, Petlack continues,

"The federal restrictions placed on white southern sympathizers during the war gave blacks an opportunity to expand their religious, educational, and social institutions."[4]

In cities like Baltimore, policing became more equitable once the Union army gained control of the area, with African American arrest rates dropping dramatically between 1859 and 1865. Arrests of black men for vagrancy also plummeted in New Orleans during Union occupation of the city. Indeed, Union occupation of Southern cities enabled local African Americans to expand their political and social horizons. The black community in Baltimore founded its first newspaper, constructed its first Catholic house of worship, and built a new building for the Ebenezer A.M.E. Church. Seven schools for black children were staffed, four industrial schools for black women were established, and by 1867 seventy-three schools for African Americans were opened across Maryland. In Alexandria, Virginia, the presence of Union troops offered security, work opportunities, schools (some even taught by soldiers), and decent burials, while in New Orleans, local African Americans created civic organizations, established newspapers, and publicly advocated for economic, political and social rights. One slave woman in the Crescent City even successfully had her former mistress arrested by Union military authorities for kidnapping and enslaving her children. Even contraband camps became places where military officers were able to offer protection from kidnapping to freed people.[5]

Confederate civilians groused that their slaves were fleeing to be "protected by Federal Bayonets." But from the slaves' perspective, this federal protection brought about a new sense of dignity for African Americans. "Drawing wages from the federal government in the nation's capital carried enormous symbolic significance for African American men and women, because before the war laws prohibiting black federal employment were so unbending that an African American was not even supposed to handle the U.S. mail," writes Manning.[6] For the first time in American history, black men and women were welcomed at the White House, and more than one hundred citizens of color felt the confidence to write directly to Abraham Lincoln.[7]

Perhaps the most notable changes in these regards took place in Cincinnati, Ohio. Race riots and violence against African Americans and abolitionists was rampant in Cincinnati during the first year and a half of the war, when a racist white Democrat served as mayor. However, after Republicans won control of the city in 1863, things took a turn for the better for the African American community. The new mayor reformed the police department to make it less political, choosing men with military experience over those with political connections. The appointment of Maj. Gen. Ambrose Burnside as commander of the Department of the Ohio in early 1863 also brought a new sense of order to Cincinnati.[8]

Burnside is perhaps most famous for issuing General Orders No. 38 on April 13, 1863—a military order that ultimately led to the military arrest, trial, and banishment of former Ohio congressman Clement L. Vallandigham.[9] But Burnside's order had far-reaching implications. "Calm pervaded the city until the war's end," writes Luci Petlack. "General Order No. 38 said nothing about race, but people of color in Cincinnati gained much from its issuance. With freedom of speech limited for whites . . . African Americans experienced freedom from assault and could partake in freedoms of speech and the press, as well as the ability to congregate publicly." Violence against African Americans in Cincinnati diminished dramatically during the second half of the war, and the city saw a broad creation of black political, social, and educational institutions. Indeed, one Ohio correspondent for the New York *Anglo-African* recognized these remarkable consequences of Burnside's edict, writing: "Under the combined influences of General Order No. 38 and loyal municipal authorities, this city, so long the theater of licensed riot and high handed outrage, has become a very model of quiet and good order. Negro-hating secession-sympathizers finding that they could neither ventilate their treason nor maltreat black men with impunity, have—to use a phrase more expressive than elegant—'simmered down.'" Petlack concludes, "For the last two years of the war, life improved for Cincinnati's African American population. This safe atmosphere allowed men and women of color to exercise forms of liberty previously unavailable to them, illustrated in the establishment of their periodical, as well as the expansion and further development of churches and educational offerings."[10]

Members of Lincoln's cabinet—as well as their opponents in the Democratic press—recognized that new political and social opportunities were becoming available to African American communities throughout the nation. In August 1864, black religious leaders in Washington, DC, gained permission to hold a fundraising event on the White House grounds on a day that Lincoln had appointed as "a day of national humiliation and prayer."

Attorney General Edward Bates observed in his diary "that the *white* and the black understand the Proclamation differently, and use the day for different and opposite purposes." "The Whites humble in fasting and prayer, as well they may, in view of their great and many sins, which have called down God's vengeance, and has brought upon us this desolating war," he wrote. "But the Blacks rejoice exceedingly, over the results of the war, already accomplished in their favor, and exult in the hope of the continuance of the war, in all its desolations." Bates concluded that this was a "reasonable" response for African Americans to take, as, to them, the war was being "waged solely for their emancipation." While Bates did not believe that African Americans "desire that the Whites shall be reduced to slavery," he knew that they welcomed "the destructive processes of the war" even if it meant that "all the civil, social and political rights of white men may be destroyed."[11] Democrats, of course, complained bitterly at the expansion of social privileges for African Americans. The *Washington Constitutional Union* groused that the White House lawn was "polluted" and "prostituted and disgraced" by the "negro revelries." White Sunday School groups had been denied the right to use these grounds. "The public grounds were too sacred—of too high a character—in too close proximity to the residence of the august Abraham Lincoln for white men to use," and "their color would remind him too forcibly of the despotism he has erected on the ruins of the republic," they wrote. "But the negro is wooed to accept the gracious permission—nay, it may be, the urgent request—and the aghast country beholds the terrible spectacle of white men rudely spurned in requesting a privilege most eagerly and anxiously thrust forward to the blacks."[12]

From the Democratic perspective, the expansion of social rights for African Americans had an inverse relationship with the rights of whites. In a litany that interspersed a variety of Lincoln's wartime policies, the *Holmes County Farmer* of Millersburg, Ohio, explicitly linked the expansion of rights for African Americans to the denial of rights of white citizens. "He suspended the writ of habeas corpus—set aside the Constitution—made a law of his own to free the niggers—rides in a carriage guarded by soldiers—admits nigger guests to the White House—sends ministers to Hayti and Liberia—buys all the niggers in the District of Columbia—muzzles the Press—[and] puts down Free Speech." A Pennsylvania newspaper similarly sneered that Lincoln "is emphatically the black man's President and the white man's curse." (Ironically, Frederick Douglass would call Lincoln "emphatically the black man's president" just a few months after the president's death.)[13] It is little wonder that editors like these feared the consequences of granting political rights to free blacks and ex-slaves. They feared that such actions would only mean fewer rights for whites.[14]

Some of the greatest wartime expansions of rights for African Americans involved the judicial system. Prior to the war, most states did not permit black men or women to testify against whites. Federal courts generally followed state laws regarding court procedure. As a consequence, African Americans were not allowed to testify in most federal courts, either. However, during the war, black soldiers and civilians gained new opportunities in the military justice system.

As Union soldiers, black men were court-martialed and permitted to offer their own defense. Historians differ over how fairly African American soldiers were treated in military courts. "If trials for black soldiers before general courts-martial were indicative of anything, it was their inconsistency," writes Joseph T. Glatthaar. Sometimes the courts proved "severe." For example, 21 percent of all Union soldiers executed were black even though black soldiers made up only 8 percent of the Union armies. "Yet," Glatthaar continues, "an examination of nearly all the transcripts of trials that resulted in executions indicates a surprising degree of fairness." In most cases, the testimony against the defendant was conclusive, although Glatthaar maintains that black soldiers often received harsher punishments than whites who committed similar crimes. While the lack of equal punishment was clearly unjust, Glatthaar points out that military discipline made black men "feel and act like soldiers rather than civilians."[15]

More recently, Christian Samito has challenged Glatthaar's interpretation, arguing that "While endemic racism in the Union army tainted the disciplinary process on other levels, the records reveal that officers on general court-martial panels wrestled with providing fair judicial process to black defendants while maintaining discipline so that African American soldiers received equal treatment and justice in cases involving capital-level crimes." From his examination of the records, Samito concludes that white officers presiding over cases often sought ways to grant leniency to black soldiers who were convicted of various crimes—particularly since those who were protesting injustice were often justified in their complaints. All told, "black soldiers enjoyed high standards of fairness and due process when facing general courts-martial."[16]

Regardless of which interpretation is more persuasive, participating in trials by court-martial played a significant role in the political socialization of African Americans of the Civil War era. Ira Berlin and the editors of the Freedmen and Southern Society Project concluded that the process of bringing black soldiers into the military justice system helped teach ex-slaves how to live under the rule of law. Military justice introduced African Americans to formal judicial procedures: they could testify against whites, cross-examine witnesses, and appeal convictions through the military chain of command. If they believed themselves wrongly convicted, they could even petition the secretary of war or Lincoln. As such, their experiences in military courts "helped prepare them for civilian life in a society at least nominally ruled by law."[17]

The absence of loyal civil courts in the South, in conjunction with the presence of Union armies, also led to situations in which black civilians were tried before Union military courts. Black men and women on trial appear to have received the same protections as black soldiers. Of course, it would be a mistake to assume that black civilians automatically received fair hearings simply because their judges were Union military officers. In many cases they did not have a lawyer to represent them. When one "poor negro" was accused of murder in Kentucky, "the *humane* lawyers of Louisville were going to allow the poor devil to be tried without Counsel." Fortunately, the defendant found counsel where he "least expected it"—Brigadier General James Brisbin of Pennsylvania "stepped forward to defend him." Brisbin told his wife, "The trial is exciting and I am much interested in it. I believe the negro is innocent and will clear him if possible. You know I would not see a dog suffer unjustly."[18]

In other cases African American civilians received notably fair trials. In one remarkable case, E. H. Williams, a black man in Norfolk, Virginia, was acquitted of murdering a Union soldier in May 1862. Williams had no lawyer, offered no witnesses or defense, and never cross-examined the prosecution's witnesses. Yet looking at the evidence offered by the prosecution, the court recognized that Williams had been unjustly assaulted by drunken Union soldiers and was therefore acting in self-defense when he shot and fatally wounded one of them.[19] These sorts of cases became more prominent after Lincoln issued the Emancipation Proclamation. In several notable cases, Judge Advocate General Joseph Holt—himself a former Kentucky slave owner who came to see the destruction of slavery as necessary to pre-

Figure 2.1. ***From left*****: Congressman John A. Bingham of Ohio, Judge Advocate General Joseph Holt, and Major Henry L. Burnett, taken during the Lincoln assassination conspiracy trial in 1865. Holt and Burnett would be key figures in the arrest and prosecution of Milligan and the other conspirators. Courtesy of the Library of Congress.**

serve the Union—held that the Emancipation Proclamation justified black men in killing whites when the accused murderers were defending their own freedom or that of their families. Indeed, during the latter half of the war (he was appointed judge advocate general of the US Army in September 1862) and into the postwar period, Holt would be a strong advocate for the expansion of civil rights to the freed people—and he used his high position as the head of the War Department's Bureau of Military Justice to try to accomplish this.[20]

Another great stride took place when slaves, contrabands, and free black civilians were allowed to testify against white defendants in military courts. As early as November 1861, a free black man testified against a Marylander known as "King Rebel."[21] The practice spread throughout the North and South during the war and persisted well into Reconstruction, with African

Americans testifying before provost courts, courts-martial, Freedmen's Bureau courts, and other federal boards of inquiry. Being able to testify was not only an important assertion of one's legal rights. As Chandra Manning argues, such testimony also "carried tremendous symbolic import and cemented bonds between the power of the U.S. government . . . and black men, women, and children."[22]

Recently, one historian has pointed out that the arrival of Union armies in the South "exposed black women to a new kind of sexual violence at the hands of soldiers," while at the same time "the passage of new military laws under Lincoln's Lieber Code of 1863 brought all southern black women under the umbrella of legal protection." The Lieber Code defined rape as a war crime without regard to the race of the victim, thus giving black women at least theoretical equality under the law. And black victims "did not hesitate" to assert their rights by bringing charges against their assailants. Indeed, a recent study found that military courts prosecuted approximately 450 men for sexual crimes, including a number that involved women and girls of color. "By not limiting its purview to accusations made by white women only, the military justice system made a stunning departure from Southern legal conventions," write historians E. Susan Barber and Charles F. Ritter. "Union courts-martial and military commissions held trials on behalf of both black and white women and based convictions of white soldiers on testimony of black witnesses. Thus, although invasion and military occupation left Southern women more vulnerable to sexual assault, paradoxically, the Union military justice system provided them with a venue to seek redress for sexual crimes."[23]

In some cases Union military officers sought to avoid military trials because they did not want the outcomes to be based on black testimony.[24] In other cases, Union officers specifically wished to use military courts for trials against whites who harmed blacks.[25] In one such case, pro-Confederate congressman Benjamin Gwinn Harris of Maryland wrote to Attorney General Edward Bates about the case of a white doctor who was charged with murdering a black woman. The prosecutors, according to Harris, "depend upon the testimony of a negro to sustain the charge and that is the reason why he is not handed over to the civil authorities upon proper application." Without giving "any remark or comment upon this course" of action, Harris asked Bates whether "you have given an opinion that negro testimony can be received, in a state which excludes such testimony, in such a trial as I have described above." Bates replied that this "question has never been before me, and I have given no opinion upon the subject. Nor can I give one now," Bates concluded, as federal law only authorized him to give legal opinions to particular government officials.[26]

White defendants and their lawyers offered numerous reasons for the "incompetency" of black witnesses. Many, like Harris, relied on state laws that prohibited blacks to testify in court against whites. In 1864 a Baltimore woman named Sarah Hutchins was tried by a military tribunal for attempting to send a decorative sword to Confederate cavalryman Harry Gilmor. One of the chief witnesses against Hutchins was a black courier named Joseph Baker. When the prosecution called Baker to the stand, Hutchins and her lawyers immediately "objected to the competency of this witness." Under Maryland law, her lawyers argued, "a colored person is not a competent witness in any case, against a white person." Any court sitting in Maryland was bound to follow local law and custom, they claimed. Allowing Baker to testify "would set the precedent." In fact, the precedent had already been set. The judge advocate replied that in military courts throughout the nation, African Americans "were now universally admitted . . . as competent witnesses." (This went back at least as far as the case of "King Rebel" in Maryland in November 1861.) The military judges agreed and decided to allow him to testify. Baker provided damning testimony of Hutchins's actions, leading to her conviction.[27]

Southern whites believed that permitting blacks to testify in court would undermine the entire Southern social system. Harrison B. Rooker, the overseer of the Neely Plantation in Madison Parish, Louisiana, was charged with murder and manslaughter for killing a freedman named Edward Johnson on October 13, 1863. The two men had gotten into an argument over a horse that Johnson was feeding and taking care of at the plantation. A local Union general had given Johnson permission to care for the horse there, but Rooker replied, "Dam[n] the general." After a heated exchange, Rooker shot the black man. He later claimed self-defense, saying that he was intimidated by Johnson and shot him before Johnson could physically attack him.[28]

The prosecution called nine African-American men and women as witnesses. Before the first witness could be asked a question, the defense objected "on the ground that he (the witness) was a Negro of African Descent, and it being contrary to the laws of the State of Louisiana for a colored man to give evidence against a white man." The objection was overruled. When asked what he knew, the witness replied, "Nothing." Perhaps this first witness was intimidated by the defense counsel's antiblack strategy. The next eight witnesses, however, offered complete accounts of what they saw. (They had not been in the room during the first witness to hear the defense lawyer's objection so they were likely not intimidated in the same way.)

Ironically, the first defense witness, Boaz Johnson, was also black, although the remainder of the witnesses for the defense were white. In their closing statement, the defense claimed that Rooker's position as overseer of the Neely Plantation gave him a special power over the victim. "The accused and deceased stood in the relation to each other of 'Master & Servant,'" claimed the defense. "Mr. Rooker representing his employers & being responsible to them for the good order & proper management of the business of the Plantation, as such agent & Representative, he was clothed with all the power and authority which his principals would have had." He continued that "it would be absurd to contend that Rooker and Ed Johnson were on terms of Equality on the Plantation, the adoption of such a principle would destroy everything like order & discipline on these leased Plantations & place the colored hirelings on equality with the owners & proprietors as well as with the agent, overseers & managers." Johnson thus owed Rooker his "obedience as his Master and Employer for the time being." With a touch of irony, the defense insisted that Johnson "had been previously in a state of rebellion[—]if I may use such a term—he had entirely ignored Mr. Rooker and his authority and in fact had claimed to have full privileges & authority to do just about what he pleased on the Plantation, regardless of the will or wishes of Mr. Rooker or those by whom he was employed." In a disingenuous attempt to sound fair-minded, the defense argued that if Johnson had been white and disobedient, he would have been treated the same way.

The defense returned to the issue of "colored" witnesses, pointing out that all of the prosecution's witnesses were black. Their race alone "may not of itself justify us in making any special objections to them—the objection we raise is far deeper & wider and underlies the whole matter." More than their color, the defense argued that their recent status as slaves deprived them of the capacity to serve as witnesses in court:

> These witnesses were until but a short time since, slaves, in absolute bondage, by act of the governmental authorities their *status* has been changed, from bondage they have been elevated to the state of freedom, would that their

> moral nature could have changed as readily as their civil or political *status*—at a bound, like Minerva from the brain of Jupiter, they sprang from a state of bondage to the conditions of liberty & freedom but they are still the untutored children of African parentage, without moral culture or Religious instruction, their moral senses obtuse & blunted,—time, careful moral & religious instruction, with other auxiliaries may remedy this, but it may be the work of centuries—the whole thing presents a problem which the wisest statesman & savant have yet been unable to solve.

The court, in other words, ought not to rush into such a monumental change. Until they were "better acquainted with the Negro character we should receive their statements with or without oath with great caution, otherwise we may find when too late that injustice has been done." The lawyer maintained that the "colored witnesses swear in many material respects at random & we fear with out any regard to truth, for they flatly contradict each other." He then proceeded to show ways in which their testimony did not agree.

The court rejected these arguments and found Rooker guilty of manslaughter, but not murder, and sentenced him to prison at hard labor in Alton, Illinois, for five years. This was a wartime case in occupied Louisiana. In many ways, cases involving black witnesses increased in importance during Reconstruction. From the perspective of wartime leaders like Judge Advocate General Holt, military courts would need to be used to remake Southern society and culture in the postwar period.

Even when blacks were allowed to testify, defense attorneys often used racial stereotypes to undercut their credibility. In August 1865, Edward W. Andrews of Orangeburg, South Carolina, was tried before a military commission for murdering a black man named Cromwell Bright in the presence of Bright's young son, "the small negro boy Israel." Andrews protested the jurisdiction of the military court, claiming that it violated his Fifth and Sixth Amendment rights, and that the US military did not have control of the area when he killed the man, so it could not claim ex post facto jurisdiction. Moreover, Andrews contended that he had been part of a provost guard and was meting out justice on the black man, whom he claimed was a thief. From Andrews's perspective, Cromwell had been "executed" for being a horse thief; he had not been murdered but had received justice under state law because in South Carolina, horse stealing was a capital offence.

(Andrews also claimed in court, quite preposterously, that Israel had urged him to kill his father.)[29]

The military commission rejected Andrews's objections and moved forward with the trial. When Israel Bright was called to testify about his father's death, Andrews maintained that he could not testify because he had not been "a free *citizen* of the United States when the crime is charged to have been committed." Moreover, federal law had never provided for blacks to be allowed to testify, and South Carolina law prohibited such testimony. If Bright could not lawfully testify in the federal courts within South Carolina, then "all other government courts should conform to the same rules of evidence, as are observed in the Federal courts." For additional support, Andrews pointed to the recently published fourth edition of *A Treatise on Military Law and the Practice of Courts-Martial* (1864), by Captain Stephen Vincent Benet, a professor at the US Military Academy:

> In the absence of all *statute laws settling this question* and in view of the utterly divergent and irreconcilable opinions on the subject of slavery held by different sections of the country, it is the policy of all Courts Martial to be guided and governed in such cases by the *rules that regulate the Federal Courts of law,* and which are in harmony with the rules of evidence of the particular states or territories in which these courts may hold their session.[30]

Again the court overruled the objection. Israel Bright testified that his father had been loaned the horse by one of Andrews's former slaves. He also denied Andrews's ridiculous claim that he had told Andrews to shoot his father.

The witnesses for the defense directly contradicted Israel's testimony; they also sought to impugn his character. One witness testified that Israel and Cromwell admitted to stealing the horse, saying, "We black people do some dark things." Israel's former owner, Solomon Legare, claimed that Israel was dishonest—"always a little run-a-way—pilfering, and doing all sorts of mischief." Other white witnesses similarly testified that Israel could not be trusted.

The military court acquitted Andrews of murder but found him guilty of manslaughter and sentenced him to ten years in prison in Albany, New York. The commanding general in the Department of South Carolina was appalled by the court's decision and returned it to them "for reconsideration," to determine whether Andrews ought to be convicted of murder. The commission reconsidered the evidence and came to the same conclusion—that he was innocent of murder but guilty of manslaughter.

Hundreds of South Carolinians petitioned President Andrew Johnson testifying to Andrews's good character and asking for a reprieve. Upon reviewing the case for the president, Judge Advocate General Holt was incensed:

> The murder was committed in the presence of the negro's son, upon whom, as an excuse for his own wickedness, the prisoner endeavored to fasten the crime of having urged the murder of his father. . . . The murder was undoubtedly committed under the influence of that brutal contempt for the lives and rights of the negro race so commonly prevailing with certain classes of the south, and in fanatical defiance of the government which has taken that race under its protection.

Holt further argued that the conduct of the military officers who composed the military commission had been "inexcusable" and that they ought to receive a reprimand of "the severest and sternest censure." He concluded with a strong statement about the role of military courts in the Reconstruction South, calling the court's decision in this case a "discreditable breach of official obligation."

> Unless the military courts now and hereafter necessarily to be organized in the southern States, for the enforcement of the laws, and especially for the protection of the negro from tyranny at the hands of his former master, shall be kept up to a proper estimate of the duties of their position by properly dealing with those who thus flagrantly violate these duties, it is to be feared that the consequences of the war for freedom, so lately brought to a successful issue, will be only misery, and a servitude worse than slavery, to that oppressed and unhappy race.

In other words, the courts must protect the freed people or they would lose their hard-won rights and freedom, and the war would be for naught.

From Holt's perspective, such a cold-blooded killing could only be the result of "the benumbing influence upon the moral sense of the system of forced labor in the midst of which the prisoner has been brought up," and it was the federal government's "bounden duty" to punish such manifestations of that Southern way of thinking. He continued:

> It shows to be so deeply seated and so widely spread the feeling of deadly hatred to the black race among those who so lately held that race in abject bondage, and the will to see them crushed without a protest or remonstrance so strong and ready, that the government is imperatively called on to carry out with the utmost resolution and sternness of purpose, undeterred by pretended signs of penitence, every measure having for its object the protection of this helpless people, which the overthrow of a treasonable war against human freedom throughout the world has placed under its almost exclusive guardianship.

Military courts, in short, must help bring about a social change in the South. Unfortunately, Andrews escaped from prison before Johnson made a decision in this case. He was never recaptured, although rumors circulated as late as 1882 that shortly after the Union troops had abandoned South Carolina he "returned home and had never been molested."[31]

When a white North Carolina woman was tried before a military court shortly after the war for the murder of a black man, her former slaves were permitted to testify against her. After her conviction, prominent politicians in the state sought her release after only two months in prison. Again disheartened by the push to show leniency to Southern whites who had shown disregard for the lives of former slaves, Judge Advocate General Holt recorded on her case file that releasing her from prison after such a short period "would be a low estimate, indeed, of the value of the life of a freedman." Unfortunately, President Andrew Johnson buckled to the political pressure and pardoned her after he came into office.[32]

Holt would be fighting an uphill battle to persuade white Southerners that their former slaves were worthy of dignity and respect. Some Southern lawyers relied on prevailing racial perceptions of African Americans to argue against their ability to testify in court. Stephen Lee, a citizen from Anson County, North Carolina, was charged with murdering a black man named Reuben on July 18, 1865. Lee did not object to the two black witnesses—John and Sallie—when the prosecution called them to the stand. But in his closing statement, Lee's lawyer made an impassioned plea for the court not to heed the words that John and Sallie had said.[33]

In an attempt to persuade the court of his good will, Lee's lawyer asserted that "no one . . . is more pained than myself at any act" that would disturb the peace of the community and "that harmony so desirable at this time between the people of the different sections, of one common country;

or between the white & collored races in our midst." Moreover, he professed to "desire especially that all lawlessness or violence towards the collored race because they are collored, & have been slaves, should cease at once." But the way to accomplish such peace and harmony was not by having "our courts, military, or civil, declaring that two ignorant collored witnesses . . . are to be credited, in prefference [*sic*] to four or five intelligent white witnesses who had a much better opportunity, to observe the transaction, than the two collored witnesses. Such a decision, would shock the community in which we live, & in its results would be most unfortunate for the collored race." This was a case in which there was "a direct & irreconcilable conflict of testimony, between the collored & the white witnesses," and he charged the commission with determining "whether two ignorant & unlettered collored witnesses" should be believed over the testimony "given by twice the number of white witnesses of good character & highly intelligent."

After impugning the black race generally, Lee's lawyer proceeded to attack the two black witnesses in particular, challenging some of the specific testimony they had given. He claimed that they could not comprehend what it meant to swear the truth, and that the court should instead rely on the white witnesses for the defense because they are "more intelligent," "have a higher moral character," and are "manifestly much more capable of understanding & of relating what actually occurred." How, after all, could the court rely on a "humble, illiterate, & dull" black woman "of great moral obtuseness"? In conclusion, the lawyer returned to the motif that black witnesses could not be trusted, recounting a case from the antebellum years in which a slave raped and murdered a white woman and then lied about it and accused other men.

The judge advocate replied that he would leave it to the members of the commission to decide the merits of the testimony, but he challenged the defense attorney's characterization of Sallie: "I consider that the assertions of the counsel with regard to the (colored) witness Sallie, being so low and dull and brutish, are altogether uncalled for and unjust; for she was decidedly *polite, bright,* & *sensible.*" The members of the military commission, in other words, could determine for themselves whether Sallie's demeanor revealed something subhuman and brutish, or human and worthy of trust.

The commission convicted Stephen Lee of murder and sentenced him to be hanged, but the decision of the court was overturned by Brevet Major General Thomas H. Ruger, the commanding general, who believed that

Figure 2.2. Biracial jury empaneled at Richmond, Virginia, for the Jefferson Davis treason prosecution, ca. 1867. Courtesy of the Huntington Library.

the evidence did not show malice and forethought. Instead, Ruger believed that Lee should have been charged with manslaughter. The prisoner was released.

Despite these setbacks, the developments that took place organically in the field eventually found affirmation from Republicans in Washington. In an 1864 appropriation bill, Congress allocated $100,000 for the purpose of counteracting the counterfeiting of US currency, "*Provided,* That in the courts of the United States there shall be no exclusion of any witness on account of color, nor in civil actions because he is a party to, or interested in, the issue tried."[34] Pointing to this statute as a precedent, Stephen Vincent Benet revised his *Treatise on Military Law and the Practice of Courts-Martial* in 1866, arguing that "Negroes may testify before a military court, notwithstanding any disqualifying statute or custom in the State where the court is held."[35] (It will be recalled that the earlier edition of Benet's treatise had been used to try to exclude black testimony from military courts.)

Permitting black men and women to testify against whites in court was a momentous step forward in American law—even if only a temporary one.[36] It demonstrated a new appreciation for the personhood of African Americans, rejecting the holding of the *Dred Scott* decision—that black people were not citizens and "had no rights which the white man was bound to respect"—well before the ratification of the Fourteenth Amendment.[37] So quickly were African Americans ushered into the legal system that in 1866 the first biracial federal jury was empaneled—in Virginia—to try former Confederate president Jefferson Davis for treason.[38] Former slaves would be prepared to sit in judgment over the nation's greatest living traitor.

NOTES

1. Court-Martial Case file LL-566, Record Group 153 (Records of the Office of the Judge Advocate General [Army]), National Archives and Records Administration, Washington, DC. (Subsequent citations will simply give the alphanumeric case number.) Unlike in civil trials, verbatim transcriptions were recorded for each court-martial and military tribunal during the Civil War.

2. Alexander Keyssar, *The Right to Vote: The Contested History of Democracy in the United States* (New York: Basic Books, 2000); Mark A. Graber, "Voting Rights and Other 'Anomalies': Protecting and Expanding Civil Liberties in Wartime," in Thomas E. Baker and John F. Stack Jr., eds., *At War with Civil Rights and Civil Liberties* (Lanham, MD: Rowman & Littlefield, 2006), 153–176; Jonathan W. White, *Emancipation, the Union Army, and the Reelection of Abraham Lincoln* (Baton Rouge: Louisiana State University Press, 2014).

3. Chandra M. Manning, *Troubled Refuge: Struggling for Freedom in the Civil War* (New York: Knopf, 2016), 4.

4. Karin Leann Petlack, "A Dilemma of Civil Liberties: Blacks under Union Military Control, 1861–1866" (PhD diss., University of California, Davis, 2013), 3, 6, 45–52, 93, 101–102, 173–176 (quotes on 3, 6). On a strong antebellum black community in the Midwest, see Mark A. Furnish, "Black Hoosiers and the Formation of an Antislavery Stronghold in the Central Ohio Valley," *Ohio Valley History* 16 (Fall 2016): 6–27.

5. Petlack, "Dilemma of Civil Liberties," 38–39, 105, 107–108; Adam Rothman, *Beyond Freedom's Reach: A Kidnapping in the Twilight of Slavery* (Cambridge, MA: Harvard University Press, 2015); Bradley R. Clampitt, *Occupied Vicksburg* (Baton Rouge: Louisiana State University Press, 2016), 125; Diane Mutti Burke, "'Slavery Dies Hard': Enslaved Missourians' Struggle for Freedom," in Jonathan Earle and Diane Mutti Burke, eds., *Bleeding Kansas, Bleeding Missouri: The Long Civil War on the Border* (Lawrence: University Press of Kansas, 2013), 151–168.

6. Manning, *Troubled Refuge*, 5, 47–48, 51, 73, 186.

7. James B. Conroy, *Lincoln's White House: The People's House in Wartime* (Lanham, MD: Rowman & Littlefield, 2016), 155–163, 185–191; Jonathan W. White, ed., "African American Correspondence with Abraham Lincoln" (unpublished book manuscript).

8. Petlack, "Dilemma of Civil Liberties," 150–162, 165–166.

9. Jonathan W. White, *Abraham Lincoln and Treason in the Civil War: The Trials of John Merryman* (Baton Rouge: Louisiana State University Press, 2011), 80–83.

10. Petlack, "Dilemma of Civil Liberties," 171–176. For the development of other economic rights by African Americans in Cincinnati during the war, see Matthew Axtell, "'At Liberty to Take Possession': How Cincinnati Riverboat Law Turned 'Have-Nots' into 'Haves' during the Civil War Era," *Ohio Valley History* 16 (Fall 2016): 48–71.

11. Edward Bates, diary entries for August 4, 6, 1864, in Howard K. Beale, ed., *The Diary of Edward Bates, 1859–1866* (Washington, DC: Government Printing Office, 1933), 393, 395.

12. *Washington Constitutional Union,* quoted in *Daily Milwaukee News,* August 14, 1864.

13. Millersburg, OH, *Holmes County Farmer,* March 26, 1863; Bloomsburg, PA, *Star of the North,* December 21, 1864.

14. On the political and economic fears of Northern whites regarding the potential influx of slaves during the war, see Leslie A. Schwalm, "'Overrun with Free Negroes': Emancipation and Wartime Migration in the Midwest," *Civil War History* 50 (June 2004): 145–174.

15. Joseph T. Glatthaar, *Forged in Battle: The Civil War Alliance of Black Soldiers and White Officers* (New York: Free Press, 1990), 116–120.

16. Christian G. Samito, "The Intersection between Military Justice and Equal Rights: Mutinies, Courts-Martial, and Black Civil War Soldiers," *Civil War History* 53 (June 2007): 174, 202. See also Christian G. Samito, *Becoming American under Fire: Irish Americans, African Americans, and the Politics of Citizenship during the Civil War Era* (Ithaca, NY: Cornell University Press, 2009), chapter 4.

17. Ira Berlin et al., eds., *Freedom: A Documentary History of Emancipation, 1861–1867, Series 2: The Black Military Experience* (New York: Cambridge University Press, 1982), 433–442.

18. James Brisbin to wife, May 26, 1865, Filson Historical Society, Louisville, KY.

19. LL-25.

20. Elizabeth D. Leonard, *Lincoln's Forgotten Ally: Judge Advocate General Joseph Holt of Kentucky* (Chapel Hill: University of North Carolina Press, 2011), 160–166, 176–180, 220. On ways that the proclamation actually freed slaves, see Mark E. Neely Jr., "Lincoln and the Theory of Self-Emancipation," in John Y. Simon and Barbara Hughett, eds., *The Continuing Civil War: Essays in Honors of the Civil War Round Table of Chicago* (Dayton, OH: Morningside, 1992), 45–59. White Southerners who kidnapped contrabands and free blacks to sell them into slavery also found themselves hauled into military courts. See, for example, KK-824, KK-825, LL-1334, LL-1344, MM-1195, MM-1217, MM-3360, and NN-2224.

21. Steven J. Ramold, *Across the Divide: Union Soldiers View the Northern Home Front* (New York: New York University Press, 2013), 64.

22. Manning, *Troubled Refuge,* 266–267. For a close analysis of how African Americans thought about citizenship when they testified in both civil and military courts, see Michael Vorenberg, "Abraham Lincoln's 'Fellow Citizens'—Before and

after Emancipation," in William A. Blair and Karen Fisher Younger, eds., *Lincoln's Proclamation: Emancipation Reconsidered* (Chapel Hill: University of North Carolina Press, 2009), 151–169.

23. Crystal N. Feimster, "'What if I Am a Woman': Black Women's Campaigns for Sexual Justice and Citizenship," in Gregory P. Downs and Kate Masur, eds., *The World the Civil War Made* (Chapel Hill: University of North Carolina Press, 2015), 256–260; E. Susan Barber and Charles R. Ritter, "'Physical Abuse . . . and Rough Handling': Race, Gender, and Sexual Justice in the Occupied South," in LeeAnn Whites and Alecia P. Long, eds., *Occupied Women: Gender, Military Occupation, and the American Civil War* (Baton Rouge: Louisiana State University Press, 2009), 51. On the rape of white women and girls by black soldiers, see William A. Dobak, *Freedom by the Sword: The US Colored Troops, 1862–1867* (Washington, DC: Center of Military History, 2011), 419–420.

24. Dobak, *Freedom by the Sword,* 116.

25. John A. Logan to John A. Rawlins, December 20, 1862, in John Y. Simon et al., eds., *The Papers of Ulysses S. Grant,* 31 vols. (Carbondale: Southern Illinois University Press, 1967–2009), 7: 506.

26. Benjamin Gwinn Harris to Edward Bates, July 2, 1864, in Record Group 60 (General Records of the Department of Justice), Entry 9 (Letters Received by the Attorney General, 1809–1870), Box 50, National Archives at College Park, MD; Bates to Harris, July 2, 1864, in RG 60, Microfilm M699 (Letters Sent by the Department of Justice: General and Miscellaneous, 1818–1904), Reel 8.

27. Jonathan W. White, "All for a Sword: The Military Treason Trial of Sarah Hutchins," *Prologue* 44 (Spring 2012): 12–20.

28. LL-2676.

29. MM-2606.

30. Emphasis added by Andrews's attorney. MM-2606. See also S. V. Benet, *A Treatise on Military Law and the Practice of Courts-Martial,* 4th ed. (New York: D. Van Nostrand, 1864), 250. This language had appeared in the 1862 edition as well.

31. This case was also investigated by Congress. See Sen. Ex. Doc. No. 11, 39th Cong., 1st Sess. (1866). Andrews had actually died in 1869. See *Orangeburg* (South Carolina), September 4, 1869. His gravesite, which is pictured at findagrave.com, is marked with a Confederate soldier marker.

32. Thomas P. Lowry, *Confederate Heroines: 120 Southern Women Convicted by Union Military Justice* (Baton Rouge: Louisiana State University Press, 2006), 143.

33. MM-3195.

34. *An Act making Appropriations for sundry Civil Expenses of the Government for the Year ending the Thirtieth of June, eighteen hundred and sixty-five, and for other Purposes,* act of July 2, 1864, 12 Stat. 351.

35. S. V. Benet, *A Treatise on Military Law and the Practice of Courts-Martial,* 5th ed. (New York: D. Van Nostrand, 1866), 305.

36. For the best recent analysis of both the expansion and limitations of rights

for African Americans in the Civil War era, see Laura F. Edwards, *A Legal History of the Civil War and Reconstruction: A Nation of Rights* (New York: Cambridge University Press, 2015).

37. *Dred Scott v. Sandford* 60 US 407 (1857).

38. Jonathan W. White, "The Trial of Jefferson Davis and the Americanization of Treason Law," in Paul Moreno and Johnathan O'Neill, eds., *Constitutionalism and the Civil War: Prelude and Legacy* (New York: Fordham University Press, 2013), 113–132.

CHAPTER 3

The Janus-Faced Character of Martial Law in the American Civil War, or the Strange Case of Lieutenant Alanson L. Sanborn and Dr. David M. Wright

Mark S. Schantz

On July 11, 1863, Dr. David M. Wright, one of his city's most respected citizens, stepped from the inside of Foster and Moore's dry goods store in Union-occupied Norfolk, Virginia, and put two bullets into Lieutenant Alanson Sanborn, a white officer, who was leading a company of troops from the First US Colored Infantry on a parade to recruit black men for the Union Army. In firing these shots, Wright put into motion a legal case of extraordinary importance for the course of the American Civil War. Tried by a military commission in Norfolk, the doctor and his legal counsel argued to be brought before a civilian court. But the Union occupiers of Norfolk would have none of that. A Confederate civilian had gunned down a Union officer on a fine summer day. And Lieutenant Sanborn was not just any ordinary Yankee. The young and idealistic man from Vermont had recruited the first eighty-one members of Company A of the First US Colored Infantry in Washington, DC, earlier that summer.[1] If ever there were a walking advertisement for the Union's resolve to recruit, train, and deploy men of color for the Union cause it was Alanson Sanborn. Think of the timing: one week after the Union victories at Gettysburg and Vicksburg. Abraham Lincoln and the Union commanders knew that more bodies would be needed to win the war, and the decisive increment would come from a massive effort to recruit black men to fight for the Union flag. In Norfolk, at the fulcrum of the Civil War, that effort stood to be compromised. If it were to become open season on Union Army officers leading black troops, the Union's war effort might be imperiled not only by resilient rebel armies but also by every civilian with a pistol. The military commission case against Wright for

Sanborn's murder became a test case of federal will to promote the cause of freedom by arming black men.[2]

Martial law and civic freedom make strange bedfellows. Uncomfortable in our national past and, perhaps, a blemish on the record of the United States as the standard-bearer for human liberty, military commissions rest uneasily in a democratic society.[3] The Sanborn-Wright case complicates in beautiful ways our reservations about military rule. Unlike most military commission trials during the Civil War, it did not take place in a border state—such as Missouri, Kentucky, or Maryland.[4] It did not step into an arena in which civic authority had already crumbled, in which flagrant lawlessness and guerrilla war were the order of the day. No horse thieving, pillaging, or bushwhacking in the streets of Norfolk or Portsmouth was involved. Nor did it take for its subject a Northern civilian on Yankee terrain—a man like Lambdin Milligan—who had allegedly threatened the Union's war effort. No draft dodgers, dissident newspapermen, or political heretics here. The Sanborn-Wright case did not seek justice for such men. On the contrary, it went after one of Norfolk's finest and most refined men for an act of murder in the streets—a murder that, if left untried—could have crippled the Union's war effort by working against the recruitment of black soldiers. The case is particularly illuminating because it shows how the Union armies could wield the power of martial law for the cause of black freedom. In this way, it challenges a conventional view of military commissions and the martial law under which they operated. While Union occupation and martial law clearly cut away at the "property" rights of white Virginians, it simultaneously served as a positive push toward freedom. In the liminal political terrain of occupied Norfolk, Virginia, martial law had at least two faces.

Emancipation in the Virginia Tidewater came in waves. Fortress Monroe, Virginia, a formidable federal position in Hampton Roads, provided the scene for extraordinary early encounters between Union troops and black Virginians looking for freedom. Designated as "Freedom's Fortress" by President Obama in a proclamation establishing a national monument there, it was the destination for enslaved Virginians seeking their freedom. Within days of Union general Benjamin Butler's arrival on May 22, 1861, black men presented themselves to him, their very bodies now demanding a determination of their legal status. Butler's now famous decision to term the runaways as "contraband of war" (while still not refuting that the people he encountered were property) was the crack in the door for hundreds and then thousands of blacks to seize the opportunity for freedom. By July 30, Butler counted at least nine hundred such "contrabands" at Fortress Monroe—among them men who also sought freedom for their entire families.[5] In making his "contraband" decision, Butler made what looked to Virginia slaves a lot like a black declaration of independence. Word of the reception of people of color at Fortress Monroe raced through Virginia, fear welling in the minds of slaveholders and hope in the hearts of their human property. The electricity of Butler's decision was verified by Union soldier Edward L. Pierce, whose 1861 article for the November issue of the *Atlantic Monthly* put it another way: "such is the mysterious spiritual telegraph that runs through the slave population."[6]

Pierce's *Atlantic Monthly* essay presented to readers his experiences as a military supervisor of contraband labor in tones that lauded the attitudes and accomplishments of his workers. He noted their willingness to work, their civility toward each other, and their disinclination to use "profane or vulgar" language—quite a change, one imagines, from soldierly discourse. Pierce's admiration for the contraband workers fairly springs off the page. "But the negroes, so dogmatically pronounced unfit for freedom," he declared, "were in this respect models of those who make high boasts of civility of manners and Christian culture." Early in his tenure at Fortress Monroe, Pierce recounted, he had the opportunity to address an "audience of sixty-four slaves and say what the Spirit moved him to utter." He went on, "I said to them that everyone of them was as much entitled to his freedom as I was to mine, and I hoped they all now secure it." With an anthropologist's eye, Pierce studied the living conditions of the slaves in the Hampton work camps, commenting especially on the great varieties of skin colors among his workers, the separation of their families, and "a universal desire among the slaves to be free." He noted particularly the desire of the contrabands to cut down a locust tree that stood in front of the jail. While his Hampton workers alleged to him that they had generally not been used severely (a judicious answer for a white man whom they did not yet know well) Pierce noted that the tree "was used as a whipping-post, and they were very desirous that it be cut down. It was used, however, only for what are known there as flagrant offenses, like running away." Running away, of course, was exactly what the contraband workers had done.

The earnest desire for freedom among the slaves and their near-reckless flight into the arms of General Butler's men (whom they did not know) hit their former masters hard. The slaveholders professed authentic astonishment that their human property had not been content. Many of Virginia's masters had agreed to put their slaves to work in building fortifications and breastworks designed to halt the advance of Union troops up the Virginia Peninsula toward Richmond, and they may have assumed their slaves shared their own political views. When their slaves bolted for Union lines, slave owners were left baffled, confused, and betrayed. Testimony from Peninsula slave owners makes this clear. Edmund Ruffin admitted, "The readiness of slaves to flee to the enemy . . . I did not expect." Another vignette: "One Hampton slaveowner was so troubled that he came to see Butler. 'I have always treated my Negroes kindly,' he informed the Union general, [and] I supposed they loved me."[7] Such were the delusions of Virginia's Tidewater aristocracy. For Norfolk resident and soon-to-be murderer Dr. David M. Wright, the signs were more ominous yet. During his closing remarks in his 1863 military commission trial, he struggled to explain his homicidal impulse: "May I be permitted to ask why a colored company was brought over to Portsmouth? Was it not known that a great feeling & fear would thus be excited in Norfolk? Who in this city has forgotten the Southampton massacre? Who does not know that these creatures, the negroes, when restraint is removed become ungovernable savages?"[8] Having first seen the flight of their slaves, then knowing of their employment as laborers in the Union Army, and now facing the prospect of their former slaves armed with muskets, Virginia's slave owners cracked. In every black soldier in a blue uniform, Wright saw another Nat Turner. The psychological shock to Virginia's masterclass of their slaves fleeing in droves to Union lines pushed one of the most level-headed and respected physicians of their city to commit a desperate act of murder.

Glimpses of the new life that Virginia's blacks began to make for themselves, all under the eye of their Union military occupiers, is provided in the pages of the newspaper the *Weekly Anglo-African,* published in New York City by Robert and Thomas Hamilton, African-American brothers born as free men. Robert Hamilton kept his eye trained on events in the Virginia Tidewater with an unwavering vision and visited there in the fall of 1863, just as the impact of Dr. Wright's trial came to its conclusion.[9] The *Weekly Anglo-African*'s columns on developments in Virginia appear in almost every extant issue from 1861 through 1863 and provide historians with an unequaled view of some of the first moments of black freedom in the American Civil War. On May 4, 1861—even before the arrival of General Butler—an article titled "What To Do With Virginia" suggested that because "Eastern Virginia is the most prolific negro nest in the United States, and almost in the world, outside of Africa," Union forces should be sent there immediately to recruit black men for service. The author cheered that "of course there are *Nat Turners* yet to be found in Southampton; in hanging one they extended the breed, and the story of the Southampton insurrection and massacre is recited by every slave mother to her children, from the Blue Ridge to the Accomac."[10] Wright's memory of Nat Turner and the memory cherished by Virginia's enslaved people could not possibly have been more at odds.

Other stories in the *Anglo-African* documented the joys of newly freed black folk of the Tidewater. They covered the free singing of songs in the growing contraband camps of Hampton, just outside Fortress Monroe.[11] Some told of General John E. Wool (who had followed Butler in command of Fortress Monroe) protecting the rights of hundreds of contrabands to learn how to read and write, cracking the sanction of laws that made it illegal for slaves to become literate.[12] The American Missionary Association was at work at Fortress Monroe, distributing reading primers and pamphlets. The Reverend Lewis C. Lockwood of the American Missionary Association presided over these efforts and established a school in the home of former United States president and slaveholder John Tyler. Mary S. Peake, "a free black woman of Hampton," could be found among the teachers.[13] Treating the contrabands as though slavery were already a dead letter, Lockwood performed the marriage rites for six couples in a single service. In this regard, he had consulted with General Wool, who "advises the administration of marriage in due form in regard to parties who, without having been married in fact, are living as man and wife."[14] The role of the Union military in making civil rights a reality for the black population of the Tidewater cannot be overestimated.

Before black men marching in blue uniforms caused Wright to pull the trigger on his pistol, black men were already signing up for military service. This he must have known. As a port city, Norfolk was home to all manner of mariners and workers familiar with rigors of life at sea. On October 19, 1861, the *Weekly Anglo-African* reported on the recruitment of black sailors for the USS *Minnesota,* the flagship of a Union flotilla deployed to attack Confederate batteries. "This is the first instance, as far as we can learn," remarks one account, "that the negro and the white man stood side by side fighting for the North. It is the testimony of an eye-witness, that the negroes fought as energetically and bravely—none more so."[15] While the canonical story of black men in military service during the Civil War begins with either the army units deployed by Thomas Wentworth Higginson and the men of the First South Carolina Volunteers or the men of Robert Gould Shaw in the Fifty-Fourth Massachusetts Regiment, it is the case that black men had been joining an integrated Union Navy before those units saw action. In this way, what was happening on the ground at Fortress Monroe, Hampton, Norfolk, and Portsmouth, Virginia, prepared the way for the much wider participation of black men during the Civil War. By the end of the conflict, black seamen made up fully one-quarter of the sailors in the Union Navy.[16]

In early May 1862, the sight of Union warships coming through Hampton Roads spelled an even more profound revolution for the white residents of Norfolk and Portsmouth. President Lincoln himself was on hand to help survey the coastal area for likely sites for the invasion and to bolster the spirits of his troops.[17] He could not possibly have grasped that in a little more than a year's time, he would wrestle with the outcome of a murder case of enormous significance that would come from the terrain he now surveyed. With the clash between the USS *Monitor* and CSS *Virginia* settled, the rebel ironclad scuttled, and the Gosport Naval Yard in ruins, Union troops landed in one of the key ports of the Confederacy. On May 10, 1862, General Wool at the head of approximately 6,000 Union troops seized Norfolk without a fight, finding the defensive positions that Confederate troops had constructed to be abandoned. It is impossible to know just how many of the city's 15,000 occupants were still in town. Before the war, Norfolk contained approximately 10,000 whites, 1,000 free blacks, and 3,200 slaves.[18] What the white population shared was a deep commitment to slavery, with virtually the entire white population either standing as slave owners or among those who employed and used slave labor. Enslaved people tested the boundaries of white authority by fleeing to the rivers and ports of Virginia in search of freedom. "In 1858, officials in Norfolk discovered the existence of a group known as the Norfolk Nine, which was assisting runaways," writes historian Glenn David Brasher, "The arrests and subsequent investigation exposed the existence of a network that allegedly stretched from Norfolk up the Peninsula to Richmond."[19] Given Norfolk's role as a port city—places that offered free blacks and slaves hiring out their time a sense of freedom—it is not surprising that it was a destination for runaways.

On May 10, 1862, when Wool's troops took charge of the city of Norfolk, the social and political revolution begun at Fortress Monroe found even wider compass. Beyond the superficial calm that may have attended Mayor William Lamb's formal surrender of the city to the general, there was deep resentment on both sides. Just days after Wool's forces arrived, Union soldier William Byrns, a lieutenant in the First Michigan Volunteers, wrote to Miss Morris Clark of New York that "The people here are of the most villainous kind & secessionists & will need a deal of kind schooling. . . . Perhaps the presence of a vigorous Provost guard will tend to bring them to a sense of right if not to a sense of the good & beautiful."[20] They would prove to be difficult pupils. On June 20, 1862, the front page of the *New-York Tribune* carried a clutch of stories that charted the simmering resentment between the white residents of Norfolk and Portsmouth and their Union invaders. "This city and Portsmouth," reported a special correspondent from Norfolk on June 17, 1862, "have been disturbed by repeated collisions between Union men and Secessionists during the last week."[21] From Portsmouth, the paper reported on an altercation between a "violent Secessionist and good Union men that ended in a "row." General Egbert L. Viele, the Union commander in Norfolk and Portsmouth (probably better suited for his craft as a cartographer rather than as a commanding general), evidently allowed the "Union men" to be handed over to the local authorities. The precise nature of the incident remains mysterious. While local government records do not reveal the trial or more details about the incident, the newspaper account continued that "The Union men say they are unwilling to be tried by Courts and Jurors who refuse to take the oath of allegiance to the Government." Unionists demonstrated their resentment of Viele's rather light hand on citizens whom they considered to be disloyal. While local court records do not illumine this incident, it certainly is evidence of the challenge mounted to Union authority by the occupants of Portsmouth and Norfolk. Women added to the resistance movement. Under the guise of ministering to the wounded on nearby hospital ships, they instead lobbed "studied insults, not only toward our officers and soldiers, but toward ladies supposed to be the wives and daughters of Union men." Across the board, resentment simmered. "These scenes are increasing and an unhappy state of things is growing up. A firm hand is required in the direction of affairs," reported the *Tribune*, "which should not be allowed to drift at random." Drift soon turned to murder.

On June 2, 1862, E. H. Williams, a "colored man" of Norfolk, stood accused of the shooting of Corporal John Hogan of Company C, in the Ninety-Ninth New York Infantry. Hogan and three fellow soldiers made their way to town, imbibing liquor purchased from local black vendors along the way, and were clearly intent on having a rowdy time. Visiting a bawdy house—staffed by two women of color—the soldiers found themselves behind the establishment in confrontation with black men. Harsh words flew. And moments later so did bullets, one of which killed Corporal Hogan. The record of this event in military commission transcripts are stunningly detailed and reveal both the close relationships and the hostility that characterized the Union troops and the black residents of Norfolk. Charged in a military court with murder of a white Union soldier, Williams would be expected to have been a doomed man. Instead, the court pronounced him "Not Guilty" of the charge. More than any other factor, it was the relentless questioning of the judge advocate, Major John Augustus Bolles, that ferreted out the details that the Union soldiers had been the ones who provoked the violence. Unraveling under Bolles's questioning, Hogan's Union comrades admitted that Williams shot only in self-defense after the Yankees had started to beat him. Whatever the facts of the case, whatever the dispositions of the men involved, it seems almost beyond belief that a black man could be acquitted by a military commission in occupied Norfolk, Virginia, of killing a Union soldier.[22]

But then again, Norfolk did not know Major John Augustus Bolles. A Whiggish intellectual from Connecticut, Bolles had studied at Brown University, where he had delivered a student oration on the memory of the dead. He was a formidable intellect with a keen sense of his role in both his family and his nation.[23] Before his military career, Bolles served in the Massachusetts state government and pledged himself to reformist causes ranging from temperance to the international peace movement. Indeed, his 1840 essay on a *Congress of Nations*—a kind of prototype for the United Nations—won a prize from the American Peace Society and served as the lead essay in a published volume. Ironically, the future soldier would argue in this essay that "the philosophy of war is absurd." Further, he contended, "The vanquished, though trampled into dust and bleeding at every vein,

Figure 3.1. Major John A. Bolles. Courtesy of the MOLLUS Collection, US Army Heritage and Education Center, Carlisle, PA.

and glad to obtain a temporary repose, is animated with the undying spirit of vengeance."[24] In these lines, it was as if John Bolles could already conjure the motivations of the man he was to prosecute in the summer of 1863. He also cast a skeptical eye toward slavery. On July 4, 1860, in addressing the people of Winchester, Massachusetts, Bolles observed "the Constitution of the United States—the most admirable frame of government ever devised by human wisdom, yet winks at slavery." Taking direct aim at the *Dred Scott* case, Bolles noted that the most exalted judicial body in the land could make "*dread*" mistakes. "Even juries," he reflected, "the palladium though they are of freedom and justice, at times render monstrous and unrighteous verdicts."[25] Lawyer and statesman, John Bolles had begun to see that exceptional measures might need to be taken to root out the evil of slavery in America. In September 1862, it is little wonder that the freshly appointed judge advocate general for the US Army, Joseph Holt, would tap John Bolles for service. "Over the next two and a half years," notes legal historian John Fabian Witt, "Holt recruited thirty-three men from among the best and the brightest of the northern antislavery elite; Lincoln personally appointed each of them judge advocates to work under Holt's direction."[26] Bolles was a perfect choice; he had thought deeply about issues of war and peace, occupiers and the conquered, slavery and freedom, and the complicity of the United States Constitution and its Supreme Court in perpetuating and then protecting chattel slavery. And in a final twist of fate, Bolles was the brother-in-law of Major General John A. Dix, who arrived in early June 1862 to relieve General Wool as commander of Fortress Monroe. His views would indeed be taken seriously by the local Union leadership in the Virginia Tidewater. Perhaps far more than any other Union officer on the scene, Bolles personified liberty in the cloak of martial power.

Into early 1863 the Union military continued to protect the political aspirations of blacks in Norfolk and Portsmouth. This was tricky business, particularly after President Lincoln's Emancipation Proclamation excluded the Union-occupied terrain of the Virginia Tidewater from its compass. This legal technicality did not stop the black residents of Norfolk from holding one of the most extraordinary celebrations in the city's history. A gathering of some five thousand black residents turned out to celebrate. Given "permission by Gen. Viele," they were led by one John Milton of North Carolina, who was Norfolk's own version of Frederick Douglass. Indeed, the *Weekly Anglo-African*'s lengthy account of the parade observed that Milton "wears his hair exactly like Frederick Douglass and is of his build. His was the marshal of the day and was seated on a fine jet-black horse, which was his own, and accompanied by ten aids, all on horseback." Drawing support from "the surrounding counties," the mass march called upon General Viele at his home; he gave them a hearty salute and favored them with little speech. The march continued to a lot in front of Cedar Cemetery to be treated to a sermon by the Reverend Richard Parker, a former slave who had hired out his time to earn his freedom at the princely sum of $3,000. He did not disappoint. He walked his listeners through the six decades of oppression and brutality during which he "had to surrender his will entirely to another." It was an occasion brimming with affirmations of freedom for black residents, and one completely orchestrated under the watchful eyes of the Union commanders. Though at times threatened by ominous rumblings from the Ninety-Ninth New York Regiment (the deceased corporal Hogan's unit), the "effect of this celebration upon the slaveholders of Norfolk has been wonderfully telling," wrote the *Weekly Anglo-African*'s correspondent. They were shaken to the core by the boldness of the procession and could hardly believe their eyes as former slaves took center stage while they watched the show. Anticipating the murderous rage of Dr. Wright a few months later, one "slaveholder on the street, no longer able to contain himself, gave vent to his feelings, and gave a young colored man a violent blow upon his head" but was then quickly corralled by men of the Nineteenth Wisconsin Regiment. "This somewhat cooled the passions of others," reported the newspaper, "which at that moment were at fever heat." The sight of so many black residents boisterously enjoying their freedom (in an area in which the Emancipation Proclamation did not apply) turned Norfolk's social order on its head.[27]

Where people of color found voice, white Virginians felt a choke hold on their rights to free speech. Nowhere was this more evident than in the case of the Reverend John H. D. Wingfield, associate rector of Trinity Church. During the month in which Union forces took Norfolk, Wingfield perpetrated a little legerdemain when he substituted "the litany for the traditional prayer that contained the petition for the president, Jefferson Davis being the chief executive for the whom Wingfield had explicitly prayed since Virginia's secession." Union troops in attendance at the service did not let it slide. They confronted Wingfield on his refusal to pray now for President Lincoln instead of Jefferson Davis. Even before Butler's General Orders No. 49 (in December 1863) Confederate clergy walked a tightrope. In March 1863, Union troops were posted at First Presbyterian Church to prevent residents from complying "with Jefferson Davis's proclamation for a day of fasting."[28] And as the Union occupation wore on, the restrictions upon Norfolk's Confederate clergy tightened, leading to the eventual incarceration of Wingfield and his Presbyterian colleague, the Reverend George D. Armstrong. The contrast here could not be starker—as newly freed black ministers and former slaves preached in the open, white Confederate ministers had to worry about Union troops showing up to clap them in irons.

Into such a white-hot environment marched the elements of the First US

Colored Troops (USCT). Recruited in Washington, DC, in May and June of 1863, the First USCT was a showcase unit for the recruitment of black men under federal auspices—something that the Emancipation Proclamation had promised. Although individual states had been about the business of recruiting regiments for the Union cause, the federal effort did not gain formal structure until May 22, 1863, when the secretary of war announced the establishment of "Boards" to recruit and to organize black men for military service. Even before General Orders No. 143 (the empowering document for this action), recruiters in Washington had jumped the gun, announcing meetings in early May to enlist men of color. With significant help from church leaders, such as Henry McNeal Turner (who became chaplain of the First USCT), the recruiters brought in a rich harvest of men.[29]

As was the case in the Virginia Tidewater two years earlier, black refugees flooded the city when the District of Columbia abolished slavery. Fully two-thirds of the men of Company A of the First USCT came from the counties and farms of Maryland and Virginia—escaping to the city to find freedom.[30] As the men began to be organized into companies and to drill, their officers moved them to the seclusion of what was known then as Analostan Island, in the middle of the Potomac River between the District of Columbia and Virginia. Previously known as Mason's Island (for James Mason, the Virginia planter, politician, and slave owner), Analostan Island was liminal terrain in 1863. The move to this place may have sprung from many motives—the urge to protect the recruits from angry white residents of the district or the wish to taunt secessionists in Virginia with the sight of black men drilling in blue uniforms, or the desire simply to train in peace. Whatever the reason, this part of the history of Roosevelt Island (as we know the place today) has, like much of our story, been hidden from history. No plaque or monument identifies the island as the place where the first two companies of the USCT were formed and trained.[31]

It was within this context that Lieutenant Alanson Sanborn began his work. Prior to joining the Union Army, Sanborn had been a young man on the move—born in New Hampshire, raised in Vermont, he spent time exploring the Midwest, found religion, taught school, and had probably encountered proslavery "border ruffians" in Missouri before returning to New England. Sanborn's thoughts and beliefs, like those of many young men of the mid-nineteenth century, were in transition, but the ideas of freedom that jelled in his head became a constant. Perhaps he found in the company

Figure 3.2. Rev. Henry McNeal Turner, African American chaplain of the First USCT. From William J. Simmons, *Men of Mark: Eminent, Progressive and Rising* (Cleveland, OH: Geo. M. Rewell, 1887).

of his men a solidarity that had eluded him in his days of rambling. Perhaps his talents as a schoolteacher made him a powerful recruiter. Details on his life are painfully slim, and since his service record with the Union Army lasted only several months, it took significant effort on the part of his mother to even apply for a pension following his assassination.[32] So fleeting was his service that the US Army appeared to have no record of it; so they told her. Still, he hungered to see all Americans freed and, according to his eulogy, for glorious death on the field of battle.[33] While a martyred death during combat eluded him, he did strike, perhaps, an even more important blow for freedom: leading men whose bodies signified a new identity for

African Americans. Unlike the much-storied Colonel Robert Gould Shaw or Colonel Thomas Wentworth Higginson, Sanborn would not find fame or a place in the history books. His work for the Union, however, was every bit as important—for it was the daily business of signing up black men for military service.

Born in 1809 in Nansemond County, Virginia (the same year as Abraham Lincoln), David M. Wright had studied in the North, earning his medical degree from the University of Pennsylvania. He moved his family to Norfolk from North Carolina and stayed through the horrendous yellow fever epidemic of 1855. One of the most important pieces of evidence in exploring Wright's background is the 139-page account book he left of the patients he visited during the summer of 1855.[34] Wright was a man of considerable energy, compassion, and precision—the book brims with multiple visits to the same families. He was a loyal physician and friend to his city. His account book makes clear that he treated not only white residents but their "servants" as well. As an owner of six slaves himself, this would not be surprising; Southern doctors routinely treated the human property of their white patients. Yet, tantalizing clues percolate from the handful of black residents he listed simply as "colored," and by their first names only, in his account book. Were they free blacks? How well did he know them? We know that Dr. Wright's medical practice embraced people of color, too, and he had come to know some of them as individuals. He had touched their bodies. Perhaps he had healed them. He was also organized and mindful of the bottom line—the account book contains meticulous records of the amounts owed and paid by his patients. An oil portrait of him at the Virginia Museum of History and Culture displays a man in heroic posture. He is seated, his head reflecting the light, face turned to the side in anticipation; he seems to be looking ahead for the next challenge.[35] He would not run from the ravages of yellow fever in 1855, nor would he run from the Yankees when they anchored their boats in Norfolk in the summer of 1862.

In Dr. Wright's view, Sanborn's work was that of the devil. On July 11, 1863, when Wright saw Lieutenant Sanborn and his detachment from Company B, First USCT marching down Main Street, he was moved to action. The details of the murder—scrupulously recorded by the military commission that sat in judgment on Wright—are so extraordinary as to seem almost unreal. And even more interesting are the variations, speculations, and outright falsehoods that surround these few brief seconds outside, and then inside, of Foster and Moore's Dry Goods store.

Earlier that day, Wright had celebrated his thirtieth wedding anniversary. It is tempting to speculate that the anniversary of his marriage called to his mind the end of the household (his family, white and black) he had cherished for so many years. Whatever the case, he was out and about in the afternoon. He found himself along Main Street where Sanborn was marching his company, evidently taking full advantage of the sidewalks as they proceeded—a clear violation of Southern racial etiquette, and a matter made much of in subsequent pro-Wright renderings of the tale. This evidently rattled the orderly physician. For Southern gentlemen such as Wright, having women and children yielding to, or being "jostled" by, black soldiers was an insult of catastrophic proportion. The most complete testimony of the next few minutes comes from Colonel Hugh C. Flood of the 155th New York Volunteers, who was close at hand. In brief, as the column passed by him, Dr. Wright was heard to say something that included the word "cowardly." Sanborn brought the column to a halt. He then approached Wright, who was standing in the doorway of Foster and Moore's Dry Goods, and the two exchanged words. There was "considerable excitement," recalled Flood, but he was unable to decipher the content of the conversation. Sanborn turned and began to walk back to his unit. "While he was in the act of turning," Flood recalled, "the Doctor fired a pistol." He fired again. Sanborn then rushed toward Wright and the two men fell into the store, grappling with the pistol—"the Doctor had it by the butt & the Lieut by the barrel." The two men clinched. And then Sanborn "slid along the counter and fell to the floor & the blood gushed out of his mouth and nostrils." The next few moments were miraculous: having watched Wright shoot and kill their lieutenant in plain view, the men of Company B were primed to exact revenge on the spot. But, fortunately for Wright, Colonel Flood intervened, held the doctor—who now offered to assist the dead Union officer—and hustled him off to the Customs House. There is much we can never retrieve from history about those first moments in Sanborn's assassination, but we do know that the quick instincts of Colonel Flood, a Union Army officer and occupier, saved Dr. Wright's life and carried him away to await justice.[36]

From the moment of the murder, white Southerners were anxious to turn Dr. Wright into a martyred victim while white Northerners thought him an outrage. From North Carolina came praise in the form of an article titled "A Southern Man Kills a Yankee," which delighted in the fact that Wright "evidently gloried in the deed he had done."[37] An anonymous imprint from Portsmouth, Virginia, began in earnest the trend of rewriting the record that was heard before the military commission. In this rendering, it was Sanborn's ignorance and barbarity that led to his death. Here, Wright confided that he had indeed "hissed" that the lieutenant was a "coward" but that he had walked toward the officer, now armed, and with his hand behind his back—"which in all countries is recognized as a warning that the accosted is armed." It was Sanborn's "persistent determination" to arrest him that led Wright to open fire—any civilized person would have known what was coming and desisted. Here was a nineteenth-century version of "blame the victim."[38]

Yankees took a different view of the murder. The *New York Times* called it "a deliberate assassination."[39] And when Wright finally dropped through the trap doors on his gallows platform, Mrs. J. N. Coan, a Sunday School teacher in Norfolk, would cheer to the *American Missionary,* "This has been a great day; justice has triumphed, and Dr. Wright has gone to his account."[40]

History, myth, and propaganda blurred in the hot and hazy days after the murder. Hence did the Sanborn-Wright case become a blank canvas upon which Confederates and federals could paint their best hopes and worst fears.

In the first moments after the murder, much had already been decided. Most important, and a matter of contention in the military commission trial, was Colonel Flood's initial move to take Wright to the provost marshal rather than to the civil constable. What might be called the "restored" (i.e., Union) government in Virginia was coming back into operation in the summer of 1863, and both Norfolk and Portsmouth had open and functioning local governments and local courts. Was the move to take Sanborn's murderer immediately to military authorities a righteous and just one?

Wright's legal team were not fire-breathing secessionists with vendettas to settle but loyal, reasonable and—most important—former Whigs, Union men, and well-respected lawyers. Lucius Henry Chandler, a Yankee-born Republican, settled in Norfolk in 1852 to pursue a law practice. A man of the Whig Party (like Lincoln), Chandler "continued to express his strong Unionist position" even as the Confederacy was born. Before the unsavory business of this trial, he had consulted with the president in the White House. Lincoln favored him by making him American consul to Cuba in late 1861. Upon his return, Chandler became United States Attorney for Virginia in 1863 and joined the Wright team: "This high-profile case brought Chandler into contact with Lincoln once again when he and his co-counsel, United States Senator Lemuel Jackson Bowden, appealed to the president to intercede."[41] Lemuel Bowden had Unionist credentials every bit as burnished as Chandler's. A Williamsburg, Virginia, man through and through, he had been a Democrat until 1855, when he supported Know-Nothing candidates. By 1860, Bowden had shucked his allegiance to the Southern Democratic order and was a presidential elector for John Bell's Constitutional Union Party. "He opposed secession so strongly in 1861," notes his entry in the *Dictionary of Virginia Biography*, "that he refused to pay state taxes until the government threatened to auction off his property." On January 23, 1863, Bowden was elected senator of the restored government of Virginia. He was sworn in on March 4 and "appointed to the Committees on Military Affairs and the Militia, on Pensions, and on Post Offices and Roads."[42] Dr. Wright's defense team was thus poised to offer a defense that might resonate with the "law and order" preferences of the Republican administration. They would be smart, reasonable, and judicious.

Chandler and Bowden based Wright's defense on the fact that the restored government existed in Norfolk at the time of Sanborn's death, and that with civil courts functioning, the military commission had no jurisdiction over Wright's case. Lucius Chandler began his defense by calling the clerk of the Corporation Court of Norfolk to the stand and asking a series of questions regarding the status of the local government. Had it met? Were its officers qualified? Yes, came the answer: "The Court met June 8, 1863 and its officers qualified on June 10, 1863." Was the government functioning? Had taxes been collected? "Yes, they have been assessed & are in process of collection." Chandler and Bowden were clearly making the case that because the local government and courts were functioning in Virginia, the Union Army had no jurisdiction over a murder case, a state crime.[43]

On July 22, 1863, squabbling continued over the matter of jurisdiction. Major Bolles punctured the case by arguing that the Virginia Constitution did not allow elections for the Circuit Court until November 15; thus, there was no legal authority to try Wright. Bowden counter-punched by saying he had evidence that the postmaster of Virginia had received "letters from Gov. Pierpont of Va., from which he learned that said Governor until within ten days last past has been since the erection of West Virginia into a State at

Wheeling engaged in adjusting & settling the fiscal & other arrangements between the old state & new." The court refused to hear the evidence, however, and the defense wished to note their exception.[44] The issue of jurisdiction, of course, was the most substantive line of legal defense. Wright did not dispute the facts of the case, or the fact that he pulled the trigger. Denying the authority of the military commission was his best hope for an acquittal.

It was precisely the issue of military authority that the judge advocate, Major John Bolles, wanted to pound home. In service of this task, he deployed the heaviest artillery at hand—Lincoln's General Orders No. 100, otherwise known as the Lieber Code. Issued on April 24, 1863, Lincoln's orders comprised 157 aphoristic pronouncements regarding how the Union would conduct war.[45] Written with emancipation firmly in mind, the orders contained provisions that protected all prisoners of war and included capacious powers for armies in terrain they had conquered—one might read here, Union armies in control of Southern terrain. So who, exactly, was under martial law? According to the Lieber Code, the answer was clear: "The presence of a hostile army proclaims its martial law." The code was scarcely eight weeks old when Major Bolles beat it like an executioner's drum at the end of July 1863. Citing no less than seven of its propositions in full, Bolles reminded his adversaries and the commission that these words "are from the pen of Francis Lieber, one of the most learned of living jurists."[46] From start to finish, Bolles grounded his case in Lincoln's new order explicating the laws of war and, particularly, in its formulation of martial law.

And martial law, as Bolles understood it, was essential to the preservation of liberty. Military rule, he argued, was the only way to preserve fairness and a sense of justice in wartime Virginia. As he reached the conclusion of his argument, Bolles hit full stride. "Is murder to go unpunished until such court may be in some way not known to the laws of Va. Created and organized." Here, he went after the argument suggested by Chandler and Bowden, that in time the newly reconstituted government of Virginia would be able to hold the reins of justice. But not now. "May any malignant Secessionists & traitors stand armed upon the sidewalks and with impunity shoot down or stab, at their own good pleasure, any soldier or citizen, whom they may solicit as their victims?" he asked as his argument drew to a close. Sounding a note that would in time ring ominously for the president, to whom the case would be appealed, Bolles posited that "the next victim may be a member of Congress, or a Senator of the United States. Who shall venture to predict what civil or military functionary may next fall under the bullet or blade of the assassin, & the murder find shelter beneath a denial of your right to bring him to certain and speedy justice?"[47]

Given the power of Bolles's argument, and the full support of the officers on the military court, Wright's defense team did not have a chance. A few snippets from the trial in July demonstrate their predicament. On July 22, as we have seen, the court refused to receive into evidence a missive from Governor Pierpont. On July 23, Wright's defense team wanted to cross-examine the provost marshal, A. E. Bovay, with respect to the question of whether Robert Kerwin, the local justice of the peace, had asked for custody of the prisoner. Bovay's answer toyed with Chandler's question regarding the written request that Kerwin had made: "This paper makes no demand on me & I have nothing to do with it as far as I can see." By the end of the day, the military commission had fully accepted Bolles's argument regarding jurisdiction and, from the defense perspective, things quickly went from bad to worse. As Bolles lined up his key witnesses—two Union army officers—the defense asked but a single cross-examination question, directed to Colonel Flood, who had protected Dr. Wright from harm following Sanborn's demise. Flood had noted in his testimony that Wright had asked to assist the fatally wounded Sanborn seconds after he had been shot down. "At the time the Doctor said 'let me do something for him' was his manner threatening or otherwise?" Flood replied: "I should judge he wanted to do something to alleviate the Lieut's pain." That was as far as it got. The defense essentially conceded the murder and was reduced to trying to introduce fragments of evidence that would reveal Wright's humanity or, perhaps, even regret.

On July 27, the last full day of the trial, Provost Marshal Bovay was recalled to the stand by the defense to elicit any words that might mitigate Wright's murderous rage. Bowden asked Bovay, "Was the accused examined before you as Provost Marshal of Norfolk on the evening of the alleged murder of Lt. Sanborn touching the charge of murdering him?" Bovay replied, "He was." Bowden proceeded, "Please describe the conduct & manner of the accused on that occasion." Bolles then immediately objected to this line of questioning, and "the Court was cleared." After a few moments, the clerk recorded that "On deliberation the Court excluded the question & decided to admit no evidence as to the conduct of the accused after the crime had been committed & the accused had been arrested and brought before the Provost Marshal." This was the last straw. Wright's team asked for thirty minutes to regroup, and when they returned to the court room "the counsel of the accused informed them that they withdrew from the case & withdrew accordingly." Frustrated at every turn by the military court, Wright's defense team had thrown their final punch.[48]

Almost. In his closing argument to the military tribunal, Wright—now representing himself—introduced a new option for his defense: the plea of insanity. Whether he had concocted this scheme with the knowledge and advice of his former lawyers, we cannot know. Indeed, it is possible that the defense's last move to examine the provost marshal about the doctor's conduct "after the crime" may have been the beginning of an attempt to cast doubt on his psychological state. What is clear is that Wright argued before the commission that "the most malignant secessionist, unless insane, would not commit an act so seemingly without motive: an act without apparent motive seems the act of a madman. What motive appears in this case? What cause can be given for my act?" Curiously, later in the same speech, Wright supplied in startlingly clear terms his motive for shooting the white officer of black troops, but now the issue of an insanity plea had been raised by the defendant himself. In his closing argument, Bolles dignified this possible line of defense. After demolishing the defense's jurisdictional case, it seems an incredible twist that Bolles himself would take up the question of insanity in such a forthright fashion: "Insanity may be set up as a defense," he conceded, "& if proven, it is a good ground for acquittal; although if the accused be acquitted upon that ground, he should be sentenced to confinement until cured, in some insane asylum." Perhaps it was at this point that John Bolles, former Whig and social reformer, imagined the possibility of rehabilitation for the man he had just convicted.[49]

The potential for an insanity plea to spare the life of Dr. David M. Wright was, in the 1860s, an authentic possibility. Growing scholarly and legal debate had been brewing since the 1840s around the question of the "homicidal impulse" and whether it might be used as a legal defense: the killer's reason temporarily dethroned due to a moment's passion. Abraham Lincoln, Secretary of State William Henry Seward, and Secretary of War Edwin M. Stanton had all—as lawyers—brushed up against the issue of the insanity plea, and it had to be taken seriously.[50] If Dr. Wright were sent to the gallows with the stain that he was not sane to stand trial, the political fallout for the Lincoln administration might have been substantial. On August 3, within days after the verdict had been rendered by the court, the president asked to see the transcript of Wright's trial.[51] A few weeks later, Lincoln telegraphed Major General John G. Foster at Fortress Monroe, declaring that he was ready now to sit down to meet with Wright's defense team.[52] Lincoln's challenge here would be to mitigate the issue of insanity while simultaneously supporting the death sentence he likely knew he would have to execute. It would be delicate business.

By early September, President Lincoln had decided on his course of action: to hire the best medical expert in the land to decide upon Dr. Wright's sanity.[53] There were two contenders for the job. One, Dr. Charles H. Nichols, held that the desire to kill might well up in an individual in the spontaneity of the moment, and "he allowed for insanity evolving from other than pure organic disease."[54] It seemed that Dr. Nichols would be open to entertaining the idea that Wright had been insane at the time he murdered Sanborn. But on September 2, Secretary of State Seward wrote to Lincoln that "Dr. Nicholl's surroundings are so disloyal as to shake public confidence in himself. Dr. Gray of Utica occurs to me as a very proper person."[55] The alternative whom Seward suggested was Dr. John P. Gray of the New York State Lunatic Asylum in Utica, New York. Editor of the *American Journal of Insanity,* the flagship research journal of the era, Gray was at once a cutting-edge scientist and an old-fashioned moralist. In his growing insistence on the organic causes of mental illness, Gray anticipated the directions of modern neuroscience.[56] But because of his dedication to the idea that mental illness, insanity included, was a matter of organic disease, Gray did not much believe in the idea that a man might temporarily take leave of his senses to commit a heinous crime. People were responsible for their actions, organic cause or not. A reliable New Yorker (according to Seward's advice) and a man who would likely find Wright to be sane, Dr. Gray emerged as Lincoln's expert selection. On September 10, 1863, he dispatched Gray to Norfolk with a lengthy charge to determine "Dr. Wright's sanity or insanity, and not to any other questions; you are to preside with power to exclude evidence which shall appear to you not pertinent to the question."[57] Here, Lincoln cautioned Gray not to be distracted by other issues, concerns, or public opinion. The doctor was empowered to cut to the core of the case, to examine Wright and those who knew him, and then to report back to the president.

One of the ironies of the defense's insanity gambit was that as they planted seeds of doubt regarding Wright's soundness of mind, Wright's

Norfolk neighbors unleashed petitions to the White House singing his praises as a model citizen. An 1853 memorial from Edenton, North Carolina, was sent that testified to Wright's abilities as he took up his duties in Norfolk: "We recommend him to the citizens of Norfolk as an able Physician; a Gentleman in all respects; and as possessing the social qualities that will endear him to the community to which he goes." On July 28, 1863, as the trial concluded, another petition was launched to the White House maintaining that Wright "be restored to his home and family or be delivered over to the civil authorities or some other tribunal; where he can have the privileges of a fair and impartial trial." Still arguing the jurisdictional issue, the July 28 petitioners seem not to have been aware that Wright's best hope for survival was that he was now insane. On August 21 came word from a fellow physician, N. B. Webster, who was a native of New Hampshire and had seen Wright practice medicine in Norfolk. "I have seen him prescribe medicines for the sick soldiers and sailors," wrote Webster, "who hearing of his professional skill in diseases incident to the climate and applied here, and these soldiers in the service of the United States, received advice and attention, as freely as his own neighbors, and always without charge." In the messages reaching Lincoln, Dr. Wright appeared clothed in the language of nobility, character, and magnanimity—hardly the portrait of a man whose incipient insanity would soon make itself known.[58]

In the end, Dr. Gray's expert medical opinion agreed with the testimony of Wright's friends and neighbors in Norfolk: the accused was perfectly sane at the time of the shooting and continued to be so even now. Such was also the opinion of the witnesses with whom Dr. Gray met. "It is a significant fact," he wrote in his report published in the *American Journal of Insanity*, "that no member of a family attended by Dr. Wright, who was on terms of social intimacy with him and his family, and who was best qualified by education to form an opinion, has appeared to give any testimony in regard to his professional conduct tending to support the allegation of insanity."[59] With Gray's report in hand, Lincoln now had the solution he needed: he had done his due diligence, he had taken the insanity defense seriously enough to hire the most able expert in the land, and now he had an answer that would support fully his decision to support the death sentence rendered by the military commission.

On October 7, 1863, Abraham Lincoln wrote to Major General John G. Foster at Fortress Monroe to proceed with Wright's execution:

> I have caused a very full examination to be made on that question [of insanity], upon a great amount of evidence, including all offered by the counsel of accused, by an expert of high reputation in that professional department, who now reports to me, as his opinion, "Dr. David M. Wright was not insane prior to or on the 11th day of July, 1863, the date of the homicide of Lieutenant Sanborn, that he has not been insane, and is not insane now. (October 1, 1863.)"[60]

The case was closed and the execution date to be determined. Nearly; Lincoln extended Wright's execution date for a week, in order to give the physician time to prepare himself for eternity on October 23. In the meantime, Wright's wife, Penelope, had made a last-ditch attempt to see the president in person to beg for her husband's life. Perhaps knowing that it would be difficult to resist the siren calls of a spouse in distress, Lincoln rebuffed the request with a brusque fatalism. "It would be useless for Mrs. Dr. Wright to come here," he telegraphed General Foster. "The subject is a very painful one, but the case is settled."[61] On October 23, 1863, Dr. David M. Wright was executed, with the elements of at least four Union regiments standing guard, among them men from the First US Colored Troops. While the white units formed a square around the executioner's scaffold, Henry F. Gladding of the Fourth Rhode Island Volunteers wrote to his mother that "the whole column marched in the square excepting the 1st D.C., they closed up the end that was open, the Dr. was led up the steps by two of his friends & the minister." The men of the First USCT occupied a prized place, joined by white soldiers from the 118th New York, the Eighth Connecticut, and the Twenty-First Connecticut, who now stood in silent judgment on Dr. Wright, representing the powerful hand of the Union military and martial law evident from start to finish in this case.[62]

Abraham Lincoln's stalwart support of the military commission's treatment of Wright is revealing for students of the American Civil War and for American citizens today. It shows, in the first instance, the power of martial law at the local level in creating opportunities for civil rights for black Americans. Federal power matters in matters of civil rights. The Lieber Code, which the president had issued as General Orders No. 100, was indeed known by Major Bolles and put into action within weeks of its announcement. If one of the goals of Lincoln's order had been to put military muscle behind the protection of black soldiers and the men who led them, then it had worked beautifully. Further, Lincoln's handling of the Sanborn-

Wright case in the days after the military commission trial reveals a deftness that indicates his full powers as commander in chief; intervening in the case, hearing out the defense, selecting a medical expert of his choosing, and then holding firm on the verdict. While Lincoln is known to have relished any opportunity to mitigate harsh sentences (the death penalty in particular) for his own men, in this case, he knew what was at stake.[63] Either the Union would stand with free black men and let them fight, or it would capitulate to waves of assassination and reprisals.[64] Lincoln knew the Union's need for manpower was acute—indeed, his October 17 message to General Foster appeared the very same day that he asked the governors of the Union states for 300,000 volunteers for service.[65] The need for manpower and the need to protect black freedom may have mingled in his mind at the very point the Wright case was being decided. That John Bolles and Abraham Lincoln handled the Sanborn-Wright case with such skill has lent it a certain measure of obscurity in the history of the American Civil War. But it could have all gone down so differently. At that pivotal moment in the Civil War, military power spelled freedom for black men and quickened the end of slavery in America.

NOTES

1. National Archives and Records Administration (hereafter, NARA), Washington, DC, Record Group 94, Record of the Adjutant General's Office, Book Records of Volunteer Union Organizations, 1st USCT Infantry, Vol. 1 of 5; see Regimental Descriptive Book detailing Sanborn's role as a recruiter for Company A, First USCT. On the formation of the First USCT, see also C. R. Gibbs, *Black, Copper, and Bright: The District of Columbia's Civil War Regiment* (Silver Spring, MD: Three-Dimensional Publishing, 2002), 1–58.

2. All references to the Sanborn-Wright case are from NARA, Washington, DC, Record Group 153, Records of the Judge Advocate General's Office, Military Commission Case MM-631, hereafter cited as MM-631.

3. Louis Fisher, "Military Tribunals: A Sorry History," *Presidential Studies Quarterly* 33 (September 2003): 484–508, situates the discussion of military commissions in the post-9/11 context and the so-called war on terror.

4. See Mark E. Neely Jr., *The Fate of Liberty: Abraham Lincoln and Civil Liberty* (New York: Oxford University Press, 1991), 168 and 166–184 more generally on this point. See also Detlev F. Vagts, "Military Commissions: The Forgotten Reconstruction Chapter," *American University International Law Review* 23, no. 2: 271–274.

5. See Glenn Larry Brasher, *The Peninsula Campaign and the Necessity of Emancipation: African Americans and the Fight for Freedom* (Chapel Hill: University of North Carolina Press, 2012), 27–49, for an excellent treatment of the Butler decision and its military and political context. See as well Louis S. Gerteis, *From Contraband to Freedman: Federal Policy Toward Southern Blacks 1861–1865* (Westport, CT: Greenwood Press, 1973), 11–32. As Gerteis wrote succinctly, "Whenever federal troops occupied slave territory, slavery as an institution crumbled and collapsed." Quote on 11.

6. Butler assigned Private Edward Pierce, "a staunch abolitionist, to organize the contrabands into a labor force." Brasher, *The Peninsula Campaign,* 44. All quotes from Edward A. Pierce, "The Contrabands at Fort Monroe," *Atlantic Monthly* (November 1861), 626–640; esp. 635, 636. Pierce's detailed article is an astonishing first-hand account documenting the first moments of black freedom in the Virginia Tidewater.

7. Both quotes from Brasher, *The Peninsula Campaign,* 37.

8. MM-631, Exhibit E, "Remarks of the accused to the commission, July 29, 1863, Norfolk, Virginia."

9. On Robert Hamilton's journey and activities see Debra Jackson, "A Black Journalist in Civil War Virginia," *Virginia Magazine of History and Biography* 116 (2008): 42–72. See also Henry Louis Gates Jr. and Evelyn Brooks Higginbotham, *African American National Biography,* vol. 4 (New York: Oxford University Press, 2008), 28–30, for entries of Robert and Thomas Hamilton.

10. *Weekly Anglo-African,* May 4, 1861, front-page article "What to Do with Virginia."

11. *Weekly Anglo-African,* September 14, 1861, "The Contrabands at Newport News, Contrabands Singing."

12. *Weekly Anglo-African,* October 5, 1861, "The Freedmen at Fortress Monroe."

13. *Weekly Anglo-African,* October 19, 1861, "The Virginia Freedmen: Their Moral and Intellectual Improvement."

14. *Weekly Anglo-African,* October 5, 1861, "The Freedmen at Fortress Monroe."

15. *Weekly Anglo-African,* October 19, 1861.

16. James M. McPherson, *Battle Cry of Freedom: The Civil War Era* (New York: Oxford University Press, 1988), 563–564, on the early entrance of black sailors into the Union ranks.

17. Anna Gibson Holloway and Jonathan W. White, "Abraham Lincoln's First Visit to Hampton Roads," *For the People: A Newsletter of the Abraham Lincoln Association* (Summer 2017): 1–3.

18. See Ervin Leon Jordan Jr., "A Painful Case: The Wright-Sanborn Incident in Norfolk, Virginia, July–October 1863" (master's thesis, Old Dominion University, 1979), 4 for population details. Jordon's thesis is the most coherent modern analysis of the Sanborn-Wright case. See also Gerteis, *From Contraband to Freedman,* 22, on the growing number of people of color behind Union lines.

19. Brasher, *The Peninsula Campaign,* 21.

20. The Mariners' Museum Library, William Byrns Letter, May, 15, 1862. I am grateful to Jonathan White for bringing this source to my attention.

21. *New York Tribune,* June 20, 1862, in possession of the author.

22. See General Orders No. 7, Head Quarters Dept. of Virginia, Seventh Army Corps, Fort Monroe, VA, February 5, 1863, indicating the "Not Guilty" verdict to the specification of murder brought against E. H. Williams on June 2, 1862. LL-25, NARA, Record Group 153.

23. See John A. Bolles, *Genealogy of the Bolles Family in America* (Boston: Henry W. Dutton & Son, 1865), ii; and John H. Eicher and David J. Eicher, *Civil War High Commands* (Stanford, CA: Stanford University Press, 2001) on Bolles, who was the brother-in-law of Major General John A. Dix, who served in military command at Fortress Monroe at the beginning of the Sanborn-Wright case.

24. John A. Bolles, *Prize Essays on a Congress of Nations for the Adjustment of International Disputes and for the Promotion of Peace without Resort to Arms* (Boston: Whipple & Damrell, 1840), quotes on 21 and 22.

25. John A. Bolles, *An Oration, Delivered before the Inhabitants of Winchester, Mass. July 4, 1860.* (Boston: Press of T. R. Marvin & Son, 1860), both quotes on 5.

26. John Fabian Witt, *Lincoln's Code: The Laws of War in American History* (New York: Free Press, 2012), 264–265.

27. All quotes from this event are from detailed coverage in the *Weekly Anglo-African,* February 14, 1863, "The Emancipation Proclamation in Norfolk, Va."

28. Sean A. Scott, "His Loyalty Was but Lip Service": Loyalty Oaths and the Military Arrests of Two Ministers in Occupied Virginia during the Civil War," *Virginia Magazine of History and Biography* (122): 300–335; quotes on 301 and 303.

29. See Jean Lee Cole, ed., *Freedom's Witness: The Civil War Correspondence of Henry McNeal Turner* (Morgantown: University of West Virginia Press, 2013), esp. 37–39.

30. NARA, Washington, DC, Record Group 94, Record of the Adjutant General's Office, Book Records of Volunteer Union Organizations, 1st USCT Infantry, Regimental Descriptive Book, Vol. 2 of 5. On early recruiting efforts for the First USCT in Washington, DC, see also C. R. Gibbs, *Black, Copper, and Bright,* 40–58.

31. I am deeply indebted to Bryan Cheeseboro, historian at the National Archives and Civil War re-enactor for the Fifty-Fourth Massachusetts Infantry, for pointing me in the direction of resources on the early history of the First USCT, particularly its time on Analoston Island.

32. See NARA, Washington, DC, Pension File of Mary H. Sanborn, 1884–1885. To prove her son's service and murder, Mary Sanborn included a press clipping from 1863 recounting the shooting.

33. See Rev. D. S. Frost, *Funeral Sermon of Lieut. A. L. Sanborn, 1st Reg't U.S. Colored Troops, Murdered at Norfolk, Va., by Dr. D. M. Wright, July 11, 1863. Preached at Thetford, VT, December 8, 1863, by Rev. D. S. Frost. Freedom's Martyrs Immortal,* esp. 13–15.

34. Account Book of Dr. David Minton Wright, 1855, Southern Historical Collection Manuscripts, University of North Carolina.

35. See Virginius Cornick Hall Jr., *Portraits in the Collection of the Virginia Historical Society: A Catalogue, published for the Virginia Historical Society* (Charlottesville, VA: University Press of Virginia, 1981), 266. The historian will use with caution and a critical eye the written accounts and biographies of Dr. David M. Wright since 1863—most are hagiographical (which is of real interest and will be treated in my forthcoming book) and are dedicated to rehabilitating his memory. Among many, William S. Powell, ed., *Dictionary of North Carolina Biography,* Vol. 6, T–Z, (Chapel Hill: University of North Carolina Press, 1996), 276, avers that Sanborn threatened Wright with a drawn sword—an important detail, but one completely missing from the military commission transcript. If such a threat occurred, Wright's defense team would surely have introduced it into evidence. No witness at the trial mentioned this, nor did the legal defense introduce a plea for self-defense. This is but one specimen of the layers of myth that were accreted on the murder in the years to come.

36. MM-631, Testimony of Lt. Col. Hugh C. Flood, 155th N.Y. Volunteers.

37. *Western Democrat* (Charlotte, NC), "A Southern Man Kills a Yankee," July 28, 1863.

38. *Trial and Execution of Dr. David M. Wright, of Norfolk, Va., for the Murder of Lieut. A. L. Sanborn,* July 11, 1863. Portsmouth, Va. October 27, 1863. Anonymous broadside, in possession of the author.

39. *New York Times,* "Affairs in Norfolk, VA; Deliberate Assassination of an Officer of Colored Troops by a Citizen–Great Excitement—The Assassin under Close Arrest," Sunday, July 12, 1863. It is worth noting that even though contemporary historians of the Civil War barely glimpse at the Sanborn-Wright case, "The case of Dr. David M. Wright was known to nearly every American in 1863," according to independent researcher and writer Thomas P. Lowry in *Merciful Lincoln: The President and Military Justice* (N.P.: Thomas P. Lowry, 2009), 100.

40. *American Missionary,* New York, December 1863, "Mission House, Norfolk, Oct. 23, 1863."

41. Jodi L. Koste, entry for Lucius Henry Chandler, *Dictionary of Virginia Biography,* vol. 3 (Richmond: Library of Virginia, 2006), 165–167.

42. Donald W. Gunter, entry for Lemuel Jackson Bowden, *Dictionary of Virginia Biography,* vol. 2 (Richmond: Library of Virginia, 2001), 131–132.

43. MM-631, proceedings of July 21, 1863.

44. MM-631, proceedings of July 22, 1863.

45. The text of General Orders No. 100 can be found in Witt, *Lincoln's Code,* 375–394.

46. MM-631; see Exhibit C for Bolles's full argument. The sections of code that Bolles cited were 1, 2, 3, 4, 12, 13, and 26. Bolles's nimble and extensive use of General Orders No. 100—scarcely two months after it was issued—confounds the arguments of historians who think the orders made relatively little difference in the

field. See Matthew J. Mancini, "Francis Lieber, Slavery, and the 'Genesis' of the Laws of War," *Journal of Southern History,* 77 (May 2011), who argues that "While No. 100 made little impact at the time on Union officers—or on subsequent historians for that matter—it went on to exert a profound and lasting influence on international law and diplomacy." See 328 for quote. Or, Frank Friedel's pioneering essay "General Orders 100 and Military Government," *Mississippi Valley Historical Review,* 32 (March 1946), which argues that "Union commanders and military governors seem to have attached relatively little importance to the Orders." See 553 for quote. Major John A. Bolles's use of the code may have been exceptional, but he deployed it at an absolutely crucial juncture in the American Civil War.

47. MM-631, Exhibit C, for all quotes.

48. MM-631 for all quotes.

49. MM 631, Exhibits E and F.

50. See Allen D. Spiegel, *A Lincoln, Esquire: A Shrewd, Sophisticated Lawyer in His Time* (Macon, GA: Mercer University Press, 2002), 245.

51. Roy P. Basler, ed., *The Collected Works of Abraham Lincoln,* vol. 6 (New Brunswick, NJ: Rutgers University Press, 1953), 362.

52. Basler, *Collected Works,* 6: 419.

53. The issue of Wright's sanity is explored by Spiegel, *A. Lincoln, Esquire,* 244–273, and in Spiegel's articles "Abraham Lincoln and the Insanity Plea," *Journal of Community Health,* 19 (June 1994): 201–219; and "Differing Views on Insanity of Two Nineteenth-Century Forensic Psychiatrists," *Journal of Community Health* 5 (October 2006): 430–451.

54. Spiegel, "Differing Views," 430.

55. Seward quoted in Spiegel, *A. Lincoln, Esquire,* 256.

56. The landmark article here is John P. Gray, *Insanity: Its Dependence on Physical Disease. Read before the Medical Society of the State of New York, at Its Annual Meeting, February, 1871* (Utica, NY: Roberts, Book and Job Printer, 1871). Gray's work on the Wright-Sanborn case—selected by Lincoln himself—vaulted Gray into the front ranks of American psychiatric practitioners.

57. Basler, *Collected Works,* 6: 437–438.

58. All petitions in MM-631 case file.

59. Dr. John P. Gray, "The Case of Dr. David M. Wright, for the Murder of Lieutenant Sanborn.—Plea Insanity," *Journal of American Insanity* 20 (January 1864): 284–300; quote on 300.

60. Basler, *Collected Works,* 6: 505. The original document, with Lincoln's signature, is part of the MM-631 case file.

61. Basler, 6: 522.

62. Henry F. Gladding Letter, October 26, 1863, Manuscripts, Virginia Historical Society, Richmond, VA.

63. The painstaking work of amateur historian Thomas P. Lowry has methodically shown that Lincoln consistently mitigated harsher sentences meted out by military courts throughout the war. See his *Don't Shot That Boy! Abraham Lincoln and*

Military Justice (Mason City, IA: Savas Publishing, 1999), 213–224; and *Merciful Lincoln: The President and Military Justice* (2009). See also Spiegel, *A. Lincoln,* 276, for discussion of a six-hour meeting with John Hay, one of Lincoln's personal secretaries, on July 18, 1863, attempting to find almost any reason to keep Union soldiers from being executed.

64. "Sanborn's public assassination severely damaged Union troop recruiting efforts in eastern Virginia for months," writes Spiegel in *A. Lincoln.* "Between March and the end of August, 1863, comments to and from Lincoln proclaimed the concrete value of Negro troops to the Union cause and set a precedent for hanging verdicts." See 271.

65. Basler, *Collected Works,* 6: 523.

Part Two

The Copperheads of the Middle West

CHAPTER 4

Race, Class, and Copperheadism: The Localist Foundations of Dissent in the Civil War's Middle Border

Christopher Phillips

In many parts of the nation, communities went to war. In the middle border states of the Union, west of the Appalachians and spanning the Ohio and Missouri Rivers and straddling the heralded line between freedom and slavery, the Civil War came to communities. Most residents of this region, generally far from the regular scenes of fighting, endured an *un*civil war in the form of daily conflicts fought in the streets, schools, churches, courthouses, and other public and private spaces of individual communities. Often violent, thoroughly politicized, and widely disruptive, this neighbors' war pitted the supporters of Abraham Lincoln, mostly Republicans, and dissenters, often anti-war Democrats, who blamed the conflict on radicals—whether the president, Republicans, or abolitionists.

Rejecting the multiplying policy pillars of the Lincoln administration's house—enrollment, conscription, the suspension of habeas corpus, and especially emancipation, all announced in the war's first fifteen months—they soon coupled them with other centralizing congressional acts, such as greenbacks, war bonds, postal regulations, homesteads, land grants, revenue taxes, high tariffs, and a transcontinental railroad, all passed without Southern opposition owing to their absence, and over border state opposition. Together, they gave the impression that Republicans, and especially the president, exerted dictatorial powers and were bent on usurping local governance. Lincoln earthily referred to the manifold and growing dissent movement, with its epicenter in his home border region, as the "fire in the rear." His supporters pejoratively labeled dissenters "Copperheads," likening them to poisonous snakes that strike without warning. (A western epithet for mulattoes, the term only hardened racialized opposition to Republicans' efforts to attach emancipation to the war goals.)

THE COPPERHEAD PARTY.—IN FAVOR OF *A VIGOROUS PROSECUTION OF PEACE!*

Figure 4.1. "The Copperhead Party—In Favor of a *Vigorous Prosecution of Peace!*" From *Harper's Weekly*, February 28, 1863.

Historians have interpreted Copperheadism either as a will o' the wisp figment of Republican propaganda or as a potent, organized "dark lantern" subversive movement bent on upending the Union war effort and destroying the Lincoln coalition. In fact, the western dissent movements were largely spontaneous, localized responses to changing war circumstances. Organizationally diffuse, their resistance efforts nevertheless proved powerfully disruptive of the war effort. Their subversion took the form of harassing war supporters and troops, discouraging enlistments, supporting desertion and deserters, and organized terrorism of anxious local Republicans with targeted threats and violence under guise of secret societies. Explanations of wartime dissent frequently center on either politics, meaning Democrats' loyal opposition to the wartime Lincoln administration and the Republican-led Congress, or ideology, with dissenters' constitutional anxieties coincident to small-R republican fears of the overweening centralization of power.[1]

By limiting the study of dissent to the free states, historians have perpetuated the familiar binary between free and slave states, their modalities centered largely on resistance to violations of civil liberties in the former and resistance to slavery interference in the latter. In fact, dissent extended across the rivers and was coextended, if by somewhat differing circumstances, by the military presence on both sides. A cross-border look at the shadowy yet intense inner civil war that plagued large sections of the western home front reveals deeper conflicts over localism, with surprisingly congruent social foundations rooted in the intersection of slavery and emancipation, racial subordination, and class anxieties, and manifested in aggregate as divisive language politics and social violence at all levels. Indianan Lambdin Milligan's 1864 arrest for subversion was only one, if telling, incident in this shadowy local war that ebbed and flowed in the western states nearly from its start until it largely ceased after Lincoln's reelection in 1864.[2]

Moreover, when studied at the ground level, this home-front conflict in the western border region reveals how both war supporters and dissenters weaponized their words to manipulate existing social and political fissures. Well known is that wartime dissenters employed race-based language to defend against Northern-style social engineering initiated by Lincoln and Republican leaders as war goals in the aftermath of the announcement of emancipation. Less studied is how war supporters—military and civilian—both proactively and reactively exploited class-based rhetoric to define and employ loyalty as a strategy to delegitimize war opponents. In this localist warfare, buttressed by the presence of military authority, Republicans shrewdly harnessed loyalty definitions to class antagonisms to protect their own claims to social and economic advantages provided by the emergent wartime economic expansion.

However pervasive were wartime divisions in these western states, dissent was more often quarantined than epidemic, clustered among families and in neighborhoods and hamlets. Families soon became known as "Union" or "secesh," with dissenters concentrating their activities on personal spheres of influence. Initially muted, dissent soon took on a class dimension that bled into its swelling ranks. An investigator in southern Illinois found that the earliest dissenting organizations were often led by lawyers, judges, physicians, merchants, ministers, and elected county officials. But poorer men, often from rural families of Southern origin referred to pejoratively by striving town dwellers as "Butternuts" (to reflect the coloring of their homespun clothing) and who supported the Democratic Party's individualistic politics, were the dissent movements' shock troops. One of

Danville, Illinois's, two competing protective organizations was "composed of almost entirely ardent, impulsive young men," according to one federal recruiting officer. "The other is composed of middle aged men property-holders, made up out of both parties but all good union men." Some dissenters who had initially joined the Union leagues were soon ostracized for opposing strong war measures. They left to join the other protective organization, or to form "Democratic regiments" to deliver blows, political and otherwise, and resist authority that might compel them to support the war. Turning the tables, these dissenters gleefully appropriated the Republicans' politicized epithet—Copperhead—as a conservative badge of populist localism while ridiculing their opponents as fanatics, authoritarians, racial egalitarians, and Yankees.[3]

Already in the spring of 1861, in contested border counties where Lincoln had mostly lost and in cities where he had won, unconditional Unionists, mostly Republicans, defined disloyalty in absolutist terms. Cincinnati editor Henry Reed was unambiguous. "In this contest there can be no neutral position," he fumed. "He who will sustain the Government is its friend, and he who will not, is its enemy. . . . *Our* enemies, [are] those who are not for the Union." To the familiar charge by dissenting Democrats that "the Administration is not the Government," Republicans responded firmly. Conditional Unionism was treason. "In time of peace we may oppose the policy of the Administration," one wrote, "but in war if we do so in a manner to weaken the Government we strike hands with the enemy." With enemies on battlefront and home front, Republicans like Illinois governor Richard Yates easily collapsed the spectrum of dissent into a single term. "Secession," wrote Yates of growing dissent in his state, "is deeper and stronger here than you have any idea."[4]

Across the rivers, among similarly divided populations in which Republicans were fewer and support for slavery was more intrinsic, dissent took a distinct form: neutrality. Union meetings among proslavery white Kentuckians and Missourians sought to squelch radical secessionism, buttressing principled dissent against Northern Republicans who now headed the national government and controlled the federal war effort. "Demagogues at the North and . . . South have divided the country," implored former Kentucky U.S. senator Archibald Dixon at an April 18 Union meeting in Louisville. "I say, for my part, I am not to be forced." The legislature agreed, and in May voted for neutrality. Such nuancing soon found its absolutist match in the president's July 4 message to Congress. Lincoln unambiguously condemned neutrality as de facto if not outright secession, and proclaimed those "*professed* Union men" who favored it as disloyal. Under the "guise of neutrality . . . the border States, so called—in fact, the middle states [claimed] being almost *for* the Union," he sneered, dismissing neutrality as a ruse to "tie the hands of the Union men." To Lincoln, this was "disunion completed. . . . This government has no choice left but to deal with [insurrectionism], *where* it finds it." That fall, arriving federal troops in the border slave states would take the president's cue.[5]

Long before this, in fact within weeks of Fort Sumter, Republicans in the border free states had launched their own defense of localism. Propagandizing support for the war and the government as protection of "law and order," and often hailing from propertied classes who drove business and controlled newspapers, they launched preemptive counterinsurgencies against perceived disloyalty against the Lincoln administration. One central Illinoisan claimed local Republicans "were forming Vigilance committees to scout the country and find out the principles of every man (and woman too I suppose) those that were not loyal to Lincoln. . . . Cellie declares he[']ll die before he[']ll ever hollor hurah for Lincoln and they going round and making men do who did not vote for him." Many dissenting organizations formed initially as mutual protection societies to counter threats by Republican hard-liners whose "partyism rises far above their patriotism," as an Indianan complained. In one Illinois village, after learning that a local teacher was allowing his school to be the site of dissent meetings that winter, war supporters "thrashed Old Lakenan about that school . . . as the old traitor deserved it." "Peace meetings" quickly found themselves squelched by Union vigilance committees, hastily formed home guard units, and federal regiments. Near Centreville, Indiana, on the National Road, one committee questioned farmer John Ketler about raising a company of "Southern rights" men to enlist in the rebel army. After the men had forced him to claim his effort was "all in jest," the local newspaper editor warned readers, "He who is not for us, is against us." Such absolutism was more pronounced when federal troops entered local communities, triggering long-standing cultural prejudices within these states. A Northern Illinois lieutenant marching southward through his home state judged the "illmannered and slovenly clad people of Carlinville . . . [as] 'Secesh' in sentiment . . . from the almost entire absence of any exhibition of joy at our arrival." When local Unionists learned in early 1862 that John Poague had left his Marion County, Indiana, home to fight for the Confederacy, authorities soon confiscated his property—some two hundred acres—and sold it at auction under the terms of Congress's recent Confiscation Act. Rarer in free states like Indiana, such confiscation incidents occurred more frequently in communities in neighboring slave states like Kentucky, where Confederate enlistments were common.[6]

Arriving federal troops from across the rivers often believed that slavery undergirded the class disparities they now viewed, and they welcomed the war as a class conflict writ large against the aristocracy of the slaveholding South. An Ohioan in Louisville dismissed local secesh as "mostly the lower Class of people," while others believed they saw everywhere the hallmarks of a fully stratified, disloyal plantation society. Williamson D. Ward wrote to his family about a farmer outside Louisville who he and his comrades "believe[d was] . . . a Secessionist [although] he said he was union. He owned several Slaves and a farm of 600 acres I asked him if that was not too much for one man to have he said no I told him if a man in Indiana had a farm of 160 acres he had all he wanted to take care of." Michigan soldier Norman G. Markham instinctually compared the slaveholding society he saw in Kentucky with those he imagined in the Deep South. "The farmers are very wealthy. They own large plantations and lots of niggers. They have the finest buildings that I ever saw, have nice horses and carriages and nigger drivers. . . . I think when this war ends these big plantations will be cut up some." Just a few miles into Kentucky in late 1861, an Indiana soldier wrote to his hometown newspaper that "the people and the country are about twenty years behind the times: they appear to think and talk of nothing but negroes and tobacco. This is their comfort by day and their song in the night; their hope, their salvation, their all. . . . They claim to be good Union men, but press them a little and they very soon let you know that they are Southern-rights men; in plain terms, they are rebels, the last one of them."[7]

Made freely, comments such as these convinced local Unionist slaveholders that federal troops just as freely used slaveholding to bar shut the doors to their loyalty. In February 1862, Missourian David Bailey, a War of 1812 veteran who, like most of his neighbors, was a "Slave holder and opposed to Emancipation and do[es] not wholley approve of all of the acts of the present Administration," complained that he was among "the class of Citizens that those in Power think proper to designate as Secessionist, disloyal Rebels and Sympathizers and treat them as Such." Based purely on ownership of slaves, local federal troops "have taken all their armes from them they have arrested them and taken them to headquarters, and made them take the oath and give bonds in Large amount—they impressed their Horses and their waggons and teams and Slaves just where and when they please in the most insulting manner."[8]

As armed federals and non-slaveholders used support for the peculiar institution against Confederate sympathizers and neutralists, they similarly leveraged proslavery Unionists who, caught in the fray, experienced a growing alienation against the national government. A generic "Southern rights," or simply "Southern," identification emerged to reflect a clandestine culture of proslavery dissent among white border residents. As with neutrality, for newly politicized Southerners theirs was dissent without treason, an expression of conservative politics by citizens who peacefully defended the nation's republican traditions protecting slaveholders' rights *within* the nation. Taking the form of grievance politics, personal and collective, it conjured a sense of victimization that easily entwined with secessionism. As a Kentucky Unionist remarked, "This secession is a disease—a disease, Sir. It can be caught in a night. I have seen people go to bed as good Unionists as there are in the country and wake up in the morning Secessionists." Many such converts had no direct connection, cultural or otherwise, with the plantation states. Often, as a Kentucky Unionist minister observed, other than slavery, they "know very little of the South or her institutions."[9]

Dissenting proslavery residents, slaveholding and not, quietly commodified their personal loyalties. Many turned sullen and resentful, while others became radicalized and rode as armed irregulars, guerrillas, bushwhackers, and partisans, targeting Unionists, federal garrisons, and free blacks. In St. Louis, Union general Henry Wager Halleck, a published expert on international and military law, prescribed capital punishment for those who assisted or joined insurgents "[who] threaten and drive out loyal citizens and rob them of their property." He asked permission to be even tougher on civilian populations in border slave states, a request the president himself went on record as supporting—with the notable exception of emancipating slaves. "Nothing but the military power can now put down the rebellion and save Union men in this State," wrote Halleck. "It is useless now to try any other remedy." Caught in a three-way crossfire between federal troops and militias, guerrillas, and non-slaveholders, slaveholding Unionists were excluded from assumptions of loyalty to any side. "Loyal men have almost despaired," a southern Kentuckian complained, "and are ready to sacrifice their property and leave." Many did just that, often migrating to occupied cities like Louisville, Lexington, and St. Louis or to neighboring free states and cities like Cincinnati.[10]

Having festered for years, the war opened old wounds that now became scores to be settled—by accusations, arrests, and violence. In what one Kentuckian called an "evening-up time . . . [when] many a man became a violent Unionist because the ancient enemies of his house were Southern sympathizers," garrisoning troops were often involved in settling personal disputes and feuds. Another Kentuckian lamented that a Unionist neighbor "has made it his business to arrest all his rebel friends that he has a spite against." The randomness of this localized conflict prompted Union general John M. Schofield to complain that in Missouri, indeed the border region generally, the war was largely "the result of old feuds, and involves very little, if at all, the question of Union or disunion." A Kentuckian affirmed that "the secret clue to this seeming capriciousness was the private business affairs of the two parties." She continued, "If a Southerner held the note of a Union man and the day for payment approached nothing would save the best government the world ever saw but the transfer of the Southerner to Camp Chase." Class resentments drove many such complaints against prominent landowners. As one Missourian of moderate means later sneered, "the cry of 'disloyal' could be very easily raised against any man who happened to have a superabundance of property."[11]

Home guard and state militia who supported or replaced garrisoning troops contributed to this private class warfare. A resident of Elk Fork, Missouri, complained that his local home guard "came from all parts of the County and Some of them have little grudges at their fellow Citizens and they make use of their opportunity to avenge themselves." Lincoln himself heard similar complaints "that arrests, banishments, and assessments are made more for private malice, revenge, and pecuniary interest than for the public good." With slave ownership the measure of the occupying troops' calculus of loyalty and disloyalty, prominent slaveholders commonly believed that Lincoln's war was a ruse for overt class warfare. "Dutch and Irish laborers," complained one, "who by becoming 'Home Guards' can prey upon their neighbors, or jayhawk . . . openly boast that they will have possession of their fine farms, and they think that the time has arrived for them to take the time to better their fortunes." Abuses of civilians by home guards were pronounced enough for Henry W. Halleck to pledge to disband such units in Missouri "as rapidly as I can supply their places" with state militia.[12]

Not surprisingly, antislavery hard-liners were quickest to judge loyalty and disloyalty along a slaveholding axis. Ephram J. Wilson, the provost marshal at Palmyra, Missouri, near the Mississippi River, was blunt. "Any man [who] would hold a slave with very few exceptions is neither a Christian, a patriot or a loyal citizen," he wrote. Such prejudice among many federals, especially Republicans, derived from cultural absolutism about inferior populations of slaveholding states. "There being so many of that class of people in Missouri," believed Edward Daniels, colonel of the First Wisconsin Cavalry garrisoning at Cape Girardeau, he lectured a crowd of residents that "the demagogues and secession leaders befooled them. . . . Indeed the great reason of the whole rebellion is, *IGNORANCE*. . . . The Col. told them this in plain words, and extorted [*sic*] them to *educate their children*." Federal soldiers, particularly from the northern portions of western states, often labeled these border slave-state residents as more than "secesh." They were bottom dwellers, hill toppers, sand hillers, and pukes.[13]

If smoldering class tensions served as a friction primer for loyalty, disloyalty, and dissent on both sides of the middle rivers, emancipation was the war's exploding projectile. Even before the president announced his Emancipation Proclamation on September 22, a range of western dissenters who opposed Northern Republicans' strategy of moral nationalism, one that they believed by dint of war would accomplish the "greater New England," were predicting that the war would soon be one waged to free slaves. Condemnations following the draft of a "rich man's war and poor man's fight" now gave way to overt racialist language as dissent's lingua franca. Amending the Democratic rallying cry to "The Constitution as it is, and the Union as it was, *and the Niggers where they are*," white westerners who favored an immediate end to the war took aim at Republican candidates and Lincoln's war policies. They had received some unexpected, and unintended, help. Only weeks before, southern Illinoisans' collective anger had boiled over at the apparent change in the war's direction. On September 18, to alleviate overcrowding at several of the border region's refugee camps, the secretary of war, Edwin M. Stanton, ordered contrabands to federal camps near Cairo and authorized their use as laborers to assist labor-strapped farmers with their harvests. Its post commandant was instructed to turn women and children over to local committees of "humane and benevolent persons" who would provide them employment. White rural Illinoisans erupted in fury at the Republicans' bald intention to "Africanize" their state in violation of its exclusion law. Many of the black refugees quickly fled back to Cairo. With the midterm election imminent, the editor of southern Illinois's *Belleville Advocate* warned that racial undertow from anti-emancipation politics assured "The Radical of yesterday . . . will be a Conservative to-day." "The great issue to be decided to-day at the polls," blared the Cincinnati *Enquirer*, "is the FREEDOM OF THE WHITE MAN." Democrats increased their congressional seats by eighteen to outnumber Republicans and won legislative majorities in Illinois, Indiana, and Ohio. In Illinois, Democrats swept the midterm elections after winning the central counties, gaining control of the state's legislature and congressional delegation. Voters rejected a new state constitution (offered by a convention with more than twice as many Democratic delegates as Republicans) but upheld the state's 1848 bans on black immigration, suffrage, and office holding by more than a five to one margin. (Four in ten Republicans joined Democrats in affirming the exclusion clause.)[14]

Emancipation galvanized smaller dissent groups into organized mobs, urban and rural and often estimated at hundreds, who now devoted themselves to subversive democracy against Republicans' wartime authority and the racial status quo. They served as a counterbalance to newfound Southerners and Conservatives in the region's slave states, whose paramount political aim was protection of slavery. They eagerly used the politicized terms "Northern" and "Northerner" to denigrate loyal supporters of emancipation and the new war measures. "We call on Northern thinkers to emancipate themselves, in order to save their own section from destruction," wrote one Cincinnatian in response to emancipation. Adherents often took the term for their own. Race riots—far more than draft riots—erupted in middle border cities that witnessed an influx of contrabands and fugitive slaves and whose employers replaced white workers, especially immigrants, with black workers. In Chicago, Toledo, Indianapolis, and Evansville, working-class whites ravaged black residential sections. In New Albany, Indiana, five days after Lincoln signed the confiscation and militia bills into law, amid Democratic newspapers' editorials claiming "the city is overrun with worthless runaway slaves," armed white supremacists roamed the city's black community to rid it of "strangers." Cincinnati's violence outstripped all others, especially after blacks retaliated by burning homes in "Dublin," its Irish section. William Wells Brown, a former Kentucky slave and prominent abolitionist, claimed that "hatred of the negro" was worse in Cincinnati "than in any other city in the West."[15]

Outside the region's cities, dissenting groups similarly organized as paramilitary units pledged to fight Republicans' attempts at racial leveling. "Prominent men are scouring the country holding meetings of secret societies almost nightly, and often daily," wrote an alarmed officer, noting that these groups drilled at night or in hill valleys and creek bottoms or on prairies in rural areas. Provost marshals and commanders alike frequently received "annonymous letters from nearly all the little towns, saying they fear an outbreak, and fear to communicate their names." Accosting Unionist speakers by shouting down or attacking them, these dissenters engaged in their own brand of absolutism by castigating all Republicans as abolitionists. Some interfered with local enrollment by blocking roads or, worse, ambushing enrollment officers and securing military arms. One dissenter, a physician, claimed in an affidavit that he "advised his copperhead friends present, 'to organize and drill publicly, not in the night as the damned abolitionists were doing, in order to be ready for the conscription, when the abolitionists commenced to enforce it.'" In Hancock County, Illinois, their boldness drew federal troops with instructions to shoot to kill. When the new legislative majority of Democrats attempted to constitute an appointed commission to oversee spending and the appointment of military officers, Richard Yates prorogued the state legislature for the remainder of the war. Some forty thousand outraged voters—including some of the most prominent men in the state—held an anti-war meeting in Springfield in late June 1863. Replete with racialized language, it called for a peace convention to be held in Louisville that would negotiate the end of the war, and resolved against martial law, arbitrary arrests and confinements, and other perceived violations of civil liberties.[16]

The strident Democratic response to emancipation rapidly destabilized Republicans' local authority. Their claims that the dissent movement was principally comprised of lower-class, undereducated younger men now made Republicans appear as elitist revolutionaries, supporting a war for racial equality in order to undermine the social fabric. To counter their opponents' racialized attacks and rebrand themselves, Union League Clubs, or "Loyal Leagues," became the operative means by which Republicans squelched dissent and coerced home-front loyalty. Begun in late 1862 by anxious central Illinois Republicans, these organizations quickly spread to other Northern cities and small towns as "patriotic fraternities" to counteract defeatism and war-weariness. By the summer of 1863, the leagues had spread to eighteen free states; by 1864, some 140,000 members were enrolled in Illinois alone. (In the region's slave states, such leagues existed mainly in cities, especially St. Louis, Louisville, and Lexington, the only sizeable locales for Republican support.) Enlisting the aid of sympathetic editors, the leagues sought "by moral and social influences" to raise troops and supplies and blunt rising disaffection. Distributing pamphlets and holding debates to promote the war effort was accompanied by economic pressure exerted by the business community, who offered rigid tests of national patriotism centering on support for emancipation and pressuring wage workers and small business owners to support the now unpopular war. "Disloyalty must be made unprofitable," argued one.[17]

With local business leaders in the vanguard, class understandings undergirded these anxious Republicans' concerns about pervasive dissent. Believing the Democratic Party was fully in league with secret societies, Republicans found an antidote to the racial venom western Peace Democrats spewed after emancipation. "Copperhead Democracy to-day means traitorism," blared one local Republican newspaper in the summer of 1863. "Those that are not for the Government *must* be against it." Those in the lowest classes of society—urban immigrants and rural whites, especially in the southernmost counties of western states that voted largely against Lincoln—came under particular scrutiny. "It is generally understood that when we speak of Democrats and Butternuts that they both mean the same thing," wrote an Illinoisan. Echoing federal officers' depictions of neighboring slave-state residents, Centralia editor John W. Fletcher, recruited from New York specifically to start a Union League newspaper in the spring of 1863, believed his new, uneducated, rural neighbors were Confederates by extension: undermining the war effort as a means of putting the bottom rail on top. "We have for our enemies," he inveighed in the summer of 1863, "every Southern sympathizer, every rebel in arms . . . the peace men, the ignorant and depraved . . . men who put in their time bawling about the Constitution, who never read it; men whose constant cry is, 'abolition,' 'abolition,' and yet are too ignorant to even define the meaning of the word."[18]

For Republicans like Fletcher, being good Union men in this existential wartime crisis required more than class standing. Faced with widespread anti-emancipation dissent, they made support for and opposition to Lincoln's proclamation the purity test for loyalty and disloyalty. Lincoln's attorney general, proslavery St. Louisan Edward Bates, was shocked at how quickly emancipation became the litmus of loyalty. "Abolition seems to be the strongest rallying point, and men who dont care a fig about it, have become all of a sudden, very zealous in that cause," he grumbled. "The radicals are making great efforts to create the belief that they are *the* Union men, and all others are against the Union. And they succeed in driving on some *cowardly patriots*." (Bates's disagreement with Lincoln over emancipation and particularly black military enlistment contributed to him leaving the administration the following year.) As a Cincinnati dissenter complained of Republicans, "They brand every man as traitor who does not Kneel at the footstool of 'Abraham' and say Amen to every edict and Proclamation that emenated from his pen." "Though you give your flesh and blood to put down the rebellion," another dissenter spat, "if you do not favor abolition you are denounced as a rebel sympathizer."[19]

Demands for loyalty made for an easy step for Loyal Leaguers to become hard-liners by demanding all-or-nothing Republicanism for loyalty residents. A southern Indiana editor complained that Republicans "conduct themselves as though 'patriotism' in these days is exclusively designed for the benefit of their party." The state's Republican senator, George W. Julian, would later admit that "loyalty to Republicanism was . . . accepted as the best evidence of loyalty to the country." Republicans in divided western states quickly made the Loyal North synonymous with the Loyal Nation, and its war supporters fell in line with Lincoln's interpretation of emancipation as military necessity, the central strategy for winning the war on the ground, in the field, and at home.[20]

Undermanned and dispersed federal garrisons and enrollment squads found ready assistance from Union leagues to weave stronger webs of restraint. In provost marshals' offices, lists of newly designated disloyalists lay alongside enrollment lists and those of known deserters. In Wayne County, Indiana, three categories of civilian loyalties existed—"Union, Traitor, Doubt"—with notations such as "go to the devil" inserted for traitors and "may be saved" and "don't give up" for those still in doubt. More often, such as in Fulton County, Illinois, lists contained little more than names of local Peace Democrats, draft evaders, or those who paid commutation fees. Increased arrests, for dissenting speech or traveling without a military pass in nearby slave states, make it difficult for non-Republicans and dissenters to avoid running afoul of military authorities. When Ohio's Robert Neil, a former Whig turned independent, received a box of clothing from cross-river relatives, instructing him to deliver to a Kentucky soldier confined at Camp Chase, he was immediately summoned to the local provost marshal's office for violating the most recent trade restrictions and threatened with prison.[21]

More than simply acting as the Republican Party's political arm, Loyal Leagues organized as local paramilitary units and vigilance committees that often overmatched dissenters' secret societies in numbers and intensity. Pekin, Illinois's, organizational document declared so, claiming it was a "home guard . . . [to] put down treason and traitors . . . maintain the laws . . . [and] keep inviolate the principles of the constitution and the Declaration of Independence." The choice of language was telling. "We dont want to fight a fare fight," admitted one Illinois Unionist, while another claimed his local Union league could "raise *one hundred men* in this town for service in scouring the county and driving these 'fellows' out on a few hours notice." As "union regulators," they rooted out dissenters' assemblages, infiltrated their organizations, assisted squads of troops to arrest leaders, attacked individual dissenters, and blamed suspicious calamities, such as the burning of churches, on "dark lantern, slung-shot and bowie-knife 'peace' men in the neighborhood." The mayor of Galesburg, Illinois, asked federal commander Jacob Ammen "how to proceed to exterminate the rebels" in his area, while another resident wanted to "Scatter Some of tham Old loffers out of our part of the country." Reports of "50 armed butternuts" across the state line near Richmond, Indiana, sent three train carloads of armed Illinoisans to assist soldiers in capturing and arresting most of them; they then remained "to gard the jail."[22]

All-or-nothing patriotism as a Republican counterinsurgency strategy received powerful assistance from the military's growing web of restraints, including new trade regulations applied in the border region's towns, cities, villages, and rural hamlets. As treasury secretary Salmon P. Chase buoyantly touted the impetus—"*let commerce follow the flag*"—a War Department order authorized special treasury agents and local commanders to appoint local boards of trade who could, and more importantly who could not, conduct trade. The order further empowered them to wield potent social weapons by affixing names to disloyalty lists if civilians were determined to have engaged in contraband trade. By March 1862, boards of trade operated in most of the middle border's cities, especially those lying on navigable rivers, as well as in many interior towns. Accordingly, business and class interests deeply influenced the emerging calculus of loyalty and order on the home front. With unconditional loyalty the baseline criteria for board membership in the western states, nearly all were prominent businessmen, merchants, editors, manufacturers, or public officials. The boards often selected the local provost marshals, charged with stopping illicit trade with the Confederacy, and in turn appointed them to the boards. In Centralia, Illinois, editor Edward S. Condit was named his district's provost marshal in 1864 owing to his "thorough-going business qualifications. . . . The locating of the Head-quarters at Centralia will naturally draw a considerable amount of business to the city."[23]

In the middle border's free states, which in 1862 were less affected by overt disloyalty than across the rivers, trade permits greased the skids for class-based partisan politics. Boards of trade expanded their responsibility to stop illegal trade by pressuring businesspeople who opposed the Lincoln administration. Rank-and-file Republicans more easily received approval for monthly applications for the Southern trade than their Democratic counterparts. When the president of Cincinnati's chamber of commerce, Joseph C. Butler, telegraphed the new secretary of war, Edwin M. Stanton, with the appointments of three members of the local board of trade, he noted they were unimpeachably loyal and prominent Republican businessmen who had received government contracts for war materiel or transportation services. The strong current of trade, politics, and loyalty distinctions soon flooded over the river region, causing non-Republican businesspeople to complain. When John Skiff, a Cincinnati merchandiser, admitted to attempting to smuggle south a load of butter marked as ale through Kentucky in May 1861, he claimed he "had done no worse than others" and grumbled that for the local board his true crime was having voted for John Bell, and not Lincoln, in 1860.[24]

In divided border slave states, among growingly hostile populations, commerce following the flag demanded strict and often biased measures of Unionism. Patriotism and profit were not mutually exclusive impulses, and the mismarking of barrels and boxes stood alongside the bribery of federal marshals, deputies, and inspectors as common smuggling practices. Federal officials blamed local boards of trade for suspect ethics, and they even questioned their loyalty. "Supposing it possible to find three unconditional Union men so to act (a fact I am not disposed to admit as far as some towns are concerned)," wrote an exasperated commander in Bowling Green, Kentucky, "their very isolation places them at the mercy, and under the control, of the disloyal population around them. Add to this family and social ties, and the chances of protection for the Government against the abuses they were appointed to correct, amount to nothing." In the fall of 1862, district commander Jeremiah T. Boyle prohibited civilians in central Kentucky from "engag[ing] in the buying, selling, or shipping of merchandise or groceries without having first obtained a certificate signed by six Unconditional Union men of good standing, that said person himself is an Unconditional Union man." Politicized manipulations of such loyalty distinctions led to widespread abuses of the permit system, compelling Kentucky's final wartime governor, Thomas E. Bramlette, to complain to Lincoln that "many *loyal men* are driven out of business . . . for no other reason than their political preferences." When the army refused to honor the Treasury Department's rescission of trade restrictions in Kentucky in early 1864, the governor condemned the permit system as "a most shameful and corrupt system of political partisan corruption and oppression." In August 1864 the federal military halted all trade in and out of Kentucky for those labeled as being disloyal.[25]

This web of military trade restraints cascaded through local economies, causing widespread suffering to those marked on the wrong side of the loyalty ledger. In May 1862 a visitor to Louisville, by then a teeming federal supply center, remarked that the city had "suffered terribly" from a year of conflict: its nonmilitary economy stagnant, its storefronts boarded and shops silent, gave it a "sleepy, drowsy look." Smaller business owners, especially, who could not conduct business could then not pay workers, who in turn could not pay bills. Many were left destitute, forced out of their lodgings, or relocated to where they could find work. Some moved into abandoned homes and buildings, or left altogether. Louisville's Alexander Jeffrey, who owned and managed several small coal gasworks, fell afoul of the city's Loyal League, which increasingly pressured local businesses not to employ any "traitor or traducer of the Administration," for his outspokenness against partisanship in awarding trade permits. After the provost marshal placed him on the disloyal list and the local board of trade prohibited him from conducting business, he fled the city, leaving his family behind to prevent their home from being vandalized. Without income in Lexington, he tried unsuccessfully to obtain clemency from the district commander and to hire or sell several of his male slaves. Frustrated, he wrote his wife, "I really think it is better to live any where than here." He raged, "K[entuck]y is a subject province under the most arbitrary military despotism. . . . I do find myself getting very savage."[26]

By contrast, residents in free states above the rivers experienced a mid-war economic boom. Similar to states below, its benefits would be experienced unevenly as loyalty politics and trade restrictions assured its beneficiaries were recognized Republicans. Loyal farmers and manufacturers found war-related production and profits sharply increased, and small-town merchants, bankers, and creditors reaped debt-driven windfalls from loyal civilians' borrowing and investing in their businesses. By the summer of 1863, Republican-led towns experienced building booms that matched up with local loyalty politics. "Mechanics and laborers are all busily engaged in renovating, repairing and building new mansions, both great and small. Business houses, dwelling houses and buildings of all sorts are springing up in every direction . . . such as it has not before presented since the great financial crash of 1857," boasted the Republican editor of Illinois's *Centralia Sentinel.* "Fine brick blocks are going up, as if by magic . . . as though no war existed. . . . The farmers are coming to the conclusion that they have lived in their old cabins about long enough, and in many cases are building houses." Conversely, dissenters judged as disloyal could not sell or borrow, relegating their production to home or local consumption. This was itself often reduced, especially with men serving in the military or, if they deserted, forced to hide out.[27]

Community streets and public spaces quickly became battlegrounds when dissenters contested perceived inequities with physical force. Then, normally placid village streets sometimes witnessed what amounted to mob warfare with class overtones. After Unionist residents of Liberty, Illinois, celebrated the unexpected news of the surrender of Fort Henry in the spring of 1862, one wrote a few months later that "we had a little battle on a small scale in town yesterday. . . . Some Seceshers came up from the bottom, armed with revolvers and knives, they flourished their arms on the street and hurrahed for Jeff. Davis. . . . [The] others surrounded the enemy opposite George Walters store, ran them into the store, charged upon them not with bayonets, but with stones. . . . It appears cruel to beat men so." Public dissent meetings were met with increasing violence from self-named "Union vigilantes," many of them discharged soldiers hardened by their own sacrifices. When a group of dissenters "tried to have a peace meeting" in Liberty, Illinois, "the Union men went in and broke the meeting up and made old Lake [nan, the organizer] Hurray for the Union." In July 1863, when local Unionists discovered a "Mutual Protection Company" meeting in a remote township house in Ohio's Butler County, formed mostly by rural dissenters from across the state line in Indiana, they drove them out violently after barely a month. The ferocity of Unionists' counterinsurgent responses caused commanders and even soldiers to call for restraint. In June 1863, Orlando B. Willcox, commander of the Department of the Ohio's division that included Indiana and Michigan, requested the disbanding of *all* secret societies, including Loyal Leagues, for the sake of public peace. "They are a constant source of dread and mistrust, and divide and provoke hostility between neighbors, weaken the dignity and power of courts of justice, expose the country to martial law, and [are] discouraging the people from enlisting in defense of the nation." By late summer of 1863, the frenzy of military efforts had gone far to quell the disturbances in many areas. After Ohio's fall election, in which the exiled Copperhead Clement L. Vallandigham lost his bid for governor (his 186,672 votes represented nearly 40 percent of votes cast, and he carried seventeen counties), a Cincinnati newspaper claimed several boxes of "Butternut breast-pins . . . [were] left behind intended for some Butternut procession, which never came off. If meant for this county, there was no demand for them."[28]

Briefly muted, waves of political rhetoric and violence crescendoed again in the summer of 1864 against the backdrop of the national election. The editor of Dayton's *Daily Empire* impressed on its readers the heightened stakes of Lincoln's reelection and Union victory. "Admitting the war to be over, and the negro free, we will then have to grant them every right, social and political of the white man, or slaughter them. There is absolutely no end to the difficulties which must grow out of the Republican endeavor to equalize, the white and black races. It is not only at Richmond, that white men protest against this unnatural and most repugnant attempt." Racial rhetoric flowed freely at competing grand rallies in local counties, as Republicans tarred Democrats as "all nigger" and Democrats responded with a recently invented term for Republicans—"miscegenationists." Divided Democratic county conventions regularly erupted into shouting matches, with "Peace

Figure 4.2. Ohio congressman Clement L. Vallandigham. Courtesy of the Library of Congress.

men" shouting down "War men" who "had better go over to the abolition party where they belong." Anti-emancipation former federal soldiers were fixtures as such rallies. As an Ohio editor reasoned, "a large majority can see no reason why *they* should be shot for the benefit of niggers and Abolitionists." At the national party's "Copperhead Convention" in Chicago, intended to draw attention to the president's vulnerability in his home state and the autocratic actions of its Republican governor, the raucous delegation compromised around a War candidate, Lincoln's former general-in-chief, George B. McClellan, while Peace delegates drove through a platform drafted by a committee headed by Ohio's notorious Copperhead, Clement L. Vallandigham, back from exile and publicly daring his re-arrest. (Lincoln instructed his generals to desist.)[29]

Ahead of the election and with military assistance, Republicans intensified efforts to bludgeon organized dissent. On March 28, 1864, in Charleston, Illinois, a violent series of furloughed soldiers' provocations against dissenters led local Democrats to organize a rally on court day. Many came armed. Federal soldiers and local Republicans clashed with dissenters in the town square. The incident, which occurred in a county known for dissent—perhaps not ironically, only a few miles from the farm near which Lincoln's father was buried and where his stepmother yet lived—lasted only a few moments. But before relief troops could arrive by train from nearby Mattoon and Indiana, nine were killed (six of them soldiers) and twelve were wounded. Fifty Copperheads were taken into custody and interrogated, and twenty-nine were retained and relocated to Camp Yates in Springfield. Many others fled the state. In July, the provost marshal at Quincy gave clear instructions to deputized subordinates that although his authority limited him to arrests of "deserters, spies and persons who resist or obstruct officers engaged in the enrolment or draft," organized Unionists should protect the polls by deadly force if needed. "If you meet with armed resistance you will give your opponents your best show of fighting without any hesitation, and in such cases use no blank cartridges."[30]

In November, Lincoln won an electoral landslide, the first president since Andrew Jackson to win reelection. Heading a National Union Party ticket alongside Tennessee Democrat Andrew Johnson, Lincoln's national margin of victory was more than 10 percent, and in most middle border states, where margins four years earlier had been thin, the president won comfortably. The outcome was less certain in the western border states. Entire federal regiments had jammed trains and riverboats heading northward. Many who did not go home held mock elections and published the results in local newspapers ahead of the election, hoping to sway voters. Overall, nearly 80 percent of soldiers gave their votes to the president. But Lincoln received overall just 380,000 more votes in 1864 than in 1860, and without the soldiers' votes Lincoln might have lost Indiana and perhaps Illinois. There, troops stationed at polling places intimidated dissenters with loyalty challenges, threats of exile, and property confiscation. Republicans swept the Illinois state legislature, took eleven of the state's fourteen congressional districts, and won the governorship. Indiana's congressional delegation included seven new members, all but one a Republican. Four had served in the war.[31]

In the border region's slave states, federal troops manned polling places and test oaths banned dissenting and disloyal voters. Consequently, just less than 40 percent fewer voters went to the polls than four years earlier. In Missouri, disfranchisement and depopulation were so complete that, although Lincoln had received just 10 percent of the popular vote in 1860, he received nearly 70 percent in 1864. As one dissuaded voter claimed, he "would not risk his life, liberty and property in any vain attempt to vote for McClelland with the vain hope of regaining our lost liberties." Despite the presence of federal troops, Kentucky voters trounced Lincoln by nearly 40 percent, giving McClellan his widest margin of victory. Cries of "Curse the president. Damn this Lincoln government" were heard freely at polling places. Dissent in all of these states virtually died with the president's victory.[32]

Amid such tumult, Copperhead vigilantism found grim successes in the border region. Armed dissenters and secret societies targeted African Americans, especially in the free states' Butternut regions. Regulators in Illinois attacked and killed prospective black recruits on their way to enlist at Quincy and Shawneetown, and a gang of dissenters stabbed to death a prominent A.M.E. minister in Evansville, Indiana. Between the fall of 1863 and the winter of 1864, dissenters involved in the subversive groups in hilly Washington County, Indiana, north of Louisville, murdered or drove out virtually all of the county's nearly two hundred black residents "who would not leave the neighborhood." Many had lived for decades in the county, having migrated as freed people with North Carolina Quakers. Now, with Lincoln's reelection having convinced local whites "that negroes would receive citizenship," one propertied black resident was shot in his doorway the following December. Most others left for Evansville and Indianapolis. In Kentucky in late November, within weeks of the president's reelection, federal troops expelled some four hundred black refugees from Kentucky's Camp Nelson, mostly families of recruits enlisted at the camp, into a bitterly cold night during an ice- and snowstorm. More than a quarter of them, all women and children, died from exposure.[33]

By the waning days of the 1864 presidential election, when Lambdin Milligan was arrested at his northern Indiana home for conspiracy and disloyalty to the federal government as a member of a subversive national secret society, the Civil War had long since unleashed deep social and political divisions that drew on long-standing local tensions in the western states. Its culture leavened by decades of peacetime expansion negotiated as conflicts between national and state authority, the angry politics of dissent were a democratic challenge to republican ideals of freedom that had not been evenly realized in a western society, waged now as war-torn struggles for home rule. War supporters, especially Republicans, used politicized class rhetoric to exploit antagonisms in part as a means to preserve their hard-won position in the region's fluid economic, social, and political hierarchy, denigrating challengers in both free and slave states. War opponents responded with racialized rhetoric, contemptuous of Lincoln's supporters who they saw as elitists and overweening nationalists and, following emancipation, freed people as illegitimate claimants to democratic promise. Copperheads easily grafted localist class antagonisms and national challenges to the racial status quo to produce the nation's first-ever populist revolt against modernization and national government, in which they would prove twice losers. Despite Abraham Lincoln's wishful first inaugural appeal to his nation's better angels in order to avoid war, once it came to the dusty streets of his home region the war's lesser angels reduced the conflict to familiar social terms that, once touched, would not easily be reined.

NOTES

1. More than fifty years ago, historian Frank L. Klement argued that the dangers of Copperheadism had been exaggerated, exploited by overly anxious and opportunistic Republicans for political gain and incapable of seriously disrupting the Northern war effort. More recently, Jennifer Weber has disagreed, arguing that dissenting organizations posed significant threats, both political and subversive, to the

national government's viability and the success of the federal war effort. She contends that Copperheads were often of Southern origin and their dissent emanated largely from a conservative Jacksonian Democratic commitment to strict constructionism. Michael F. Holt observed that historians had neglected to adequately study Democratic war dissent at local political levels, locating these politics in the most formal realm of county and state voting totals in order to measure how fully formed was anti-war opposition to necessary war measures and military participation. Taking up some of Holt's challenge, Jonathan W. White has argued that traditional vote tallies obscure the level of Democratic soldiers' political dissent. A considerable number of them rejected the Republican platform, and many who voted for Lincoln disagreed openly with his positions on slavery and wartime emancipation. See Frank L. Klement, *The Copperheads in the Middle West* (Chicago: University of Chicago Press, 1960) and *Dark Lanterns: Secret Political Societies, Conspiracies, and Treason Trials in the Civil War* (Baton Rouge: Louisiana State University Press, 1984); Jennifer L. Weber, *Copperheads: The Rise and Fall of Lincoln's Opponents in the North* (New York: Oxford University Press, 2006); Michael F. Holt, "An Elusive Synthesis: Northern Politics during the Civil War," in James M. McPherson and William J. Cooper Jr., *Writing the Civil War: The Quest to Understand* (Columbia: University of South Carolina Press, 1998), 112–113; and Jonathan W. White, *Emancipation, the Union Army, and the Reelection of Abraham Lincoln* (Baton Rouge: Louisiana State University, 2014). See also Jennifer L. Weber, "Lincoln's Critics: The Copperheads," *Journal of the Abraham Lincoln Association* 32 (Winter 2011): 33–47.

2. As Jennifer Weber explains, "one would naturally expect resistance in the border states, [so] I do not consider what happened in Kentucky, Missouri, Delaware, or Maryland." Weber, *Copperheads,* 220 n10.

3. Henry B. Carrington to [Samuel]. P. Heintzelman, March 26, 1864, RG 393, Pt. 1, Ser. 3349: Letters Received, Northern Department, Box 1, RG 393; James M. McPherson, *Battle Cry of Freedom: The Civil War Era* (New York: Oxford University Press, 1988), 450–453; Weber, 17–19; *Centralia (IL) Sentinel,* July 16, 1863.

4. George H. Porter, *Ohio Politics during the Civil War* (New York: Columbia University, 1911), 75–78; *Cincinnati* [*Enquirer,* June 9, 1861; Henry H. Haviland to Susan Terrell Scrogin, April 25, 1861, Folder 6, Scrogin-Haviland Collection, Mss. 2001 SC20, Kentucky Historical Society, Frankfort; John A. Trimble to Dear Brother, March 7, 1861; Trimble to Jack Trimble, May 4, 1861, both in John A. Trimble Papers, Mss. 249, Box 10, Folder 2, Ohio Historical Society, Columbus, Ohio (hereafter cited as OHS); *Daily Times* (Cincinnati), April 16, 1861; *Catholic Telegraph and Advocate* (Cincinnati), April 27, 1861; Jacob P. Dunn to Oliver P. Aiken, May 6, 1861, Oliver Perry Aiken Papers, Mss. SC7, Indiana Historical Society Library, Indianapolis, Indiana (hereafter cited as IHSL); Rutherford B. Hayes Diaries, vol. 2, April 25, 1861 [transcript p. 12], Manuscript Division, Rutherford B. Hayes Presidential Center, Fremont, OH; McPherson, *Battle Cry of Freedom,* 560; Richard Yates to Abraham Lincoln, July 11, 1862, Richard Yates Papers, Mss. SC421, Abraham Lincoln Presidential Library and Museum, Springfield, Illinois (hereafter cited as ALPL); Richard

Yates and Catherine Yates Pickering, *Richard Yates: Civil War Governor,* ed. John H. Krenkel (Danville, IL: Interstate Printers and Publishers, 1966), 173–182; Weber, *Copperheads,* 48; Adam I. P. Smith, *No Party Now: Politics in the Civil War North* (New York: Oxford University Press, 2006), 59–63, 101–102.

5. E. Merton Coulter, *The Civil War and Readjustment in Kentucky* (Chapel Hill: University of North Carolina Press, 1926; reprint Gloucester, MA: Peter Smith, 1966), 43; Message to Congress in Special Session, July 4, 1861, in Roy P. Basler, ed., *The Collected Works of Abraham Lincoln* (Springfield, IL: Abraham Lincoln Association, 1953), 44: 426–428.

6. Weber, *Copperheads,* 26–27; Smith, *No Party Now,* 71–72; Klement, *Copperheads in the Middle West,* 179; Anonymous to Annie Cooper, April 28, [1861], Cooper-Phillips Family Papers, Mss. 66M37, Manuscripts and Special Collections Library, University of Kentucky, Lexington, (hereafter cited as UK); Nancy Mann to J[ohn]. Preston Mann, February 11, 1862; Alfred M. Mann to J[ohn]. P. Mann, March 20, 1862; and Civil War Diary of John Preston Mann [transcription, vol. 6], February 22–23, 1862, all in Mann Family Papers, Coll. 111, Box 1, Special Collections/Morris Library, Southern Illinois University, Carbondale [hereafter cited as SIU]; Victor Hicken, *Illinois in the Civil War* (Urbana: University of Illinois Press, 1966), 2, 5, 13; Emma Lou Thornbrough, *Indiana in the Civil War Era, 1850–1880* (Indianapolis: Indiana Historical Society, 1965), 124, 170, 395; John A. Trimble to Jack Trimble, May 4, 1861, John A. Trimble Papers, Mss. 249, Box 10, Folder 2, OHS; James Pickett Jones, *"Black Jack": John A. Logan and Southern Illinois in the Civil War Era* (Carbondale: Southern Illinois University Press, 1995), xiii–xiv; *Cairo (IL) City Weekly Gazette,* April 25, 1861; Daniel Harmon Brush, *Growing Up in Southern Illinois,* ed. Milo Milton Quaife (Madison: University of Wisconsin Press, 1944), 119; *Illinois State Journal* (Springfield), June 5, 6, 10, 11, 1861; *Jonesboro (IL) Gazette,* June 29, 1861; John S. Tarkington to Marion Trust Co., August 5, 1905, Churchman Family Papers, Mss. M53, IHSL; Richard E. Nation and Stephen E. Towne, eds., *Indiana's War: The Civil War in Documents* (Athens: Ohio University Press, 2009), 48–49; Robert J. Price to Dear Father, October 16, 1861, Robert J. Price Letters, Mss. SC1221, Folder 2, IHSL; Stephen Rockenbach, "'The Weeds and the Flowers Are Closely Mixed': Allegiance, Law, and White Supremacy in Kentucky's Bluegrass Region, 1861–1865," *Register of the Kentucky Historical Society* 111 (Autumn 2013): 563–589.

7. John H. Tilford Diary, September 5, 1862, Mss. A/T572, vol. 1, Filson Historical Society, Louisville, Kentucky (hereafter cited as FHS); Allen to Eliza, April 5, 1862, Mss. VFM 802, OHS; Paulina H. Stratton Diary [typescript], October 12, 1862, Paulina H. Stratton Papers, Mss. C0842, Joint Collection/Western Historical Manuscript Collections, University of Missouri–State Historical Society of Missouri, Ellis Library, University of Missouri, Columbia, Missouri (hereafter cited as SHSM); John A. Higgins to Nancy Higgins, October 19, 1861, John A. Higgins Papers, Mss. SC1918, Folder 1, ALPL; Williamson Dixon Ward Civil War Journal, October 25, 1861, Mss. SC627, Manuscripts and Special Collections, Kentucky Library, Western Kentucky University, Bowling Green, (hereafter cited as WKU); Norman G. Markham

to My Dear Eunice, October 25, 1862, and Markham to Dear Wife and Boy, February 3, March 20, 1863, N. G. Markham Papers, Mss. A/M345, Folder 1, FHS; *The Illinois Free Press* (Hillsboro), April 4, 1861; Watson Goodrich to Alvin C. Woolfolk, November 26, 1861, Watson Goodrich Letters, Mss. C/G, FHS; Daniel M. Davis to Dear Father, September 22, 1862, Daniel M. Davis Letters, Microfilm 48; and Daniel Berry to Mary B. Crebs, November 30, 1862, Daniel Berry Letters, Misc. Vol. 53, both SIU; *The Stars and Stripes* (Sullivan, IN), December 26, 1861; *The Advance Guard* (Fredricktown, MO), August 28, 1861.

8. David Bailey to Hamilton R. Gamble, January 13, 1862, Record Group 133: Adjutant General Missouri Volunteers, 27th Regiment Infantry, Regimental Correspondence—Miscellaneous, Box 1, Missouri State Archives, Jefferson City, (hereafter cited as MSA).

9. Edwin Smith to Maria Smith, October 14, 1862, Smith Family Papers, Cincinnati (OH) Historical Society Library, (hereafter cited as CHSL); J. T. K. Hayward to John C. Fremont, August 10, 1861, *War of the Rebellion: Official Records of the Union and Confederate Armies*, 4 ser., 128 vols. (Washington, DC: Government Printing Office, 1881–1901), ser. 1, vol. 3, 434 (hereafter cited as *OR*); "Sermon Delivered in the Lexington Presbyterian Church," June 3, 1862, p. 12, Lyle Family Papers, Mss. 62M49, Box 1848–72, UK; [Elizabeth Pendleton Hardin], *The Private War of Lizzie Hardin: A Kentucky Confederate Girl's Diary of the Civil War in Kentucky, Virginia, Tennessee, Alabama, and Georgia*, ed. G. Glenn Clift (Frankfort: Kentucky Historical Society, 1962), 51.

10. Mark Grimsley, *The Hard Hand of War: Union Military Policy toward Southern Civilians, 1861–1865* (Cambridge: Cambridge University Press, 1995), 190–204; Halleck to Lorenzo Thomas, January 18, 1862, *OR*, ser. 1, vol. 8, 503; Stephen V. Ash, *When the Yankees Came: Conflict and Chaos in the Occupied South, 1861–1865* (Chapel Hill: University of North Carolina Press, 1995), 50–53; General Orders No. 8, November 26, 1861, General Orders No. 13, December 4, 1861, and Halleck to Charles Whittlesey, January 2, 1862, all in *OR*, ser. 1, vol. 8, 380–381, 405–406, 481.

11. Proclamation, "To all peaceably-disposed citizens of the State of Missouri, greeting," November 1, 5, 1861, *OR*, ser. 1, vol. 3, 563–564; Ettie Scott to Susan Grigsby, August 3, 1862, Grigsby Family Papers, Mss. A G857, Folder 173, FHS; Williamson Dixon Ward Civil War Journal, October 12, 1861, Mss. SC627, WKU; J[ohn]. M. Schofield to E[dwin]. M. Stanton, May 16, 1862, *OR*, ser. 1, vol. 13, 386; Elvira A. W. Scott Diary [typescript], Mss. 1053, Folder 4, pp. 116–1131, SHSM; Samuel S. Hildebrand, *The Autobiography of Sam S. Hildebrand: The Renowned Missouri Bushwhacker*, comp. James W. Evans and Abraham Wendell Keith (Jefferson City, MO: State Times Printing House, 1870), 47.

12. Edward Conrad Smith, *The Borderland in the Civil War* (New York: Macmillan, 1927), 367–368; William Crawford to H[enry]. W. Halleck, January 5, 1862, Records of the US Army Continental Commands, 1821–1920, Record Group 393, Pt. 1, Ser. 2593: Letters Received, Department of the Missouri, 1862–1867, Box 2, National Archives and Records Administration, Washington, DC (hereafter cited as RG 393);

Elvira A. W. Scott Diary [typescript], Mss. 1053, Folder 4, p. 99, SHSM; Abraham Lincoln to Samuel R. Curtis, January 5, 1863, and H[enry]. W. Halleck to George B. McClellan, December 19, 1861, both in *OR,* ser. 1, vol. 22, pt. 2, 17–18; vol. 8, 448–449.

13. Grimsley, *Hard Hand of War,* 1–6, 23, 35–36; Ephram J. Wilson to Odon Guitar, July 27, 1863, Odon Guitar Papers, Mss. C0882, SHSM; Daniel E. Sutherland, *A Savage Conflict: The Decisive Role of Guerrillas in the American Civil War* (Chapel Hill: University of North Carolina Press, 2009), 61; *Cape Girardeau (MO) Eagle* [Union Series], May 6, 1862, Special Collections and Archives, Southeast Missouri State University, Cape Girardeau (hereafter cited as SEMO); Michael Fellman, *Inside War: The Guerrilla Conflict in Missouri during the American Civil War* (New York: Oxford University Press, 1989), 13–15, 161.

14. V. Jacques Voegeli, *Free But Not Equal: The Midwest and the Negro* (Chicago: University of Chicago Press, 1967), 18, 60–62; Weber, *Copperheads,* 48–49; McPherson, *Battle Cry of Freedom,* 506–508, 591–592; *Cincinnati Daily Enquirer,* April 11, 18, September 26, 1862; *Belleville (IL) Advocate,* December 4, 1863.

15. Frank L. Klement, "Sound and Fury: Civil War Dissent in the Cincinnati Area," *Cincinnati Historical Society Bulletin* 35 (Summer 1977): 100; Charles Ray Wilson, "Cincinnati's Reputation during the Civil War," *Journal of Southern History* 2 (November 1936): 476; *Cincinnati Daily Enquirer,* April 11, 1862; *Defiance (OH) Democrat,* July 26, 1862, in Christine Dee, ed., *Ohio's War: The Civil War in Documents* (Athens: Ohio University Press, 2006), 79–81; *Daily Ledger* (New Albany, IL), July 22, 29, October 20, November 10, 1862; *Catholic Telegraph and Advocate* (Cincinnati), July 23, 30, 1862; McPherson, *Battle Cry of Freedom,* 591–592; Clinton W. Terry, "'The Most Commercial of People': Cincinnati, the Civil War, and the Rise of Commercial Capitalism, 1861–1865," (PhD diss., University of Cincinnati, 2002), 80–94; Leslie Ann Schwalm, "'Overrun with Free Negroes': Emancipation and Wartime Migration in the Upper Midwest," *Civil War History* 50 (June 2004): 145.

16. D. S. Brown to J[ames]. A. Wilcox, September 28, 1864, and Benjamin F. Cory to James A. Wilcox, October 7, 1864, Pt. 1., Ser. 3349: Letters Received, Northern Department, Boxes 1, 3, RG 393; Smith, *No Party Now,* 89; Affidavit, March 21, 1863; J. F. Dunn to Jacob Ammen, April 25, 1863; R. U. Mallory and S. G. Nesbitt to Ammen, May 19, 1863; N[apoleon]. B. Buford to [Alexander S.] Asboth, April 27, 1863, all in Jacob Ammen Papers, ALPL; Ammen to L. Richards, July 23, 1863, RG 393, Pt. 1, Ser. 3514: Letters Received, Department of the Ohio, Box 2, RG 393; Robert E. Sterling, "Civil War Draft Resistance in Illinois," *Journal of the Illinois State Historical Society* 64 (Autumn 1971): 255–258; Nation and Towne, *Indiana's War,* 167–169.

17. Paul Taylor, *The Most Complete Political Machine Ever Known: The North's Union Leagues in the American Civil War* (Kent, OH: Kent State University Press, 2018), 44–66; Smith, *No Party Now,* 68–75; Bentley Hamilton, "The Union League: Its Origin and Achievements in the Civil War," *Transactions of the Illinois State Historical Society* 28 (1921): 110–115; Charles H. Coleman, "The Use of the Term 'Copperhead' during the Civil War," *Mississippi Valley Historical Review* 25 (September 1938): 263–264; Melinda Lawson, "'A Profound National Devotion': The Civil War

Union Leagues and the Construction of a New National Patriotism," *Civil War History* 48 (December 2002): 338–344; Phillip Shaw Paludan, *"A People's Contest": The Union and Civil War, 1861–1865* (New York: Harper & Row, 1988), 237–238; *Centralia (IL) Sentinel,* December 3, 1863; *Grayville (IL) Independent,* April 10, 1863; Frank L. Klement, *Dark Lanterns: Secret Political Societies, Conspiracies, and Treason Trials in the Civil War* (Baton Rouge: Louisiana State University Press, 1984), 36–39.

18. *Centralia (IL) Sentinel,* July 16, 30, August 20, 1863, February 11, 1864; Bryon C. Andreasen, "'As Good a Right to Pray': Copperhead Christians on the Northern Civil War Home Front" (Ph.D. diss., University of Illinois, Urbana-Champaign, 1998), 4, 10 n8, 162; Weber, *Copperheads,* 3; Grapeland [Will T. Hart] to Susan Preston Shelby Grigsby, February 23, 1863, Grigsby Family Papers, Mss. A/G857, Folder 180, FHS.

19. [Edward Bates], *The Diary of Edward Bates 1859–1866,* ed. Howard K. Beale (Washington, DC: American Historical Association, 1933; reprint New York: Da Capo Press, 1971), 321–322, 292; Arthur C. Cole, *The Era of the Civil War, 1848–1870* (Chicago: A. C. McClurg, 1922), 301; James B. Boyd to David T. Statham, July 19, 1863, David T. Statham Papers, Mss. 688, OHS; *Grayville (IL) Independent,* April 10, 1863; *Centralia (IL) Sentinel,* February 11, 1864, August 6, 20, 1863; *The Scion* (West Union, OH), September 19, 1862; *The Free Nation* (Cincinnati), December 7, 1861; Taylor, *Most Complete Political Machine,* 117–119; Anonymous, *For Peace, and Peaceable Separation. Citizen's Democratic Address to the People of the State of Ohio, and the People of the Several States of the West and North* (Cincinnati: Author, 1863), iii–iv, 10; *Cincinnati Daily Enquirer,* March 18, 1863.

20. George W. Julian, *Personal Recollections, 1840–1872* (Chicago: Jansen, McClurg, 1884), 222–223.

21. Hamilton [OH] Telegraph, undated [January 1865]; Pomeroy [OH] Weekly Telegraph, May 26, 1864; Thomas A. Cobb to Dear Father, May 12, 1863, Thomas A. Cobb Letters, Mss. SC251, IHSL; Statement of Frank Howe, August 15, 1864, Pt. 1, Ser. 2229: Correspondence, Affidavits, Oaths Regarding Civilians Charged with Disloyalty, Department of Kentucky, Box 1, RG 393; Jon G. Taylor to Robert Neil, September 21, 1863, Robert Neil Family Papers, Mss. 259, OHS.

22. J. F. Dunn to Jacob Ammen, April 25, 1863, and Campbell Young to Ammen, June 4, 1863, both in Jacob Ammen Papers, ALPL; Alfred M. Mozley to My Dear Uncle, August 4, 1863, Alfred M. Mozley Letters, Mss. VFM 1642, SIU; Charles W. Starr to W. C. Starr, May 3, 1863, W. C. Starr Papers, Mss. SC1400, Folder 4, IHSL.

23. William A. Blair, *With Malice toward Some: Treason and Loyalty in the Civil War Era* (Chapel Hill: University of North Carolina Press, 2014), 100–159 passim; Report of Capt. Nelson Cole, May 16, 1861, *OR,* ser. 1, vol. 3, 10–11; Martha M. Jones to My Dear Father [W. S. Buford], December 21, 1862, Jones Family Papers, Mss. A/J78, Folder 1, FHS; Coulter, *Civil War and Readjustment in Kentucky,* 80; General Orders No. 10, March 28, 1862, *OR,* ser. 1, vol. 8, 834; *The Western Citizen* (Paris, KY), March 7, 1862; E. Merton Coulter, "Commercial Intercourse with the Confederacy in the Mississippi Valley, 1861–1865," *Mississippi Valley Historical Review*

4 (March 1919): 382 n15; Salmon P. Chase to William P. Millen, July 4, 1863, Record Group 56—Department of the Treasury Records, Pt. 56, Ser. 40: Letters Sent Related to Restricted Commercial Intercourse, Box 60, Book 13, Entry 3/6, pp. 321, 362–364, National Archives and Record Administration, Washington, DC (hereafter cited as NARA); Ross Jekyll to Bernard G. Farrar, May 7, 1863, Union Provost Marshals' File of Papers Relating to Individual Citizens, Record Group 109: War Department Collection of Confederate Records, File M345, Microfilm Reel 199, NARA; E. W. Bradley to Gen. [J. M.] Judah, April 13, 1863, and Thomas M. Redd to D. G. Barnitz, January 25, 1865; J. M. Judah to A. C. Semple, April 18, 1863; Charles B. Colton to J[eremiah]. T. Boyle, December 22, 1862; William P. Millen to S[tephen]. G. Burbridge, October 27, 1864; S. Meredith to J. Bates Dickson, February 7, 1865; all in RG 393, Pt. 1, Ser. 2173: Letters Received, Department of Kentucky, 1862–1869, Boxes 1, 4, 5, RG 393; Clinton W. Terry, "'Let Commerce Follow the Flag': Trade and Loyalty to the Union in the Ohio Valley," *Ohio Valley History* 1 (Spring 2001): 7 (emphasis Chase's). Chase included the phrase in his 1861 annual report on government finances. Cities with boards of trade operating in them included Pittsburgh, Wheeling, Mayville, Cincinnati, Madison, Lawrenceburg, Louisville, New Albany, Evansville, Paducah, Cairo, Quincy, St. Louis, Hickman, Cadiz, Hopkinsville, Bowling Green, Catlettsburg, and Rolla. By August 2, 1861, the Confederacy had banned the trade of cotton, tobacco, sugar, rice, molasses, and naval stores with the United States. On January 5, 1865, Stephen E. Burbridge banned boards of trade in his Kentucky department owing to corruption.

24. Joseph C. Butler, W[illia]m. McCreary, and Geo[rge]. H. Thurston to Edwin M. Stanton, all March 26, 1862, in *OR*, ser. 3, vol. 1, 950–951; Terry, "Let Commerce Follow the Flag," 1–3, 7–9; Charles B. Colton to J[eremiah]. T. Boyle, December 22, 1862, RG 393, Pt. 1, Ser. 2173: Letters Received, Department of Kentucky, 1862–1869, Box 1, RG 393; Coulter, Civil War and Readjustment, 80 n142; *Centralia (IL) Sentinel*, February 11, March 31, 1864.

25. J. M. Judah to A. C. Semple, April 18, 1863, and enclosures; J. P. Jackson to J. Bates Dickson, August 20, 1864; Thomas M. Redd to William P. Millen, October 3, 1864, all in Pt. 1, Ser. 2173: Letters Received, Department of Kentucky, 1862–1869, Boxes 1, 4, RG 393; *Cincinnati Enquirer*, September 4, 1861; Terry, "'Let Commerce Follow the Flag,'" 7; Salmon P. Chase to William P. Millen, May 29, 1861, Record Group 56, Department of the Treasury Records, Part 56, Ser. 40: Letters Sent Related to Restricted Commercial Intercourse, Box 60, Book 11, pp. 16–17, NARA; [William Conrad], *The Journal of Elder William Conrad: Pioneer Preacher*, ed. Lloyd W. Franks (Lexington, KY: R. F. Publishing, 1976), 81; Lowell H. Harrison, *The Civil War in Kentucky* (Lexington: University Press of Kentucky, 1975), 99–100; J. H. Hammond to J. Bates Dickson, September 3, 1864, RG 393, Pt. 1, Ser. 2173: Letters Received, Department of Kentucky, 1862–1869, Box 4, RG 393.

26. Edward Dicey, *Spectator of America*, ed. Herbert Mitgang (Chicago: Quadrangle, 1971; reprint Athens: University of Georgia Press, 1989), 175–181; Contract, Rule and Bro. to Alexander Jeffrey, July 21, 1862, and Jeffrey to Rosa V. J. Jeffrey, Jan-

uary 6, 7, 1863, all in Rosa V. J. Jeffrey Papers, Mss. A/J46r, Folder 83, FHS; Kentucky Union League to National Union League, November 21, 1864, Abraham Lincoln Papers, Series 1, General Correspondence, 1833–1916, Library of Congress.

27. *Centralia (IL) Sentinel*, June 4, 1863, July 14, 1864.

28. James F. Lee to Brother Junius Fee, October 15, 1861, James Frank Fee Letters, Mss. SC567, Folder 1, IHSL; "The Civil War and Activities in Union County. As related by E. R. Jinnette, late of Oakland, California; formerly of Union County, Illinois," unpublished interview [typescript], John Willis Allen Papers, Mss. 76–3-F1, Box 25, SIU; Nancy Mann to J[ohn]. Preston Mann, February 11, 1862, Mann Family Papers, Coll. 111, Box 1, SIU; William Houghton to Walter Houghton, July 26, 1862, William Houghton Papers, Mss. M147, Box 1, Folder 5, IHSL; Jasper Cross, "Divided Loyalties in Southern Illinois during the Civil War" (PhD diss., University of Illinois, Urbana-Champaign, 1940), 134–143; Nation and Towne, eds., *Indiana's War*, 177–178, 185–188; Mary A. Crebs to My Own Dear Husband, November 16, 1863, July 11, August 14, 1864, Mary A. Berry [Crebs] Letters, Misc. Vol. 88, SIU; Nancy C. Mann to J[ohn]. Preston Mann, July 7, March 13, September 16, and undated, 1863, January 25, 1864, Mann Family Papers, Coll. 111, Boxes 1–2, SIU; Leo D. Sirrania to Friend Monroe, November 22, 1863, Amos C. Weaver Papers, Mss. SC1545, Folder 2, IHSL; Jeptha V. King to Dear Uncle, February 7, 1863, Jeptha King Letters, Mss. SC916, IHSL; Daniel L. Thomas, June 18, 1863, Daniel Lafayette Thomas Papers, Mss. SC1445, IHSL; *Corydon (IN) Weekly Democrat*, July 14, 1863.

29. John A. Trimble to Jack Trimble, June 23, 1861, John A. Trimble Papers, Mss. 249, Box 10, Folder 2, OHS; Smith, *No Party Now*, 86, 117–120; George Q. Langstaff Jr., ed., *The Life and Times of Quintus Quincy Quigley, 1828–1910: His Personal Journals, 1859–1908* (Brentwood, TN: Tallant Group, 1999), 74; T. F. Blakeman to Jack Harding, May 16, 1862, John Harding Collection, Mss. A/H263, Folder 5, FHS; *Dayton (OH) Daily Empire*, January 14, 1864; Sidney Kaplan, "The Miscegenation Issue in the Election of 1864," *Journal of Negro History* 34 (July 1949): 274–343 passim; McPherson, *Battle Cry of Freedom*, 789–791; *Valley Democrat* (McConnelsville, OH), May 25, 1864; [William McKnight,] *Do They Miss Me at Home? The Civil War Letters of William McKnight, Seventh Ohio Volunteer Cavalry*, ed. Donald C. Maness and H. Jason Combs (Athens: Ohio University Press, 2010), 72; *McArthur (OH) Register*, June 2, 1864.

30. Anthony Miller to Sam Beck, April 26, 1863; G. C. W. to Jacob Ammen, June 9, 1863; B. Pilkington to N[apoleon]. B. Buford, June 16, 1863; J. W. Woodruff to S. R. Holmes, July 15, 1864, all in Jacob Ammen Papers, ALPL; Mary A. Berry to My Own Dear Husband [Daniel Berry], July 11, August 14, October 2, November 10, 1864, Mary A. Berry [Crebs] Letters, Misc. Vol. 88, SIU; M. D. White to Lazarus Noble, June 23, 1863, in Nation and Towne, *Indiana's War*, 173; *The Free South* (Newport, KY), October 26, 1864; Hicken, *Illinois in the Civil War*, 263; *Centralia (IL) Sentinel*, June 30, August 18, 1864; Henry Carrington to Carroll H. Potter, March 30, 1864, and Hiram Sandford to Samuel B. Heintzelman, September 6, 1864, both in RG 393, Pt. 1., Ser. 3349: Letters Received, Northern Department, Boxes 1–2, RG 393; Stephen E.

Towne, "'Such Conduct Must Be Put Down': The Military Arrest of Judge Charles H. Constable during the Civil War," *Journal of Illinois History* 9 (June 2006): 57; Cole, *Era of the Civil War,* 307–308.

31. Weber, *Copperheads,* 196–200; Smith, *No Party Now,* 95–100; John Cook to C. H. Potter, November 8, 1864, Pt. 1, Ser. 2249: Letters Received, Northern Department, Box 1, RG 393; James M. McPherson, *Ordeal by Fire* (New York: Knopf, 1982), 457–458; Dixon Wecter, "The Soldier and the Ballot," *Huntington Library Quarterly* 7 (August 1944): 397–400; Benjamin P. Thomas and Harold M. Hyman, *Stanton: The Life and Times of Lincoln's Secretary of War* (New York: Knopf, 1962), 331–334; Robert P. Howard, Illinois: *A History of the Prairie State* (Grand Rapids, MI: William B. Eerdmans, 1972), 305–312.

32. McPherson, *Battle Cry of Freedom,* 756–758, 784–788; Gienapp, "Lincoln and the Border States," 19–20; John B. Helm to Samuel Haycraft, October 7, 1864, Haycraft Family Papers, Mss. 69; M690 [microfilm], UK; John B. Helm to Samuel Haycraft, October 7, 1864, Haycraft Family Papers, Mss. 69M690 [microfilm], UK; James D. Hardin to the President of the United States, October 17, 1864; RG 393, Pt. 1, Ser. 2173: Letters Received, Department of Kentucky, Box 4, RG 393.

33. Elliot Jaspin, *Buried in the Bitter Waters: The Hidden History of Racial Cleansing in America* (New York: Basic Books, 2007), 16–29; Darrel E. Bigham, *On Jordan's Banks: Emancipation and Its Aftermath in the Ohio River Valley* (Lexington: University Press of Kentucky, 2006), 92–93, 94–95; Emma Lou Thornbrough, *The Negro in Indiana Before 1900: A Study of a Minority* (Indianapolis: Indiana Historical Bureau; reprint Bloomington and Indianapolis: Indiana University Press, 1993), 225; Amy Murrell Taylor, *Embattled Freedom: Journeys through the Civil War's Slave Camps* (Chapel Hill: University of North Carolina Press, 2018), 182–205.

CHAPTER 5

"The State Was Honeycombed with Secret Societies": Governor Oliver P. Morton and the Copperheads in Indiana

A. JAMES FULLER

The bullet flew past Indiana governor Oliver P. Morton's head as he stepped out of the door of the state capitol, where he had been working late in his office in the summer of 1863. The sound of the shot shattered the silence of the warm night in Indianapolis, and the governor moved quickly to escape the assassin whose bullet had narrowly missed him. Rushing to the quarters of his friend and colleague in the Union war effort, General Henry B. Carrington, Morton told the army officer about the assassination attempt. Carrington dressed and accompanied Morton home, hoping to safeguard the Indiana governor from whatever enemies lurked in the darkness. As they approached Morton's house another shot rang out, and the assassin again missed his target. General Carrington searched the area but could not find the shooter. Although they told several others about the incident, the governor and the general agreed to keep the shooting quiet, as they did not want to frighten Morton's family and did not want the news to bolster support for the Copperheads who were behind the assassination attempt. The term "Copperheads" derived from the poisonous snake, and Republicans applied it liberally to their Democratic political foes. While many Democrats opposed the war and criticized the Republicans in the government for raising taxes, using the draft to conscript soldiers into the army, and for limiting civil liberties in the name of putting down the rebellion, the Copperheads crossed the line into treason by actively working to thwart the Union cause.[1]

Governor Morton worked with General Carrington and other military officers to investigate the Copperheads, and they discovered that there were numerous clandestine organizations operating in the state of Indiana. As Morton later put it, "the state was honeycombed with secret societies," and

Figure 5.1. Indiana governor Oliver P. Morton, ca. 1863. Courtesy of the Library of Congress.

he believed that a fifth column of traitors might rise up in the Union rear to aid the rebels of the Confederacy. If that happened, the rebels might win the Civil War and the Union would be destroyed. Carrington and Morton were convinced that the dissenters presented a danger to the war effort and urged the federal authorities to take action. Recognizing that the threat of traitors would rally support for the Union cause, the governor decided to take political advantage of the situation and pushed the army investigators to move against the Copperheads. The resulting arrests and the Indianapolis treason trials of men like Lambdin P. Milligan came just in time to help the Republicans in the elections of 1864. These events showed that the Copperheads were real, that Morton believed them to be a peril to the Union, but that he also opportunistically turned the military investigations and trials of the traitors to his political benefit.[2]

Figure 5.2. Copperhead leaders arraigned at Indianapolis for treason. *Clockwise from top*: William A. Bowles, Andrew Humphreys, Stephen Horsey, Horace Heffren, and Lambdin P. Milligan. From Benn Pittman, ed., *The Trials for Treason at Indianapolis* (Cincinnati, OH: Moore, Wilstach & Baldwin, 1865).

Historians continue to disagree about the Copperheads and Morton's role in opposing them. Nineteenth-century writers generally took a Unionist or nationalist perspective that favored the governor and saw the Copperheads in the Midwest as a genuine threat. This understanding continued in the early twentieth century, even as the scholars of the Progressive era challenged the prevailing view and developed new interpretations that emphasized economics and conflict in history. During World War II, Progressive historian Wood Gray saw the Copperheads as a serious threat to the Union in his 1942 book, *The Hidden Civil War,* and positively portrayed Morton as the Union leader who rooted out the traitors in the rear. George Milton's *Abraham Lincoln and the Fifth Column,* a popular history published in the same year, took a similar view: Morton was a Union hero who led the effort to thwart the traitorous Copperheads.[3]

After World War II, revisionist scholarship challenged the long-standing narrative of Morton and the Copperheads. The reinterpretation began with William B. Hesseltine's classic book, *Lincoln and the War Governors,* a 1948 work that saw Abraham Lincoln as a master statesman who outsmarted the Union state leaders and outmaneuvered them in ways that helped defeat the rebellion. Hesseltine saw Morton as the best of the inferior governors, a man of talent and great energy, but he thought that the Indiana governor was paranoid. Thus, he argued that the Hoosier leader's alarmist tendencies caused him to panic and exaggerate the danger of the Copperhead conspiracies.[4]

Another revisionist argument appeared in 1949 when Kenneth M. Stampp published *Indiana Politics during the Civil War.* Stampp saw the past through an economic lens and framed his analysis in the terms of class conflict. He cast Morton as a ruthless dictator who joined other Republicans in supporting capitalism and big business against the agrarian interests of the farmers. Although he admitted that Morton was talented and worked hard to save the Union, Stampp saw him as a tyrannical opportunist who would do whatever it took to keep power. In this influential study of Indiana in the war years, then, Morton crushed dissent by toying with the Copperheads like a cat played with a mouse. The opponents of the war made legitimate criticisms of the government's expansion and abuse of power. Far from being a real threat, they were used by Morton to his political advantage. According to Stampp, there was no reason for the government to fear the secret Copperhead network in Indiana "as a menace to domestic peace."

But the authorities moved against the secretive traitors, and Morton manipulated the situation to his party's advantage. Stampp quoted Morton's nineteenth-century biographer William Dudley Foulke in saying, "the Governor held the society 'as a plaything in his hands,' allowed it to grow, and 'even coerce[d] it into his service.'" In this account, Morton was the mastermind who actually encouraged the Copperheads in order to use them to his advantage.[5]

But the most important revisionist interpretation came in the work of Frank L. Klement, whose arguments became the definitive account for nearly half a century. He first offered his interpretation in his 1960 book, *The Copperheads in the Middle West*, but repeated it in later books as well. According to the Klement thesis (as it came to be called) Morton concocted the threat of traitors in the rear, the Copperheads were legitimate critics of Republican policies, and only a handful of them actually planned treasonous activities. First writing in the wake of the Red Scare of the 1950s, Klement portrayed Morton as a ruthless opportunist who whipped up hysteria to create fear among the voters and to crush the loyal opposition. Like Stampp, Klement had been trained by Progressive scholars and saw history in terms of economics and class conflict. In his hands, Morton became a political mastermind representing the forces of capitalism while the Copperheads became the defenders of liberty and the agrarian way of life.[6]

For decades the Klement thesis held sway, although historians such as Emma Lou Thornbrough offered somewhat more balanced accounts of Morton, arguing that the governor was an "organizational genius" and praising his leadership of the state throughout the rebellion. By the end of the twentieth century, however, the view of Morton as a ruthless opportunist who concocted the Copperhead threat to win elections was the dominant theory. But in the age of the War on Terror, the literature took another turn. In her 2006 book, Jennifer L. Weber argued that the Copperheads were a real threat and, had they timed their actions correctly, might have seriously damaged the Union war effort. Stephen E. Towne set out to fully dismantle the Klement thesis in his 2015 work, *Surveillance and Spies in the Civil War*. Arguing that the Copperheads constituted a true threat, Towne mined previously unused primary sources, especially military records, to show that the secret societies of traitors were widespread. The Copperheads collaborated with the Confederates and not only planned treason but also took action against the government. Only through the efforts of diligent military authorities and political leaders like Morton was the Union saved from an internal civil war. Although his work necessarily relied too heavily on Union Army sources and, thus, gave a largely one-sided view, Towne effectively challenged the Klement thesis and raised serious doubts about its validity.[7]

Despite the divided nature of the literature, the situation in Indiana during the war reveals that the Copperheads did exist; that regardless of their actual potential, Morton believed that they constituted a threat; *and* that he used the opportunity to gain a political advantage. If there really were traitors in Indiana, it means that the military officers and Governor Morton were not merely trampling civil liberties in the name of political opportunism. Instead, their actions were taken in the name of saving the Union from a serious threat of an internal attack that would aid the rebellion. The fact that whatever records the secret organizations might have kept were destroyed makes it nearly impossible for historians to find out more about the Copperhead side of the story—accounts that might confirm either historical interpretation of their actions. Given that caveat, this analysis closely follows Towne's excellent and detailed research and Weber's insightful and well-documented interpretation in their convincing challenges to the Klement thesis. Drawing heavily on Towne's account, this chapter accepts that the Copperheads existed and that their plans were a danger to the Union. Because they were unsuccessful or unable to carry out most of their schemes, the full extent of the peril remains unclear. But however serious their potential to do harm actually was, Morton and other authorities believed that they threatened the cause. This chapter also agrees with Towne's argument that the Indiana governor was a consumer of intelligence information who collaborated with the military. Thus, this approach rejects the view of scholars like Stampp and Klement, who portrayed the Hoosier leader as the mastermind behind the investigations.

At the same time, however, there was some substance to the mid-twentieth-century revisionist interpretation. The governor sometimes painted with too broad a brush and portrayed legitimate Democratic critics as traitors. And he was clearly not afraid to take advantage of a situation to further his party's interests. That Morton pushed the army to move in time to help the Republicans win the elections in 1864 shows that he did indeed seize the chance to bolster his political ends. But rather than looking at the arrests and resulting Indianapolis treason trials as either a political concoction or a legitimate move to thwart a treasonous uprising, this chapter argues that the situation was both a real threat and an opportunistic political move. Therefore, this argument fits comfortably between the Klement thesis and the recent attempts to refute that long-standing interpretation. It explains as well the historical context that set the stage for *Ex parte Milligan.*[8]

THE COPPERHEADS

Even before the War of the Rebellion actually started, there were Hoosiers who expressed sympathy for the South and thought that the Confederate states should be allowed to secede peacefully. By 1862, rumors and reports of traitors on the Indiana home front had become widespread, as citizens worried about the activities and Confederate leanings of their neighbors. Such concerns only increased as the months rolled by. In the confusing context of the war, it became difficult to ascertain who was actually a Copperhead and who was simply complaining about the government's actions or about a particular leader or specific policy. Evidence emerged, however, showing that there were networks of anti-war Democrats who were planning to undertake sabotage and even insurrection in the name of fighting against Republican tyranny.

Politically, the Democratic Party in the Union states split into factions during the rebellion. Some, like Andrew Johnson of Tennessee, John Brough of Ohio, and Benjamin Butler of Massachusetts, became War Democrats who supported the government's efforts to defeat the Confederacy. In Indiana, prominent War Democrats included Lew Wallace, Robert Dale Owen, Joseph McDonald, and William English. Such men joined the Republicans in the Union Party (and some of them would eventually switch to the Republican Party itself), which claimed to be nonpartisan and dedicated only to preservation of the nation. Others worked as Peace Democrats, offering criticism of the Republican-led government while remaining committed to the Union, becoming a legitimate loyal opposition. Peace Democrats included New York's Horatio Seymour and Fernando Wood, while Ohio's Clement Vallandigham and George Pendleton ranked among the most famous critics of the Republican-led war effort. In Indiana, this faction was led by prominent politicians such as Daniel Voorhees and Thomas Hendricks. Still other Democrats took their opposition to the war and/or sympathies with the rebels to such extremes that they crossed the line into treason. It was this last faction who were the Copperheads. Of course, the lines often blurred and individuals sometimes had mixed loyalties and political views. Issues like taxation, property rights, conscription, racism, slavery, emancipation, and state's rights all played a role in the context of the war. One could legitimately criticize the government within the bounds of the law on a whole range of questions. And one could engage in treason in the name of any of them. Further clouding the picture was the fact that Republicans like Morton were quick to label any Democrat who did not join the Union Party a "Copperhead." During the war, patriotism and allegiance were redefined to mean alliance with the government or treason. Thus, many Republicans thought of men like Voorhees and Vallandigham as Copperheads, while many Democrats thought of them as the loyal opposition or Peace Democrats. Such realities lent to the confusion, making for a political "fog of war" for state officials and military authorities in the region.

Even the name "Copperhead" raised controversy, as it employed a poisonous snake in the grass as a symbol of those who so stridently opposed the war. In the heat of political discourse, the term could be hurled at an opponent too easily, and politicians like Morton were prone to using it indiscriminately. Even after the war, when he was serving as a US senator, Morton called all Southern Democrats "rebels" and all Northern Democrats "Copperheads." Such rhetoric became his stock in trade as he helped lead the Radical Republicans during the political battles over Reconstruction that he saw as a continuation of the war. It was a practice he had developed during the rebellion, when he often attached the term "Copperhead" to Democratic rivals.

In the states in the lower Midwest—Ohio, Indiana, and Illinois—large portions of the population hailed from the South or claimed Southern ancestry, and this was especially true in places like southern Indiana. Often called Butternuts (because of the use of butternuts, or white walnuts, to dye their homespun clothing), these white residents had often left Southern states like Kentucky, Virginia, and North Carolina to avoid living in a slave society, and many of them held strongly racist views. In fact, some of these so-called upland Southerners had opposed slavery *because* of racism, as their hatred of black people meant that they did not want to live around them. Thus, they supported states like Indiana, Illinois, and Ohio passing exclusion laws forbidding blacks from settling within their borders and approved the passage of Black Codes that ensured white supremacy. These

Butternuts usually maintained strong connections to their family members and friends who still lived in the South. Such ties could nurture sympathies that led to pro-Southern and anti-war political views. At the very least, a Butternut living in the Midwest worried about how a war to put down the rebellion might adversely affect friends or relatives in the South. It might also mean that such an individual opposed the war outright or thought that it should be conducted in a very limited way. Of course, not all Butternuts were Copperheads and not all Copperheads were Butternuts. Furthermore, in Indiana, anti-war sentiment could be found in the northern parts of the state as well as in the southern regions. And some who opposed the war in extreme ways traced their heritage to the North—or if they were recent immigrants, to Europe—not to the South. But they were united in their opposition to the war and were ready to take treasonous actions against the government.[9]

The secret societies of Copperheads used different names for their clandestine networks but often took the title Knights of the Golden Circle (KGC). The KGC originated in the 1850s as an organization dedicated to the territorial expansion of the United States. Operating secretly because their plans for annexing new areas often involved illegal activities, they hoped to carve out territory in the Southwest by taking more land from Mexico. When the rebellion began, some KGC members turned the organization toward aiding the Confederacy and resisting the government. Later, the secret societies in Indiana would call themselves the Order of American Knights (OAK). By 1864 the Copperhead secret organization called their network the Sons of Liberty. Whatever the name—and they may have coexisted for a time—their membership overlapped, and only the inner circle of leadership had an idea about the full extent of their actual numbers and their plans.[10]

Reports of Copperheads in Indiana arrived on Governor Morton's desk as early as the summer of 1861, although a number of citizens had notified him of secessionists and pro-Confederate sympathizers that spring. In August, pro-Union authorities in Michigan City in northern Indiana arrested a photographer they suspected of being a recruiter for the KGC. Other reports came from across the state about possible disloyalty, and Morton gave a speech to a Union meeting in Rockville urging Hoosiers to be vigilant in watching for traitors in their midst. That fall, an informer told the government about the "Mutual Protection" organizations that had been formed across western Indiana and eastern Illinois. These groups opposed the policies of the Lincoln administration, especially increased taxation to pay for the war, and included a number of prominent Democratic officeholders. Their plans to resist the government involved sabotaging troop trains and assassinating Republican political leaders. In light of such information, Morton began to more earnestly gather intelligence on the Copperheads, as he feared that an internal threat existed and might become more widespread as the rebellion continued.[11]

In 1862 opposition to the war increased in the wake of military setbacks and Union policies. When General George B. McClellan's Peninsular Campaign ended in defeat, many worried that the rebellion might well be successful, and this lent credence to the arguments that secession was legal because of state sovereignty. Perhaps putting down the rebellion was not really worth all of the blood and treasure it would take to defeat the Confederacy. Meanwhile, the War Department ordered the military to clamp down on anti-war sentiment expressed in act or speech. This led to the arrests of many Democratic newspaper editors and other citizens who dared to speak out against the government. Army officials also investigated and arrested those they suspected of encouraging soldiers to desert. When the Militia Act of 1862 authorized the president to enlist members of state militias into national service, it was seen as a draft and added fuel to the growing fires of dissent. That the law also allowed for the enlistment of black soldiers only further enflamed the racist fears of the Copperheads. That summer Colonel Henry B. Carrington arrived in Indianapolis and began collaborating with Governor Morton in investigating the Copperheads and working to stop their actions against the war.[12]

Sent to the Hoosier state as commander of the Eighteenth US Infantry regiment, Carrington helped organize the vast numbers of troops being recruited in the state. Governor Morton had grown impatient with the army commander on the scene and requested a new bureaucratic officer who would keep up with the governor's breakneck speed in recruiting and supplying troops and responding to needs and crises when they arose. Carrington, whose headquarters was in the state capital, proved to be as energetic and effective as an army officer as Morton was as governor. The two became friends as well as allies for the Union, and the governor counted on the officer to carry out the work that his predecessors had been slow to undertake. In addition to organizing and preparing the soldiers to fight, Carrington sent troops to restore order when draft riots broke out in Hartford City in northern Indiana and oversaw efforts to stop desertion. Late in 1862 the colonel received reports about dissent and disloyalty within the ranks of the army. He gathered information on Copperhead conspiracies among the soldiers, including details about codes, passwords, and secret handshakes used by the disloyal men who had joined the clandestine movement.[13]

Carrington's worries about Copperheads in the army stemmed from the shifting political situation. In September, President Lincoln issued the Preliminary Emancipation Proclamation, a measure that made the war about slavery as well as rebellion. This upset many in the Northern states, especially those who held racist views and/or thought the war should be only about restoring the Union. Further, Lincoln's Emancipation Proclamation, which was officially issued in January 1863, was carried out through executive order. This was seen as an expansion of presidential power at the expense of Congress, and many Democrats argued that it was unconstitutional because it violated property rights firmly established by law. Even some Republicans disliked emancipation, but the party (including Morton) followed the lead of President Lincoln, who explicitly pitched the issue as being a war measure, a means of putting down the rebellion. They pointed out that Lincoln's preliminary proclamation gave the Confederates months to make peace and give up their rebellion. And the measure freed only those slaves in territory still in rebellion, not those in loyal states or areas. When combined with mounting battlefield casualties, increased taxation, and the draft, however, emancipation became a hot-button issue that rallied dissent against the government and lent credence to those who cried out against Republican tyranny. In Indiana this political perfect storm allowed the Democrats to sweep to power in the mid-term elections, as they took seven of the state's congressional seats (the Republicans had enjoyed a 7–4 advantage in the state's delegation before the election, but the contest flipped the numbers and the Democrats had a 7–4 edge) and won a majority in the state legislature that set the stage for a conflict with Governor Morton.[14]

Dismayed by the election results, Morton worried about the growing strength of the Copperheads and feared that the newly elected Democrats might implement the anti-war plans devised by the secret societies. Earlier in the year, Thomas A. Hendricks, who would soon be elected to the US Senate by his fellow Democrats, had delivered an anti-war speech in which he had envisioned a "Northwestern Confederacy" that would secede from the Union and be independent of both the South and the Northeastern bankers and capitalists. In October the governor's secretary informed the Lincoln administration about Copperhead plans for making the Northwestern Confederacy a reality. Morton himself wrote to the president and detailed the reasons to fear such a plan. He explained that Democratic arguments about how those in the heartland were exploited and abused by the Northeast appealed to Hoosiers. And the governor reminded Lincoln that geography tied many regions in the midwestern states to the South. Social and cultural connections to the South were strengthened by economic interests created by river trade, and the Democrats were using the political situation to support their call for independence. Following the disastrous defeat at Fredericksburg in December, Ohio Copperhead congressman Clement L. Vallandigham vehemently attacked the Lincoln administration and rallied anti-war protestors across the Midwest. Vocal critics in Indiana hoped to use the growing momentum to score political points in their state.[15]

In January, things came to a head. Violent resistance to the war took place in Morgan County, just a few miles to the west and south of Indianapolis, when cavalrymen hunting deserters made some arrests and were fired upon by riders trying to free the prisoners. Finally, the cavalry charged the shooters, captured several of them, and brought them back for trial. This minor "Battle of Waverly" was only one of many conflicts across the Midwest, but coming when and where it did, it added to the concern that the Democrats and Copperheads were working together and might take Indiana out of the Union. The Morgan County resistance coincided with the opening of the legislative session and a political battle between the governor and the legislature.[16]

THE DEMOCRATS VERSUS GOVERNOR MORTON

In preparation for the legislative session, Morton prepared his annual message reporting on the state of the state. His written report defended the Republicans and himself, arguing that all of their actions had been done legally and in good faith in the name of saving the Union. He couched his message in nationalist terms and dismissed the idea of state sovereignty and the right of secession. Having defended his party in partisan fashion, Morton then denounced partisanship, calling for unity to preserve the national republic. The governor's message proved to be the opening salvo in the grand political battle that played out on the stage of Indiana state politics in the first half of 1863.

The Democrats in the legislature refused to receive Morton's message and, instead, voted to accept the message of Governor Horatio Seymour of New York, a Democrat who criticized the Republican war effort and attacked the Emancipation Proclamation. The Indiana Democrats then elected first David Turpie and, then, Thomas Hendricks, to the US Senate. This election of a senator was necessary because the US Senate had expelled Democrat Jesse Bright, who had been charged with treason when it came to light that he had written a letter of introduction for a friend to rebel leader Jefferson Davis. Bright had addressed Davis in honorific terms and called him the president of the Confederacy. Morton had appointed Joseph Wright, a War Democrat and former governor and long-time enemy of Bright, to fill the vacancy until the legislature convened. The senate seat's term would end in about a month, and they wanted to elect Hendricks to fill the slot for the next six years. But the Democrats wanted to resist Morton and slapped at him by refusing to wait until the term ended to replace Wright. Instead, they elected Turpie to serve out the vacancy, and then they would choose Hendricks. Hoping to stop the election of Hendricks, the Republican minority in the legislature bolted the session to deny a quorum. This marked a turn to bitter partisanship, as the Republicans failed to live up to their own talk about unity and a nonpartisan Union Party. Given the reality of the Democratic majority, the Republicans failed to stop the election of Hendricks and returned to the legislative seats in defeat. Their attempt to thwart the election backfired when their bolt became controversial because most Hoosiers did not agree with the Republicans who called the Democratic candidate a traitor. Morton fired at Hendricks in his annual message, remarking on the Democrat's hints at a Northwest Confederacy and calling such ideas "hollow," saying that peace on such terms "would be a dishonorable and shameful surrender." The Republicans called Hendricks a Copperhead and a cowardly traitor, but this had no effect. Hurling angry epithets at the Democrats did little and, given the mood of the voters, might well hurt the Republicans in the next election.[17]

Having flexed their muscles in electing a senator, the Democrats turned to investigating the governor, who they had charged with corruption throughout the campaign. They claimed that he had misused and stolen funds from the state treasury. In response, Morton opened the books to a full accounting and the resulting audit proved his honesty, although it did uncover a mistake made by the Democratic state auditor that involved money being deposited in the wrong account. The investigation also showed that the state arsenal that Morton had created in Indianapolis actually turned a profit. Unsatisfied, the Democrats appointed a committee to investigate whether the governor and his administration had been corrupt in their purchasing of arms for Hoosier soldiers. Morton cooperated with the inquiry, finding funds in the budget to cover the expenses of the legislators on the committee to travel to New York to review arms purchases. In the end, the committee found no wrongdoing and reported that the administration had been honest in its expenditures. Far from misusing government funds, the governor proved to be trustworthy and efficient.[18]

Disappointed that they had not caught their enemy in corruption, the Democrats turned to blaming him for the military arrests made of anti-war activists who had criticized the government. Because the arrests were ordered by the federal government, it was hard to pin them on Morton. But his opponents claimed that he had not publicly denounced the arrests; therefore he was guilty of making them. In reality, Morton sometimes fought the arbitrary arrests—even when they involved men that he suspected of being Copperheads—because he worried that such incidents only strengthened the opponents of the war. But in the opening weeks of the 1863 legislative session, his enemies accused him of cooperating too readily with the army and pointed to his work with officers like Carrington as proof that he supported the violation of civil liberties. Desperate to defeat Morton, the Democrats in the legislature formed a committee to investigate his involvement in the arbitrary arrests.[19]

Unable to bring the governor down with investigations of corruption and by blaming him for what the Lincoln administration had done, the Hoosier Democrats decided to take away his control of the state's war effort. To do this, they introduced legislation that would dissolve the Indiana Legion—which was the state militia that Morton had raised in 1861 to defend the state. They also proposed to create a four-man military board made up of the state treasurer, secretary of state, auditor, and attorney general that would direct Indiana's war effort instead of the governor. These four state officers would direct the recruitment, training, and supplying of troops.

They would appoint and commission officers. And they would command the state militia. Of course, Morton had been doing all of those things under the authorities granted to the governor under the state constitution and laws passed many years before. Although the Democrats argued that the board would be balanced, with two members from each party, the governor saw the new legislation as an unconstitutional threat to his power and to the survival of the Union.

To thwart the Democratic power grab, Morton encouraged his fellow Republicans in the state legislature to bolt the session and deny the majority a quorum. Although the tactic had failed to stop the election of Hendricks earlier in the year, the minority bolted and quietly took a train to Madison, a river town from where they could slip into Kentucky if they needed to avoid marshals sent by the Democrats to bring them back. This time, the bolt worked and the legislative session ended without the majority being able to pass their military bill. But they also failed to pass an appropriations bill, leaving the state government unfunded. Without a budget, Morton would be forced to call a special session to get the needed money. The Democrats thought that they would seize that opportunity to push through their plan to take over the war effort. But Morton defeated them again. Instead of calling a special session, he simply ran the state himself for the next twenty-two months (from March 1863 to January 1865). During this period of one-man rule, he borrowed money from county governments, banks, and the War Department. He crossed legal bounds when he took funds from the state arsenal to help pay for the government without a budget. In the end, it worked, and subsequent investigations led by the Democrats proved that, once again, Morton was honest and did not steal or misuse government money.[20]

THE CONSPIRACIES UNCOVERED AND EXPOSED

Even as the political drama in Indianapolis unfolded in early 1863, military investigations of the Copperhead conspiracies continued. From his headquarters in Cincinnati, General Horatio Wright, the commander of the Department of the Ohio, oversaw the operations of district commanders who led the army in Illinois, Ohio, and Indiana, as well as in West Virginia and Kentucky. Of course, Wright was concerned with more than just the Copperheads, as the sprawling department needed to be defended and troops were continually being mobilized and moved about the region as well as to the front. But Wright recognized the importance of military intelligence and facilitated the work of his officers like Carrington who directed the investigation of the secret societies of disloyal men working within the department. The army used spies and detectives to gather information and infiltrate the Copperhead networks. In late 1862 and early 1863, the military discovered the sale and shipment of arms and ammunition to the rebels and to Copperheads. They uncovered schemes for sabotage, assassination, and armed uprisings. There were indications that prominent Democrats were involved in the conspiracies, including Hendricks and Congressman Daniel Voorhees. From across the state came reports of veterans and soldiers home on furlough taking action against suspected traitors. In some communities, the loyal Union Leagues fought with opponents of the war. In such cases, those who attacked the disloyal men called their targets Copperheads and accused them of treason. Some might have been members of the secret societies, while others were probably legitimate critics of government policies. But the growing climate of fear and distrust gave dire meaning to any such accusations.[21]

In March of 1863, General Ambrose Burnside took command of the Department of the Ohio. Fresh from his humiliating defeat at Fredericksburg and removal as commander of the Army of the Potomac, Burnside hoped to redeem himself in his new role. This meant taking military action. The general learned about the situation in the Midwest as he prepared to lead some of the troops in his department into East Tennessee. There, he hoped to be in a position to fight another battle against the rebels and erase the stain of Fredericksburg. But the political unrest, widespread dissent, and increasing incidence of violence in the department hampered his ability to move his men to Tennessee. So, Burnside issued General Orders No. 38, which stated "that hereafter all persons found within our lines who commit acts for the benefit of the enemies of our country will be tried as spies or traitors, and, if convicted, will suffer death." The order also declared that the military would suppress disloyal speech and publication: "The habit of declaring sympathy for the enemy will not be allowed in this department. Persons committing such offenses will be at once arrested, with a view to being tried" or sent to the rebels. This military censorship threatened the civil liberties of American citizens, as the army would decide what was loyal and what was disloyal.

In the wake of the order, violence in Indiana again erupted, as Democratic opponents of the war battled with Unionists in Hendricks County and a former state legislator killed a cavalry trooper in an argument over the soldier's attempts to round up deserters in Brown County. When the army moved to arrest the Democratic former lawmaker, a large group of armed citizens moved in to protect him. The Republicans called them Copperheads and said that they were members of the KGC; the Democrats, in turn, insisted that they were true patriots who had formed a posse comitatus to check the tyranny of the government.[22]

When General Carrington's (he was promoted to brigadier general in March 1863) response to these events seemed to Burnside too panicky, the department commander removed the district officer from his position. Burnside suspected that his subordinate was unreliable and a troublemaker because of reports and insinuations he had received from others before taking over the department. He saw Carrington's response as evidence of such insubordination and promptly removed him. Shocked and distressed by this, Morton tried unsuccessfully to persuade Burnside to return Carrington to his post. Burnside did allow the outgoing district commander to stay in Indianapolis to put his office in order, but the governor worried that his replacement, General Milo Hascall, would not perform as competently as the hardworking Carrington. At the very least, the new commander did not yet fully understand the dangerous situation in the state of Indiana. Because of this, Morton canceled plans to travel to Washington and stayed in Indianapolis, where he could help Hascall in the event of an emergency.[23]

Later that spring Morton decided to travel East to conduct business with the federal authorities, and while he was gone, Hascall thwarted a planned uprising in the state capital. On May 20, 1863, the Indiana state Democratic Party held a convention in Indianapolis. By this time, many Hoosier Democrats feared the tyranny of the Republicans as expressed in the draft, the suppression of free speech, what they perceived as executive overreach in policies like emancipation, and in Morton's refusal to recall the legislature. Prepared to take violent action to protect civil liberties if necessary, many Democrats headed to Indianapolis with pistols in their pockets. Some of the Copperheads among them hoped that they could turn the meeting into a full-scale uprising. If the impassioned speeches made by anti-war critics to a large crowd of Jacksonian Democrats could rouse enough men, perhaps the Copperheads could even manage to overthrow the state government. Short of such dramatic action, many no doubt carried their guns out of fear that Morton and the army might try to shut down their meeting, and they would try to defend democracy against such tyranny.

With the governor gone to Washington, the state's defense rested in the hands of General Hascall. When the district commander learned of the planned uprising from officers in Cincinnati, who were directing the work of the network of spies and detectives, he quickly posted artillery and armed guards at strategic points around Indianapolis. This dampened the rebellious spirits among the Democrats, and their meeting proved to be much less fiery and more moderate than anticipated. Clearly, the sight of armed Union soldiers with cannon had intimidated most of the Democrats, although a few went ahead and blasted away at the Lincoln administration with their rhetoric.

When the Democrats boarded the train to leave town, however, Hascall gave them another opportunity to offer armed resistance to the government. He had his men stop the train and board the cars to search for the weapons he knew so many of the opposition party were carrying. Rather than fight, the men aboard the train chose to throw their revolvers out the windows of the train, which had been stopped at a point where the passenger cars were positioned on a bridge over a creek.[24]

This so-called Battle of Pogue's Run became further evidence that the Copperheads existed and that many mainstream members of the Democratic Party were connected to the secret societies and anti-government conspiracies. Yet, at the same time, it could be construed as proof that there was no actual armed conspiracy but that the opposition merely wanted to defend democracy and did not rise up in an attempt to overthrow the government. Although the incident demonstrated that Hascall would move quickly and efficiently against a threat, Morton not only mistrusted the general but also feared that he was making the situation worse. In his eagerness to implement Burnside's General Orders No. 38, Hascall had issued his own General Orders No. 9 for the District of Indiana. This order announced that the military would hold all speakers and writers to strict accountability, and that anyone who criticized the draft or government policies would be "considered as having violated the order" and would be arrested. A Democratic congressman from Fort Wayne confronted Hascall, demanding clarification of the order. The general informed him that he meant to suppress all speech that attacked government policies including conscription, emancipation, the war tax, and the confiscation of rebel property. The Democratic politician denounced the order and asked where Governor Morton stood on the issue, since he was the one with the constitutional authority in Indiana, where civilian government remained in effect. Since the state was not in rebellion, the military should not have the power to make such rules there. The opposition party criticized Morton for not speaking out against Hascall's order and the usurpation of power that it entailed.[25]

Morton remained silent in public, but he privately agreed with the Democrats on this issue. Far from crushing dissent, Burnside and Hascall were making things worse, feeding the underground networks of opposition by attacking legitimate disagreements. Suppressing the freedom of speech made the Copperhead arguments about tyranny all the more credible. And, frankly, Morton resented anyone exercising power that he believed rightly belonged to him. The governor met with Hascall and told him that he did not think that the generals' orders could be enforced. Furthermore, Morton worried that the policies would only exacerbate the political tensions in the state. He also argued against some of the arrests that had been made.

Hascall wrote to Burnside and informed his superior officer of the conversation with the governor—and admitted that he was embarrassed by the confrontation. He said that he thought Morton was actually jealous of his own power and that the real "trouble seems to be that you issued order 38 without consulting him and removed Genl. Carrington." Hascall warned Burnside to remember that Morton had a lot of influence and had successfully undermined other commanders and had them removed from their commands. Even as they shared similar motives with state officials in hoping to crush the Copperheads, the military men had to be careful in the dangerous political waters where jurisdictions and authorities overlapped.[26]

But the general's warning came too late. By the late spring of 1863, Morton had decided to try to have both Burnside and Hascall removed from their commands. Although he failed to dislodge Burnside, the governor did manage to have Hascall replaced, and General Orlando Willcox took over the military operations in the district in June. The following month brought Morgan's Raid, as Confederate cavalry forces under General John Hunt Morgan crossed the Ohio River from Kentucky in mid-July 1863 and struck out across southern Indiana. Burnside had sent most of the troops in the state to Kentucky in anticipation of fighting there, and the state draft had already taken many men from the militia. The cavalry troops needed to chase the fast-moving raiders were especially in short supply, but Morton organized the Indiana Legion and urged his commanders to intercept the Confederates. Rumors spread that the raiders planned to work with the Copperheads, who were to rise up and overthrow the state government, by freeing rebel prisoners held at Camp Morton in Indianapolis. The traitorous uprising did not materialize, and Morton mobilized 65,000 men to defend the state. The raiders, numbering somewhere around 2,000 men, were in Indiana four days before they rode on into Ohio, where most of them were eventually captured. While the raid did little to help the Confederate cause militarily, it struck fear in the minds of Hoosiers and convinced Morton, who had worried about a rebel invasion throughout the war, that the Copperheads might well cooperate with the enemy for a future incursion that might be more damaging to the Union. Fortunately, July brought positive developments with the news of the victories at Vicksburg and Gettysburg. And that same month, General Carrington returned to Indiana, where he resumed collaborating with the governor. Morton watched and gathered information from citizens and monitored the accounts he received from the military. Carrington composed official reports to his superiors and shared the information with the state leader.[27]

Summer 1863 also brought the assassination attempt on the governor, and draft and race riots across the country further added to the growing unrest within the United States. Meanwhile, army detectives and spies continued gathering information on the Copperheads. They uncovered conspiracies across the Midwest and discovered that some Copperhead leaders were in communication with Confederate agents, with whom they worked to devise elaborate strategies for an internal war behind Union lines. As the year progressed, so did the investigations. That fall, army officers in Indiana reported that one of their detectives had infiltrated a secret society called the Order of American Knights that operated in Illinois as well as the Hoosier state. This Copperhead network raised money, bought weapons, and planned to carry out the scheme to free the prisoners at Camp Morton.[28]

In early 1864 the investigations continued and widened, as General William Rosecrans took command of the Department of the Missouri and began cooperating with other military and civilian leaders to coordinate a unified response to the internal threat. Meanwhile, in Indiana, Carrington continued overseeing the efforts against the disloyal enemies within the Union lines. His operatives infiltrated the Copperhead underground in

1864. One spy, Felix Stidger, provided detailed information about the Sons of Liberty, a secret society that succeeded the Order of American Knights. This group claimed to have thousands of members and was planning an insurrection in Indiana. Carrington collected evidence of an armed uprising and identified the leaders of the conspiracy as well as some members. His spies implicated several prominent Democrats, including former state legislator and army officer Horace Heffren and congressman Daniel Voorhees, although it was unclear to what extent the latter was actually involved. Voorhees would later claim that paperwork related to the Sons of Liberty found in his office had been planted by the government. Whatever the congressman's role, it was clear that the Copperheads were up to something, and the general dutifully reported his findings to the War Department and shared the details with Morton.

The two men hoped to move against the Copperheads to prevent them from carrying out their planned rebellion, but the federal authorities proved reluctant to agree to such action. President Lincoln seemed unable to fathom that there were large numbers of traitors in the Midwest, his home region, which had given him such strong political support. In fairness, Morton had bombarded the War Department and the administration with reports and plans that ranged from sensible suggestions to outlandish strategies that would give him command of troops to win the war. Sometimes his concerns about the defense of Kentucky, Indiana, and the other midwestern states seemed overly fearful or panicky. Because Carrington continued to have political difficulties within the army, his reports were also greeted with leisurely skepticism.[29]

Clement Vallandigham had been tried and exiled to the Confederacy under General Orders No. 38 in May 1863, but he had then gone to Canada and fired written missiles against the government from there. He even ran for governor of Ohio in absentia in the fall of 1863, but lost the election. In June 1864 he returned to the United States and gave a rousing anti-war speech in Hamilton, Ohio. His oratory coincided with another raid by General Morgan, with his cavalry striking this time from Tennessee into Kentucky. The timing of these events convinced Morton and Carrington that the Confederates were preparing to aid the Copperheads in their planned insurrection. But the War Department and the president refused to heed the warnings and did nothing. Finally, Morton decided to take matters in hand and spur the federal bureaucracy to action. So, he leaked information to the media to do it. In June he passed on a story about one of the Copperhead leaders in Indiana. Then, when the national leaders still dragged their heels, he leaked Carrington's report to the *Indianapolis Journal,* the chief Republican newspaper in the state and a publication that was rightly seen as the governor's mouthpiece. The newspaper exposé included fascinating details about the Sons of Liberty, including loyalty oaths, secret handshakes, and a general sketch of their plans. Carrington felt betrayed by the leak and expressed his displeasure to his superiors, but he learned that the governor had actually cleared his maneuver with Secretary of War Edwin Stanton before doing it. This coincided with the War Department authorizing military commanders to arrest conspirators in Kentucky. Despite Morton's badgering and the stream of intelligence coming from army officers, what convinced the federal authorities to move was a fact-finding mission through the region by Joseph Holt, Lincoln's trusted judge advocate general. Holt confirmed the existence of conspiracies and plots against the Union.[30]

But the army made no immediate arrests. In late July, Stidger—who was still working undercover as a member of the Sons of Liberty—reported that the headquarters of the secret network were located in the offices of Indianapolis printer Harrison H. Dodd. He also passed on the proposed start date and the plan for the insurrection, which would begin with a mass meeting in the state capital that would then launch the rebellion by taking Camp Morton and freeing the Confederates held there. They would arm the prisoners of war and overthrow the government, sparking a rebellion across the state as well as in Kentucky, Illinois, and perhaps elsewhere. Morton, Stidger, and some military commanders in the region wanted to move quickly to make arrests and stop the insurrection before it started. But Carrington wanted to take a more cautious approach and continued gathering intelligence about the uprising. The general and the governor both watched carefully and worried about how to respond, especially since there were few Union troops available to act against the traitors. The early August arrival of Hoosier soldiers who had been mustered out of the army after finishing their enlistments as well as some other reinforcements relieved Carrington and Morton, who had feared that they would be unable to offer even a token defense against the planned insurrection.[31]

The appointed date for the uprising came and went—and nothing happened. As tensions mounted, Governor Morton received an anonymous tip that shipments of arms and ammunition were being sent to Indianapolis for the coming insurrection. Using this information, soldiers seized shipments of guns in both New York and Indianapolis. They also searched the offices of Dodd and Voorhees and seized piles of papers filled with information about the secret societies. Dodd fled, disappearing before the authorities could arrest him. Still, General Carrington refused to move against the Copperheads, arguing that the longer he waited, the more evidence he uncovered to expose the full extent of the plot. At that point, he was relieved of his command. While the exact reasons for his removal were unclear, the change was ordered by Stanton, and General Alvin P. Hovey took command of the district. Carrington and Morton disagreed that summer over when to strike, and the governor's growing sense that a disloyal uprising was imminent fed his impatience to make arrests. Thus, it is possible that the state leader pushed the War Department to remove his old friend. It seems unlikely that Stanton would have listened to the complaints of the Democrats, who railed against Carrington and accused him of drunkenness. Perhaps the bitterness of other Union officers hurt the general. Combined with his reluctance to move against the Copperhead conspiracy, this seems to have cost him the position in Indiana. Morton knew and trusted Hovey, an Indiana Legion commander who was eager to work with the governor in his new position.[32]

Meanwhile, spies reported on Copperhead plans to rise up in Illinois during the Democratic Party's national convention in Chicago. The Sons of Liberty planned to cooperate with Confederate agents in the city to free prisoners held at Camp Douglas and to spark a wider rebellion. Army commanders moved available troops to the area and prepared for a possible insurrection, but the news of General William Tecumseh Sherman's victory in taking Atlanta and the presence of armed Union soldiers thwarted any action by the traitors. While a number of them went to Chicago and carried arms with them, they simply failed to act, just as they had in Indianapolis in 1863 and thus far in the summer of 1864. Meanwhile, Morton sought reelection as governor and Republicans hoped to return Lincoln for a second term as the campaign for the fall elections heated up. Throughout the summer, Morton squared off in a series of public debates with his opponent, Joseph McDonald, a War Democrat and a friend of the governor's. Hoping to secure an overwhelming victory that would give him a mandate and a legislative majority to approve his one-man rule, Morton used the situation with the Copperheads to his advantage. He knew that McDonald could not afford to alienate the Peace Democrats and thus would not want to denounce them. Nor could he afford to support them as that might taint him with charges of treason and drive away the War Democrats and other loyal voters.[33]

Despite Sherman's taking of Atlanta, Morton and other Republicans worried that an unexpected defeat and the sheer number of casualties suffered that summer in General Ulysses S. Grant's Overland Campaign in Virginia might turn the election against them. Hoping to add to his political advantage, Morton continued to leak information about the Copperheads to the press and to urge the military to make arrests and hold a trial of the conspirators before the election. In late August and early September, the authorities finally moved against the Sons of Liberty. Although Dodd escaped, they arrested other leaders of the planned insurrection and brought them to trial before a military tribunal. Carrington had opposed military trials, arguing that civilians should be tried by the civilian courts that were still operating in Indiana. But Morton supported the plan and used the resulting deliberations and convictions to his advantage, persuading voters that the Indianapolis treason trials proved that the Copperheads were a fifth column in the rear and that the rebels were cooperating with traitors in order to win the war.[34]

The men brought to trial were all Democrats who had been implicated by the spies and detectives who had spent the previous two years or more investigating the disloyal networks. Lambdin P. Milligan was a Huntington, Indiana, lawyer who had sought to participate in legitimate political opposition to the expansion of government power before turning to the underground conspiracies after his bid for the Democratic nomination for governor failed. Horace Heffren, a former state lawmaker and soldier, had resigned his commission as a protest against the Emancipation Proclamation and joined the Sons of Liberty as a means to resist the government's new policies. William Dodd was an eccentric veteran of the US-Mexican War who had been a colonel in the army and was a notorious alcoholic with a checkered past. He had been arrested many times for a variety of crimes and had gotten drunk at the Battle of Buena Vista just in time to cause his regiment to collapse, nearly costing the United States the battle. He lived in French Lick, where he had established a resort at the mineral springs there and loudly proclaimed his Southern sympathies. Harrison Dodd, an Indianapolis printer, feared the expansion of government power at the expense of civil liberties and saw himself as a freedom fighter standing up to tyranny. Although he fled, the court tried him in absentia.

J. J. Bingham of Indianapolis was the editor of the state's leading Democratic newspaper, the *Indiana Sentinel,* but he was quickly released after his arrest, probably because apprehending him smacked of overt partisanship and reminded citizens of the suppression of free speech in the previous months. Furthermore, Bingham had refused to cooperate with the conspirators and also agreed to testify against them. Stephen Horsey was a Martin County, Indiana, resident who saw himself as a defender of the US Constitution and joined the Sons of Liberty to defend individual liberty against the encroaching power of the government. Andrew Humphreys, of Greene County, Indiana, was another former state legislator who had been appointed as an Indian agent in Utah in the late 1850s. He held similar views to those of Horsey and Milligan and had earned a reputation as a Democratic firebrand. Heffren turned state's evidence and, in late October, the court convicted the other four. Milligan, Bowles, Dodd, and Horsey all received death sentences, while Humphreys was given hard labor for the duration of the war. Soon after, Republicans elsewhere arrested Copperheads and brought them to trial in their states.[35]

The treason trials were conducted and concluded at just the right time to help the Republicans win the 1864 elections. To be sure, Union military victories did more to secure the election, but the sensational story of traitors in the rear being splashed across headlines that fall further aided the party of Morton and Lincoln. Both the governor and the president won reelection in Indiana by wide margins, and the Republicans retook most of the congressional seats and the state legislature. Governor Morton had urged the military to act in time to benefit him and his party politically, and his plan worked. The voters reacted to the news of the conspiracies and the treason trials exactly as he hoped they would: they rallied around the flag and supported the government.[36]

Certainly, Morton seized the opportunity to add to his advantage and to win the election. But he was not merely an opportunist playing a political game in which he toyed with his opponents to manipulate the electorate. Instead, he seized the moment politically while also genuinely believing that the Copperheads were a threat to the Union. He had urged action even earlier in the year, when the arrests would have been less likely to help the Republicans at the ballot box. While it was true that all of those who were arrested were Democrats, Morton was not a simple partisan.

Rather, his partisanship stemmed from his nationalist ideology of freedom, Union, power, and party. As he put it in his debates with McDonald, "my position is easily defined: I am in favor of sustaining the National government, restoring and maintaining the Union of these States, and suppressing the rebellion by force of arms." He challenged his opponent to explain what was meant when the Democrats argued that they defended the Constitution and opposed freeing the slaves. Morton insisted that secession was unconstitutional and rebellion was treason. This meant that there could be no middle ground: "There can be no neutrals in this war. There is not half-way house. There is no place in the Constitution where a man can stand midway between the rebellion and the Government." In his mind, the Democrats who opposed the war either directly participated in the conspiracies against the government or enabled those who did. Their criticism of the Lincoln administration and of Morton aided and abetted the rebels. Their attacks on government policies strengthened the Copperheads. This made them complicit in plots to destroy the Union, which he sincerely believed embodied and defended the freedom bestowed upon Americans by the Founding Fathers.

To defeat this internal threat, the government needed to exercise its power—by spying on citizens, investigating anti-government plots, and arresting those who were about to carry out an insurrection that might lead to a Confederate victory. Because the Democrats acted in ways that helped both the rebels and the Copperheads, only the Republicans—including Morton and Lincoln—could be trusted to wield such power. Morton declared that "we will conquer this rebellion, we will crush it out, unless we shall be defeated by men in the North who seek to divide our people." If the Democrats won the election, the rebellion would be lost and the nation would be destroyed.[37]

In the final analysis, then, Morton's actions against the Copperheads show that he was indeed an opportunist, but that he was also a man of principle. He saw a real threat in the secret societies that actually existed and that planned and carried out attacks on the Union war effort. Even if the military and the government too readily believed their spies and detectives and exaggerated the scope of the underground networks and the potential threat they posed, the governor was correct when he said that "the state was honeycombed with secret societies" of disloyal men planning to commit treason. Thus, Morton believed that he was fully justified in urging the army to take action against the traitors operating clandestinely in Indiana. After all, any doubts he had about the potential danger easily disappeared when he remembered the sound of a bullet fired at him from the darkness of a summer night in Indianapolis. Whether or not the course of action that he advised and the military took was legally sound under the Constitution mattered little in the heat of rebellion. Yet the aftermath of those actions and their historical legacy raised important questions about how the government should respond to internal threats.

NOTES

1. For a full study of Morton's life, see my biography of him, A. James Fuller, *Oliver P. Morton and the Politics of the Civil War and Reconstruction* (Kent, OH: Kent State University Press, 2017). The account of the assassination attempt is found in William Dudley Foulke, *Life of Oliver P. Morton, Including His Important Speeches,* 2 vols. (Indianapolis: Bowen-Merrill, 1899), vol. 1, 383–384. Horace Heffren, a Democratic state legislator involved in the anti-war conspiracies, turned state's evidence and testified at the Indianapolis treason trials in 1864, confirming that the Copperhead organizations had plotted to assassinate the governor; see *Farmer's Cabinet,* November 11, 1864. For a later example of the Republicans using the assassination attempt as a means to rally Union veterans to vote for Morton's party, see *Indiana American,* January 17, 1868.

2. For Morton's later account about the state being laced with secret organizations, see *Congressional Record,* 44th Congress, 1st Session, May 3, 1876, 2900–2903; and Oliver P. Morton, *Personal Explanation. O.P. Morton, Governor of Indiana. Alleged Misapplication of $250,000. Revolutionary Policy of Democratic Legislature. In the Senate of the United States, May 3, 1876* (Washington, DC: Chronicle Printer, 1876).

3. Wood Gray, *The Hidden Civil War: The Story of the Copperheads* (New York: Viking Press, 1942); George Fort Milton, *Abraham Lincoln and the Fifth Column* (New York: Vanguard Press, 1942). Throughout this chapter I use the term "Midwest" instead of "Northwest," which was common in the mid-nineteenth century. I employ the anachronism for sake of clarity and to place this chapter within the emerging field of midwestern history. In using "Midwest" here, I mean Ohio, Indiana, Illinois, Michigan, Wisconsin, and Minnesota—the states carved out of the old Northwest Territory.

4. William B. Hesseltine, *Lincoln and the War Governors* (New York: Knopf, 1948).

5. Kenneth M. Stampp, *Indiana Politics during the Civil War* (Indianapolis: Indiana Historical Bureau, 1949; repr., Indiana University Press, 1978), 241; Foulke, *Life of Oliver P. Morton*, vol. 1, 374.

6. Frank L. Klement, *The Copperheads in the Middle West* (Chicago: University of Chicago Press, 1960); Klement, *The Limits of Dissent: Clement L. Vallandigham and the Civil War* (Lexington: University Press of Kentucky, 1970); Klement, *Dark Lanterns: Secret Political Societies, Conspiracies, and Treason Trials in the Civil War* (Baton Rouge: Louisiana State University Press, 1989).

7. Emma Lou Thornbrough, *Indiana in the Civil War Era* (Indianapolis: Indiana Historical Society, 1965); Jennifer L. Weber, *Copperheads: The Rise and Fall of Lincoln's Opponents in the North* (New York: Oxford University Press, 2006); Stephen E. Towne, *Surveillance and Spies in the Civil War: Exposing Confederate Conspiracies in America's Heartland* (Athens: Ohio University Press, 2015). Towne relied too heavily on the military records, which means that his work is biased positively toward the Union and the Republicans while perhaps being too negative about the Copperheads. This slant was the result of the source material because whatever records the secret societies kept were destroyed and scant evidence of their inner workings remains. Another recent scholar who largely accepted the Klement thesis but still took the Copperheads seriously was Robert H. Churchill, *To Shake Their Guns in the Tyrant's Face: Libertarian Political Violence and the Origins of the Militia Movement* (Ann Arbor: University of Michigan Press, 2009). In his study of the Union governors, Stephen Engle drew on Towne's work and treated the efforts of Republicans like Morton more positively: Stephen D. Engle, *Gathering to Save a Nation: Lincoln and the Union's War Governors* (Chapel Hill: University of North Carolina Press, 2016).

8. I make this argument more extensively in Fuller, *Oliver P. Morton*, passim.

9. Fuller, *Oliver P. Morton*, 146–150. Useful insights on how connected the lower-tier of the midwestern states were to the South can be found in Christopher Phillips, *The Rivers Ran Backward: The Civil War and the Remaking of the American Middle Border* (New York: Oxford University Press, 2016).

10. Fuller, *Oliver P. Morton*, 166–167.

11. The Rockville speech is conveniently reprinted in Foulke, *Life of Morton*, 1: 172–174. I take these incidents from the more complete treatment of them in Towne, *Surveillance and Spies*, 18–21. The account given here depends heavily on Towne's research, both because his work was so impressive and because his analysis of the military sources is so persuasive. He carefully pieced together the story of the complicated twists and turns of the army intelligence operations in the heartland. However, this piece differs in its focus on Morton and Indiana rather than on the broader region that Towne examined and in its nuanced interpretation. I think that Towne was too accepting of the Union/Republican view of the situation. Also, while Klement was too prone to seeing the investigations as hysterical because of the Red

Scare of his own times, Towne might too readily see the reports of spies and citizens as real rather than as stemming from a climate of fear or from self-interest. I admire Towne's work and accept much of his reinterpretation of the Copperheads. He has convincingly destroyed the Klement thesis. But without sources from the Copperheads themselves—one member of the secret societies admitted to destroying records—it is difficult to tell both sides of the story. That leaves us with Towne's excellent but pro-Union/pro-government perspective. Because of his research, his book will stand the test of time as the definitive study of the military side of the story. Therefore, most of the details in this section closely follow Towne's work.

12. Towne, *Surveillance and Spies*, 38–45; for 1862 examples of Morton's ongoing investigations from the governor's office, see Oliver P. Morton to E. B. Allen, May 10, 1862, July 15, 1862, in Edward B. Allen Papers, William Henry Smith Memorial Library, Indiana Historical Society, Indianapolis.

13. Towne, *Surveillance and Spies*, 40–78.

14. Fuller, *Oliver P. Morton*, 123–126. For studies on the Emancipation Proclamation, see John Hope Franklin, *Emancipation Proclamation* (New York: Doubleday, 1963); Allen C. Guelzo, *Lincoln's Emancipation Proclamation: The End of Slavery in America* (New York: Simon & Schuster, 2004); and Harold Holzer, Edna Greene Medford, and Frank J. Williams, *The Emancipation Proclamation: Three Views* (Baton Rouge: Louisiana State University Press, 2006).

15. Thomas A. Hendricks, "The Issues of the War: Speech Delivered to the Democratic State Convention, Metropolitan Hall, Indianapolis, Jan. 8, 1862," in John W. Holcombe and Hubert M. Skinner, eds., *Life and Public Services of Thomas A. Hendricks with Selected Speeches and Writing* (Indianapolis: Carlton & Hollenbeck, 1886), 451–465; for Morton's secretary reporting to the White House on Copperhead plans to create the Northwest conspiracy, see William R. Holloway to John G. Nicolay, October 24, 1862, Oliver P. Morton Letterbooks, Indiana State Archives, Indianapolis; Morton to Lincoln, October 27, 1862, repr. in W. H. H. Terrell, *Indiana in the War of the Rebellion: Report of the Adjutant General*, vol. 1. (Indianapolis: Indiana Historical Bureau, 1960; originally published 1869), 25–28.

16. Towne, *Surveillance and Spies*, 53–55.

17. Morton, "Governor's Message, January 10, 1063," printed in *Evansville Daily Journal*, January 12, 13, 1863; Fuller, *Oliver P. Morton*, 123–131.

18. Fuller, 128–129.

19. Fuller, 129–130. The committee's report was eventually published; see *Report and Evidence of the Committee on Arbitrary Arrests in the State of Indiana, Authorized by Resolution of the House of Representatives, January 9, 1863* (Indianapolis: J. J. Bingham, State Printer, 1863).

20. Fuller, *Oliver P. Morton*, 129–131. For an example of how Republicans defended the governor during his battle with the legislature, see *Evansville Daily Journal*, March 30, 1863; For a later account of the conflict by Morton, see Oliver P. Morton, "The History of Indiana Democracy Ventilated: Speech of Oliver P. Mor-

ton at LaPorte, Indiana." *Indianapolis Journal*, August 15, 1876. For Democratic criticism of Morton's one-man rule, see *Indiana Sentinel*, December 21, 1863; April 9, 18, 30, July 13, 1864.

21. Towne, *Surveillance and Spies*, 61–75. For a splendid study that shows the internal conflicts in one community in Indiana, see Nicole Etcheson, *A Generation at War: The Civil War Era in a Northern Community* (Lawrence: University Press of Kansas, 2011).

22. Towne, *Surveillance and Spies*, 61–77; "General Orders No. 38," April 13, 1863, in *The War of the Rebellion: A Compilation of the Official Records of the Union and Confederate Armies*, 128 vols. (Washington, DC: Governmental Printing Office, 1880–1901), ser. 2, vol. 5, 480.

23. Towne, 77–80.

24. Foulke, *Life of Morton*, 1: 273–278.

25. Fuller, *Oliver P. Morton*, 134–139.

26. Hascall's report to Burnside and his warning about Morton's wrath are related in Stephen E. Towne, "Killing the Serpent Speedily: Governor Morton, General Hascall, and the Suppression of the Democratic Press in Indiana, 1863," in *Civil War History* 52 (March 2006): 56–58.

27. Fuller, *Oliver P. Morton*, 139–141; Towne, *Surveillance and Spies*,116–136.

28. Towne, 116–136.

29. Towne, 174–209; Fuller, *Oliver P. Morton*, 83–93, 119.

30. Towne, 209–220; 221–245. For the newspaper printing the report, see *Indianapolis Journal*, July 30, 1864.

31. Towne, 256–263.

32. Towne, 264–271.

33. Towne, 271–275; Fuller, *Oliver P. Morton*, 146–166.

34. Fuller, 146–166.

35. Fuller, 166–175. Morton had urged the arrest of Milligan in the summer of 1862, but the federal authorities had not pursued such action; see William R. Holloway to John Hanna, August 15, 1862, John Hanna Papers, Lilly Library, Indiana University–Bloomington.

36. Fuller, 166–175. For the detailed account of the case in the transcripts of the Indianapolis treason trials, see Benn Pittman, *The Trials for Treason at Indianapolis: Disclosing the Plans for Establishing a North-Western Conspiracy, etc.* (Cincinnati: Moore, Wiltstach & Baldwin, 1865).

37. Fuller, 146–166; *The Gubernatorial Canvass: Debate between Gov. Oliver P. Morton and Hon. Joseph E. McDonald, at LaPorte, Wednesday, Aug. 10, 1864* (Indianapolis: n.p., 1864).

CHAPTER 6

"These Scoundrels Stand in No Fear of the Civil Courts; They Do, of the Military": The Decision to Use Military Commissions to Try the Indiana Conspirators in 1864

STEPHEN E. TOWNE

The standard historical explanation for why Union authorities used a military commission in 1864 to try the Indiana conspirators, including Lambdin P. Milligan, points to the central role of Governor Oliver P. Morton. Having infiltrated his spies into the conclaves of the secret society that plotted upheaval and exposed them to the public eye, the story goes, the forceful and energetic state executive decided, in concert with President Abraham Lincoln's secretary of war, Edwin M. Stanton, that trials in civil courts would not suffice. "More drastic measures were required," explained Morton biographer William Dudley Foulke of their decision, "to strike terror into the hearts of the conspirators."[1] Historian Kenneth M. Stampp, who characterizes Morton as a devious political genius, asserts that the governor acted alone and made his decision "late in August" 1864 to arrest the leaders of the secret organization "at once" to save his and the Lincoln administration's chances in the fall elections, knowing full well that the "ludicrous" schemers posed no threat.[2] Generations of historians have oscillated between the Foulke view of shared responsibility and Stampp's take. Perhaps representative of current mainstream thinking on the matter, Chief Justice William H. Rehnquist's analysis of constitutional issues during wartime follows Foulke in arguing that Morton and Stanton together "resorted to the more expeditious mode of a military tribunal."[3]

In fact, the process of deciding to employ a military commission to try the conspirators was more complicated and long in coming than either the Foulke or Stampp views suggest. Many hands contributed to the effort, which resulted from the failure of civil law-enforcement officers and the civil courts to get a handle on the threat of organized resistance on the Northern home front during the war. In their place, the United States Army deployed military detectives across the North to collect information on persons and groups who obstructed the war effort, as part of the Lincoln administration's militarization of the government's response to domestic opposition. The army's spies (not Morton's) gathered intelligence on secret organized efforts to subvert the Union war effort in Indiana and neighboring states. Military commanders received this intelligence and shared it with their superiors and civilian leaders in Washington, DC. Working in concert with sympathetic Republican governors in northwestern states wracked by internal unrest, commanders in the region devised plans to counter the growing threat. Initially, President Lincoln dismissed the generals' and governors' requests for assistance against organized conspiracy. But in the summer of 1864 the president, recognizing that his chances for reelection were ebbing away, authorized the army to increase surveillance and arrests of those perceived as "disloyal," and to try them by military commissions. He used the military power at his disposal to save the Union.

To understand the federal government's choice to employ military commissions to try the Indiana conspirators, the historian must turn back to 1861, when the seceded Confederate states commenced armed rebellion against the national Union. During the first weeks and months after the attack on Fort Sumter, angry men and women in the states of the Old Northwest—now called the Midwest—demanded vengeance against the South. Men volunteered to fight to crush the rebellion and reunite the nation. Similarly, patriotic women sent their husbands and sons off to war. But while indignation against the Confederates was widespread and loud, it was not universal. Many Northerners believed that the Southern rebels were fully within their rights under the federal Constitution to secede. The Constitution protected slavery, they believed, and the slave states could preserve their institutions against the onslaught of abolitionism by seceding. Accordingly, some residents of the Northwest expressed sympathy for the South in its actions to preserve slavery. One such figure was Lambdin P. Milligan, a prominent Democrat of Huntington County in northeastern Indiana, who expounded his Calhounite state-sovereignty views in speeches throughout his part of the state. In a public event in August 1861, for example, he rallied war opponents by addressing them as the "*Genuine* friends of the Union, &

the Constitution—those who are *opposed to waging an unjust and unprofitable crusade* against the Southern people."[4]

But beyond public rallies, residents of the northwestern states of Illinois, Indiana, and Ohio perceived that quiet, hidden movements were afoot. Citizens reported to state and federal officials that they had evidence that neighbors conspired in secret against the federal government. Worried constituents sent letters to their political leaders. Illinois governor Richard Yates received word that secession flags flew in different parts of the state, that expressions of sympathy with the South were frequent, and that Illinois men forded the Ohio River to join and fight in Confederate units. Men swore that they would not aid any effort to free slaves. Even prominent future civil libertarians like David Davis and Orville Hickman Browning shared the fear that "traitors" were in league with rebels to the south. Reports of a secret organization called the Knights of the Golden Circle (KGC)—heretofore openly active in the South as a filibustering organization to spread Southern-style slavery into Central and South America—stated that it was active in Illinois. Yates deemed many of these reports to be "reliable" and as posing an internal threat.[5] Indiana governor Oliver P. Morton fielded similar reports from constituents who wrote of US flags being cut down and of cheering for Confederate president Jefferson Davis. Warning of potential sabotage, the governor advised officials in Washington, DC, "not to suffer affairs to drift on until it is too late."[6] Ohio governor William Dennison likewise warned federal leaders to keep an eye on growing secret societies in his state.[7]

Newly appointed federal law enforcement officers—US attorneys and marshals—also received reports of underground activities from concerned citizens. Residents wrote of efforts to smuggle arms and other contraband to the Southern rebels. They alerted officers to the existence of secret armed organizations in their communities that aimed to oppose the war effort and aid secessionists. Officers credited the reports and worked to investigate them. Indeed, they found evidence of conspiracy to undermine the Union cause in the northwestern states by discouraging enlistments and smuggling materiel to the rebels. They reported their findings to Attorney General Edward Bates and asked for assistance. But, overwhelmed by the demands that civil war placed on him and his tiny staff, Bates gave little help to his beleaguered subordinates. Similarly, when asked for funds to hire detectives to investigate criminal conspiracy, the attorney general had none to share.[8] The Judiciary Fund, established by Congress to pay court-related costs, could not be used to hire detectives, and Secretary of the Interior Caleb B. Smith, who controlled the fund, jealously made sure monies were not so used.[9]

While starved for funds to make investigations, some federal law-enforcement officers managed to make significant discoveries of criminal conspiracy. The most notable instance occurred in the summer and fall of 1861 in northern Ohio, where a detective working for the US attorney and marshal in Cleveland infiltrated secret armed groups spread across several counties. Marshals arrested several locally prominent Democrats for collecting and hiding arms with which to oppose the government. In hearings before a federal magistrate, testimony showed the existence of the KGC across the region. However, before defendants could go to trial, the case collapsed when one witness died suddenly and another fled under threats to his life.[10] Investigatory efforts by federal officials elsewhere similarly failed. In Indiana in mid-1862, the US attorney brought over two hundred witnesses before a grand jury to learn details about secret organizations in that state. But no indictments or trials resulted. While Congress had passed legislation to broaden the definition of criminal conspiracy, civil investigations largely failed to present indictments. The root cause was lack of money with which to hire detectives to develop leads.

Owing to the failure of civil authorities to investigate conspiracy in the North, the US Army stepped into the breach. The army was ubiquitous throughout the North, with recruiting offices, volunteer rendezvous camps, and other posts scattered in every state. The activities of secret organizations to dissuade volunteering and encourage desertion impinged on military recruiting and unit strength, thus attracting the attention of officers. Starting in the summer of 1862, commanders sent out soldiers as detectives to spy on local anti-war activities. The War Department's order of August 8 authorized civil officers to arrest and jail anyone who discouraged volunteer enlistments or gave "aid and comfort" to the enemy; the order also suspended the privilege of the writ of habeas corpus to persons arrested. Spurred on by the order, the army gave significant attention to investigating dissent and active "disloyalty" in the North; however, Governor Morton's private secretary could not successfully persuade the US attorney in

Indiana to arrest Lambdin P. Milligan for giving speeches that discouraged enlistments.[11]

Military investigations in the Northwest broadened in late 1862 and early 1863. Working in an uncoordinated and ad hoc manner, applying to the home front intelligence techniques learned on the battlefield, commanders across the region responded to increasingly loud opposition to the war and massive desertion from the army's ranks.[12] Soldiers in civilian clothes and hired detectives fanned out in search of deserters and those who harbored them. They investigated and intercepted arms shipments to persons considered disloyal, gathering information about armed groups that intended to defend deserters from arrest. With the passage of the Enrollment Act in early March 1863, reports flowed into headquarters that armed secret organizations vowed resistance to the draft. Responding to these challenges, Brigadier General Horatio G. Wright, commander of the multistate Department of the Ohio, established a small detective bureau attached to his headquarters in Cincinnati.[13] Detectives operated from Ohio to Illinois to track down arms shipments and arrest deserters. Major General Ambrose E. Burnside, who succeeded Wright in command of the department, continued his policies. Burnside's arrest and military-commission trial of Ohio politician Clement L. Vallandigham for seditious speech in May 1863 was the product of a military-intelligence operation run out of his Cincinnati headquarters.[14]

The Enrollment Act required a large national bureaucracy called the Provost Marshal General's Bureau to administer the draft. Part of that bureaucracy was a national detective force that blanketed the North, placing "special agents" (also known in army records as secret agents, detectives, and spies) in every county of the Union. Together with detectives working for military commanders, these hundreds of investigators, aided by thousands of local informers, tracked down deserters and draft dodgers, intercepted secret arms shipments to groups hostile to the government, opened private mail, and identified persons involved in secret organizations active in efforts to weaken the war effort.[15] By the summer and fall of 1863, army intelligence in the Old Northwest chalked up several successes. Commanders arrested KGC founder George W. L. Bickley while en route from the South to the North and packed him off to prison without charges. Army spies infiltrated a group who plotted an attack on the Camp Chase prisoner-of-war facility in Columbus, Ohio. Troops and US marshals together arrested the leaders and obtained indictments for treason and conspiracy in the federal court in Cincinnati.[16] Commanders received word of a similar plot to attack Camp Morton, an Indianapolis prison for Confederate POWs, and detectives who crossed the international border into British North America (i.e., Canada) exposed an effort by Confederate agents operating out of Canada to attack the Johnson's Island prison in Lake Erie. Moreover, army spies discovered that the KGC had changed its name to the Order of American Knights (OAK) and that the revived secret group was active and growing throughout the Northwest. Acting on President Lincoln's direct orders, commanders later arrested OAK leader Phineas C. Wright in Michigan and packed him off to a military prison without charges.[17]

By 1864, army intelligence efforts in the Old Northwest had amassed significant evidence that secret organizations existed that aimed to subvert the war effort. Indeed, it became increasingly clear to commanders that conspirators in the North, some of whom were prominent persons active in the Democratic Party, were in communication with Confederate government agents operating out of Canada. Conspirators and rebels together hoped to weaken the Union war effort with increasingly ambitious efforts, including releasing Confederate prisoners of war to raise insurrection in the North. Army spies operating throughout the North and across the border in Canada successfully infiltrated the secret organizations working with Confederate agents and learned the plans of their leaders. The key figure in military intelligence efforts in the Northwest was Brigadier General Henry B. Carrington, who in the first half of 1864 served on Governor Morton's staff. A Yale-educated attorney and abolitionist who had been active in Ohio politics, Carrington's efforts as a spymaster started in December 1862, when, as post commander in Indianapolis, he had discovered that soldiers in military camps around the city were members of secret organizations that aimed to aid deserters. His intelligence efforts became indispensable to Morton, who pulled strings in Washington to retain Carrington in Indiana. The officer worked indefatigably to expose KGC (and, later, OAK and Sons of Liberty) activities in the state. Carrington's hard work and knowledge came to the attention of Major General Samuel P. Heintzelman, appointed to command the Northern Department (encompassing Ohio, Michigan, Indiana, and Illinois) in January 1864, and whose headquarters were in Columbus, Ohio. Soon, Carrington functioned as de facto chief of intelligence for Heintzelman. With a stable of spies working for him as well as coordinating information from other sources, Carrington regularly reported to Columbus headquarters on the threat posed by secret organizations in the multistate region.[18]

Carrington achieved a coup when Felix G. Stidger, a detective loaned to him from military headquarters in Louisville, successfully infiltrated both Indiana and Kentucky branches of the Sons of Liberty organization, the renamed KGC/OAK. Installed as the secretary of the Kentucky branch, in early June 1864 Stidger borrowed a sheaf of secret paperwork from his Indianapolis counterpart and smuggled it into Carrington's hands. The general's staff feverishly copied the records overnight and returned the originals to Stidger. The records provided new details of the secret organization.[19]

With the new information in hand, government authorities possessed important leverage that offered them the opportunity to take the offensive against the conspirators. Governor Morton, a brilliant and ruthless politician then embroiled in a tight election fight, saw the possibilities. The copies of incriminating records presented avenues to strike back at Democrats who held leadership positions in the organization. He immediately pressed Carrington to allow him to splash the records across the pages of the state Republican Party newspaper to create a public furor and embarrass his Democratic opponents. But Carrington appealed to Heintzelman to back him in opposing Morton's importunities. Both generals wished to withhold disclosure of the records in order not to compromise their spies and their ability to collect more information. They asked for guidance from the War Department in Washington.[20] Undeterred, Morton traveled to Washington to make his case. After weeks of pressure, Secretary Stanton sided with the governor. At the end of July, Morton had the smuggled secret records published in the main Republican newspaper in Indiana. The exposé created a sensation.[21]

By this time, the generals and Republican governors in Ohio, Indiana, and Illinois had been quietly sharing among themselves intelligence about the conspiracies alive in their states. In April 1864, Governor John Brough of Ohio and General Heintzelman traveled to Indianapolis to confer with General Carrington and Governors Morton of Indiana and Yates of Illinois regarding "copperhead demonstrations," as Heintzelman termed them.[22] Thereafter, officers from Detroit, Michigan, to Lexington, Kentucky, compared notes about their intelligence. Major General William S. Rosecrans, commander of the Department of the Missouri, headquartered in St. Louis, aggressively employed his expansive intelligence resources to gather information on the secret organization active in his realm. He shared his findings with Heintzelman and Governors Yates and Morton. All were keenly concerned about the threat of insurrection. All believed that they required more troops. All agreed in the need to ask Washington for help and guidance.[23]

But other war matters preoccupied President Lincoln. During the spring and summer of 1864 he focused his attention on military campaigns in Virginia and Georgia, where armies under Ulysses S. Grant and William T. Sherman, respectively, engaged in nonstop attacks to wear down Confederate forces. Appeals to send troops to the Northwest would weaken armies in the field and were dismissed out of hand. Previous requests to the president for help against unrest in the North had met with his denials that a problem existed. In early 1863, when his friend Governor Yates sent an Illinois general (and mutual friend) to Washington to carry a letter reporting on the dangers of secret groups in their state and the need for troops, the president, "in response to the letter of the governor, handed him by me, answered with one of his jokes which cannot be repeated, and said: 'Who can we trust if we can't trust Illinois!' and referred me to the secretary of war."[24] A year later, Yates sent another Illinois general and mutual acquaintance to meet with Lincoln about the domestic threat to Illinois and received a similar dismissal.[25] General Rosecrans wrote similarly urgent appeals to Lincoln regarding the existential threat from secret organizations in the Northwest and Missouri. Highly distrustful of Rosecrans and his motives, Lincoln would not allow the general or his chief spymaster, Colonel John P. Sanderson, to travel to Washington to present their findings, but dispatched his private secretary, John Hay, to St. Louis to confer and report. Hay met with Rosecrans and Sanderson and returned to the White House fully convinced of the significant threat of insurrection from secret organizations. But the president again waved away the threat. Wrote Hay in his private diary, "He treats the Northern section of the conspiracy as not especially worth regarding, holding it a mere political organization, with about as much of malice and as much of puerility as the Knights of the Golden Circle." According to Hay, contrary to Rosecrans's intelligence, Lincoln thought that the secret return of Clement Vallandigham to Ohio from his exile in Canada would actually aid the Union cause by dividing the Democratic Party between the pro-war and anti-war factions. Instead, the president would put his trust in "the people," the "honest though misguided masses," who would not be led to insurrectionary violence.[26]

When no help or promise of help arrived from Washington, Rosecrans sent Sanderson east in early July to rally support. Forbidden to enter Washington himself, Sanderson sent a detective to the Capitol to gather congressmen to call on the president and present a massive report of intelligence on the secret conspiracy. Lincoln met with them, but nothing came of the effort.[27] He remained unconvinced that a dangerous problem existed in the Northwest. Days before, he had offered no advice or assistance to Brough and Heintzelman when Vallandigham had snuck back into Ohio in defiance of Lincoln's exile order.[28] Lincoln would trust in the people not to rise up in violence. The governors and generals were on their own.

Lacking support from national leaders and left to fend for themselves, the military men and governors made their own plans to combat the conspirators. In July the commander of the District of Kentucky, Major General Stephen G. Burbridge, played an important role at this stage. His own spies and informers alerted him to the growing threat of revolutionary violence in the commonwealth and the states across the Ohio River. Convinced that aggressive measures were necessary, Burbridge lobbied the governors and generals over the river to preempt an uprising by arresting the known state leaders of the secret group and trying them by military commissions. Morton and Heintzelman fell in with his plan, but both Brough and Yates feared there were insufficient troops on hand to put down uprisings should the rank and file of the organizations react violently to the arrest of their leaders.[29] Burbridge and Rosecrans—both with thousands of troops at their disposal, many more than available north of the Ohio River—went ahead and swept up many leaders of the conspiracy in their states.

While seemingly rebuffed by the president, the governors and generals never stopped their appeals for help and reinforcements. To appease the clamorous governors, Secretary Stanton sent Judge Advocate General Joseph Holt, an influential and trusted figure in the War Department, on a mission to Louisville and St. Louis. He was to see for himself if the secret plots were as dire as reported.[30] Holt arrived in mid-July and met with commanders and politicians. In three written reports sent back to Washington, his view was unequivocal: conspirators plotted armed cooperation with Confederates to foment insurrection and revolution throughout the

Northwest. In his report of July 29 from Louisville, he stated the situation "indicates clearly the existence of a conspiracy . . . looking to an armed rising against the government." Two days later, writing from St. Louis, he noted that the organization was strongest in Illinois and Indiana, adding: "It is not to be endured that these conspirators should be permitted" to act. Shortly afterward, on his return to Washington, he concluded: "It is for the Government to determine whether, consistently with its own safety or with its duty to the country, it can longer endure this knife of the domestic traitor at its throat."[31]

Holt's powerful words shook off the torpor in Washington, and in the White House particularly, regarding the situation in the Northwest. "The Government," meaning Lincoln's administration, had to decide. Evidence shows that it did. Thereafter, to bolster prisoner-of-war camp garrisons the War Department sent reinforcements, additional arms, funds, and other assistance to the governors and generals in Ohio, Indiana, and Illinois. The assistance had an immediate impact. In mid-August, for example, the timely arrival of troops in Indianapolis intimidated plotters poised to rise up, attack Camp Morton, and release thousands of rebel soldiers.[32] Significantly, at the time that Holt's reports arrived in Washington in early August, Stanton distributed lists of names and issued orders to all army commanders in the North and occupied regions of the border and Southern states to keep these "disloyal persons" under surveillance. Officers were to arrest any person detected to have committed hostile acts.[33] This national watch list was undoubtedly the first of its kind in US history.[34]

It is no coincidence that the decisions to reinforce the Northwest to guard against domestic conspiracy, and the surveillance and arrest orders blanketing the North and occupied regions, occurred at that time. Lincoln's government realized that the war effort in the South was going badly. General Grant's army in Virginia was mired in trench warfare and suffering monstrous casualties, while General Sherman's forces stalled outside Atlanta in the face of fierce rebel resistance. The Northern voting population was exhausted and restive, and Democratic opposition appeared to be rallying around Major General George B. McClellan to be the party's presidential nominee. Suggestions from Major General Henry W. Halleck, the army's chief of staff, to detach significant numbers of troops from the armies in the field and send them north to guard against feared insurrection met with firm dismissals by General Grant, with the president's enthusiastic blessing. "Hold on with a bulldog grip, and chew and choke as much as possible," Lincoln encouraged Grant, opposing Halleck's suggestions to reinforce Heintzelman.[35] In August, Lincoln concluded that if Union military fortunes did not improve significantly, he would lose reelection in November. On August 23 he penned a note and required his cabinet members to sign on its back without allowing them to see it. The note read: "This morning, as for some days past, it seems exceedingly probable that this Administration will not be re-elected. Then it will be my duty to so co-operate with the President elect, as to save the Union between the election and the inauguration; as he will have secured his election on such ground that he can not possibly save it afterwards."[36] Lincoln did not trust that McClellan would continue the war to crush the Confederate rebellion. He was also finally cognizant (thanks to Holt) that the threat of insurrection loomed in the Northwest. Lincoln had to win the war in the field, prevent domestic uprising, and continue to battle for votes. Loath to weaken Union armies in the field, the president chose to employ other tools available to him to counteract the threat of conspiracy. These tools included the military intelligence apparatus. Army surveillance of "disloyal persons" would afford the government knowledge of conspirators' plans and allow commanders to marshal their meager forces. The army's unchecked ability to arrest Northern disloyalists was another arrow in Lincoln's quiver.

Back in Indianapolis, General Carrington, the de facto chief of intelligence in the Northern Department, planned how to prosecute the leading conspirators once they were arrested. In June, he had informed departmental headquarters that he wished to try plotters in federal civil courts; he desired a judge advocate be appointed to the District of Indiana who would prepare evidence and forward it to a federal grand jury to obtain indictments.[37] He had had good results with civil trials in the previous year, though at the time he had faulted the federal judge in Indiana for passing down light punishments.[38] But Carrington's preference for civil trials for the conspirators was not widely held. To date in other northwestern states, prosecutions of secret plotters in civil courts had been ineffectual. As previously shown, in 1861 law enforcement officers in Cleveland, Ohio, had failed to bring members of the KGC organization to trial. In 1862 the US attorney in Indianapolis released a grand jury report showing widespread activity of the KGC in Indiana; however, no prosecutions resulted. In the summer of 1863 a federal grand jury in Cleveland investigated the activities of "secret societies" in northern Ohio, focusing on extensive organized resistance to the draft enrollment. Troops and federal marshals worked together to arrest scores of Ohioans involved in violent enrollment resistance in June, including the Holmes County rebellion. The US attorney brought charges of treason, conspiracy, and assault against them. However, authorities managed to take only two defendants to trial in federal court and convicted just one person.[39]

The most notable instance of the ineffectualness of the civil courts emerged from arrests of plotters who planned an attack on Camp Chase, in Columbus, Ohio, to free rebel prisoners. After army spies infiltrated the plot, in November 1863, federal marshals and troops arrested the leaders, including prominent Democratic politicians in Columbus, Cincinnati, and Covington, Kentucky. The federal attorney in Cincinnati, Flamen Ball Jr., traveled to Washington to consult with his superiors. Returning to Ohio, he secured indictments for treason and conspiracy against the defendants. However, trial preparation ground to a standstill amid intense procedural wrangling. Months passed with no progress in the cases. In a letter to Attorney General Bates, Ball confessed his frustration that proving a case of treason was highly difficult.[40] He dropped the treason charge and relied on lesser conspiracy charges. Still, the cases dragged. In the end, the war concluded before the cases came to trial and prosecutors dropped all charges.[41] Overall, the federal government's track record in the northwestern states for bringing conspiracy cases in civil courts was poor.

Whereas Carrington was an advocate of civil trials for the leading conspirators, by the summer of 1864 Governor Morton was not. A keen political observer, Morton and other Republicans were nervous about their election prospects in the fall in light of how badly the war was going.[42] In 1863 the governor had resisted General Burnside's intrusive use of military commission trials in the case of Clement Vallandigham and others. In the hands of foolish generals, such tribunals only had the effect of energizing Democratic opposition.[43] But, a year later, trials in federal civil courts, especially the prosecution of the Camp Chase conspirators, were going nowhere fast. Like the exposés of secret-organization records in the press, Morton needed something to rally Unionists. Wanting to land a blow on his Democratic rivals, some of whom, he knew, were implicated in conspiracy, the governor wished to publicize intelligence findings, while Carrington (and Heintzelman) sought to keep their work quiet.[44] These differences over tactics meant that General Carrington, who for two years had been a close ally and friend, was now a hindrance to the governor.

Just days after Carrington buried his infant son, Morton, named after his friend, the governor requested the War Department to remove the general from command of the District of Indiana. Chief of staff Halleck ordered Heintzelman to make the move, replacing Carrington with Brevet Major General Alvin P. Hovey, an Indiana War Democrat, former justice of the Indiana Supreme Court, and US attorney, who was known to favor the use of military commissions.[45] His appointment came at the high point of the threat of insurrection in Indiana and the Northwest. Days before, the arrival of new troops in Indianapolis had caused conspirators to pause, but, thanks to good spy work, authorities knew that plotters planned further attempts. Hovey asked the War Department for instructions. After delay, in September the department sent orders for him to work closely with Morton and not to declare martial law, which Hovey believed would afford cover for employing military commissions. Instead, Stanton "authorized [Hovey] to exercise, within your district, the powers of the commander of a Department, in making military arrests, in the organization of courts-martial, and in carrying their sentences into effect."[46] In this way, in bland bureaucratic language, authority to arrest and try conspirators by military commission came from the nation's leaders.

The orders bypassed departmental commander Heintzelman, who was slowly—too slowly—working up his own military commission to try conspirators, and who did not relish doing what he considered the Lincoln administration's political dirty work. Earlier, in August, when Heintzelman issued orders banning arms and ammunition sales throughout the department, the career soldier angrily complained in his journal that Stanton feared making difficult decisions of political significance but left them to him to do and face the consequences. "The copperheads are arming," he wrote. "The War Dept. won't take the responsibility, so I have to."[47] Later, he vented: "I have not been radical enough—won't arrest people without orders—will not take the responsibility of doing what Mr. Stanton would not do without Mr. Lincoln's orders. They can't make me a radical[.] I will do what I think best for the country and not for a party. I have served my country too long to now commence to serve a party."[48] Clearly, Heintzelman believed that Stanton made politically charged decisions only on the orders of President Lincoln. The War Department would replace him shortly with Major General "Fighting Joe" Hooker.

Work had already begun to try conspirators by military commissions under the authority of the Northern Department. The key figure was Major Henry Lawrence Burnett. A young Ohio attorney (born in 1838) who saw action in an Ohio cavalry regiment until injured in a fall, he served as judge advocate for both the Northern Department and the District of Kentucky. Busy trying hundreds of cases, from simple infractions of military regulations to long, complicated frauds involving civilian contractors, Burnett had met with Heintzelman and Burbridge in August in Cincinnati, where they agreed to arrest leaders of the secret organizations and try them by military commission.[49] On September 16 he visited Indianapolis to meet with Hovey and Carrington (the latter retained in Indiana at Morton's behest to continue his espionage work). Carrington suggested that the first conspirator tried should be William A. Bowles from French Lick, a fiery Mexican War veteran, Democrat, and number-two figure in the Sons of Liberty in the state, who had divulged secrets to spy Felix Stidger. But Hovey had already arrested Harrison H. Dodd, top leader of the secret organization in Indiana, an Indianapolis printer and prominent Democrat. He believed Dodd was the bigger fish to fry. Convinced that Carrington's evidence would be sufficient to convict, Burnett wrote to headquarters that he decided to proceed with a military trial of Dodd, reasoning that if he was to be "tried by the Military Authorities at all it should be well tried."[50] He would prosecute Dodd himself. The next day, Hovey received his orders from the War Department granting him departmental powers to convene courts-martial. With this authority and eager to start, Hovey telegraphed Heintzelman to say he would assume charge of the conspiracy trials. He quickly lined up trial witnesses and assembled a military commission composed of high-ranking officers.[51] Most were from Indiana volunteer regiments, reliable Republicans appointed by Morton. He sent troops to arrest Bowles and an army officer who had supplied conspirators with grenades filled with "Greek Fire," a highly flammable chemical that had already been used to destroy military warehouses in Louisville and shipping on the rivers. Hovey ordered the formation of the commission on September 17; it met for the first time on September 19.

The commission gathered in the federal courtroom in Indianapolis, later

Figure 6.1. Drawing of the Indianapolis trial scene. Courtesy of the Chicago History Museum.

moving to the chamber of the Indiana Supreme Court. Behind the scenes, General Carrington fed evidence to Burnett to use in his prosecution. He also conferred with Joseph Holt, judge advocate general, who oversaw all military trials, to anticipate defense arguments contesting the commission's jurisdiction to try civilians. He "endeavored," he wrote, "to conform to the President's Proclamation [of the suspension of the privilege of the writ of habeas corpus], & the precedents of Gen Halleck's order [of January 1862 regarding military commissions], and such few antecedents as are accessible, to neutralize or meet the question of 'jurisdiction.'" He also asked Holt's advice on modifications to Dodd's charges and those to be brought against Bowles.[52] In this way, while far away, Joseph Holt had a guiding hand over events in Indianapolis.

The presentation of the army's evidence against Dodd opened on September 27. The courtroom was open to the public, citizens packed into the hall, and newspaper reporters took detailed notes of proceedings to satisfy intense public interest. The first witness called was the army's star secret agent, Felix G. Stidger, who was secretary of the Kentucky branch of the Sons of Liberty. Court reporter Benn Pitman, who compiled a verbatim account of proceedings for the army and later published a printed edition for public consumption, described the scene: "At the moment of Stidger's appearance on the witness stand, Dodd stared at him in bewildered surprise."[53] Up to that moment, neither Dodd nor any of the other conspirators had known that Stidger was a government spy. Burnett carefully walked

Figure 6.2. The judge advocate and officers of the military commission that convicted Milligan. *Standing, from left*: Brigadier General Silas Colgrove (formerly colonel of the Twenty-Seventh Indiana), Colonel Thomas J. Lucas (Sixteenth Indiana), Colonel Thomas Bennett (Sixty-Ninth Indiana), Colonel Benjamin Spooner (Eighty-Third Indiana), Colonel Richard P. DeHart (128th Indiana), Major Henry L. Burnett (Second Ohio Cavalry). *Seated, from left*: Colonel Ambrose A. Stevens (Veterans Reserve Corps, formerly Twenty-First Michigan), Colonel William E. McLean (Forty-Third Indiana), Colonel Charles D. Murray (Eighty-Ninth Indiana), Colonel Reuben Williams (Twelfth Indiana), Colonel Ansel D. Wass (Sixtieth Massachusetts), Lieutenant Colonel Albert Heath (100th Indiana). Courtesy of the Indiana State Library.

Stidger through his experience as an army spy inside the secret organization. Stidger occupied the witness stand for four days, including answering questions posed by defense lawyers. He told of meetings to plan uprisings and attack prison camps in collaboration with Confederate agents, and of the leadership of important Democratic politicians, including Clement Vallandigham. Other witnesses took the stand to provide damning details. Each day newspapers published verbatim or nearly verbatim accounts of the trial, reaching thousands of rapt readers. It was a sensation.

The trial halted unexpectedly on the morning of October 7 with the announcement that Dodd had escaped his prison cell in the federal building.

Angry and embarrassed officers scrambled to capture him, but soon word arrived that the fugitive had reached Canada.[54] Burnett recommended that the commission adjourn temporarily, as in previous days Hovey had issued orders to arrest more Indiana leaders of the Sons of Liberty. Troops went to Greene County to arrest Andrew Humphreys, to Martin County to arrest Stephen Horsey, and to Washington County to arrest Horace Heffren. Troops did not travel far to arrest Joseph J. Bingham, editor of the *Indianapolis Daily State Sentinel* and chairman of the Democratic state central committee. As well, on October 5 a company of troops traveled by train to Huntington County and early the next morning arrested Lambdin P. Milligan in his house.[55]

After a week's hiatus, the trial of Dodd resumed with the defendant in absentia. During that week, Indiana voters went to the polls and gave Morton and other Republicans resounding majorities, bigger than the most optimistic Republicans had expected. Burnett announced that he would submit no more evidence to the tribunal regarding Dodd. After closing prosecution and defense arguments, the commission found him guilty. However, officers delayed public announcement of the verdict. Trials of the new prisoners commenced shortly thereafter, with some defendants turning state's evidence against others. In November, the focus turned to Milligan's leadership of the secret organization in northern Indiana. The presidential election and state elections elsewhere passed off with more Republican victories, including Lincoln's reelection. The trial continued into December. In their concluding arguments, the defense counsel attacked the testimony of witnesses like Stidger, arguing that they were *agents provocateurs* and could not be relied on. Burnett, in reply, stated that army spies had demonstrated that the KGC, OAK, and the Sons of Liberty "were all one and the same general conspiracy" that attempted to raise revolt in the North and turn its people against the war to suppress the Confederate rebellion. In the end, the commission found all defendants guilty and sentenced them (except Humphreys) to death. The verdicts were kept secret until President Lincoln reviewed the findings with Joseph Holt and confirmed the sentences, whereupon Hovey announced them to the public.

Before the end of the Indianapolis trials, Burnett communicated to Joseph Holt in Washington that he foresaw convictions for the Indiana conspirators. He believed the trials would induce voters to abandon the Democratic Party and support the government. He asked the judge advocate general to exert his influence on Lincoln to confirm the expected execution orders.[56] Later, in another letter to Holt, the young officer stated that once he completed the Indianapolis trial he would move on to trying the Chicago conspirators. He opined that "these cases must to a certain extent stand as precedents, and by making the right of military tribunals, to take jurisdiction of that class of offenses and offenders clear and unquestioned, we will have achieved a great work for the government. These scoundrels stand in no fear of the civil courts; they do, of the military."[57] Previously, army commanders in Illinois and Kentucky had desired to try leaders of the Sons of Liberty by military commission, but Major Burnett was busy with the Indianapolis trials and turned them down.[58] High-profile military commission trials continued after the elections. Military intelligence efforts broke up a plot by Confederate agents working in concert with Chicago conspirators to attack the Camp Douglas prison camp on the eve of the November elections. Commanders in Chicago arrested Confederate soldiers and local citizens implicated in the plot.[59] Before the arrests, the War Department issued orders to commanders in Chicago to try by military commission anyone attempting to free rebel prisoners.[60] Therefore, the post commander in Chicago, Colonel Benjamin J. Sweet, contacted Burnett to initiate trials of the Chicago conspirators by military commission. There was no thought given to civilian trials. As several of the prisoners were rebel officers and soldiers, a military tribunal was appropriate. Thus, following War Department orders, commanders tried the Chicago civilians together with the Confederates.

While General Sherman's military victory in Atlanta in early September undoubtedly factored in Republican election successes in October and November, the astonishing revelations in the Indianapolis military commission trials surely played an important part in swaying voters to the Republicans. Other military commission trials occurred in October and November that may have influenced voters. For example, military authorities in Pennsylvania tried organized draft resisters before state elections there; the trials received much newspaper attention and probably factored in Republican electoral victory in the Keystone state. But the Pennsylvania defendants were small-fry citizens, not prominent political figures as in Indiana.[61]

During a break in the Indianapolis trial in December, Burnett traveled to Chicago to confer with Sweet and review evidence.[62] As he was busy with many other trials, he insisted on trying the Chicago conspirators at army headquarters in Cincinnati. Proceedings began in January 1865, shortly after the end of the Indianapolis trials. As several officers on the Indianapolis commission sat on the Cincinnati tribunal, the new trial was in effect a continuation of the administration's efforts to break the secret organizations in the Northwest. Proceedings were again open to the public, and press coverage was extensive. Once more, army spies and informants formed the majority of the prosecution's witnesses. The proceedings continued for months, with defense counsel calling prominent Democratic leaders, among them Clement L. Vallandigham, to portray the secret organizations as benign and peaceful political groups that merely aimed to protect Democrats from rapaciously radical Republicans. Witness testimony ended on April 10, and defense summations began. During this time, news of Robert E. Lee's surrender and the murder of President Lincoln arrived in Cincinnati. Secretary Stanton telegraphed Burnett to report to Washington immediately to aid the investigation of the assassination. The next day, Burnett hurriedly wrapped up his reply to defense statements. He justified the jurisdiction of the military commission, claiming that a *lex non scripta* existed in wartime when the civil power was sometimes powerless to challenge lawlessness. The war was not limited to areas where armies fought each other on the battlefield but existed "all over the limits of this government." The army's operations and jurisdiction were, he said, "co-extensive with the geographical lines of our country."[63]

Military commanders, acting on orders from Washington, DC, used the Indianapolis and Cincinnati trials to embarrass and weaken the compromised Democratic Party. Elsewhere, however, authorities in Washington turned down opportunities to arrest and try more conspirators. In 1864, General Rosecrans's widespread intelligence system in Missouri had uncovered an extensive secret organization with ties to sabotage, guerrillas, and Confederate plans to invade the state. He had arrested dozens, some of whom had confessed to leadership in the group. In February 1865, while that department's judge advocate prepared to try them by military commission, Joseph Holt sent word that he had conferred with Secretary Stanton about more military commission trials. He reported that Stanton ordered the trials of the Missouri conspirators be put on hold until after the final disposition of the Indianapolis cases, which were then "under advisement" by President Lincoln.[64] In the end, military trials of Missouri conspirators did not take place.

Further evidence that the Lincoln administration dropped the plan to employ military commissions came from Ohio. In September 1864, Confederate agents based in Canada launched an attack on the Johnson's Island prison camp in Lake Erie near Sandusky, where the army confined two thousand rebel officers. Agents commandeered a small passenger steamer called the *Philo Parsons* with the plan to attack and seize the USS *Michigan,* a warship that guarded Johnson's Island, and force the surrender of the camp. But a rebel turncoat informed on the plotters, and military and naval forces prepared for the attack. At the last moment, the Confederates on the *Philo Parsons* lost their nerve in sight of the *Michigan* and Johnson's Island. They turned back, fleeing to the safety of Canada. Military authorities arrested the Confederate officer residing in Sandusky who helped plan the attack, as well as some local citizens who collaborated with him. The generals sent to the scene initially planned to try the rebel officer by military commission. But in the end, in June 1865, civil authorities tried two Sandusky citizens in the federal district court in Cleveland. They were found not guilty.[65] While the generals and Republican governors genuinely feared the threat of revolution from their partisan foes, perhaps the Indianapolis and Chicago convictions sufficed to tarnish Democratic opposition.

Recently, legal historian John Fabian Witt has argued that during the Civil War, President Lincoln and his administration expanded the scope of the laws of war to afford his administration and the army greater ability to put down the Confederate rebellion. The Lieber Code, developed by legal scholar Francis Lieber at the request of the War Department and adopted by the US Army in 1863, increased the number of violations with which civilian noncombatants could be charged as long as the offense had some connection to the war. Accused civilians were, under this expanded authority, military prisoners covered by military law and liable to be tried by military commissions, even when and where civil courts were open for business. Earlier in the war, military commanders in Kentucky had employed military commissions in an extensive range of cases involving noncombatants.[66] General Burbridge, commander in the commonwealth in 1864, understood that precedent when he advised the generals and governors north of the Ohio River to arrest the leaders of the secret organization in their states and try them by military commission. Witt argues that Burbridge was abetted by Judge Advocate General Holt, who aggressively pushed the use of military law "as an instrument for increasing the power of a nation at war."[67] In addition, historian Harold Hyman has pointed out that the Lincoln administration and commanders distrusted the civil courts, both state and federal. A result was the Habeas Corpus Act of March 1863, which moved suits against federal officers out of state courts and into federal ones.[68] Still, federal judges appointed by Democratic presidents posed a challenge; several such jurists still presided in district courts in the Old Northwest. Courts presided over by judges appointed by Lincoln were slow, and the sentences handed down by the judges were sometimes mild. Hence, Major Burnett could boast to his superior, Joseph Holt, that only military tribunals could strike fear into the hearts of the conspirator "scoundrels."

Throughout, we see leaders at the national level making decisions and taking steps to combat organized opposition to the war effort in the Old Northwest and elsewhere. After Lincoln repeatedly expressed his faith and trust in the people of the region not to be drawn into violence against the government, he and his administration changed course. In August 1864 the president's subordinates directed measures to counteract conspiracy, issuing orders for national surveillance, arrests, reinforcements for the prisoner-of-war camp garrisons, and arms for loyal state militia troops. This shift was consistent with the militarization of action under the expansion of the law of war: Lincoln's administration would take whatever steps necessary to defeat the rebellion and restore the Union. It occurred at a time when the president thought the war effort was failing and he would lose reelection. The decision to try the Indiana conspirators was not made by Governor Morton, though the governor had fallen in with Burbridge's July plan to arrest the leading conspirators and likely lobbied the president aggressively to that end. The decision was not Morton's to make. It was Lincoln's to decide.

NOTES

1. William Dudley Foulke, *Life of Oliver P. Morton, Including His Important Speeches*, vol. 1 (Indianapolis: Bowen-Merrill, 1899), 419.

2. Kenneth M. Stampp, *Indiana Politics during the Civil War* (Indianapolis: Indiana Historical Bureau, 1949, reprinted Indiana University Press, 1978), 246–247. See also Stampp, "The Milligan Case and the Election of 1864 in Indiana," *Mississippi Valley Historical Review* 31 (June 1944): 41–58.

3. William H. Rehnquist, *All the Laws but One: Civil Liberties in Wartime* (New

York: Knopf, 1998), 83. In his account of the Indianapolis Treason Trials, Rehnquist relies heavily on works by historian Frank L. Klement, even though Klement sides with Stampp to aver that Morton acted alone to try the conspirators by military commission. See Klement, *The Copperheads in the Middle West* (Chicago: University of Chicago Press, 1960), 196–197; Klement, *Dark Lanterns: Secret Political Societies, Conspiracies, and Treason Trials in the Civil War* (Baton Rouge: Louisiana State University Press, 1984), 161–162, 172; Klement, "The Indianapolis Treason Trials and *Ex parte Milligan*," in Michal R. Belknap, ed., *American Political Trials* (Westport, CT: Greenwood, 1981), 107–108.

4. J. F. Duckwall to Laz Noble, August 3, 1861, Adjutant General of Indiana Records, Indiana State Archives, Indiana Archives and Records Administration, Indianapolis, Indiana (hereafter ISA). (Italics original.) The letter is printed in Richard F. Nation and Stephen E. Towne, eds., *Indiana's War: The Civil War in Documents* (Athens: Ohio University Press, 2009), 127–128. See also Stephen E. Towne, "The Persistent Nullifier: The Life of Civil War Conspirator Lambdin P. Milligan," *Indiana Magazine of History* 109, no. 4 (December 2013): 303–354.

5. Thomas A. Burgess to Oziah M. Hatch, April 27, 1861, Oziah M. Hatch Papers, Abraham Lincoln Presidential Library, Springfield, Illinois (hereafter ALPL); Browning diary entry of April 22, 1861, in *The Diary of Orville Hickman Browning,* Theodore C. Pease and James G. Randall, eds., 2 vols. (Springfield: Illinois State Historical Library, 1925–1933), I: 465; David Davis to Richard Yates, May 9, 1861; R. J. Wheatley to Yates, July 26, 1861; J. M. Galbraith to Yates, August 4, 1861, Lewis Hammach to Yates, April 20, 1861, all in Yates Family Papers, ALPL; Richard Yates to J. I. McCawley, August 10, 1861, Wabash Yates Papers, ALPL.

6. William C. Kise to Oliver P. Morton, August 6, 1861, Tenth Indiana Volunteer Infantry Regiment Correspondence, Adjutant General of Indiana Records, ISA; Morton to Thomas A. Scott, August 31, 1861, in Governor Oliver P. Morton Telegraph Books, vol. 1, 182–183, ISA (reprinted in *The War of the Rebellion: A Compilation of the Official Records of the Union and Confederate Armies,* 128 vols. (Washington, DC: Governmental Printing Office, 1880–1901), series 3, vol. 1, 473–474 (hereafter *OR*).

7. Diary of William T. Coggeshall, entries of July 28 and 31, 1861, ALPL.

8. David L. Phillips to Caleb B. Smith, May 12, 1861, Record Group 60, General Records of the Department of Justice, Southern Illinois, 1860–1863, Letters Received re Judiciary Accounts; Phillips to Edward Bates, May 13, 1861, RG 60, Southern District of Illinois (US Marshal), Letters Received, both National Archives and Records Administration, College Park, Maryland (hereafter NARA-CP); Phillips to Yates, September 21, 1861, Richard Yates Papers, Southern Illinois University–Carbondale Special Collections, Morris Library, Carbondale; Richard Bates to Flamen Ball, May 4, 1861; Titian J. Coffey to Montgomery Blair, May 8, 1861; Edward Bates to Asa S. Jones, May 21, 1861; Bates to Robert F. Paine, May 24, 1861; Coffey to Paine, September 19, 1861; Coffey to Ball, September 2, 1861, all in RG 60 Letters Sent by the Department of Justice: General and Miscellaneous, 1818–1904, NARA-CP.

9. See Stephen E. Towne, *Surveillance and Spies in the Civil War: Exposing Con-*

federate Conspiracies in America's Heartland (Athens: Ohio University Press, 2015), 32–36.

10. Towne, *Surveillance and Spies in the Civil War*, 28–32. Cleveland's three daily newspapers provided extensive coverage of the pre-trial hearings before the federal magistrate. See the *Cleveland Daily Plain Dealer*, the *Daily Cleveland Herald*, and the *Cleveland Morning Leader* starting October 8, 1861.

11. Mark E. Neely Jr., *The Fate of Liberty: Abraham Lincoln and Civil Liberties* (New York: Oxford University Press, 1991), 52–53; William R. Holloway to John Hanna, August 15, 1862, John Hanna Papers, Lilly Library, Indiana University–Bloomington; Towne, "The Persistent Nullifier," 323.

12. For studies of government efforts to suppress dissent in the North, see Neely, *The Fate of Liberty*; and William A. Blair, *With Malice toward Some: Treason and Loyalty in the Civil War Era* (Chapel Hill: University of North Carolina Press, 2014). The army's top commander reported that over a third of total manpower was absent, mainly due to desertion. See Maj. Gen. Henry W. Halleck to Edwin M. Stanton, February 18, 1863, Edwin M. Stanton Papers, Manuscripts Division, Library of Congress, Washington, DC (hereafter LC).

13. Captain Andrew C. Kemper to Major N. H. McLean, March 17, 1863, and Kemper to James L. Ruffin, March 15, 1863, both in RG 393, US Army Continental Commands Records, Part IV, Post of Cincinnati, Ohio, Records, E 212, Letters Sent, vol. 1, 116, 118, National Archives and Records Administration, Washington, DC (hereafter NARA-W).

14. Kemper to Captains Harrington R. Hill and John A. Means, April 30, 1863, RG 393, Part IV, E 212, Letters Sent, vol. 1, 147, NARA-W.

15. Works detailing the operations of the conscription system include Eugene C. Murdock, *Patriotism Limited, 1862–1865: The Civil War Draft and the Bounty System* (Kent, Ohio: Kent State University Press, 1967); Murdock, *One Million Men: The Civil War Draft in the North* (Madison: State Historical Society of Wisconsin, 1971); James W. Geary, *We Need Men: the Union Draft in the Civil War* (DeKalb: Northern Illinois University Press, 1991), and Robert E. Sterling, "Civil War Draft Resistance in the Middle West" (PhD diss., Northern Illinois University, 1974). None of the above focuses on the espionage system in the Provost Marshal General's Bureau created with the hiring of special agents. See Towne, *Surveillance and Spies in the Civil War*, 89–115.

16. See Stephen E. Towne, "Exposing Confederate Conspiracies in Ohio: Camp Chase Plot," *Timeline* 34, no. 2 (April–June 2017): 14–27; Towne, *Surveillance and Spies*, 123–127.

17. Lincoln's order to arrest P. C. Wright survives in two locations. See Col. James A. Hardie to Major General Samuel P. Heintzelman, April 20, 1864, in Stanton Papers, and in the Samuel P. Heintzelman Papers, both in LC.

18. Carrington is the special target of abuse of historian Frank L. Klement, who wrote extensively on the anti-war or Peace Democrats of the Civil War era, also commonly called "Copperheads." Klement defended these Democrats from what he

termed "fabrications" and "smears" concocted by Republicans and army commanders for political purposes. Carrington comes in for heavy censure from Klement for his efforts to uncover and counteract organized conspiracy. See Klement, *The Copperheads in the Middle West* (Chicago: University of Chicago Press, 1960); *The Limits of Dissent: Clement L. Vallandigham and the Civil War* (Lexington: University Press of Kentucky, 1970); *Dark Lanterns: Secret Political Societies, Conspiracies, and Treason Trials in the Civil War* (Baton Rouge: Louisiana State University Press, 1984), and "Carrington and the Golden Circle Legend in Indiana during the Civil War," *Indiana Magazine of History* 61, no. 1 (March 1965): 31–52. Klement's works have had significant influence among historians and legal scholars. However, most of Klement's arguments about Carrington and government efforts against the conspirators are undermined and rendered unreliable by his numerous errors of fact and interpretation. Indeed, Klement invented events based on no documentation or other evidence in order to cast Carrington and others in a bad light. Many of these errors and inventions are noted in the endnotes of my book *Surveillance and Spies in the Civil War.*

19. Brigadier General Henry B. Carrington to Capt. Carroll H. Potter, June 6, 1864, RG 393, Part I, Northern Department Records, E 3351, Confidential Correspondence re OAK, 21–26, NARA-W, printed in *OR,* series 2, vol. 7, 341–342. Stidger's memoir is remarkably accurate and useful. See Felix G. Stidger, *Treason History of the Order of Sons of Liberty . . .* (Chicago: Author, 1903).

20. Carrington to Edwin M. Stanton, June 17, 1864, Box 2, Carrington Family Papers, Yale University Library, Manuscripts and Archives, New Haven, Connecticut, printed in *OR,* series 2, vol. 7, 376; Carrington to Potter, June 18 and 25, 1864, both RG 393, Part III, District of Indiana Records, E 218, Letters Sent, vol. 1, 20–21, 31–32, NARA-W; Heintzelman to Carrington, June 23, 1864, RG 393, Part III, E 221, Letters Received, vol. 1, 292, NARA-W.

21. *Indianapolis Daily Journal,* July 30, 1864. Carrington to Potter, July 30, 1864, RG 393, Part I, E 3349, Letters Received, Box 1, NARA-W.

22. Journal entries of April 16 and 17, 1864, Heintzelman Papers, LC.

23. Towne, *Surveillance and Spies in the Civil War,* 188–194.

24. John M. Palmer, *Personal Recollections of John M. Palmer: The Story of an Earnest Life* (Cincinnati: Robert Clarke, 1901), 152–153.

25. Brigadier General Julius White to Yates, June 19, 1864, Wabash Yates Papers, ALPL.

26. Diary of John Hay, entry of June 17, 1864, in John Hay, *Inside Lincoln's White House: the Complete Civil War Diary of John Hay,* ed. Michael Burlingame and John R. Turner Ettinger (Carbondale: Southern Illinois University Press, 1997), 207–208.

27. Towne, *Surveillance and Spies in the Civil War,* 229–233.

28. According to Hay's diary entry of June 17, 1864, Lincoln had told Hay that he would write to the Ohio governor and general with instructions concerning the return of Vallandigham. The letter he drafted contained merely vague statements

saying nothing. Though signed by Lincoln, he did not send the letter. Lincoln to Brough and Heintzelman, June 20, 1864, Abraham Lincoln Papers, LC.

29. Lieutenant Colonel Thomas B. Fairleigh to Captain J. Bates Dickson, July 4, 1864, RG 393, Part I, District of Kentucky Records, E 2173, Letters Received, Box 4; Carrington to Potter, July 14, 1864, RG 393, Part I, E 3349, Box 3; Carrington to Potter, July 30, 1864, RG 393, Part I, E 3349, Box 1, all NARA-W.

30. E. D. Townsend to Joseph Holt, July 12, 1864, *OR*, series 3, vol. 4, 488. See Elizabeth D. Leonard, *Lincoln's Forgotten Ally: Judge Advocate General Joseph Holt of Kentucky* (Chapel Hill: University of North Carolina Press, 2011).

31. Holt to Stanton, July 29, 1864, vol. 22, Stanton Papers, LC; Holt to Stanton, July 31 and August 5, 1864, *OR*, series 1, vol. 39, part 2, 212–215 and series 3, vol. 4, 577–579.

32. Towne, *Surveillance and Spies in the Civil War*, 260–263.

33. Charles A. Dana to Heintzelman and Burbridge, August 1, 1864, RG 107, Records of the Office of the Secretary of War, E 5, Letters Sent by the S of War Relating to Military Affairs, 1800–1889, vol. 56A, M-6, roll 55, 378, NARA-W. The War Department sent similar orders to commanders of the Department of the East, the Department of Washington, the Department of the Cumberland, and other armies in the field. See ibid., vol. 56A, 370, 377–378, 383, 394, 395, and vol. 56B, 424, 425, and 428.

34. Histories of government surveillance and espionage in the United States have overlooked the scale of domestic intelligence efforts in the North during the Civil War in general, and this first mass-surveillance order in particular. See Joan Jensen, *Army Surveillance in America, 1775–1980* (New Haven, CT: Yale University Press, 1991); Rhodri Jeffreys-Jones, *Cloak and Dollar: The History of American Secret Intelligence*, 2nd ed. (New Haven, CT: Yale University Press, 2003); and Jeffreys-Jones, *We Know All About You: The Story of Surveillance in Britain and America* (New York: Oxford University Press, 2017).

35. Lincoln to Grant, August 17, 1864, *OR*, series 1, vol. 42, part 2, 243.

36. Lincoln memorandum, August 23, 1864, in *The Collected Works of Abraham Lincoln*, 9 vols., ed. Roy P. Basler (New Brunswick, NJ: Rutgers University Press, 1953), 7: 514.

37. Carrington to Potter, June 1, 1864, E 3351, 20–21; Carrington to Major Henry L. Burnett, June 8, 1864, E 218, vol. 1, 18, both NARA-W.

38. Carrington to Holt, March 5, 1863, RG 94, Records of the Adjutant General of the United States, M-619, roll 165, NARA-W.

39. See Stephen E. Towne, "A Lesson for All Rebels at Home: The Holmes County, Ohio, Rebellion of 1863 Revisited," *Ohio History* 126 (Fall 2019): 5–37. Lincoln pardoned the one person convicted. See Patrick J. Drouhard, *It Don't Look Right for the Times: The Factual History of the Holmes County Rebellion* (privately printed, 2007).

40. Flamen Ball to Bates, April 26, 1864, RG 60, E 9, Letters Received, Ohio "Southern District of Ohio (US Attorney), NARA-CP. A Cincinnati newspaper noted Ball's return from Washington, DC after the arrests. *Cincinnati Daily Times*, November 11, 1863.

41. Towne, "Exposing Confederate Conspiracies in Ohio," 15–27.

42. Morton, et al., to Stanton, September 12, 1864, and Schuyler Colfax to Stanton, August 29, 1864, Stanton Papers, LC.

43. See Stephen E. Towne, "Worse Than Vallandigham: Governor Oliver P. Morton, Lambdin P. Milligan, and the Military Arrest and Trial of Indiana State Senator Alexander J. Douglas during the Civil War," *Indiana Magazine of History* 106, no. 1 (March 2010): 1–39.

44. Carrington to Holt, September 22, 1864, RG 107, E 17, Letters Received by the Secretary of War Main Series 1861–1870, M-221, roll 257, NARA-W.

45. Alvin P. Hovey to Essie Hovey, August 25, 26, and 30, 1864, all in Alvin P. Hovey Papers, Lilly Library, Indiana University–Bloomington. See also Donald E. Dewey, ed., "Hoosier Justice: The Journal of David McDonald, 1864–1868," *Indiana Magazine of History* 62, no. 3 (September 1966): 188.

46. Townsend to Hovey, September 14, 1864, RG 94, E 159, subseries 2, Generals' Papers, Alvin P. Hovey, Box 16, Folder 9, NARA-W; also in Stanton Papers, LC.

47. Journal entry of August 22, 1864, Heintzelman Papers, LC.

48. Journal entry of September 30, 1864, Heintzelman Papers, LC.

49. Journal entries of August 9, 10, 11, and 12, 1864, Heintzelman Papers, LC; Burbridge to Burnett, August 9, 1864, RG 393, Part I, E 2174, Letters Sent, vol. 119, 160, NARA-W.

50. Burnett to Lieutenant Colonel S. H. Lathrop, September 16, 1864, RG 393, Part III, District of Indiana Records, E 222, Letters Received, Box 3, NARA-W.

51. Hovey to Heintzelman, September 17, 1864, RG 393, Part I, Northern Department Records, E 3350, Telegrams Received, NARA-W.

52. Carrington to Holt, September 22, 1864, RG 153, Judge Advocate General Records, E 6, Letters Received, Box 4, NARA-W.

53. Benn Pitman, ed., *The Trials for Treason at Indianapolis, Disclosing the Plans for Establishing a North-Western Confederacy* (Cincinnati: Moore, Wilstach & Baldwin, 1865), 19.

54. Historian Kenneth M. Stampp erroneously claims that "Military authorities had taken no precautions against such an [escape] attempt, and inexplicable delays occurred before the alarm was sounded. Nor was any real effort made to secure his capture." See Stampp, "The Milligan Case and the Election of 1864 in Indiana," *Mississippi Valley Historical Review* 31, no. 1 (June 1944): 55. Stampp implies that authorities let Dodd escape as a way to cement his guilt in the court of public opinion. On the contrary, army officers were furious about the escape and made sedulous efforts to capture him.

55. Towne, "The Persistent Nullifier," 335–336.

56. Burnett to Holt, November 8, 1864, RG 153, Judge Advocate General Records, E 6, Letters Received, Box 6, NARA-W.

57. Burnett to Holt, November 24, 1864, RG 153, Judge Advocate General Records, E 6, Letters Received, Box 6, NARA-W.

58. Confession of James Ingraham Adams, September 27, 1864, in RG 393, Part I,

Department of the Missouri Records, E 2786, Letters Received, Box 2, NARA-W. On October 29, Burnett endorsed the document: "Resp[ectfull]y returned to Capt. C. H. Potter. . . . I do not think it advisable to make the arrests recommended by Genl. [Halbert E.] Paine. The evidence is not of that intelligent conclusive character that would [?] the putting these men on trial." Burbridge ordered his spy chief to select imprisoned Kentucky conspirators who "can be convicted without implicating your detectives to be brought before a military commission." He meant "to remove all doubts" among those in Washington that a conspiracy existed. However, Burnett could not try the Indiana and Kentucky plotters at the same time. Dickson to Fairleigh, September 13, 1864, RG 393, Part IV, Post of Louisville, Kentucky Records, E 734, Letters Received, Box 1, NARA-W.

59. See Stephen E. Towne, "Quelling the Camp Douglas Conspiracies," *Chicago History* 40, no. 1 (Winter 2015): 26–39.

60. Major G. Bladen to Col. Benjamin J. Sweet, November 7, 1864, RG 393, Part IV, Post of Chicago, Illinois Records, E 418, Letters, Telegrams, and Orders Received, vol. 2, 17, NARA-W.

61. See Richard A. Sauers and Peter Tomasak, *The Fishing Creek Conspiracy: A Story of Civil War Draft Resistance* (Columbia: University of Missouri Press, 2012); Jonathan W. White, "Remembering the Fishing Creek Confederacy," *Pennsylvania Heritage* 40 (Summer 2014), 6–13.

62. *Chicago Tribune*, December 13, 1864, and *Cincinnati Daily Commercial*, December 16, 1864.

63. The complete transcript of the Chicago Conspiracy military commission trial appears in print. See *Executive Documents Printed by Order of the House of Representatives during the Second Session of the Thirty-ninth Congress, 1866–1867* (Washington, DC: Government Printing Office, 1867), 577–579. The original transcripts of the trials of G. St. Leger Grenfell, Charles Walsh, Buckner Morris, R. T. Semmes, and V. Marmaduke, et al., are to be found in RG 153, Judge Advocate General Records, Court Martial Case Files, NARA-W.

64. Holt to Lucien Eaton, February 10, 1865, in RG 393, Part I, Department of the Missouri Records, E 2786, Letters Received, Box 2, NARA-W.

65. A detective who participated in the investigation recorded later that commanders initially planned to try the rebel officer by military commission: "They talked at first of trying [rebel officer] Cole by a military commission." See John Wilson Murray, *Memoirs of a Great Detective: Incidents in the Life of John Wilson Murray*, ed. Victor Speer (New York: Baker & Taylor, 1905), 28.

66. John Fabian Witt, *Lincoln's Code: The Laws of War in American History* (New York: Free Press, 2012), 233, 268–271.

67. Witt, *Lincoln's Code*, 274.

68. Harold M. Hyman, *A More Perfect Union: The Impact of the Civil War and Reconstruction on the Constitution* (New York: Knopf, 1973), 234–242.

Part Three

The Milligan *Decision*

CHAPTER 7

Ex Parte Milligan in Context and History: David Davis and the Constitutional Politics and Law of Civil Liberty

MICHAEL LES BENEDICT

In the summer of 1866, David Davis, associate justice of the Supreme Court, appointed by his long-time friend Abraham Lincoln, was hard at work in the study of his farmhouse on the site of the beautiful mansion and garden that he and his wife Sarah would build five years later and which still graces one of the nicest neighborhoods of Bloomington, Illinois. He was writing the Supreme Court's opinion in the case *Ex parte Milligan*, which had been decided a few months earlier but announced without an opinion, which was promised for the following winter. It was, he knew, the opportunity of a lifetime for a lawyer and judge—indeed, for an American.

DAVID DAVIS AND CIVIL LIBERTIES IN THE CIVIL WAR

During the Civil War, Davis had been dismayed at how the struggle challenged traditional and deeply felt commitments to civil liberty—freedom of speech and press, but most especially the principle that one could not be deprived of life or liberty except by "due process of law." That general concept of "due process" was guaranteed in the Bill of Rights of the Constitution, along with specific procedures central to the common law: indictments or presentments before grand juries, the right to confront witnesses, a jury trial. If the government detained someone without observing these procedural rights, he or she could petition a court to issue a writ of habeas corpus, ordering the jailor literally to "bring the body" or explain on what legal basis he or she was being held.

Of course, Davis knew that the Constitution provided that the privilege of getting this writ could be suspended in time of invasion or rebellion. His friend President Lincoln had proclaimed such suspensions several times since the war had begun, finally applying them to the whole country, and Congress had passed a law in 1863 regularizing the process.[1]

But military commanders, relying on Lincoln's authority, had done more. All over the country they had not only detained people but tried them before military commissions and sentenced them to imprisonment and even death.[2] Military commissions did not have juries. The prisoners tried by them were not indicted by grand juries. The commissioners who heard the cases, applied the rules of evidence, decided guilt or innocence, and determined the punishment were military officers, often not even lawyers. According to the judge advocate general and the leading contemporaneous treatise on military law, they were to use the same procedures as courts martial,[3] which were not bound by common-law precedents and rules. Despite the principle established by the judge advocate general, when he wrote his seminal treatise on military law twenty years later William Winthrop described military commission procedures as less formal and technical than courts-martial.[4]

In establishing these tribunals, the army and navy relied on the law of war, expounded in General Henry W. Halleck's just-published treatise on international law, two-thirds of which was devoted to the laws of war,[5] and then on the army's General Orders No. 100, prepared by Francis Lieber and issued in 1863.[6] Military commissions were an inherent part of military, not civil, administration. Congress recognized their existence in various statutes, but it did not itself authorize them. The rule was that military commanders could use military commissions to punish enemy combatants acting outside the laws of war—like spies, guerrillas, and bushwhackers—and to supplant ordinary courts in occupied enemy territory.[7] Military commanders, backed by President Lincoln, held that to mean that they could punish acts that threatened their forces even in places like Ohio, Indiana, and Illinois if the threat was serious enough and the ordinary courts could not be relied on to deal with it expeditiously.

Lincoln's Democratic opponents denounced every bit of this. As far as they were concerned, Lincoln was a despot willing to destroy American liberty to win the war—a war not worth winning at that price. When Lincoln issued the Emancipation Proclamation, they redoubled their denuncia-

Figure 7.1. Associate Justice David Davis. Courtesy of the Library of Congress.

tions. Now he and the Republican Party were destroying American liberty in a mad effort to free the slaves and make them American citizens. Democrats made the Lincoln administration's violations of civil liberties, and their own defense of them, a staple of Civil War politics, complementing their attack on emancipation. These were constitutional issues, and Democrats engaged Republicans mightily in what we now identify as "constitutional politics"—reliance on constitutional interpretation in struggles over public policy.[8]

Davis did not totally agree with the Democratic criticism, but he was worried nonetheless. The suspension of access to the writ of habeas corpus had led to the detention of civilians who actively tried to obstruct Union forces near the theater of battle, as well as those who advocated Confederate independence in the border states and in occupied Confederate territory. It had led to the detention of those who helped to hide draft dodgers and deserters, even ambushing soldiers looking for them, well behind Union lines.[9]

But it had also led to the detention of Northerners who had too belligerently criticized the administration, who insisted that there was no hope of defeating the South and that it was wrong even to try. Such criticisms discouraged young men from enlisting, forcing Lincoln and Congress to institute an unpopular draft, which led to even more dissatisfaction. Everyone knew that the Confederates were counting on such defeatism to terminate the Union war effort. How far could Unionists tolerate opposition? At what point would an arrest be justified? Democrats said never. Radical Republicans urged vigorous suppression of anti-war sentiments. Lincoln and his subordinates vacillated, detaining many dissenters in the first months of the war and again after draft resistance grew. But decisions on the ground were often made by low-level officials, and higher-ups had trouble even keeping track of them.[10]

Still, even if detentions went too far, they were temporary. They were designed to prevent the disruption of the war effort, not to punish people for what they had done or said. As soon as detainees promised to abstain from going too far, the authorities released them. What bothered Davis was punishing people without due process of law, especially in this environment where it was hard to distinguish the right to criticize from the wrong of disrupting the war effort. Davis told Lincoln that punishing people through military commissions was not permissible where they could be tried in ordinary civil courts. Military commissions could be used legitimately in the South, where there were no loyal courts to enforce federal law or maintain law and order. But they could not be used to punish civilians in the North, where the ordinary courts were open to provide trials according to due process of law.[11] Davis had been upset when the military had refused to turn over to civilian authorities the prisoners accused of killing Union soldiers in a riot in Charleston, Illinois, in March 1864. "The Govt. ought not to have taken these men out of the hand of the law," he admonished the president.[12]

Davis's narrow conception of military commissions was clear. Authorities on military law stated clearly that military commanders were responsible for protecting their troops from attack from any source and could utilize military commissions to punish offenders. In Davis's view, however, they had no such authority when the attackers were civilians: "[The] fight was brought on purposely by bad men who were not in the military service to kill & murder. How can they be tried by military law[?] They violated no military law."[13]

Davis knew that Lincoln did not like military commissions. The president often moderated their sentences, and he expressed his ambivalence even when he defended them. As Davis was drafting his opinion, he convinced himself that Lincoln had fully shared his misgivings. He took time to write Lincoln's law partner and biographer, William H. Herndon, that he was "satisfied that Lincoln was thoroughly opposed to these Military Commissions, especially in the free States, where the Courts were open—& free."[14] Perhaps Davis reached this conclusion because Lincoln had finally followed Davis's recommendation to turn the Charleston rioters over to the civil authorities. But he was clearly exaggerating. Lincoln had explicitly authorized military commissions.[15] He vigorously defended their use even in the doubtful case of Ohio Democrat Clement L. Vallandigham, convicted by a military commission of uttering "disloyal sentiments" designed to weaken the government's ability to suppress the rebellion.[16] As historian Stephen E. Towne has shown, Lincoln had cooperated with Governor Oliver P. Morton of Indiana in securing the military trial of subversives there.[17] He turned the Charleston rioters over to the civil authorities only as the public sustained his position by reelecting him and because Davis assured him that the civil courts were doing their job.[18]

Many Unionists—the wartime coalition of Republicans and strongly pro-war Democrats—shared Davis's concerns. They had limited the duration of detentions in the Habeas Corpus Act of 1863. Detainees were to be released if they were not indicted for their activities before the end of the federal court term following their arrest. Secretary of War Edwin M. Stanton and Secretary of State William H. Seward were required to provide Congress with lists of all those detained. Not only did they generally fail to do so, pleading bookkeeping problems, but the War Department claimed that the time limit did not apply to those brought to trial before military commissions.

By 1865 a number of frustrated Republicans determined to stop the use of military commissions altogether in the Northern states and in those border states that had not seceded. They were led by one of the most radical of

Republicans in the House of Representatives, David Davis's cousin Henry Winter Davis. In the debate, Henry L. Dawes of Massachusetts, another respected Republican leader, worried, "We seem to have lost sight . . . of the guarantees of the Constitution. We seem to forget that civilians charged with offense have any right to trial by jury, or a knowledge of the offense for which they are frequently incarcerated. . . . We seem to be taking very little note of the direction in which we are drifting."[19] We have to stop it, Winter Davis urged, "before every vestige of American liberty is buried beneath the waters."[20] The House passed the proposal in March 1865, during the closing moments of the Thirty-Eighth Congress, over the bitter objections of the Republicans' grim House leader Thaddeus Stevens. Although Lyman Trumbull, the chairman of the Senate Judiciary Committee, backed the proposal, the upper chamber soundly defeated it, and it never became law.

So Davis knew that as the war closed, many Republicans shared his fears. Neither they nor he had raised the issue earlier. Davis had not wanted the Supreme Court to intervene, to give ammunition to the Democrats by sustaining their objections to infringements of civil liberty. He was probably relieved when Lincoln expelled Vallandigham from the country after his conviction. That meant there was no jailor on which to serve a writ of habeas corpus. Instead, Vallandigham tried to appeal the decision of the commission itself, something Davis and the rest of the justices could agree they had no authority over.[21]

But he had hated it. "During the late wicked Rebellion, the temper of the times did not allow that calmness in deliberation and discussion so necessary to a correct conclusion of a purely judicial question," he wrote two years later in *Milligan*. "Considerations of safety were mingled with the exercise of power; and feelings and interests prevailed."[22] In fact, as he later wrote his brother-in-law and fellow lawyer Julius Rockwell, at the time he had been afraid that civil liberty "w[oul]d be all gone."[23]

With the Union safe, it was time to act. As his cousin Henry Winter Davis tried to persuade Congress to put a stop to military commissions, David Davis worked to get the issue before the Supreme Court. He thought a clear case had arisen within his circuit. A locally important Indiana Democrat, Lambdin P. Milligan, had joined a number of other outspoken opponents of the war to organize a secret society they called the Sons of Liberty. They had intended to organize disaffected Democrats who were already engaging in sporadic violence to resist the draft. Milligan and his confederates had been certain that liberty was on the line and that Lincoln was already establishing a tyranny through his arbitrary arrests. They had expected the administration to use its powers to steal the 1864 congressional and presidential elections. In that case, they were determined to fight. "Arm yourselves with pikes and scythes, with long guns, with short guns," Milligan urged his neighbors. It is better to be "snuffed out" in "a glorious struggle for right, than flicker a little longer with the scintillations of expiring liberty." The organizers persuaded the exiled Vallandigham to become their titular leader and planned out an elaborate organization with Milligan as one of the Indiana commanders. Confederate agents in Canada were happy to finance the operation, and they encouraged the leaders to embark on a more ambitious plan to aid the South by local uprisings and raids on prisoner-of-war camps.[24]

It was exactly the kind of thing Union military commanders thought justified trial by military commission. An ordinary court would prove slow, and it would only take one disaffected juror to prevent a conviction. Quick action would deter imitation. The tribunal quickly convicted Milligan and his fellow conspirators, condemning Milligan to death in December 1864. Milligan's lawyer persuaded Lincoln to commute the sentence, but although he delayed the execution, Lincoln was assassinated before he could act further. Lincoln's successor, Vice President Andrew Johnson, wanted to be tougher on treason, and the executions were rescheduled for May 19, 1865. But Davis himself intervened to persuade the new president to delay the sentence again so that Milligan's lawyers could petition his circuit court for a writ of habeas corpus. Then he and Judge David McDonald, a Lincoln appointee who sat with Davis on the US circuit court in Indiana, agreed to disagree on whether Milligan was entitled to the writ.[25] This formality was required to take the case to the Supreme Court, which prepared to hear it in March 1866, almost a year after the Confederate surrender. In reality, however, there was no disagreement. McDonald doubted the commission's constitutionality as much as Davis did. When he heard that those accused of conspiring to assassinate Lincoln would also be tried by military commission, McDonald expostulated in his diary, "What folly and madness! What unpardonable disregard for the Constitution." The conspirators all deserved execution, "but why not put them to death according to law?"[26]

Everyone knew *Ex parte Milligan* was a great case. The Court assigned seven days for oral argument. Two of the foremost Democratic constitutional lawyers in the country, former US attorney general Jeremiah S. Black—a close personal friend of Davis[27]—and David Dudley Field, appeared for Milligan to argue that the commission trial was unconstitutional. They added one of the young Republican congressmen who had expressed reservations about military commissions in the House of Representatives—future President James A. Garfield. Garfield provided the added benefit of having served as a major general in the Union army before being elected to Congress. No one could accuse him of being sympathetic to traitors. Davis arranged for his wife Sarah to sit in the ladies' gallery. She reflected his excitement when she wrote their son, "It is considered the most important case *ever* brought before the court."[28]

The arguments ended on March 13. The Court decided in favor of Milligan three weeks later. All the justices agreed that Milligan's trial had violated his constitutional rights, but four of the nine indicated some reservations about what seemed to be minor points. Chief Justice Salmon P. Chase, who was among the four, naturally assigned the majority opinion to Davis, who had done so much to get the case before the Court. Like Chase, Davis was a Republican. It was safer to assign the opinion to him than to a justice who sympathized more openly with the Democratic critics of Lincoln's record on civil liberties. And it was best for the Supreme Court too. If the Court was going to side with Lincoln's opponents on this issue, better to have a Republican friend of Lincoln write the opinion than a Democratic critic.

By the time the justices reached their decision, the differences over Reconstruction between congressional Republicans and President Johnson were becoming apparent. As a justice, Davis intended to remain nonpartisan. He was growing more and more disenchanted with the more radical congressional Republican leaders, for whom "the idea that the negro must have suffrage, & all other rights, . . . rides higher than all material things," like economic and industrial interests. "The country needs quiet and rest," he wrote his brother-in-law. "Fraternal relations should be cultivated, instead of hatred."[29] But he had no use for "the discordant elements" that were gathering to support Johnson. "The distinctive feature of politics here is, to do anything to prevent rebels from again gaining power," he wrote.[30] He determined to ignore the Reconstruction issue as he prepared his *Milligan* opinion.

DAVID DAVIS AND WHIG JURISPRUDENCE

In reality, Davis was not much of a Republican. He approached his task from the perspective of an old Whig jurisprudent. Before his party collapsed, Davis had been a Whig opponent of the Jacksonian Democratic Party. A conservative, he had been appalled as the slavery issue took over American politics. Raised on a plantation on the eastern shore of Maryland, he had remonstrated with his New England–raised wife when she praised *Uncle Tom's Cabin.* He told her that it did not represent the slave system he had known. At his urging, she read a counter-novel by a proslavery apologist. He was not happy when she told him it "does not compare."[31] Reading his biography, one gets the distinct impression that he became a Republican only to support the political ambitions of his slightly less reluctant friend Abraham Lincoln. In 1866 Davis was still referring to Democrats as "Loco Focos," the old and by then anachronistic Whig term of derision.[32] His preferred newspaper was the old Whig organ, the *Washington National Intelligencer,* which still put on the masthead of its editorial page Webster's famous *pronunciamento* from his debate with Hayne: "Liberty and Union, now and forever, one and inseparable."

Whigs had insisted that democracy could be reconciled with liberty only if the people were committed to the rule of law. This was the central commitment of what historians have identified as Whig constitutionalism.[33] The *National Intelligencer,* in the 1860s still representing the attitudes of conservative Whigs, recorded proudly that it "has, from its origin, been distinguished for its reverence for law."[34] The young Lincoln provided a classic statement of the Whig philosophy in an early address in Springfield, Illinois. Tasked to discuss whether a democratic government could really persist for any great length of time, he saw an "ill-omen"—"I mean the increasing disregard for law which pervades the country; the growing disposition to substitute the wild and furious passions, in lieu of the sober judgment of Courts." A democracy required "general intelligence, sound morality, and in particular, a reverence for the constitution and the laws."[35]

Whigs had blasted Jackson and his party for their dismissive attitude toward law. They assailed Jackson and his supporters for ignoring the Supreme Court's decision in favor of the Cherokee in their dispute with Georgia over control of their territory.[36] Whigs attacked him for discounting the

Court's decision in *McCulloch v. Maryland* upholding the constitutionality of the national bank.[37] They condemned his determination to withdraw federal money from the bank in the teeth of the law that had chartered it.[38] In the Illinois state legislature, Lincoln denounced Democrats who were trumping up charges that would enable them to revoke the state bank's charter. He would address his remarks "exclusively" to "the law-loving and law abiding part of the House," he declared. "To those who claim omnipotence for the Legislature, and . . . disposed to disregard the Constitution, law, good faith, moral right and every thing else, I have not a word to say."[39]

Whigs believed that respect for the judiciary was an essential element of respect for law. As a young Whig, Davis had been outraged when Illinois Democrats reconstituted the state's supreme court because they feared its Whig majority might rule against allowing unnaturalized immigrants (mostly Democrats) to vote.[40] Of special relevance to the issue raised by the *Milligan* case was a famous fight between Whigs and Democrats that blazed from 1842 to 1844, when Davis was still a young Whig politician. Democrats in Congress proposed to reimburse their great leader for the fine a district judge had imposed on him some twenty-five years earlier, during Jackson's controversial administration of martial law in New Orleans. Jackson had been typically high-handed, jailing critics and even moving to expel the entire Creole French population. When the federal judge issued a writ of habeas corpus on behalf of one of his victims, Jackson not only ignored the writ but arrested the judge and banished him from the city. Jackson refused to respond to the judge's demand for an explanation after peace returned, and he was fined for contempt of court. The fight over reimbursement turned into a donnybrook over martial law and respect for the judiciary. For two years, according to historian Matthew Warshauer, Whigs and Democrats "fought over Jackson's refund . . . as though it was the biggest issue facing the nation."[41]

Ironically, given their Civil War concern for civil liberty, in 1841 and 1842 Democrats had argued that necessity and national defense in wartime justified these violations of constitutional norms. "The law which justified the act, was the great law of necessity," explained one of the proponents of reimbursing the general. "This great law of necessity—of defence of self, of home, and of country—never was designed to be abrogated by any statute, or by any Constitution."[42] Stephen A. Douglas, then a freshman representative, made his maiden speech in the House during this debate. He mocked "vague generalities," like "the horrors of arbitrary power" and "the supremacy of the laws, and the glorious privileges of the writ of habeas corpus." "These things sound very well," he said, but "talk to me not about rules and forms in court, when the enemy's cannon are pointed at the door. . . . I care not whether his proceedings were legal or illegal, constitutional or unconstitutional, with or without precedent, if they were necessary to the salvation of that city."[43]

During the Civil War, Lincoln exercised the sort of power that Whigs had denounced twenty years before. Lincoln himself never lost his commitment to the rule of law; he never conceded that his actions transcended constitutional limitations.[44] But Davis believed that his old friend's course, taken to extremes by more radical Republicans, had put civil liberty itself in jeopardy. In this regard, he had silently agreed with other old Whigs, like former justice Benjamin R. Curtis and Harvard law professor Joel Parker, both of whom went public with their opposition.[45]

Now, having convinced himself that Lincoln would have blessed the effort, Davis intended to write an opinion for the ages. He hoped to do more than merely establish a precedent binding in the courts. Whigs like Davis had believed the courts to be the bulwarks of constitutional liberty, but they had recognized that the opinions of judges carried weight only as long as Americans recognized their authority. Davis would go beyond a formal opinion aimed at judges and lawyers. He would address the American people and restore their commitment to the rule of law.

DAVIS, CONSTITUTIONAL POLITICS, AND CONSTITUTIONAL LAW

In undertaking to write an opinion that would command popular assent, Davis was engaging not only in constitutional law but constitutional politics. To restore what he considered proper deference to the Supreme Court, he would have to convince the American people that its decision was right. He could not have liked the idea that the Court's opinions had to secure public approbation. It implied that Jacksonian Democrats had been correct when they argued that the sovereign people retained final authority to decide how the Constitution applied to public policy. According to Jacksonian jurisprudence, the people, rather than the judges, had the final say. Judges' articulations of constitutional law might carry great weight, but they were not dispositive. To the dismay of many former Whigs, Republicans were no more willing than the Democrats to concede final authority over constitutional interpretation to the Supreme Court. They could not, because the judges, and especially the justices of the Supreme Court, were solidly supportive of the slave regime.

Nowhere was this clearer than in their response to the Court's effort to give that regime the imprimatur of the Constitution in the *Dred Scott* case in 1857. Democrats suddenly argued that all were bound by the decision. Republicans scoffed at the idea. "We shall treat the so-called decision of that Court an utter nullity," expostulated the Republican *Pittsburgh Gazette.* "It is not law, and it has no binding force upon either the people or the government. . . . The Constitution was made *by* the people and *for* the people; and *to* the people, the sovereign power in the confederacy, we appeal from this decision."[46] John A. Bingham, the future author of the Fourteenth Amendment, stated the proposition more carefully: "I recognize the decisions of that tribunal as of binding force only as to the parties and privies to the suit, and the rights particularly involved and passed upon. . . . I deny that the Supreme Court is the final arbiter on all questions of political power, and assert that the final arbiter on all such questions is the people—the people which ordained the Constitution."[47]

Abraham Lincoln, with his deep Whig commitment to the rule of law, had grappled with the problem more painfully than most. Even after the *Dred Scott* decision, he had conceded that the Supreme Court's decisions "when fully settled, should control . . . the general policy of the country, subject to be disturbed only by amendments of the Constitution." But he had come to believe that the Court's decisions "are of greater or less authority as precedents, according to circumstances." Given the context of the decision and its shortcomings, "it is not resistance, it is not factious, it is not even disrespectful, to treat it as not having yet quite established a settled doctrine for the country."[48] By 1861 he had arrived at the conclusion that while Supreme Court decisions bound the parties involved, they were only "entitled to very high respect and consideration . . . by all other departments of the government." He continued, "If the policy of the government, upon vital questions, affecting the whole people, is to be irrevocably fixed by decisions of the Supreme Court, the instant they are made, the people will have ceased to be their own rulers."[49] As Lincoln expert Phillip Shaw Paludan has observed, Lincoln had come to believe that the Constitution "would be defined by many voices, not one."[50]

The old Whig in Davis, in contrast, relished the opportunity the *Milligan* case offered to reassert the primacy of the Supreme Court in constitutional interpretation and to link that primacy to liberty instead of slavery.

THE MILLIGAN *ARGUMENTS*

Davis could draw on some powerful legal arguments as he prepared his opinion. Jeremiah S. Black and David Dudley Field had presented elaborate oral arguments in the *Milligan* case. Reverdy Johnson, the foremost constitutional lawyer in the US Senate and, like Davis, an old Whig, had challenged the jurisdiction of the military commission that tried the Lincoln assassination conspirators. Johnson had been instrumental in saving Maryland for the Union. A slave owner, he had backed the Thirteenth Amendment to end the slavery issue forever. But like other conservatives he had been dismayed by the erosion of civil liberties during the war. Denying the right of the president to establish such commissions, Johnson, like Black and Field, stressed the tradition of opposition to arbitrary executive power that Americans had inherited from their English ancestors. "Hatred of a monarchy . . . and a deep-seated love of constitutional liberty . . . constituted them a people who could never be induced to delegate any executive authority not so carefully restricted and guarded as to render its abuse or usurpation almost impossible," Johnson had intoned.[51]

Young Congressman Garfield, a college professor as well as a lawyer, provided a dry and detailed account of the English and American precedents that subordinated the military department and its tribunals to "definitely prescribed law."[52] One example and citation after another, presented without the florid language that his colleague Jeremiah Black would adopt, provided a thorough description of the English struggle to establish due process of law against arbitrary royal government. He extolled "the progress and development of Anglo-Saxon liberty; its conflicts with irresponsible power; its victories, dearly bought, but always won—victories which have crowned with immortal honors the institutions of England, and left their indelible impress upon the Anglo-Saxon mind."[53] As a Republican, he rejected the

Figure 7.2. David Dudley Field. Courtesy of the Library of Congress.

crabbed view of government power that Lincoln's Democratic critics—including his fellow defense counsel—had often avowed. The Constitution gave the government ample power to crush the rebellion, he argued. Congress had exercised that power by suspending the privilege of the writ of habeas corpus, authorizing the detention of ill-disposed citizens under the Habeas Corpus Act. But the act had explicitly required those arrested to be released if they were not indicted in due time. Congress had passed laws to make dangerous conduct illegal. If the detained merited punishment, let the government try them in civil court for violating those laws.[54]

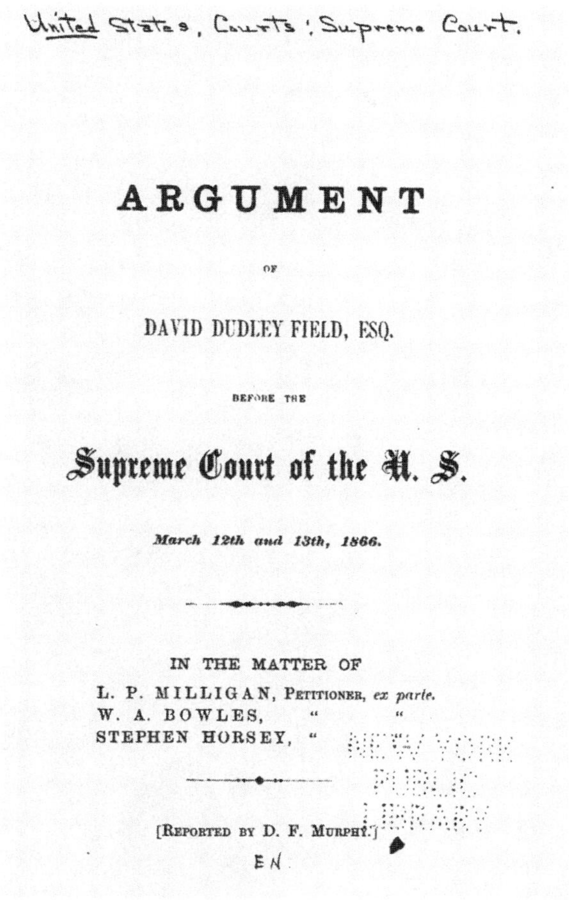
United States, Courts; Supreme Court.

ARGUMENT

OF

DAVID DUDLEY FIELD, ESQ.

BEFORE THE

Supreme Court of the U. S.

March 12th and 13th, 1866.

IN THE MATTER OF
L. P. MILLIGAN, PETITIONER, *ex parte.*
W. A. BOWLES, " "
STEPHEN HORSEY, "

[REPORTED BY D. F. MURPHY.]

EN

Figure 7.3. *Argument of David Dudley Field, Esq. Before the Supreme Court of the U.S.* (New York: W. J. Read, 1866).

Davis's friend Black made an impassioned speech, reflecting all the commitment to civil liberties that Democrats had articulated during the Civil War. "We submit that a person not in the military or naval service, cannot be punished at all until he has had a fair, open public trial before an impartial jury, in an ordained and established court, to which the jurisdiction has been given by law to try him for that specific offense," he said.[55] He was pleading before the Supreme Court. He knew to exalt the judiciary, to appeal to the professional pride of the justices. And he probably believed it. Having gained control of the Supreme Court, by the 1850s many Demo-

Figure 7.4. Jeremiah S. Black. Courtesy of the Library of Congress.

crats developed a new respect for its primacy in determining constitutional questions. President Buchanan had expressed misplaced confidence that all would defer to the Court's *Dred Scott* decision.[56] At the time Black was a close advisor whom Buchanan was preparing to name attorney general. He certainly knew how to appeal to the old Whig in Davis: all knew "that it was the intention of the men who founded this Republic to put the life, liberty, and property of every person in it under the protection of a regular and permanent judiciary, separate, apart, distinct, from all other branches of government," he said—"upright, honest, and sober men, learned in the laws of their country" and "above the clamors of the mere mob."[57] He enlisted the professional jealousy of the common-law justices: Milligan had been convicted by "this strange tribunal, . . . after a proceeding, which it would be mere mockery to call a trial," conducted before officers "unable to comprehend either the law or the facts of a criminal cause."[58] A claim of power to "capture, imprison, and kill" an offender "without the intervention of the judiciary . . . in its very essence, is despotic and lawless."[59] He listed and praised, one by one, all the constitutional protections for those accused of crime. "If these provisions exist in full force, unchangeable and irrepealable, then we are not hereditary bondsmen. . . . They are in force, and they will remain in force. We have not surrendered them, and we never will."[60]

Black converted Jackson's despotic course in New Orleans into a bulwark of judicial supremacy. Out of necessity he had "made his own will for a time the only rule of conduct." But afterward he accepted the decision of the courts that his conduct was illegal, "and he paid the penalty without a murmur," Black pointed out (none too accurately). Congress had refunded the fine, Black admitted, but proponents of the expenditure had admitted his conduct had been illegal.[61] Of course, Davis knew better, but Black's formulation—a repudiation of the actual Democratic argument at the time—must have been gratifying indeed.

Field had followed. Everyone knew that the case had immense political implications, with Milligan's lawyers restating Democratic criticisms of Lincoln's despotism. But an overt attack on the administration might have alienated Davis and other Lincoln appointees, and Field knew it. "I ventured to call myself a personal friend of the late President, and I was happy to believe that he so regarded me," he said. Field had told Lincoln that he was worried about how far "some of his subordinate officers were carrying military power; but this did not diminish my personal regard for him, nor, as I believe, his friendship for me." He praised Lincoln's "great heart, his forgiving spirit," adding, "He is far above any praise or blame of mine."[62] Field lauded even Stanton, praising his "indominatable energy" and "absolute devotion to public service." "After the great President and his minister of finance, the country owes more to the Secretary of War than to any other civilian."[63] Field was laying it on thick, since the "minister of finance" to whom he was referring was now Chief Justice Chase.

The case had nothing to do with the South or the looming issue of Reconstruction, Field continued. "What may or may not be the rightful interference of the military in the States lately in rebellion—to what extent they may go, how long continue, and when and how to cease . . . are not questions in this case," Field assured the justices.[64] He pointed to the presence of Garfield among defense counsel to demonstrate that the case was above politics.[65] Following all those assurances, Field made a careful and masterly argument that the letter and spirit of the Constitution, and the American understanding of the history of liberty, militated against the president being able to establish a military commission of his own volition.[66]

Against this mountain of talent, the government relied on Attorney General James Speed and the bombastic, sarcastic, slash-and-burn debater Benjamin F. Butler, who had utilized military commissions as military governor in New Orleans, including a controversial tribunal that had hanged a rebel sympathizer for tearing down an American flag as the city was being occupied by Union forces.[67] Speed was out of his depth, demonstrating his "utter want of ability as a lawyer," said Justice Samuel F. Miller. He was "one of the feeblest men" to appear before the Court.[68] Butler may have been a better lawyer, but he was the worst possible choice to address the Court on this case. He knew no restraint, delivering a jeremiad in support of untrammeled presidential war power. "After war is originated . . . the whole power of conducting it, as to manner, and as to all the means and appliances . . . is given to the President," he declared. "He is the sole judge of the exigencies, necessities, and duties of the occasion, their extent and duration."[69] He dismissed the provisions of the Bill of Rights as "all peace provisions of the Constitution," which "like all other conventional and legislative laws and enactments, are silent amidst arms, . . . when the safety of the people becomes the supreme law."[70] To confirm his claim, he cited Congress's decision to reimburse the fine Jackson had incurred for his actions in New Orleans, scouting Black's benign account. Jackson's congressional supporters had not acknowledged his culpability but had denied it, insisting that the law of necessity trumped the Constitution. It was "the test case of martial law in this country."[71]

Butler had gone far beyond Halleck and Lieber's argument that military commanders must establish military commissions to punish acts that threatened their forces and violated the laws of war. He did not stress, as Halleck and Lieber had, the nature of the offense. He did not explain why civil courts were incompetent to punish it. He did not challenge Milligan's lawyers' characterization of Milligan as a mere civilian, when in fact the conspirators had acted in communication with and on behalf of the Confederacy. Instead, Butler had backed unconstrained military trials of civilians at commanders' discretion. His argument focused on the location of the commission—on justifying the use of a military commission in Indiana—not on the nature of the crime or whether its perpetrators should be considered Confederate agents rather than civilians, the issue that military lawyers thought definitive. He insisted that Indiana was vulnerable to Confederate attack and that its courts operated only because the military protected them—an argument that was not without some foundation but made in such exaggerated terms that Davis, who knew the Indiana situation well, was bound to disregard it.

Butler's belligerent defense of wide-ranging military commissions was the justification that the people had come to accept during the war, Davis lamented. This was the argument he intended to scotch. He may not himself have thought about whether Milligan was truly a civilian or whether the offense was in fact a military one. The government had not made the issue, and Davis would have found it a distraction from the issue he cared about if they had. He had maneuvered to get the case before the Court to decide whether and when military commissions could try civilians, not to define who were civilians or to parse different kinds of wartime crimes. So while the holding of *Ex parte Milligan* had to do with the precise circumstances in which civilians could be tried by military commissions, the constitutional principle the Court articulated was far broader and more fundamental.

THE MILLIGAN *DECISION*

In April 1866 the justices had all agreed that the military commission that convicted Milligan and the other Indiana conspirators had no legal standing. The president could not authorize a military commission to try a civilian outside the theater of war where the civilian courts were functioning properly. Davis read his opinion in December. Four other justices joined it, enough for a majority, including three appointed by Democratic presidents, and Stephen J. Field, a California Democrat appointed by Lincoln.

Like Milligan's lawyers, Davis chronicled the great English struggle for liberty that had culminated in the American Revolution and the ratification of the Constitution. That heritage could not be chucked away. "The Constitution of the United States is a law for rulers and people, equally in war and in peace, and covers with the shield of its protection all classes of men, at all times, and under all circumstances," he wrote. "No doctrine, involving more pernicious consequences, was ever invented by the wit of man than that any of its provisions can be suspended during any of the great exigencies of government." He blasted the idea propounded by Butler—and by Jackson's defenders more than twenty years earlier—that necessity trumps constitutional limitations. "The theory of necessity . . . is false; for the government, within the Constitution, has all the powers granted to it, which are necessary to preserve its existence; as has been happily proven by the result of the great effort to throw off its just authority."[72] He was not echoing Lincoln's Democratic critics, who had said winning the war was not worth losing liberty. He was echoing Republicans like Garfield and his cousin Henry Winter Davis. A government with broad powers did not need to suspend the Constitution that delegated them.

But his language confused matters. The question in the *Milligan* case was whether Milligan and his coconspirators could be tried by a military commission. Davis listed all the provisions of the Bill of Rights that such a trial violated. But when he turned to the situation in Indiana, he and his colleagues added strictures on the imposition of martial law in general. Martial law was "properly applied" when in an invasion or civil war "the courts are actually closed, and it is impossible to administer criminal justice according to law." If it is "continued after the courts are reinstated, it is a gross usurpation of power," they opined. "Martial rule can never exist where the courts are open, and in the proper and unobstructed exercise of their jurisdiction."[73] Davis seemed unable to distinguish martial law from military commissions. If the ordinary courts were open and able to enforce the law, neither the president nor Congress could authorize military commissions or, it seemed, martial law. As Davis put it, "Martial rule can never exist where the courts are open and in the proper and unobstructed exercise of their jurisdiction. It is also confined to the locality of actual war. Because, during the late Rebellion, it could have been enforced in Virginia, where the national authority was overturned and the courts driven out, it does not follow that it should obtain in Indiana, where that authority was never disputed and justice was always administered."[74]

Davis would not weaken his argument by acknowledging that national authority *had* been disputed in Indiana. The Milligan conspiracy had been serious. Davis's circuit court colleague McDonald, not yet appointed to the bench at the time, had been terrified. "We now seem in great danger of civil war in Indiana," he had recorded in his journal. "May God avert it!" A few days later: "The cloud of civil war that threatens the state grows darker." If the disaffected are arrested, "I think war will follow." A week later, McDonald wrote, "It seems that what is called the Democracy seriously, desperately meditate a general uprising. What shall be the end can only be conjectured."[75]

Whether he intended it or not, Davis's opinion said nearly everything the Democratic lawyers had wanted. Black was ecstatic. "The court has saved us from nothing less than the total overthrow of our free institutions," he told fellow Democrats. The opinion "will be a guide and a landmark for all future time and identify its author forever with the sacred cause of constitutional liberty." It gave Davis "a position to which no earthly station can add any dignity."[76]

Chief Justice Salmon P. Chase filed a separate opinion, joined by three other justices, all but one Lincoln appointees. To Davis's surprise, the reservations they had expressed about the majority's reasoning in conference proved to be substantial. They did agree that Milligan must be discharged. Milligan's trial by military commission was unauthorized on the grounds Garfield had stressed: it was inconsistent with the terms of the Habeas Corpus Act of 1863. That law said that detainees must be released if not indicted by the end of the term of the next circuit court. The provisions of the act "obviously contemplate no other trial or sentence than that of a civil court," Chase observed.[77] But Chase and his colleagues rejected the idea that the president and Congress were precluded from authorizing military commissions wherever the civil courts were open and unobstructed in their operation.

The dissenters[78] did not address whether Lincoln might have had inherent power to establish the *Milligan* commission in the absence of congressional legislation. It did not matter. The Court could not uphold the conviction "without disregarding the plain directions of Congress."[79] But, the dissenters added, Congress could have authorized the military commissions had it wanted to. "When the nation is involved in war, and some portions of the country are invaded, and all are exposed to invasion, it is within the power of Congress to determine in what states or districts such great and imminent public danger exists as justifies the authorization of military tribunals for the trial of crimes and offences against the discipline or security of the army or against the public safety."[80]

Davis complained privately that he had been blindsided. Had he known that the disagreement was on the issue of Congress's power, he would have addressed that question more directly.[81] Clearly, over the summer Chase and the others in the minority had contemplated the implications of the decision for Reconstruction, a consideration Davis had avoided. Did Davis's opinion preclude military commissions in the South, where President Johnson had declared peace was restored, with civil governments and local courts reestablished, and where the federal courts were now open? He had acknowledged that there was "a necessity to furnish a substitute for civil authority" in a civil war, where the legally constituted courts were "actually closed." But he had added that language indicating that it was "a gross usurpation of power" to continue martial law after the courts are reinstated.[82] Chase and his confreres did not want to leave any doubt that Congress could authorize military commissions in the South as part of Reconstruction if it thought necessary. Chase's opinion carefully distinguished *martial law* in the loyal states from *military government* in the former Confederacy. The *Milligan* decision pertained to the former and not to the latter. He made clear that Congress could authorize military commissions as part of both martial law and military government, but he did not want Americans to conflate the two—to judge what was appropriate in the South by what was appropriate in the North.[83]

Despite the intention of Davis and the other justices in the majority, it is unclear what *Milligan* held as a matter of law. The actual case before the Court involved a conviction by a military commission authorized by the president on his own authority. All the justices had agreed that such a trial was unconstitutional. The majority had gone further, saying that Congress could not have authorized such a tribunal either. But was that part of the legal holding, or was it merely *obiter dictum*—a "further word"—that detailed what the Court *would* hold if the circumstances arose but not part of the holding itself?

Davis considered the reasoning all of a piece. The majority had held presidentially authorized military commissions unconstitutional where civil courts were open because the due-process provisions of the Constitution were "irrepealable," he wrote Rockwell. "Did it not logically follow that

Congress could not repeal" them either, he asked. "How can a provision be irrepealable, & yet Congress repeal it, disregard it, or suspend it?"[84] The general reasoning of the opinion was the important thing, not the specific facts. Americans had to return to their constitutional commitments.

Davis was proud of what he had done. He had reminded Americans of their heritage of civil liberty. He had positioned the Supreme Court to be the great defender of that heritage. Previously, the Court had treated the Constitution as the culmination of efforts to forge a stronger union. The Court's primary job was to police the boundaries between state and federal power and to decide whether state legislation violated express constitutional limitations. The Court explicitly denied that the Bill of Rights was among those limitations.[85] Only three times had the justices even considered whether a congressional enactment might have violated the Bill of Rights. On two of those occasions they had dismissed the objection with hardly a thought.[86] On the third—the *Dred Scott* decision—they had defended the due-process rights of slaveholders! So Davis was pioneering new ground in *Milligan,* making constitutional liberty, not federalism, the touchstone of the Constitution. In doing so, he hoped that he had restored the Court's prestige, so tarnished by its subservience to slavery. He would be devastatingly disappointed.

NOTES

1. Habeas Corpus Act of 1863, *US Statutes at Large* 12: 755 (March 3, 1863).

2. David Glazier, "Precedents Lost: The Neglected History of the Military Commission," *Virginia Journal of International Law* 46 (Fall 2005): 5–82.

3. *Digest of Opinions of the Judge Advocate General of the Army* (Washington, DC: Government Printing Office, 1865), 76; S. V. Bent, *A Treatise on Military Law and the Practice of Courts-Martial,* 5th ed. (New York: D. Van Nostrand, 1868), 204.

4. William Winthrop, *Military Law,* 2 vols. (Washington, DC: W. H. Morrison, 1886), 2: 74–75.

5. Henry W. Halleck, *International Law, or Rules Regulating the Intercourse of States in Peace and War* (New York: D. Van Nostrand, 1861).

6. Adjutant General's Office, *Instructions for the Government of Armies of the United States in the Field, General Orders No. 100* (Washington, DC: Government Printing Office, 1898).

7. Louis Fisher, *Military Tribunals and Presidential Power: American Revolution to the War on Terrorism* (Lawrence: University Press of Kansas, 2005), 50–51.

8. Michael Les Benedict, "Lincoln and Constitutional Politics," *Marquette Law Review* 93 (Summer 2010): 1335–1366.

9. William Winthrop, *Military Law and Precedents* (Washington, DC: Government Printing Office, 1920), 838–841; Mark E. Neely Jr., *The Fate of Liberty: Abraham Lincoln and Civil Liberties* (New York: Oxford University Press, 1991), 40–50, 160–175.

10. The best account is Neely's *Fate of Liberty.*

11. After the war, Davis wrote Lincoln's law partner and biographer William Herndon that "Mr. Lincoln was advised as Presdt that the various military trials in the Northern States . . . were unconstitutional and wrong" and would be overturned by the Supreme Court. It seems likely that he was one of those doing the advising. Douglas L. Wilson and Rodney O. Davis, eds., *Herndon's Informants: Letters, Interviews, and Statements about Abraham Lincoln* (Urbana: University of Illinois Press, 1998), 348–349.

12. Peter J. Barry, "'I'll Keep Them in Prison Awhile . . .': Abraham Lincoln and David Davis on Civil Liberties in Wartime," *Journal of the Abraham Lincoln Association* 28 (Winter 2007): 28.

13. Barry, "'I'll Keep Them in Prison Awhile."

14. Wilson and Davis, *Herndon's Informants,* 348–349.

15. Proclamation, September 24, 1862, in James D. Richardson, ed., *A Compilation of the Messages and Papers of the Presidents,* 20 vols. (New York: Bureau of National Literature, 1897), 7: 3299–3300.

16. Lincoln, "Letter to Erastus Corning and Others, in Roy P. Basler et al., eds., *The Collected Works of Abraham Lincoln* (New Brunswick, NJ: Rutgers University Press, 1953), 6: 260–270; Lincoln, "Letter to Matthew Birchard and Others," in Basler et al., *Collected Works of Abraham Lincoln,* 6: 300–307.

17. Stephen Towne, "Civil or Military Courts? The Decision to Use Military Commissions to Try the Indiana Conspirators in 1865" (paper presented at the conference "*Ex parte Milligan* at 150" at Illinois State University, September 2016, now chapter 6).

18. John Moreland, "David Davis: Jurist and Civil Libertarian" (paper presented at the conference "*Ex parte Milligan* at 150").

19. *Congressional Globe,* 38th Cong., 2nd Sess., 1324 (March 2, 1865).

20. *Congressional Globe,* 38th Cong., 2nd Sess., 1327.

21. *Ex parte Vallandigham,* 68 US (1 Wall.) 243 (1864). For an explanation of the jurisdiction issue, see Charles A. Fairman, *Reconstruction and Reunion, 1864–88: Part One* (New York: Macmillan, 1971), 193n, 491n.

22. *Ex parte Milligan,* 71 US (4 Wall.) 2 at 109 (1866).

23. Davis to Julius Rockwell, February 24, 1867, Davis Mss., Library of Congress. Fairman published the letter in *Reconstruction and Reunion,* 232–233.

24. Stephen E. Towne, "The Persistent Nullifier: The Life of Civil War Conspirator Lambdin P. Millign," *Indiana Magazine of History* 109 (December 2013): 303–354. Towne corrects for accounts that minimize the seriousness of the conspiracies rife

in the lower Midwest during the war. See also Jennifer L. Weber, *Copperheads: The Rise and Fall of Lincoln's Opponents in the North* (New York: Oxford University Press, 2006). For the older, more skeptical version see Frank L. Klement, "The Indianapolis Treason Trials and *Ex parte Milligan*," in Michal Belknap, ed., *American Political Trials*, rev. ed. (Westport, CT: Greenwood Press, 1994), 97–118.

25. Donald O. Dewey, ed., "Hoosier Justice: The Journal of David McDonald, 1864–1868," *Indiana Magazine of History* 62 (September 1966): 203–204 (May 9, 11, 1865).

26. Dewey, "Hoosier Justice," 204 (May 12, 1865).

27. Black was a regular guest at Davis's home. Davis's wife, Sarah, noted that Black "stays late but [is] the pleasantest talker I know of." Sarah W. Davis to [George Davies?], January 28, 1866. Davis Mss., Illinois State Library.

28. Quoted in Willard King, *Lincoln's Manager, David Davis* (Cambridge, MA: Harvard University Press, 1960), 245.

29. Davis to Rockwell, March 11, 1866, Davis Mss., Library of Congress.

30. Davis to Rockwell, August 9, 1866, Davis Mss., Library of Congress.

31. Willard King, *Lincoln's Manager, David Davis* (Cambridge, MA: Harvard University Press, 1960), 99.

32. Davis to Rockwell, August 9, 1866, Davis Mss., Library of Congress.

33. For conservative Whig commitment to the rule of law, see Daniel Walker Howe, *The Political Culture of the American Whigs* (Chicago: University of Chicago Press, 1979), 268–271. See also his discussion of Whig values in general, 23–42. See also Mark E. Steiner, *An Honest Calling: The Law Practice of Abraham Lincoln* (DeKalb: Northern Illinois University Press, 2006), 55–63, 131–136, and Steiner, "Does Lawyer Lincoln Matter?" in Roger Billings and Frank J. Williams, eds., *Abraham Lincoln, Esq.: The Legal Career of America's Greatest President* (Lexington: University Press of Kentucky, 2010), 45–64.

34. *Washington National Intelligencer*, December 22, 1866, 2.

35. "The Perpetuation of Our Political Institutions: Address before the Young Men's Lyceum of Springfield, Illinois, January 27, 1838," in Basler et al., *Collected Works of Abraham Lincoln*, 1: 108–115.

36. *Worcester v. Georgia*, 31 US (6 Peters) 515 (1832). For the controversy, see Jill Norgren, *The Cherokee Cases: The Confrontation of Law and Politics* (New York: McGraw-Hill, 1996).

37. *McCulloch v. Maryland*, 17 US (4 Wheat.) 316 (1819).

38. See Robert V. Remini, *Andrew Jackson and the Bank War: A Study in the Growth of Presidential Power* (New York: W. W. Norton, 1967).

39. "Speech in the Illinois Legislature Concerning the State Bank," in Remini, *Andrew Jackson and the Bank War*, 67.

40. King, *Lincoln's Manager, David Davis*, 41.

41. Matthew Warshauer, *Andrew Jackson and the Politics of Martial Law* (Knoxville: University of Tennessee Press, 2006), 81.

42. Senator Robert Walker, *Congressional Globe*, 27th Cong., 3rd Sess., 141 (January 10, 1844).

43. *Congressional Globe,* 27th Cong., 3rd Sess., appendix, 43–44 (January 6, 1844).

44. Herman Belz, "Lincoln and the Constitution: The Dictatorship Question Reconsidered," *Congress and the Presidency* 15, no. 2 (1988): 147–164; Michael Les Benedict, "'The Perpetuation of Our Political Institutions': Lincoln, the Power of the Commander in Chief, and the Constitution," *Cardozo Law Review* 29 (January 2008): 927–960; Allen C. Guelzo, *Lincoln's Emancipation Proclamation: The End of Slavery in America* (New York: Simon & Schuster, 2004); Philip Shaw Paludan, *The Presidency of Abraham Lincoln* (Lawrence: University Press of Kansas, 1994); William Michael Treanor, "Learning from Lincoln," *Fordham Law Review* 65 (March 1997): 1781–1786. There is a large political science literature that sees Lincoln as a benign dictator who acted beyond the Constitution. For an overview, see Philip Shaw Paludan, "'Dictator Lincoln': Surveying Lincoln and the Constitution," *OAH Magazine of History* 21 (January 2007): 8–13.

45. Joel Parker, *War Powers of Congress and the President* (Cambridge, MA: H. O. Houghton, 1863); Benjamin R. Curtis, *Executive Power* (Boston: Little, Brown, 1862). See Stuart Streichler, *Justice Curtis in the Civil War Era: At the Crossroads of American Constitutionalism* (Charlottesville: University of Virginia Press, 2005).

46. *Daily Pittsburgh Gazette,* March 8, 1857, 2.

47. *Congressional Globe,* 36th Cong., 1st Sess., 1837 (April 24, 1860).

48. Lincoln, Speech at Springfield, Illinois, June 26, 1857, in Basler et al., *Collected Works of Abraham Lincoln,* 2: 401.

49. Lincoln, First Inaugural Address—Final Text (March 4, 1861), in Basler et al., *Collected Works of Abraham Lincoln,*4: 262, 268.

50. Phillip Shaw Paludan, "Taney, Lincoln, and the Constitutional Conversation," in Jennifer M. Lowe, ed., *The Supreme Court and the Civil War* (Washington, DC: Supreme Court Historical Society, 1996), 29. See Michael Les Benedict, "Lincoln and Constitutional Politics," *Marquette Law Review* 93 (Summer 2010): 1333–1366.

51. Reverdy Johnson, Defense of Mary E. Suratt, in John D. Lawson, ed., *American State Trials: A Collection of the Important and Interesting Criminal Trials Which Have Taken Place in the United States from the Beginning of our Government to the Present Day,* 17 vols. (St. Louis: Thomas Law Books, 1914–1936), 8: 249.

52. "Argument of James Abram Garfield for the Petitioner," in Samuel Klaus, ed., *The Milligan Case* (New York: Knopf, 1929), 93–120 (quoted at 95). The complete arguments were published as pamphlets and are reprinted in this collection. Abbreviated versions were published in the official report of the case.

53. Klaus, *The Milligan Case,* 112.

54. Klaus, 114–118.

55. *Argument of Jeremiah S. Black for the Petitioner,* in Klaus, 124.

56. James Buchanan, Inaugural Address, in Richardson, *A Compilation of the Messages and Papers of the Presidents,* 6: 2962.

57. Argument of Jeremiah S. Black for the Petitioner, in Klaus, *The Milligan Case,* 125–126.

58. Klaus, 122.

59. Klaus, 143.

60. Klaus, 130.

61. Klaus, 136.

62. *Argument of David Dudley Field for the Petitioner,* in Klaus, *The Milligan Case,* 149.

63. Klaus, 149.

64. Klaus, 148

65. Klaus, 149.

66. Klaus, 148–208.

67. Alan G. Gauthreaux, "The Beast Turned Loose in New Orleans," *America's Civil War* 25 (May 2012): 30–35; Hans L. Trefousse, *Benjamin F. Butler—The South Called Him Beast!* (New York: Twayne, 1957), 114–116.

68. Charles Fairman, *Mr. Justice Miller and the Supreme Court, 1862–1890* (Cambridge, MA: Harvard University Press, 1939), 118.

69. "Argument . . . on the Side of the United States, in *Ex parte Milligan,*" in Klaus, *The Milligan Case,* 90.

70. Klaus, 91.

71. Klaus, 215–216.

72. *Ex parte Milligan,* at 209.

73. *Ex parte Milligan,* at 127.

74. *Ex parte Milligan,* at 127.

75. Dewey, "Hoosier Justice: The Journal of David McDonald," 186 (August 15, 1864), 187 (August 17, August 22 to 28, 1864). Neither Davis nor McDonald believed that the actual threat was relevant. In their view, the government could have arrested the conspirators and held them until the courts were able to deal with them.

76. *Washington National Intelligencer,* January 10, 1867, 3.

77. *Ex parte Milligan,* at 136.

78. Chase and three other justices concurred in the result but dissented from the majority's reasoning. The report of the case simply reported "The CHIEF JUSTICE delivered the following opinion," without characterizing it further.

79. *Ex parte Milligan,* 136.

80. *Ex parte Milligan,* 140.

81. Davis to Rockwell, Feb. 24, 1867, Davis Mss., Library of Congress.

82. *Ex parte Milligan,* at 127.

83. *Ex parte Milligan,* at 141–142.

84. Davis to Rockwell, February 24, 1867, Davis Mss., Library of Congress.

85. *Barron v. Baltimore,* 32 US (7 Pet.) 243 (1833).

86. *Parsons v. Bedford,* 28 US (3 Pet.) 433 (1830); *Murray v. Hoboken Land & Improvement Co.,* 59 US (18 How.) 272 (1855).

CHAPTER 8

To Leave Behind the Law of Force: Salmon Chase and the Civil War Era

MICHAEL HAGGERTY

On May 31, 1866, Supreme Court Justice Salmon P. Chase wrote to his friend and former congressman Gerrit Smith about the prospect of peace. In his letter to Smith, Chase acknowledged, "I have not been able to regard peace as fully reestablished." He argued that peace would not arrive until Southern states were restored to the Union "with substantial security in each state for the safety & security of all its inhabitants & especially of that portion whose freedom the nation, during the war as a war measure, pledged itself to maintain." In this letter, Chase asserted that the safety and security of the South's newly emancipated population would be part of any meaningful peace. Achieving peace on these terms, however, would prove to be an enduring challenge. More than a year after Robert E. Lee surrendered at the Appomattox Court House, peace still eluded the United States.[1]

In the spring of 1866, the federal government continued to utilize war powers in an effort to establish effective civil rights and protect newly emancipated people. In his effort to win the Civil War, Abraham Lincoln suspended habeas corpus, closed newspapers, and instituted military commissions to try civilians. Across the South, the US Army swept aside local officials while military officers named and introduced new ones. In 1865 the bill creating the Freedmen's Bureau allowed military officers to take charge of criminal and civil cases involving newly freed people. In order to secure victory and extend liberty to the nation's formerly enslaved population, the country suspended its traditional commitment to the civil liberties of white Southerners and their Northern allies. After formal military engagements ceased, however, Southerners returned home from war and sought control over regional legal systems along with the reestablishment of their rights.

In the weeks before Chase wrote to Smith about the prospect of peace, Confederate soldiers returned home, joined local police departments, and ran for office in their local communities. In Memphis, Tennessee, Confederate veterans joined the local police department and carried out a massacre of the city's black community. A few months later, another massacre would be carried out against the freed men and women of New Orleans. As the nation came to terms with the end of the Civil War, this continued threat of violence presented the country with a legal and political dilemma. Once white Southerners gained control over regional legal systems, these systems could not be trusted to safeguard the rights and security of newly emancipated people. The federal government could extend liberty to freed people or it could relinquish legal power to former rebels, but it could not do both. In the context of this dilemma, the Supreme Court of the United States freed a Copperhead named Lambdin Milligan and set off a national debate about the future of Reconstruction and the end of the Civil War. Although *Ex parte Milligan* has often been interpreted as a postwar decision that reigned in the wartime extension of federal power, it is better understood as part of a larger violent struggle for freedom that extended beyond the boundaries of a formal military conflict. Examining Chase's role in this struggle forces a reevaluation of his concurrent opinion and highlights his continued support for federal power as a means of securing the liberty of formerly enslaved people.[2]

In the spring of 1866 the Supreme Court determined that the military had violated Lambdin Milligan's right to due process. A military commission convicted Milligan of conspiracy against the US government and inciting insurrection. The Supreme Court, however, decided that because Milligan had been convicted in Indiana, a region where civilian courts were operating and remained unobstructed during the war, he was entitled to a trial carried out by civil authorities, not a military tribunal. The Court's decision threw into question the future of Reconstruction and sparked a national debate about the federal government's use of force during the war. Southern editors and Northern newspapers that were sympathetic to the South used the decision to criticize the "arbitrary arrest[s]" that had been carried out during the conflict. These papers applauded the Supreme Court, claiming that "the Democracy of the nation has now been vindicated." In turn, many Northern newspapers vilified the Court's decision, arguing that *Ex parte Milligan* threatened to undermine every conviction carried out during the war. The *New York Herald* claimed that this decision had "spurred a movement" for the release of the men who conspired to assassinate President

Lincoln, while the editors of the *Chicago Tribune* worried that more decisions might soon emanate from the Court, striking down other federal war measures, including "the Freedmen's Bureau and Civil Rights bills, together with all the legislation of Congress since the close of the war." Indeed, continued the paper, "our Washington correspondent telegraphs us that Secretary [of War Edwin M.] Stanton holds that the decision already rendered in the Milligan case 'overthrows the Freedmen's Bureau, and renders the army utterly powerless in the South,'" thus "turn[ing] the negroes over to the tender mercies of the rebel legislatures and courts in the South." If this proved true, the editors concluded, "it will be necessary for Congress to devise other methods for their protection. There is certainly power under the Constitution to maintain the freedom of the blacks and protect them from the discriminating and oppressive laws by which it is sought to re-enslave them."[3]

Even the Supreme Court itself was divided over the implications of its own decision. Although the justices unanimously agreed that Lambdin Milligan should be released, Chief Justice Salmon Chase and three other justices filed a separate concurrence that differed on one key point with David Davis's Opinion of the Court. Davis maintained that Congress could not authorize the use of military tribunals to try civilians, while Chase argued that it could. Moreover, whereas Davis believed that the need for military protections had come to an end, Chase left open the possibility that civil courts could be "wholly incompetent" in the South and would therefore need military oversight. Davis stated that during the war, "considerations of safety were mingled with the exercise of power." However, he noted, "now that the public safety is assured" the Court was free to consider terminating the military's exercise of power. This was the key point of contention between the two justices. While Davis believed that public safety was secure in 1866, Chase did not.[4]

This chapter reframes *Ex parte Milligan,* taking it out of the context of postwar Washington, DC, or Indiana, and placing it within the context of a continuous legal struggle between slavery and freedom. During the Civil War era, the suspension of civil liberties was not just a characteristic of war but also a catalyst for violence in antebellum Ohio. In the borderlands between slavery and freedom, violent force was common, as state and federal officials continued to ignore the civil liberties of fugitive slaves. In this environment, Chase began to defend the use of force as a means of securing liberty. Over the course of his legal career, Chase defended fugitive slaves

Figure 8.1. Chief Justice Salmon P. Chase. Courtesy of the Library of Congress.

in antebellum Cincinnati and criticized police brutally in postbellum New Orleans. For Chase, individual rights were tangible forces that could be marshalled in order to protect the liberties of a formerly enslaved people. Ultimately, Chase fought for the enforcement of an egalitarian legal standard where constitutional rights were extended to all people, regardless of race or status.

During the Civil War era, the federal government's relationship with slavery changed dramatically. Prior to the war, enslaved people often crossed state boundaries in their search for freedom. In turn, Northern communities faced a dilemma. With only one federal judge in each judicial district, the enforcement of fugitive slave law was often dependent on local officials who operated in decidedly free spaces. Throughout the 1830s and 1840s, these officials denied black people due process and re-enslaved them under the federal Fugitive Slave Act of 1793. In response, Salmon Chase and other antislavery activists fought to extend constitutional protections to fugitive slaves. In the postwar period, however, former antislavery activists faced a different problem. Federal interference was needed, as Southern officials continued to deny the political and legal rights of black people. In the antebellum period, the denial of legal rights was rooted in federal authority. In the postbellum period, however, this authority was crucial for extending legal rights to the South's newly freed population. Federalism had changed, but Chase's opposition to slavery and his support for extending constitutional protections to black people had not. When Chase authored his concurrence and affirmed the "inestimable value" of the "constitutional safeguards of civil liberty," he did so on the condition that Congress could authorize military tribunals during times of "war or public danger." Chase conceptualized the public as an inclusive body that included the nation's formerly enslaved population. Therefore, he deemed that the use of military tribunals was constitutional if expressly approved by Congress.[5]

Historians have addressed *Ex parte Milligan* from different perspectives, often incorporating it into a broader history of Reconstruction. Some revere the Court's decision and focus on its affirmation of due process. In his magisterial history of the Supreme Court, Charles Warren noted that this decision was considered one of the "bulwarks of American liberty," protecting citizens from an overzealous federal government. Historian William Dunning claimed that the decision was evidence of the Court's disdain for a radical Congress that sought to oppress the American South. These interpretations were predicated upon the assumption that Radical Reconstruction was an unnecessary and intrusive violation of state and individual rights. In recent years, however, historians have acknowledged the role of the federal government in securing freedom during the Civil War era. Over the past half century, historians have criticized Dunning and his contemporaries for marginalizing the government's role in securing freedom for newly emancipated people. James M. McPherson and Eric Foner have argued that the Civil War marked a revolutionary moment, when regional legal systems steeped in racism and bigotry were overwhelmed by federal authority. The federal government became a guarantor of liberty through the Freedmen's Bureau and the occupation of the American South. This revolution was short lived, but for a brief moment it appeared as though federal force might secure freedom for millions of people.[6]

However divergent interpretations of Reconstruction may be, most are predicated on the assumption that by the spring of 1866 the war was over and questions of peace were at hand. As a result, historians often interpret *Ex parte Milligan* within the context of a postwar period. In the spring of 1866, however, Chief Justice Salmon Chase understood that peace had not yet arrived. As Congress and the Supreme Court struggled for authority in Washington, DC, the US military continued to occupy the American South. In recent years, historians have reimagined the Civil War era as a period defined less by blanket state authority and more as a consistent struggle over police power, waged between local actors and state officials. This framework extends across the mid-nineteenth century, from antebellum communities on the American frontier to Southern cities resisting military occupation in the years after Robert E. Lee's surrender. In these regions, force was a necessity precisely because laws were often disregarded or disputed. It was in this contested space, a space between slavery and freedom, that Chase sought to secure constitutional protections for all people.[7]

Chase is often written off as a politician with national ambitions, but his jurisprudence is best understood not as a product of Washington, DC, but of the borderlands of freedom along the Ohio River. Cincinnati, Ohio, located on the Ohio River, grew rapidly during the first half of the nineteenth century. The city's expanding economy provided ample opportunities for a variety of diverse peoples. Therefore, it is not surprising that Chase chose the city as the location to begin his legal career. Although Chase was born in New England, he spent much of his early childhood on the Ohio frontier. Faced with raising ten children, Chase's mother sent him to Ohio at a young age to live with his uncle, Philander Chase. As a child, he excelled in school, attending Cincinnati College before returning to New England and enrolling at Dartmouth. After studying law in Washington under US Attorney General William Wirt, Chase returned to Ohio in 1830. As Chase received his first clients, Cincinnati was evolving into a burgeoning frontier metropolis. While German and Irish migrants from the Northeast sought jobs and land ownership, black men and women escaping slavery sought freedom on Cin-

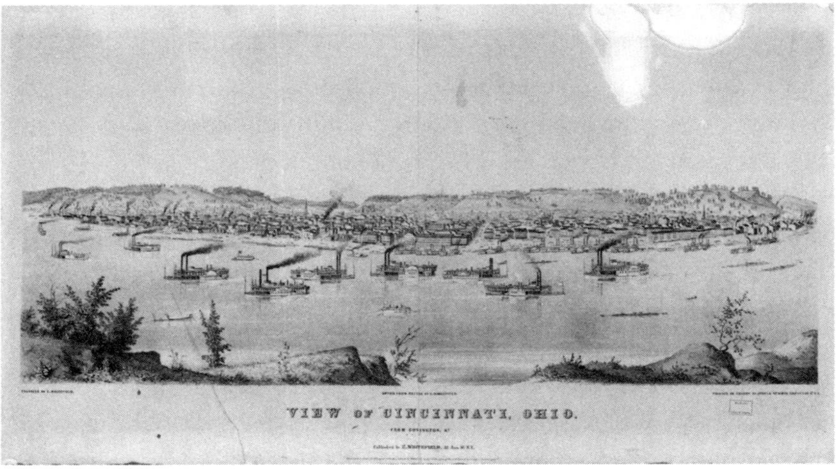

Figure 8.2. "View of Cincinnati, Ohio." In this nineteenth-century depiction of Cincinnati's cityscape, Edwin Whitefield presents a view of the city from the Ohio River's southern shore. Enslaved people standing in the slave state of Kentucky could look across the Ohio River and see the growth of America's urban frontier in the free state of Ohio. Courtesy of the Library of Congress.

cinnati's streets. By 1850 the city contained roughly 100,000 people, making it a cornerstone of America's urban frontier. By the mid-nineteenth century, it had the largest black population of any community in the Old Northwest. This population, however, faced a daily struggle in a region that was socially and economically tethered to the American South.[8]

Because of Cincinnati's dependence on Southern consumers, members of the city's merchant class went to great lengths to ensure that legal force protected the property of Southern clients. On the streets of Cincinnati, this meant the kidnapping of African Americans and the enforcement of slavery through the application of both state and federal law. Merchants in Cincinnati depended heavily on supplying Southern slave owners with food and goods for their enslaved workforce. By the 1840s, city workers annually packed half a million hogs onto river boats, many of which were sent down river to feed the South's enslaved population. The framers of Ohio's constitution prohibited slavery in the state, keeping the region in line with the Northwest Ordinance of 1787. Throughout the nineteenth century, however, the state assembly passed laws restricting the movement and political activities of black people. State law barred them from serving in the military and required them to register their families with a local clerk's office. In 1807 state officials even passed a law requiring black migrants who entered the state to post bond as a means of ensuring good behavior. Despite these laws, however, enslaved people continued to break free from bondage and take their chances in Ohio's urban frontier.[9]

Like many white antislavery activists, Chase accepted the legal consensus that acknowledged limitations on the federal government's ability to bar slavery throughout the Union. He believed that the federal government could not interfere with slavery in states that expressly protected the institution. Chase's early legal career, however, was shaped less by federal intervention in slave states and more by federal intervention within the free state of Ohio. Even as a growing number of people argued for freedom as America's national standard, kidnappers continued to re-enslave black men and women in decidedly free territories. In turn, Chase utilized the Constitution as a means of aiding fugitive slaves who escaped across the Ohio River. Aiding these fugitives was the basis of his constitutional approach to antislavery politics. Throughout the 1830s and 1840s, Chase maintained that slavery was only legal as a result of positive, local law. Ultimately, he used this position as a means of affirming the personhood of slaves and their rights to due process.[10]

In April 1842, John Van Zandt came across nine escaped slaves walking in the road while he traveled north of Cincinnati. He offered these travelers safe passage on their journey and hid them in his wagon. However, two white men named Hargraves and Hefferman soon stopped the group. These men threatened Van Zandt and loaded seven of his companions into a wagon while two fugitives escaped into the woods. Hargraves and Hefferman detained seven people without any knowledge of who they legally belonged to, whether or not they were, in fact, fugitives, and without any kind of legal proceeding. Their victims were transported to a jail cell in Covington, Kentucky, where local officials rewarded Hargraves and Hefferman with $450. Initially, a local jury found Van Zandt guilty of aiding fugitives and fined him. Van Zandt, however, continued to proclaim his innocence and denied any knowledge of the fugitive statuses of his companions. He appealed his case all the way to the US Supreme Court, providing Salmon Chase with an opportunity to fight slavery at the highest judicial level.[11]

When Chase submitted his argument in defense of Van Zandt, he went beyond questions of state's rights and challenged the constitutionality of the Fugitive Slave Act of 1793 on the basis that the law denied enslaved people due process under the Fifth Amendment. Chase maintained that slavery was a product of local law and tied the significance of this claim to the personhood of slaves. "The very moment a slave passes beyond the jurisdiction of the state, in which he is held as such, he ceases to be a slave," he argued, "not because any law or regulation of the state confers freedom upon him, but because he continues to be a man and leaves behind him the law of force." According to Chase, slavery had to be a product of state law because slavery was not a person's natural state. Slavery required the force of law; personhood did not.[12]

Furthermore, Chase argued that the Constitution acknowledged the personhood of slaves and protected their natural rights. He maintained that the federal enforcement of slavery contrasted directly with the Constitution, which acknowledged the personhood of slaves as part of Article IV, Section 2, which opens, "No person held to service or labor in one state. . . . " Chase highlighted the use of the word *person* and argued, "Under the Constitution, all inhabitants of the United States are, without exception, persons—persons, it may be, not free, persons, held to service—persons who may migrate or be imported, but still persons." The Constitution expressly acknowledged the existence of persons, not slaves. Chase argued that if slaves were persons who could be re-enslaved under Article IV, Section 2, then they were also persons entitled to all the other rights guaranteed to them by the Constitution, including due process of law.[13]

After establishing the personhood of enslaved people, Chase focused on how the Fugitive Slave Act of 1793 violated the Fifth Amendment of the Constitution. This amendment granted that "No person shall . . . be deprived of life, liberty, or property without due process of law." Chase argued that the Fugitive Slave Act of 1793 was unconstitutional because it authorized the seizure and confinement of individuals "without legal process." The Fifth Amendment guaranteed all persons, including enslaved people, a right to this legal process. He concluded, "unless it can be shew[n] that no process of law, at all, is the same thing as due process of law, it must be admitted that the act which authorizes seizure without process, is repugnant to a constitution that expressly forbids it." Nevertheless, the Supreme Court rejected Chase's argument, maintaining that the federal government had a responsibility to protect slavery. The Court determined that a federal commitment to slavery was an integral part of the nation's founding. If not for this commitment, Southern states might never have joined the Union. For the individuals who were kidnapped north of Cincinnati, this decision was irrelevant. By the time Chase presented his argument to the Supreme Court, they had already been re-enslaved in Kentucky. The law of force that protected slavery had come before the rights of fugitive slaves.[14]

Three years later, Congress affirmed the Supreme Court's *Jones v. Van Zandt* decision when it extended the federal government's role in safeguarding slavery through the Fugitive Slave Act of 1850. The law of force that underwrote slavery now had unprecedented reach into free territories. This new law authorized federal commissioners, judicial officials who were appointed by US circuit court judges, to oversee the return of fugitive slaves. Jury trials in a local court were no longer permitted, and the decision of a federal commissioner was final and not subject to appeal. In addition, the law allowed for federal commissioners to organize a "posse comitatus" if local law enforcement proved unwilling to assist in the detainment of suspected fugitives. As the nation edged closer to war, this extension of federal force would have dire consequences on the streets of Cincinnati.[15]

On the morning of January 28, 1856, Margaret Garner killed her own daughter so that she would not be kidnapped by federal marshals and returned to slavery. The night before, Garner and her husband, along with his parents and four children, had smuggled themselves across the frozen Ohio River. Once they reached the river's northern shore, they took refuge with relatives in Cincinnati. Unfortunately, the owners of the Garner family quickly discovered their escape and tracked the family into the city. A posse of kidnappers began searching throughout Cincinnati's black community. After kidnappers cornered her family, Garner proclaimed that her children would not be taken back to Kentucky as she slit the throat of her two-year-old daughter.

While newspapers across the country sensationalized Garner's crime, her case created a political firestorm over legal jurisdictions in the Queen City. The primary legal dilemma was whether Garner was to be re-enslaved by federal officials or tried for murder in a state court. Despite the abuse and torment that motivated her actions, Garner's kidnappers insisted that she be returned to Kentucky as a fugitive slave. In turn, her defense attorney argued that she should be detained and tried for murder within the city limits. Chase, serving as governor of Ohio during the trial, was incredulous when federal officials had Garner and her family removed from the custody of a

Figure 8.3. "The Story of Margaret Garner." Thomas Noble's 1867 painting *Margaret Garner,* reprinted here in *Harper's Weekly,* conveys slavery's horrific nature by depicting the tragic actions of a fugitive slave.

local sheriff. Even worse, a newly appointed federal commissioner utilized a writ of habeas corpus as a means of disputing local authority. The writ was secured, not on behalf of Garner or her family, but on behalf of a federal marshal in an attempt to challenge the local sheriff's claim of custody. Chase saw this action as a "manifest abuse of the writ of habeas corpus." According to Chase, Margaret Garner's right to challenge her own detainment had been effectively transformed into a "summary replevin" that allowed her enslaver to claim ownership. In the state courts, her attorney secured a writ of habeas corpus on her behalf, but federal officials prioritized her status as a suspected slave. After two weeks of deliberation, a US district judge determined that federal law should prevail. The federal government re-enslaved Margaret Garner and her family. Federal support for the South's peculiar institution was so strong that even a murder charge could not keep a fugitive out of bondage.[16]

The experiences of enslaved people prior to the Civil War contrast sharply with Justice David Davis's characterization of America's commitment to civil liberties in his *Ex parte Milligan* opinion. In his decision, Davis described America's peacetime commitment to civil liberties as unwavering.

While discussing the historical importance of trial by jury, Davis asserted, "when peace prevails . . . there is no difficulty of preserving the safeguards of liberty for the ordinary modes of trial are never neglected." In addition, he noted that prior to the Habeas Corpus Act of 1863, "this great writ had never before been withheld from the citizens [of the United States]." This was prior to the Fourteenth Amendment. Perhaps like Roger B. Taney but contrary to his friend Abraham Lincoln, Davis believed that enslaved people were not entitled to the rights of citizenship. Or, perhaps he merely failed to consider the legal consequences of the nation's fugitive slave laws. Either way, Davis was guilty of callous disregard for the African American point of view, as have been many historians of *Milligan*. No one familiar with the controversies surrounding fugitive slaves in the 1840s and 1850s could have agreed with Davis's characterization of American legal history without dismissing or forgetting black citizenship. In the years immediately preceding the Civil War, Chase witnessed firsthand as the federal government denied the civil liberties of fugitive slaves, including, first and foremost, the denial of habeas corpus.[17]

The denial of Margaret Garner's civil liberties was the impetus for Governor Chase to pursue the passage of Ohio's personal liberty laws. In the days after her hearing, Chase reached out to his friend and legal protégée James Monroe to ask if he would sponsor legislation in the Ohio General Assembly. According to Monroe, Chase arrived on his doorstep in the days following Garner's re-enslavement and asked, "What are you Republicans doing . . . when a mother who is a free woman is compelled to kill her children on the soil of Ohio to save them from slavery, and that because there is no efficient law to protect them." Within a few weeks, Chase signed several pieces of legislation in an effort to secure the liberties of fugitive slaves. He closed Ohio jails to the confinement of suspected fugitives and instituted penalties for individuals who participated in the kidnapping of any free black or mulatto person. In addition, he signed legislation in an attempt to extend the right of habeas corpus to all Ohioans. Finally, the state government prohibited slaves from being brought voluntarily into the state by their enslavers. This new legislation set the stage for a violent clash between state officials and federal officers. If fugitive slaves could not leave behind the law of force, then a new force had to be marshalled to secure liberty for all Ohioans.[18]

In the coming months, state force met federal force as county sheriffs battled federal marshals on the back roads of Ohio. In May 1857 a deputy US marshal entered Mechanicsburg, Ohio, in pursuit of a fugitive slave. After the marshal's posse exchanged gunfire with the suspected fugitive they retreated, empty-handed, back toward Cincinnati. A few days later, the posse returned and arrested four members of the local community after accusing them of harboring a fugitive slave. In turn, a county judge issued a writ of habeas corpus, challenging the detainment of local civilians. The federal posse ignored this writ, however, as they continued toward Cincinnati in search of a conviction from a US district judge. Soon, the Clark County sheriff set off in pursuit of the federal band. Following a gun battle, the US marshal and his posse nearly beat County Sheriff John Layton to death. As the federal posse continued toward Cincinnati, a second county judge issued an additional writ. Finally, a posse led by the Green County sheriff captured the group of federal officials and detained them in a county jail. Once again, state and federal authorities clashed over the enforcement of civil liberties. Eventually, a US district judge freed the marshal and his posse after a writ of habeas corpus was secured on their behalf. The very right that the US marshal ignored while detaining local civilians under the Fugitive Slave Act of 1850 had proven crucial to securing his freedom.[19]

As state and federal officials exchanged gunfire in Ohio, Governor Chase remained resolute in his support for state officials. In the coming weeks, he traveled to Washington and met with President James Buchanan to ensure that further hostilities would be avoided. After brief negotiations, the two men agreed that all charges would be dropped and the federal posse, as well as their detainees, would not be charged with a crime. The state of Ohio had fought the federal government to a draw. After the negotiations, Chase wrote to his friend John T. Trowbridge emphasizing his belief that Ohio was enforcing the Constitution: "I exerted all the power the Constitution gave me for the vindication of the rights which the Constitution guaranteed." As the nation edged closer to war, Chase had come to accept the use of force as a means of securing personal liberties. If the federal government continued to insist on enforcing slavery, the state of Ohio would insist on enforcing constitutional rights. Unfortunately, Chase's legal victories were short lived. In 1858, Democrats took control of the Ohio General Assembly by capitalizing on the outbreak of antislavery violence. They labeled Republican candidates as dangerous radicals. After taking office, the Democrats repealed many of the state's personal liberty laws, undermining Chase's efforts to forcibly protect the legal rights of fugitive slaves. Nevertheless, Chase soldiered on. If he was going to effectively combat slavery, he would have to do it from inside the federal government.[20]

Throughout the Civil War, enslaved people who once ran across state lines began to run toward the US military. As secretary of the treasury, Chase utilized legal principles he had helped develop along the Ohio River in the antebellum era to assist freed men and women. Before the war, Chase had utilized a series of Ohio statutes known as "watercraft laws" to aid steamboat workers when boat owners withheld their wages. Now, during the war, he paired this egalitarian approach to the collection of debt with the wartime extension of federal power. As treasury secretary, he oversaw the application of federal regulations that controlled inland river commerce. As the military gained control over America's waterways, Southern property was increasingly confiscated and sold. Chase made sure that former slaves who turned over property for confiscation were entitled to military bounties. Thus, under Chase's authority, the US government began paying slaves and freedmen for their labor.[21]

Yet, despite Chase's efforts, as the war came to a close, freedom remained out of reach in many Southern communities. Although the US Army occupied much of the American South, the end of battlefield engagements and the assassination of President Lincoln shifted America's political landscape. In the spring of 1865, President Andrew Johnson issued an amnesty proclamation, opening the door for former secessionists and Confederate veterans to run for local office. Just when victory was achieved, the US military began to lose its grasp on power as local offices were filled with Southern sympathizers. In turn, formerly enslaved people continued to live in a country where their legal and political rights were denied by the law of force.

In the summer of 1866, local officials in New Orleans carried out a violent massacre of the city's black community. The previous year a Free State legislature in Louisiana had drafted a new state constitution. This document, however, did not include a provision that extended suffrage to the state's black population. In response, the black community of New Orleans called on delegates to reconvene the constitutional convention at the New Orleans Mechanics Institute. These former slaves and US Army veterans understood that the freedom they secured during the war must be protected by their votes. In the days leading up to the convention, newly reinstated mayor John Monroe, a Confederate sympathizer who had been removed from office during the war, ordered the city's police department to prepare for a violent conflict. The commanding military officer in New Orleans, Major General Philip H. Sheridan, expressly ordered that no troops should be stationed to guard the Mechanics Institute. Sheridan feared that the presence of troops would make it appear as though the army supported the convention. As a result, the city's police department, largely composed of former Confederate soldiers, was poised to intervene with the convention's proceedings.

On the morning of the convention, a procession of US Army veterans paraded through the French Quarter to show their support for black male suffrage. As they marched, a growing number of white men began trailing the procession, shouting racist slurs, throwing rocks, and trading insults with the black marchers. Soon the procession arrived at the Mechanics Institute, only to face off against a growing mob of Confederate sympathizers. Before long, the two groups exchanged gunfire and a young clerk ran to inform police chief Thomas Adams of the disturbance. Adams used the city's network of telegraph lines to sound an alarm, informing police officers across the city. Dozens of armed officers descended on the convention. The delegates and their black supporters were overwhelmed as police officers forced their way into the building. The policemen fired at will, killing spectators and delegates alike. The total number of casualties may never be known, but the military commission that investigated the massacre placed the final number at approximately forty-eight people, forty-seven of whom supported reconvening the convention.[22]

Salmon Chase believed that the New Orleans massacre was a direct result of Confederate veterans and Southern sympathizers regaining control over local law enforcement. He laid blame for the massacre at the feet of Mayor Monroe. In the summer of 1867, Chase wrote to *New York Tribune* editor Horace Greeley and maintained that in the months after the massacre it would have been "undesirable" to displace General Sheridan. However, he felt strongly that "Monroe . . . ought to have been put on trial." Despite Chase's wishes, however, many local officials involved in the attack escaped prosecution. In the days following the massacre, a local grand jury was convened by Judge Edmund Abell. Local officials, including Mayor Monroe and Police Chief Adams, testified that members of the black community started a riot. The grand jury found that the violent use of force by the city's law enforcement officials had been justified. In the end, several convention delegates were indicted, but no local officials or police officers faced charges. It was clear that local officials could not be trusted to police themselves and ensure the security of newly emancipated people.[23]

The New Orleans massacre provides vital context for appreciating a primary distinction between Salmon Chase's concurrence in *Ex parte Milligan* and the majority opinion written by Justice David Davis. As part of the Court's decision, Davis argued that the US Constitution "covers with the shield of its protection all classes of men, at all times and under all circumstances." And yet, while Davis wrote these words in 1866, the United States Army struggled to give his claim meaning in Louisiana. If "all classes of men" were protected, it was clear that local officials could not be trusted to do the protecting. This detail was ignored by Davis but explicitly acknowledged by Chase in his concurrence. Chase noted that civilian courts could be "wholly incompetent to avert threatened danger, or to punish, with adequate promptitude and certainty, the guilty conspirators." In his opinion, Chase expressly acknowledged the possibility that local officials may not carry out their responsibilities within their respective communities. Therefore, Chase affirmed the constitutionality of military oversight in these regions if it was approved by Congress. This was a key point of contention between the two justices. While Davis asserted "the public safety is assured," Chase knew that courts could falter in their commitment to averting danger and protecting citizens. He expressly noted, "In times of rebellion and civil war it may often happen, indeed, that judges and marshals will be in active sympathy with the rebels, and the courts their most efficient allies." Chase understood that if the federal government ceded power to local authorities, those individuals could not be trusted to act in accordance with federal law. This was especially true when those communities had just carried out a rebellion against the federal government. Chase knew that a region that had just rebelled in defense of slavery could not be expected to enforce federal laws that guaranteed the legal and political rights of newly emancipated people.[24]

In 1866 the federal government continued to depend upon wartime powers to secure effective civil rights for formerly enslaved people. In order to construct freedom, military authority had to remain intact. If it was going to enforce the liberties of newly emancipated people, the military still needed to displace Southern sheriffs, police officers, and judges, as well as override state laws. Therefore, Chase maintained that Congress could still utilize wartime powers to establish military commissions, writing, "it was within the power of Congress to determine in what states or districts such great and imminent danger exists as justifies the authorization of military tribunals for the trial of crimes and offenses against the discipline or security of the army or against the public safety." For Chase, wartime powers could be utilized in accordance with the Constitution as long as Congress affirmed that public safety remained under threat. Chase highlighted danger to the public as a justification for the use of these powers, a public that he had spent his entire legal career arguing included formerly enslaved people. If, as Chase noted in his letter to Gerrit Smith, the US government had "pledged itself" to maintain the "safety and security" of newly emancipated people, then wartime powers could be used as long as their security was at risk and local officials could not be trusted to protect them.[25]

In 1866, Chase's concurrence took into account his egalitarian approach to constitutional protections. His support for the outcome in *Ex parte Milligan*—a decision that has often been interpreted as a blow to federal authority—was, in fact, an affirmation of the important role that federal force played in securing the liberty of emancipated people. This is why Chase's concurrence left open the possibility of federal intervention. The law of force could not be left behind, but it could be utilized to secure the legal and political rights of the South's newly freed population. Ultimately, the federal government could not threaten liberties that did not exist in the first place. Chase understood that America's legal system had always been a contested space, where questions of safety and security were at stake. His understanding of constitutional protections was informed by real-world experiences in the borderlands of freedom.

NOTES

1. Salmon Chase, *The Salmon P. Chase Papers, Vol. 5, Correspondence, 1865–1873*, ed. John Niven (Kent, OH: Kent State University Press, 1998), 98.

2. For the necessity of force during military occupation see Gregory P. Downs, *After Appomattox: Military Occupation and the Ends of War* (Cambridge, MA: Harvard University Press, 2015).

3. *Daily Clarion* (Jackson, MS), December 30, 1866; *Maryland Free Press* (Hagerstown), December 27, 1866; *New York Herald*, December 28, 1866; *Chicago Tribune*, December 26, 1866.

4. *Ex parte Milligan*, 71 US 109, 140–141 (1866).

5. *Ex parte Milligan*, 71 US 137–138 (1866); US Const., 5th amend. (1791).

6. Charles Warren, *The Supreme Court in United States History in Three Volumes*, Vol. 3 (Boston: Little, Brown, 1922), 149. Also see John P. Frank, "*Ex parte Milligan* v. The Five Companies: Martial Law in Hawaii," *Columbia Law Review* 44, no. 5 (1944): 639; William A. Dunning, "The Constitution of the United States in Civil War," *Political Science Quarterly* 1 (June 1886): 163–198; and Dunning, "The Constitution of the United States in Reconstruction," *Political Science Quarterly* 2 (December 1887): 558–602. For works that argue the Republicans attempted to marginalize the US Supreme Court in favor of Reconstruction see James G. Randall, *The Civil War and Reconstruction* (Boston: D. C. Heath, 1937); and W. R. Brock, *An American Crisis: Congress and Reconstruction, 1865–1867* (New York: St. Martin's Press, 1963). Stanley Kutler argues that the push for congressional supremacy existed but failed because Republicans lacked a party consensus. Stanley I. Kutler, *Judicial Power and Reconstruction Politics* (Chicago: University of Chicago Press, 1968), 65; James M. McPherson, *Abraham Lincoln and the Second American Revolution* (New York: Oxford University Press, 1991; Eric Foner, *Reconstruction: America's Unfinished Revolution, 1863–1877* (New York: Harper & Row, 1988).

7. For the contest over power between the federal government and regional actors during the Civil War era see Gregory P. Downs and Kate Masur, eds., *The World the Civil War Made* (Chapel Hill: University of North Carolina Press, 2015). For nineteenth-century law as a space of negotiation see Laura F. Edwards, *A People and Their Peace: Legal Culture and the Transformation of Inequality in the Post-Revolutionary South* (Chapel Hill: University of North Carolina Press, 2009).

8. For Chase as a politician with national ambitions see Doris Kearns Goodwin, *Team of Rivals: The Political Genius of Abraham Lincoln* (New York: Simon & Schuster, 2005); Richard Sewell, *Ballots for Freedom: Antislavery Politics in the United States, 1837–1860* (New York; Oxford University Press, 1976); David Donald, *Charles Sumner and the Coming of the Civil War* (New York: Knopf, 1960); and William E. Gienapp, *Abraham Lincoln and Civil War America* (New York: Oxford University Press, 2002). Works that are critical of Chase within the framework of state politics include Stephen Maizlish, *The Triumph of Sectionalism: The Transformation of Ohio Politics, 1844–1856* (Kent, OH: Kent State University Press, 1983); and Theodore Clark Smith, *The Liberty Party and Free Soil Parties in the Old Northwest* (New York: Longmans, Green, 1897). More complimentary works include John Niven, *Salmon P. Chase: A Biography* (New York: Oxford University Press, 1995); and Frederick Blue, *Salmon P. Chase: A Life in Politics* (Kent, OH: Kent State University Press, 1987). Harold Hyman has explored how Chase's personal history shaped his Supreme Court opinions *In Re Turner* and *Texas v. White;* Harold Hyman, *The Reconstruction Justice of Salmon P. Chase: In Re Turner and Texas v. White* (Lawrence: University of Press of Kansas, 1997). For Cincinnati as an example of the nineteenth-century urban frontier see Daniel Aaron, *Cincinnati: Queen City of the West, 1819–1839* (Columbus: Ohio State University Press, 1992); and Richard Wade, *The Urban Frontier: The*

Rise of Western Cities 1790–1830 (Cambridge, MA: Harvard University Press, 1959).

9. By 1850 the African-American population of Cincinnati had become a powerful political force with its own identity and interests; see Nikki M. Taylor, *Frontiers of Freedom: Cincinnati's Black Community, 1802–1868* (Athens: Ohio University Press, 2005). For Cincinnati as a site of conflict between Northern and Southern sensibilities see Henry Louis Taylor Jr., *Race and the City: Work, Community, and Protest in Cincinnati, 1820–1970* (Urbana: University of Illinois Press, 1993). For the Ohio River Valley as a borderland space see Christopher Phillips, *The Rivers Ran Backward: The Civil War and the Remaking of the American Middle Border* (New York: Oxford University Press, 2016); and Matthew Salafia, *Slavery's Borderland: Freedom and Bondage along the Ohio River* (Philadelphia: University of Pennsylvania Press, 2013).

10. For the "federal consensus" see William Wiecek, *The Sources of Antislavery Constitutionalism, 1760–1848* (Ithaca, NY: Cornell University Press, 1977), 16. Some have interpreted the Supreme Court decision confirming the constitutionality of the Fugitive Slave Act of 1793 in *Prigg v. Pennsylvania* as a turning point among the antislavery community. After this decision, many radical abolitionists began to condemn the Constitution as a proslavery document. Chase, however, continued to believe the Constitution was antislavery. Harold Hyman and William Wiecek, *Equal Justice under Law: Constitutional Development 1835–1875* (New York: Harper & Row, 1982), 109. For Chase's success in bridging moral opposition to slavery with party politics see Eric Foner, *Free Soil, Free Labor, Free Men: The Ideology of the Republican Party before the Civil War* (New York: Oxford University Press, 1970), 73. Chase's argument for slavery as a product of local law has its roots in the case of James Somerset. For the specific fugitive slave trial that brought about Chase's "neo-Somerset" approach to antislavery activism see Wiecek, *The Sources of Antislavery Constitutionalism, 1760–1848,* 21; John Niven, *Salmon P. Chase: A Biography* (Oxford: Oxford University Press, 1995), 50; J. W. Schuckers, *The Life and Public Services of Salmon Portland Chase* (New York: D. Appleton, 1874), 38; and Paul Finkelman, *An Imperfect Union: Slavery, Freedom, and Comity* (Chapel Hill: University of North Carolina Press, 1981), 160.

11. For secondary recountings of *Jones v. Van Zandt* see Niven, *Salmon P. Chase: A Biography,* 77–83; and Schuckers, *Life and Public Service of Salmon Portland Chase,* 52–66.

12. Salmon Portland Chase, *Reclamation of Fugitives from Service: An Argument for the Defendant, Submitted to the Supreme Court of the United States, at the December Term, 1846, in the Case of Wharton Jones vs. John Vanzandt* (Cincinnati, OH: R. P. Donogh, 1847), 84. Chase's insistence that slavery was a product of force was built upon the legal arguments of Massachusetts Supreme Court justice Lemuel Shaw. In 1836 Shaw secured the freedom of an enslaved girl after affirming her right to a writ of habeas corpus in the case *Commonwealth v Aves.* Niven, *Salmon P. Chase: A Biography,* 80; Frederic Chase, *Lemuel Shaw: Chief Justice of the Supreme Judicial Court of Massachusetts 1830–1860* (Boston: Houghton Mifflin, 1918), 164.

13. US Const., Article IV, Sec. 2 (1791); Chase, *Reclamation of Fugitives from Service,* 82.

14. US Const., 5th amend. (1791); Chase, *Reclamation of Fugitives from Service,* 89.

15. For the Fugitive Slave Act of 1850 as a turning point on the road to the Civil War see R. J. M. Blackett, *The Captive's Quest for Freedom: Fugitive Slaves, the 1850 Fugitive Slave Law, and the Politics of Slavery* (New York: Cambridge University Press, 2018). In the years after 1850, state and federal officials debated whether members of the military could be organized as part of the "posse comitatus." In most cases, the posse was organized by deputizing local civilians. Although the military was never utilized in Ohio, in 1854 it was utilized in Massachusetts during the trial of Anthony Burns. Robert W. Coakley, *The Role of the Military Forces in Domestic Disorders, 1789–1878* (Washington, DC: Center for Military History, 1988), 128–144.

16. During Garner's hearing, abolitionists Lucy Stone highlighted the light skin of Garner's children and gestured at sexual violence as a possible motivation for her actions. For a detailed discussion of the case see Mark Reinhardt, *Who Speaks for Margaret Garner: The True Story That Inspired Toni Morison's Beloved* (Minneapolis: University of Minnesota Press, 2010); and Steven Weisenburger, *Modern Medea: A Family Story of Slavery and Child-Murder from the Old South* (New York: Hill & Wang, 1998). For the trauma that women experienced in slavery and the forces that might have driven Margaret Garner to kill, see Nikki M. Taylor, *Driven toward Madness: The Fugitive Slave Margaret Garner and the Tragedy on the Ohio* (Athens: Ohio University Press, 2016). For the argument that Chase could have done more to intervene and prevent the re-enslavement of Margaret Garner and her family, see Niven, *Salmon P. Chase: A Biography,* 184. A replevin is a legal procedure whereby seized goods may be provisionally restored to their owner, pending an outcome of an action to determine the rights of parties involved. Schucklers, *The Life and Public Service of Salmon Portland Chase,* 173–175.

17. *Diary and Correspondence of Salmon P. Chase* (New York: Da Capo Press, 1971), 222; *Ex parte Milligan,* 71 US 124, 115 (1866).

18. James Monroe, *Oberlin Thursday Lectures, Addresses, and Essays* (Oberlin, OH: Edward J. Goodrich, 1897), 117; Schucklers, *The Life and Public Service of Salmon Portland Chase,* 174.

19. For a detailed discussion of the battles surrounding Ohio's personal liberty laws see Niven, *Salmon P. Chase: A Biography,* 208; and Schucklers, *The Life and Public Service of Salmon Portland Chase,* 177–182.

20. It is important to note that while Chase accepted the use of legal force to resist slavery, he did not condone extra-legal violence. When an abolitionists mob rescued John Price in 1858, members of the mob were put on trial for violating the nation's fugitive slave laws. Chase traveled to northern Ohio and cautioned the community against taking the law into their own hands: ironic, since this was exactly what the mob had done by freeing John Price in the first place. Eventually the

case was dropped. Blue, *Salmon P. Chase: A Life in Politics*, 106. For efforts to undermine Chase see Niven, *Salmon P. Chase: A Biography*, 208.

21. Matthew Axtell, "'At Liberty to Take Possession': How Cincinnati Riverboat Law Turned 'Have–Nots' into 'Haves' during the Civil War Era," *Ohio Valley History* 6 (Fall 2016): 48–71.

22. James G. Hollandsworth Jr., *An Absolute Massacre: The New Orleans Riot of July 30, 1866* (Baton Rouge: Louisiana State Press, 2001), 141.

23. Chase, *The Salmon P. Chase Papers, Vol. 5, Correspondence, 1865–1873*, 171. After Congress passed the Military Reconstruction Acts of 1867, Major General Sheridan removed Mayor Monroe and Judge Edmund Abell from office. For a discussion of the New Orleans Massacre as one conflict among many in Louisiana during the Reconstruction period, see James Hogue, *Uncivil War: Five New Orleans Street Battles and the Rise and Fall of Radical Reconstruction* (Baton Rouge: Louisiana State University Press, 2006).

24. *Ex parte Milligan*, 71 US 109, 140–141 (1866).

25. *Ex parte Milligan*, 71 US 140 (1866); Chase, *The Salmon P. Chase Papers, Vol. 5, Correspondence, 1865–1873*, 98.

CHAPTER 9

The Least Naive Position: The Lincoln Administration and International Law in American Wars on Terror

STEWART L. WINGER

As I sat down to write, there appeared in my inbox a link to a story with the headline, "Trump Administration Wants to Release US Citizen Enemy Combatant in Syria." The article stated, "The unnamed 2018 defendant seeks not to be released in Syria. The unnamed person's attorneys, who are scheduled to fight his detention in court later this month, call the potential release a 'death warrant.'"[1]

The headline neatly illustrates the renewed relevance of the decision in *Ex parte Milligan* (1866) and other Civil War–era precedents for the use of presidential power—and not merely because one of the unnamed person's attorneys was Jonathan Hafetz, a contributor to this volume. In a cousin case to *Milligan*, *Ex parte Vallandigham* (1864), Abraham Lincoln famously released former Ohio representative Clement Vallandigham behind Confederate lines. *Ex parte Milligan* and *Ex parte Vallandigham* were each concerned with the Lincoln administration's use of military commission trials during the Civil War and, more broadly, the degree to which the executive was bound to answer to the judiciary in its conduct of the war. When Vallandigham petitioned for a writ of habeas corpus, the federal district judge ruled that the use of military commission trials accorded with the president's commander-in-chief authority. After Lincoln banished Vallandigham, his attorneys challenged the manner in which the military commission had been conducted. The Supreme Court dismissed the case, arguing Congress had not granted the Court appellate jurisdiction over military tribunals.[2]

Unlike the 2018 case, Lincoln did not subject Vallandigham to the threat of extra-judicial execution; instead, Vallandigham was sentenced to confinement in military prison. And technically speaking, both his sentence and his subsequent banishment actually avoided the option of execution as provided for by Union general Ambrose Burnside's General Orders No. 38. The crimes for which Vallandigham was so ignominiously banished were also considerably less serious than the unlawful combatancy of the 2018 ISIS operative originally detained in Syria. Burnside's General Orders No. 38 declared that "all persons found within our lines who commit acts for the benefit of the enemies of our country will be tried as spies or traitors and if convicted will suffer death." Among other acts prohibited was the "habit of declaring sympathies for the enemy." The order issued by General Burnside declared that "persons committing such offences would be at once arrested, with a view to being tried as above stated, or to be sent beyond his lines into the lines of their friends; that it must be distinctly understood that treason expressed or implied, would not be tolerated in his department."[3]

Lincoln later argued that Vallandigham had encouraged desertion and discouraged enlistments.[4] Nevertheless, he was in fact convicted for uttering disloyal sentiments, which should have been protected by the First Amendment, or so we now assume.[5] In principle then, Lincoln's Civil War use of the commander-in-chief power, *seemingly* unchecked by either the Bill of Rights or the judiciary, to arrest civilians—and in the case of Milligan, to try them by military commission and sentence them to death—strikes us as dangerous to liberty in the extreme. Moreover, in an era of extraordinary rendition, the comically benign banishment of Vallandigham now raises troubling concerns about the denial of due process by the Lincoln administration.

Lincoln's wartime civil liberties record has long been a red flag for Copperhead, neo-Confederate, and libertarian writers, and something of an embarrassment for other legal liberals. Lincoln's opponents and later detractors have seen him as attempting to set up a centralized despotism or even a personal one, while his defenders have noted that it was an emergency; Lincoln had not intended to destroy constitutional liberty but instead acted to save the Union. His was a "benevolent dictatorship," but a dictatorship nonetheless.[6] Herman Belz credited Lincoln's textual arguments as well as his forthright willingness to engage in public constitutional debate, while Mark E. Neely, by contrast, found Lincoln cavalier or "indifferent" regarding the Constitution.[7] A few have openly celebrated Lincoln's vigorous use of what they see as extra-constitutional executive power and cited it as a model for vigorous executive action in the present. Not surprisingly, such defenders arose during World War II and more recently during the War on Terror, when legal counsel for the George W. Bush administration found succor in his perceived assertion of unchecked executive power.[8]

In light of recent scholarship, however, each of these responses is open to question. All of them presume a modern dichotomy of liberal individualism versus totalitarianism, rather than making the distinction between monarchy and aristocracy on the one hand and majoritarian republicanism on the other, the distinction almost everywhere assumed in Lincoln's America, not least by Lincoln himself.[9] In retrospect, elements of what right and left now celebrate as liberal constitutionalism were stirring in the 1860s, particularly on opposite fringes, among abolitionists and their archenemies, the Copperheads. But even among Lincoln's constitutional opponents, the Copperheads, such limits as there were on government were designed to thwart despotic monarchs and aristocratic minorities, not to put limits on local, self-governing, republican majorities. Lincoln's constitutional views and those of his administration were far more consonant with prevailing constitutional doctrine and small *r* republican practice than most earlier historical treatments have led us to believe.

Reading modern liberal constitutional developments into the past, most interpretations side with David Davis over Lincoln in one way or the other. With some exceptions, those that do side with Lincoln either apologize for him on pragmatic as opposed to doctrinal grounds—he did what was necessary in spite of some rough legal edges—or they celebrate his willingness to exercise an extra-constitutional prerogative power.[10] Unappreciated in these accounts is that where Lincoln and his administration innovated, it was *not* in the development of lawless prerogative. In fact, where Lincoln may be said to have innovated was in his expansion of earlier traditions that read the US Constitution in view of "universal law"[11] and the law of nations,[12] what we now refer to as "international law."

For most modern interpreters, Lincoln's actions rather than Davis's opinion present the problem. They go against our assumptions about Bill of Rights protections. But in fact, Lincoln was probably more rooted in the constitutional thinking of the time than was Davis. Davis's opinion was the more anomalous at the time, and this explains its rocky reception prior to the mid-twentieth century.

For Americans right and left, raised in the sunshine of liberal democratic expectations, to explore *Milligan,* its reception, and its current implications is to go down a dark and troubling path. In the comforting teleological narrative of the Warren Court era, the Bill of Rights spoke clearly about individual liberties. With the Declaration of Independence and the Bill of Rights, the founders planted the seeds. *Milligan* sent out shoots by extending civil liberties protections to individuals in wartime. Like a wide and powerful trunk, the great Reconstruction amendments further extended those protections to all persons regardless of race. We had only to apply those principles of civil liberty to blacks, to other disadvantaged minorities, and to women, to live in the shelter of a broad oak, the liberal democratic legal order. Enforced by the judiciary, the system of checks and balances and legal due process would result in a substantively fair system. Why wouldn't we favor checks on executive power by the "least dangerous branch"?

There are at least three problems with this view, each of which points to further troubled waters. First, Abraham Lincoln appears to be on the wrong side of this cherished story. In his *Milligan* opinion, Davis chastised his lifelong friend, the man for whom he had labored so hard in the Republican presidential nomination fight of 1860, and who had named him to the Supreme Court in 1862. Lincoln had sanctioned the use of military commissions to, if necessary, execute men during the Civil War even when and where civilian courts were open in states that had not been in rebellion. And contrary to a good bit of persistent confusion about Lincoln and black freedom, Lincoln and his administration supported civil liberties for black people in ways Copperheads and Whiggish conservative Republicans like Davis did not.

There is of course a long-held Copperhead and Confederate narrative dismissing Lincoln's commitment to human liberty as a sham.[13] And this line of reasoning has been taken up by neo-Confederate and libertarian writers more recently.[14] But even when they set out to challenge Lincoln with titles like *With Malice toward Some,* careful historians like William Blair find Copperhead, neo-Confederate, and libertarian portraits overdrawn.[15] At times and places, Lincoln, his administration, and Republicans across the country overstepped from a modern perspective, perhaps most troubling when Lincoln furloughed troops to supervise polling places and administer test oaths to determine qualifications for voting in the border states in 1863.[16] But it was never to establish a permanent dictatorship or centralize power the way his critics then as now have contended. More importantly, it was rarely out of step with prevailing nineteenth-century prac-

Figure 9.1. "The Great American WHAT-IS-IT? Chased by Copperheads," an anti-Lincoln satire showing the Republican incumbent and his supporters menaced by giant "Copperheads" (Peace Democrats). At far left is Ambrose Burnside, who holds a flaming torch and is being choked by a snake representing Clement Vallandigham. The significance of the torch is unclear, although it resembles the lanterns of the Wide-Awakes, active in Lincoln's 1860 presidential campaign. At right, a skeleton has just risen from the grave of abolitionist martyr John Brown, whose tombstone is inscribed "Hung in Virginia by [Virginia governor Henry A.] Wise." The "What Is It?" in the title refers to a deformed African man recently featured at P. T. Barnum's Museum on Broadway. Courtesy of the Library of Congress.

tice. In cases like Vallandigham's, Lincoln backed overzealous subordinates (or preferred to be seen that way). But in others, he in fact encouraged local officials and subordinates to restore civil liberties.[17] How is this to be explained? What were men like Lincoln, Henry Wager Halleck, Joseph Holt, and Francis Lieber thinking?[18] Such anomalies from our perspective suggest a problem with the prevailing paradigm of interpretation.

A robust neo-abolitionist tradition also questions Lincoln's commitments to black freedom. There is no way to hash through those arguments here. Suffice it to say only that emancipation required conscription, and that in the short run, these twin policies created a Copperhead opposition virulently opposed to any fight for black freedom whatsoever. This opposition in turn nearly derailed the war effort by discouraging enlistment, encouraging desertion, and suborning resistance to the draft. This provoked fears for the war effort resulting in the curtailment of civil liberties in the North during the Civil War. Copperheads won off-year election at the state and congressional levels, capturing key governorships, and they threatened to defeat Lincoln well into 1864.[19]

The second problem is the reverse of the first. Recent historians, some of them represented in this volume, have learned more about Lincoln's "Copperhead" opponents, and the picture they paint is not a pretty one. Actively racist, their dissatisfaction grew as much out of an intense hatred of African Americans as it did out of constitutional principle, which in some sense they were inventing for the occasion. In the 1850s, Democrats, including especially future Peace Democrats or Copperheads, had most emphatically opposed the granting of habeas petition rights to alleged fugitive slaves. Jeremiah Black himself, who now appeared for Milligan, had once argued in *Ableman v. Booth* (1859) that state courts only had power to issue writs of habeas corpus for state prisoners, not for prisoners held by the federal government. This argument was taken up by the same Roger Taney who later took Lincoln to task in *Ex parte Merryman* for, of all things, waving off a writ of habeas corpus. Taney was a federal judge and so he had not directly reversed himself. But much of the constitutional theorizing in the period was clearly a matter of whose ox was being gored. *Ableman* was the antithesis of a states' rights decision. With self-conscious irony Republicans used the Fugitive Slave Act of 1850 as a model and precedent for the Civil Rights Act of 1866 and for continued use of federal commissioners in the Reconstruction South.[20] The Democratic Party position on African Americans remained adamantine, but there was nothing consistently libertarian or even liberal about the antebellum Democratic Party.

Reading negative liberty civil libertarianism into the Davis opinion, later legal liberals (on both the right and the left of the political spectrum) have ironically tended to credit Copperhead complaints regarding civil liberties under Lincoln without much inquiry into the powerful local regulatory regimes for which they spoke, or into the costs borne by African Americans. But among the very inventors of the use of the US Constitution as the guardian, not of community and states' rights, but of *individual rights,* were men bent on the reestablishment of a terrorist regime in the South and white supremacy everywhere else. Recent inquiries into *Ex parte Milligan* therefore highlight a surprising history of constitutionalism in America.

This raises a third troubling question for the teleological history of liberal constitutionalism: the possibility that establishing domestic tranquility may be a necessary precondition for meaningful liberty rather than the other way around. Though we have tended to lecture Lincoln about civil liberties, here we may find that instead, nineteenth-century small *r* republicanism more generally, and 1860s capital *R* Republicanism specifically, hold important lessons for us. There can be no return to localist majoritarian republicanism of the nineteenth century, the kind of government of the people that Lincoln extolled at Gettysburg. Yet the relationship between freedom and power may perhaps be more fraught than modern liberal constitutional myths have led us to assume. Recent histories of the Republican war on terror in the 1860s and 1870s suggest that a more realistic assessment of the necessity of state power and the laws of war may again be necessary. If the Radical Republicans rather than the Liberal Republicans were right about the necessity of a vigorous and active state in the creation of meaningful liberty for African Americans, up to and including the use of military commissions, the tragic outcome of Reconstruction may hold important lessons for us in the war on terror.

In the fall of 1864, Milligan was arrested and charged with conspiracy against the US government, offering aid and comfort to the Confederates, and inciting rebellion, disloyal practices, and violations of the laws of war. In a kind of mirror image of John Brown's raid, a military commission found that Milligan and his co-conspirators plotted to liberate Confederate prisoners, seize a federal arsenal, and foment a general insurrection that would establish a breakaway Northwestern confederacy.[21] The case was heard in March 1866 and decided without opinion in April. Later that summer, Justice David Davis returned to write the opinion of the Court at his home in Bloomington, Illinois. President Lincoln and his administration had held that under the laws of war and as a matter of "public safety" in a time of actual war, invasion, or rebellion, the commander in chief had authority to arrest, detain, and sentence unlawful combatants or others who impeded the Union war effort. But less than two years after Lincoln's death, Davis wrote that trial by military commission was *un*acceptable "where the courts are open and their process unobstructed" and *acceptable* only "where war really prevails." The laws and usages of war "can never be applied to citizens in states which have upheld the authority of the government."

Davis emphasized that Milligan was a long-standing resident of Indiana and not a member of the military. In Davis's view, Milligan was not what we now call a "combatant." Milligan was apprehended in Indiana, where the courts were open and unobstructed, and where, according to Davis at least, there was no war. As to when war did or did not exist, Davis declared that "martial law cannot arise from a threatened invasion. The necessity must be actual and present; the invasion real, such as effectually closes the courts and deposes the civil administration."[22]

To the satisfaction of Peace Democrats or "Copperheads," of old Whigs like Davis himself uncomfortably housed for the moment in the Republican Party, and of civil libertarians ever since, Davis went on to hold that the Lincoln administration had violated Milligan's rights to a jury trial under Article III, Section 2 of the Constitution. The administration had violated his rights to be free from warrantless search under the Fourth Amendment. In addition, it had failed to indict him in a civil court as prescribed by both the Habeas Corpus Act of 1863 and the Fifth Amendment, thus threatening to deprive him of life without due process of law. Finally, it had denied him procedural rights including rights to an impartial jury under the Sixth Amendment. In what would seem to be a landmark civil liberties holding, Davis concluded that "the Constitution of the United States is a law for rulers and people, equally in war and in peace, and covers with the shield of its protection all classes of men, at all times and under all circumstances."[23]

In the twentieth century, particularly after the tragedy for civil liberties of *Korematsu v. US* and the triumphs for liberal constitutionalism of the *Steel Seizure* case and *Brown v. Board of Education,* praise for the decision in *Milligan* could sometimes be effusive.[24] In 1962, for example, Allan Nevins said that the Supreme Court had established the supremacy of the civil authority over military authority. "Wherever such civil authority is established and its ordinary judicial procedures are operating, its protections of the citizens shall remain absolute and unquestionable. The heart of this decision is the heart of the difference between the United States of America and Nazi Germany or the Soviet Union."[25]

Ex parte Milligan could well be considered a landmark. In our popular discourse, we often speak of the Bill of Rights as if it were intended from the beginning to protect individual citizens from presumably tyrannical majority government. Prior to its incorporation of the Fourteenth Amendment, the Bill of Rights of course did not apply to actions taken by the individual states. (States could and did have religious establishments, for example.) Less widely appreciated has been the way that even against federal action, the Bill of Rights was seldom if ever used as we use it today, to carve out a sphere of individual private action free from government interference. The holdings in *Milligan*, by contrast, sound eerily familiar to modern ears.

But through most of the nineteenth century, participation in republican self-government was the basic definition of a free citizen. Legal historian William Novak has argued that until well after the Civil War, "liberty" was almost exclusively taken to be a collective attribute of self-governing communities.[26] And according to Michael Les Benedict, the only areas where the federal courts had protected individual rights against majority action prior to *Milligan* were in cases involving the contracts clause (Article I, Section 10). In addition to holding that the Bill of Rights was not applicable to state, as opposed to federal, action, *Barron v. Baltimore* (1833) signified the Supreme Court's desire to avoid a broader role in protecting rights against government action. Benedict argues that the fact that no one brought suit to protect citizens against state government actions under the Article IV privileges and immunities clause, except for the abortive attempt of Massachusetts to challenge the South Carolina Negro Seaman's Law, was a telling indication of how little Americans regarded the Court as the protector of individual rights. In part, this was because Americans did not have much of a conception of individual as distinct from popular rights before the Civil War.[27]

It would not be impossible, then, to view Davis's opinion in *Ex parte Milligan* not just as a landmark case but as the very big bang of the Bill of Rights, the arrival to the Supreme Court of liberal constitutionalism as we know it. It was precisely during the Civil War that some conservative former Whig and Copperhead Democratic legal thinkers began to explore using the courts to protect individual rights from a majority perceived to be overbearing. In this, they traded places with antislavery radicals who had begun making similar appeals before the war.[28] Davis's opinion brought this line of thinking into a majority Supreme Court opinion.

As Benedict points out, after *Marbury v. Madison* and *Dred Scott, Milligan* is only the third instance of an act of the federal government being struck down by the Supreme Court as unconstitutional.[29] It was only the second time such an act was struck down based on the Bill of Rights. In *Dred Scott,* Taney's "majority" opinion held that the prohibition of slavery in territories in the Louisiana Purchase north of the 36°30′ parallel deprived slaveholders crossing into the territories of their property rights under the Fifth Amendment without due process of law. But *Dred Scott* was a dark and dubious precedent, one that in any case would soon be reversed by the Fourteenth Amendment. Thus, one might even ask why *Milligan* is not as familiar to high school students as *Brown v. Board,* the one constitutional opinion they can generally name. Or why David Dudley Field and Jeremiah Black, whose arguments on Milligan's behalf were largely accepted by Justice Davis, are not as familiar to first-year law students as Louis Brandeis and Oliver Wendell Holmes Jr. Viewed in this light, the truly remarkable thing about the Davis opinion in *Milligan* was not that it spoke for the past, but that it resonated so well in the future.

But there are good reasons to qualify this picture of constitutional history. This was not yet a world of limited government as we now think of it. In *Milligan,* Davis held that the Lincoln administration had violated Milligan's rights to a jury trial under Article III, Section 2 of the Constitution, his rights to be free from warrantless search under the Fourth Amendment, his due process rights under the Fifth Amendment, and his right to an impartial jury under the Sixth Amendment, all of which sounds like a very modern summation of the achievements of the Warren Court. Nevertheless, such a reading would be anachronistic. It is therefore important to realize just how Davis innovated in his application of the Bill of Rights in *Ex parte Milligan.*

Waving Milligan's trial record, Davis argued that Milligan could not have been a belligerent because he lived and remained in Indiana. For Davis, membership in the Sons of Liberty, a group that conspired to release Confederate prisoners of war by force and even to create a breakaway Northwest Confederacy, did not make him a belligerent under the laws of war.[30] As Benjamin Butler pointed out, this appellate case seemed to turn not on a point of law but on what should have been a point of fact stipulated in the record: was Milligan a belligerent, and was he in fact conducting war, be it in Indiana or anywhere else?[31] Taking no apparent cognizance of the laws of war or the determinations of the military commission, Davis felt free to render an entirely parochial and textualist decision based only on the Habeas Corpus Act of 1863 and the US Constitution. As a former trial judge, he read the Constitution like a mere statute.

Davis also disregarded without comment Lincoln's own argument in the Corning letter. When Albany Democrats argued that military arrests should not take place outside of the lines of necessary military occupation and the scenes of insurrection, something very close to the Davis opinion in *Milligan,* Lincoln answered that

> inasmuch . . . as the constitution itself makes no such distinction; I am unable to believe that there is any such constitutional distinction. I concede that the class of arrests complained of, can be constitutional only when, in cases of Rebellion or Invasion, the public Safety may require them; and I insist that in such cases, they are constitutional wherever the public safety does require them—as well in places to which they may prevent the rebellion extending, as in those where it may be already prevailing—as well where they may restrain mischievous interference with the raising and supplying of armies, . . . as where the rebellion may actually be.[32]

As historian Herman Belz has noted, Lincoln could cite constitutional text, and in this case he generalized plausibly from the suspension clause.[33] After Fort Sumter, he repeatedly used its language of "public safety."[34] Not coincidentally, this was entirely consonant with the meaning of the Bill of Rights at mid-nineteenth century as well as with common-law understandings of the people's welfare. After the rise of the mass corporation and with it the mass state, we tend to take a jaundiced view of this kind of assertion of public power. But in the small-town world of Lincoln's America, members of the US House likely met and even personally knew many of their constituents, and jury duty gave citizens some assurance that public power would remain controlled.[35] Lincoln's constitutional views comported almost entirely with this world.

Less clear is how well they comported with the new federal Provost Marshal General's Bureau, the first extensive federal police power after the demise of the 1850 Fugitive Slave Act. As a temporary wartime measure, Lincoln granted the federal government the full scope to preserve order routinely granted to state governments on all sides. This was the heart of Davis's disagreement with Lincoln. Without habeas corpus and civilian trial, detained citizens, whether they be deserters, draft avoiders, underage draftees or even unlawful combatants or spies would never see a judge, let alone a locally empaneled jury. A distant federal power now made salient the old Antifederalist fear for the autonomy of local juries. The argument was not about individual rights; it was about federalism and republicanism.

Though a trial judge for fourteen years in state circuit court, Davis likely had never fielded a litigant's claim to a right under the US Constitution.[36] Nevertheless, he now turned to the Bill of Rights. Lincoln, in comparison, had vast appellate legal experience, being involved in some way in 410 Illinois Supreme Court cases, at least one of which dealt with the Illinois Bill of Rights. He or his partners also handled 234 cases in federal circuit court. Some twenty of Lincoln's cases reached the US Supreme Court, of which he was attorney of record in five.[37] This illustrates two important points: first, Davis had no particular experience in constitutional law while Lincoln certainly did, and second, for that generation, the US Bill of Rights was not a constitutive part of the legal order. Action even on state bills of rights remained comparatively rare. This is what made Davis's holding in *Ex parte Milligan* so exceptional, even odd.

Davis cited the text of the Constitution. Nevertheless, his constitutional politics edged across the line into what by modern standards would be considered inappropriate activism from the bench. As Michael Les Benedict explains in chapter 7, before Lincoln's death, Davis had privately tried to advise Lincoln about the requirements of habeas corpus and the inappropriateness of using military commissions in the North. Through Governor Oliver P. Morton of Indiana, he had urged President Johnson to commute Milligan's execution so he could get the matter before the Court.[38] Mark E. Neely Jr. has stated that "the activism of the mid-century judiciary reveal[ed] itself in sharp and contentious terms." The judiciary in the Civil War period was highly political and often highly activist. Davis most certainly would not have wanted to admit it, but similar to Chief Justice Taney in *Merryman*, he "was seeking a cause of difficulty with the government."[39]

Davis had sought out the case and brought it before the Court with a particular outcome in mind, namely to rule based on the amendments to the US Constitution that military commission trials were unconstitutional in Indiana because the courts were open. Davis was not alone, as John Lupton makes clear in chapter 10. Many state judges held it to be the rule that war was defined by whether or not their own courts were open, once again indicating not only that there was a turf battle at play, but that from their point of view, republican government was being threatened by a distant imperial power. The rights in question were incidentally individual, but in essence collective.[40] In *Vallandigham,* the US Supreme Court had dismissed the case, holding that it did not have direct appellate jurisdiction over military commissions, and the Lincoln administration had routinely ignored circuit court decisions in a range of habeas cases, but especially in cases of draft avoidance and desertion. Davis therefore wanted the matter before the Supreme Court again. Finding jurisdiction in an 1802 statute, in their capacity as circuit court judges in a circuit that included Indiana, Davis and US district judge David McDonald agreed to disagree and certified their disagreement to the Supreme Court, where Davis would again hear the case.[41] Clinton Rossiter concluded that Davis had been lured into saying things about limits on the war powers that were simply not true.[42] Davis had reached in this case to make a point he was already eager to make.

And Davis *was* innovating. When thinking about nineteenth-century constitutional history, constitutional historian Akhil Amar cautions us not to read the Bill of Rights through the lens of the Fourteenth Amendment, as protecting minorities from the majority. As originally conceived the Bill of Rights was majoritarian, rather than counter-majoritarian.[43] It "protected the ability of local governments to monitor and deter federal abuse, ensured that ordinary citizens would participate in the federal administration of justice through various jury provisions, and preserved the transcendent sovereign right of a majority of the people themselves to alter or abolish government and thereby pronounce the last word on constitutional questions."[44]

In light of the twentieth-century experience, it is tempting to assume that Davis in *Milligan* accepted the views of David Dudley Field, making the judiciary (conceived as the elite judges rather than as republican juries) the guardian of individual constitutional rights. The decision in *Milligan* seems, in Amar's telling neologism, "liberal-ish" in that way.[45] Davis certainly had a high Whig view of a judge's authority.

But if Amar is correct, Davis was looking backward to a rule of participatory republican self-government rather than anticipating the civil libertarianism of the Warren era and the necessity of protecting the individual from a potentially totalitarian mass state. Entirely in line with the republican origins of the Fourth, Fifth, and Sixth Amendments, Davis said that if upon a plea of necessity the executive could set aside the constitutional provisions regarding criminal justice, "republican government is a failure, and there is an end of liberty regulated by law."[46] Davis's concern was not for the individual rights of poor Milligan to be free from majoritarian constraint, but that a future tyrant might use the plea of necessity to subvert participatory local republican government—precisely the fear that Copperheads mistakenly had had of Lincoln.[47] In other words, when Copperhead Democrats, David Davis, or former Confederates cited the Bill of Rights in ways that seem modern to us, they were nevertheless doing so not from within the liberal paradigm of limited government but from an older paradigm of powerful but mostly local self-government.

In defense of subsequent liberal readings, the case is ambiguous; the Fifth and Sixth Amendments speak of "persons" and "the accused," singular nouns, rather than the rights of "the people" as a republican political collective. But the Fourth Amendment speaks of "the right of the people to be secure in their persons, houses, papers, and effects." Protecting individual "persons" from undue search and seizure was necessary to preserve free republican majority government ("the people") from any oppressive, self-dealing, aristocratic minority in the government, rather than protections of the minority from the majority.[48] When it came to the rights of the accused, the effect can seem similar. At mid-twentieth century, reading Davis in *Milligan* as a prophet of constitutional liberalism was an easy mistake to make.

Nevertheless, it is anachronistic, and it would be best to see *Milligan* as a transitional case in the history of the Bill of Rights, part of the beginning of a long shift from republicanism to liberal constitutionalism, rather than its sudden, unlooked-for fulfillment. *Milligan* did not shape our modern understanding of the Bill of Rights. Instead, the liberal implications of *Milligan* lay dormant until after *Schenck* and *Abrams* (1919) when, somewhat miraculously, the relevance of *Milligan* was rediscovered.

Davis came from a Whig Party devoted to energetic government even at the federal level. But his conception of liberty centered on small-town and state-level republican governance, and he viewed the Radical Republicans as a tyrannical threat to the liberty of a self-governing republic. With the exception of emancipation, he wished relations with the South restored quickly and with as little damage to the previous constitutional regime as possible. This meant self-governing white men would remain in power in the South, and in the nineteenth century, self-governing communities routinely exercised awesome powers.[49] Constitutional majorities in the South had a right to rule there or republican government was dead. The Radicals did not represent a real majority but merely the majority of a rump parliament, a classic usurpation. Thus, despite the ways Davis's sometimes-lofty constitutional rhetoric resonated in the Warren era, it was not born in an era of limited government or counter-majoritarian thinking.

The Lincoln administration also worked within the framework of nineteenth-century law, in some ways more thoroughly than Davis did. And the Lincoln administration also showed creativity. Both Lincoln and Davis (and this ought to be axiomatic) innovated from within the existing paradigm. Through his successive iterations of the Emancipation Proclamation, Lincoln had learned a good bit about the laws of war and of nations (what we now call international law). With the final Emancipation Proclamation, he had concluded that some of his important commander-in-chief powers over confiscation, emancipation, military detention, and military trial derived not from Congress but from the laws of war, or as his attorney general put it, the practice of "civilized warfare."[50] Via the commander-in-chief clause, Lincoln derived powers (and constraints) from "the common law of war."[51] As if groping for the vocabulary of "unlawful combatant," which they did not have, elements of the Lincoln administration after his death claimed Milligan was a "prisoner of war," albeit one subject to military trial for violations of the law of war.[52]

Under the Habeas Corpus Act of 1863, the Lincoln administration was required to provide a list of those detained under the president's authority and either bring them to a judge or release them. Lincoln may have dismissed this unwelcome section of the Habeas Corpus Act as simply beyond the powers of Congress, just as he had dismissed Taney's judicial ruling in *Ex parte Merryman.* In *Merryman,* his attorney general presented a version of the Jacksonian departmental theory whereby each of the coordinate branches alike were responsible for determining the meaning of the Constitution and following it.[53] Earnestly fearing the loss of the republic in 1864, public safety and military necessity remained for Lincoln both the overriding practical consideration *and* his constitutional standard.

Rather than the mechanics of the exclusionary rule or *Miranda* warnings meant to forestall abuse of public power, the nineteenth-century legal order instead held officials personally libel at common law for such abuse after the fact.[54] Common-law juries rather than judges of constitutional law decided the limits of police action. We can only presume Lincoln signed the Habeas Corpus Act because its indemnity provisions shielded his officers from civil suit for unlawful detention.[55]

A holdover from the Lincoln administration, Attorney General Speed argued in *Milligan* that the Habeas Corpus Act spoke only of "state or political offenders" and therefore applied only to the arrest and detainment by the attorney general, and not to arrest and detainment by the military. The distinction actually originated with Judge Advocate General Joseph Holt back in 1863. John Fabian Witt concludes, "as Holt saw it, the act's constraints on the president's power had no bearing on prisoners held pursuant to the president's law of war authority. In so construing the act, Holt set the stage for a radical expansion in the scope of the laws of war."[56]

Witt explains that "nearly 1000 individuals were charged with violating the laws of war." Regular Confederate soldiers were sometimes so tried for spying, breaking loyalty oaths, or violating parole. More commonly, guerrillas or what we now call unlawful combatants were also tried for things like robbing and killing Unionists, which we might well call acts of terror today. But in addition to this, Witt finds that military commissions regarded as violations of the laws of war things farther from the conflict, including using disloyal language, kidnapping a "contraband negro," forging false discharge papers, assisting desertion, making a false claim for damages against the US armed forces, corruptly facilitating the release of convicts to serve as substitutes for conscripted men, neglect of duty by military contractors, forging medical certificates to extend furloughs, evading militia service, harboring rebel guerrillas, refusing to take the oath of allegiance, blockade running, obstructing the recruitment of black soldiers, killing a freedman, sending blacks deeper into Confederate territory after Emancipation, attacking black soldiers' families, conspiring to deprive soldiers of the vote, desecrating the Union dead, trading with the enemy, going to the South without a pass, joining the rebel army (only for citizens of nonseceding states), and writing encouraging letters to the South. The whole point of using law of war charges was to avoid the reporting requirements of the Habeas Corpus Act under what Witt calls "Holt's aggressive interpretation."[57]

Davis struck most if not all of this down in *Milligan*.[58] And in the twenty-first century, it would indeed seem like extravagant executive overreach to erect domestic military commissions to try many or most of these offenses. But in fairness to Lincoln, he did not have an FBI or a bureaucracy of federal prosecutors on hand. He had no Department of Justice, let alone a Civil Rights Division. Nor did he have sweeping regulatory authority under the commerce clause or the enforcement clauses of the Thirteenth, Fourteenth, and Fifteenth Amendments, or a bevy of congressionally authorized statues pursuant thereto. In *this* legal order, what he had was the US Army, and beginning in March 1863, the Provost Marshal General's Bureau. And he had the laws of war. Out of these, the Lincoln administration fashioned a temporary federal police power not otherwise established in the United States until well into the twentieth century. And he did so not to destroy federalism, let alone to create a dictatorship, for he everywhere conceived of this as temporary power in defense of republican government both majoritarian and egalitarian. As even the mere listing of the typical military commission charges makes clear, he did all this for two intimately connected reasons: to prosecute the war and to sustain black freedom.

Jonathan Hafetz's point in his chapter is therefore correct: it is *emphatically not the case* that Lincoln intended to establish a permanent regime of military commission trials. Seconding this, Mark Neely's investigations uncovered a Lincoln eager to restore civilian process, for instance in Missouri, even though Republicans there still feared violence from an unreconstructed proslavery party.[59]

We might say "too eager." As several chapters in this volume suggest, it is important to consider what a return to regular civilian process meant for newly freed African Americans. Locked in a republican understanding, Lincoln saw republican institutions as the solution to the problem of terrorism in Missouri.

> It seems that there is now no organized military force of the enemy in Missouri and yet that destruction of property and life is rampant every where. Is not the cure for this within easy reach of the people themselves? It cannot but be that every man, not naturally a robber or cut-throat[,] would gladly put an end to this state of things. A large majority in every locality must feel alike upon this subject; and if so they only need to reach an understanding one with another. Each leaving all others alone solves the problem. And surely each would do this but for his apprehension that others will not leave him alone. Can not this mischievous distrust be removed? Let neighborhood meetings be every where called and held, of all entertaining a sincere purpose for mutual security in the future, whatever they may heretofore have thought, said or done about the war

> or about anything else. Let all such meet and waiving all else pledge each to cease harassing others and to make common cause against whomever persists in making, aiding or encouraging further disturbance. The practical means they will best know how to adopt and apply. At such meetings old friendships will cross the memory; and honor and Christian Charity will come in to help.[60]

In this letter to Missouri governor Thomas C. Fletcher, the most basic building block of nineteenth-century self-government is here, the local meeting or convention. This was an institution of almost direct democracy that went back to the colonial era and whose preservation had been the chief concern of the Antifederalists. Local conventions were where much important legislation began in Lincoln's legislative career as well. Rather than relying on a distant federal judiciary backed by force to create and maintain domestic tranquility by checking tyrannical local majorities, as late as February 1865, Lincoln still hewed to government quite literally "by the people." But by pressing Republicans in Missouri to return to normal republican process with "charity," Lincoln risked exposing African Americans to further terror.

As noted in the introduction, there are two mutually exclusive anti-Lincoln traditions, the one holding that Lincoln was insufficiently concerned with black freedom and the other maintaining that he unconstitutionally disregarded white civil liberties. But one cannot complain both that Lincoln curtailed white civil liberties *and* that he was insufficiently concerned with black freedom. Throughout the war he was forced to choose between the two, a situation that persisted for Republicans through Reconstruction and beyond. Nowhere was this more glaringly apparent than in Lincoln's decision to end prisoner exchanges because the Confederacy failed to treat black soldiers as legitimate combatants. As historian John Fabian Witt notes, Walt Whitman, certainly no Lincoln hater, "took to the newspapers to decry Secretary Stanton for turning thousands of white soldiers into hostages for the benefit of a few black men."[61] Davis chose to protect local white majorities. Lacking the language and institutions of the modern Bill of Rights, Lincoln nevertheless chose black freedom, which he could only conceptualize in the republican terms of citizenship rooted in things like arms bearing, sole proprietorship, jury service, and local meeting.

The words "Christian Charity" in the Fletcher letter are also evocative. Faced with a tragic choice between white and black civil liberties, we should perhaps reconsider whether nationalist and neo-Confederate historians

Figure 9.2. "The Coming Man's Presidential Career," inspired by Charles Blondin, who crossed the Niagara Falls on a tightrope in June 1859 with his manager on his back. Published on August 25, 1860, this oracular drawing seems to capture the precarious position of Abraham Lincoln, African Americans, and the Constitution during the fraught emancipation process that was to come. Courtesy of the Library of Congress.

alike have unduly neglected that rare pair of Lincoln phrases that have not been made into book titles: "firmness in the right" and "as God gives us to see the right." The absence of these phrases from our book and chapter titles speaks volumes about our desire to create for ourselves a liberal rather than a republican past. Lincoln's final formulation, twelve days later, reveals that there was a tension here between "malice toward none and charity for all" on the one hand, and "firmness in the right as God gives us to see the right," on the other. Considering the lasting effects for African American freedom, it is worth considering whether in his earlier letter to the Missouri governor, Lincoln might have erred on the side of "malice toward none" rather than "firmness in the right" (to say nothing of "malice toward some"[62]).

"Firmness in the right as God gives us to see the right" may well have been the more important phrase in the closing of the Second Inaugural. It hearkened back to Lincoln's Cooper Institute address, in which he exhorted his fellow Republicans to proceed in the faith that right makes might. In his last public address, just over a month after the Second Inaugural, he suggested black suffrage. Importantly, it was black suffrage, specifically for soldiers and the well-educated, and participation in local republican government, rather than permanent judicial imposition from Washington, that for Lincoln might solidify the gains of the Civil War for blacks. The alternative was colonization.

Lincoln's frustration with the slow return to normal civilian rule in Missouri and elsewhere may have prompted Justice Davis to assume that Lincoln had come to share his view of the invalidity of military commission trials in areas not in rebellion. It will ever remain unknowable whether, in the face of postwar black codes and terror campaigns, Lincoln would have sustained military rule under the "grasp of war" theory or looked for a different legal solution—the guarantee clause, for instance,[63] or the enforcement clause of his Thirteenth Amendment project. Given his wartime record on civil liberties, it is highly unlikely he would have watched the rise of the Ku Klux Klan with equanimity. But the resistance of local republican majorities to inclusion of African Americans provoked a crisis for republicanism conceptually greater than the secession crisis itself. Along with the rise of mass industrialism at the end of the nineteenth century, this crisis proved to be the undoing of localist republicanism for which Lincoln assumed the Civil War was fought. The protection of local minorities would eventually require a shift in power to federal government.

Lincoln, however, still read the Constitution as a framework for the expression of popular power. In *Milligan,* his government essentially argued that if the Fourth, Fifth, and Sixth Amendments were restraints on the war-making power, fighting a war would be impossible. Holt had held that the requirements of the Habeas Corpus Act were at odds with "the exigencies" of the Union war effort.[64] Now Butler noted that Washington, DC, was under martial law throughout the Civil War and yet the courts were open and functioning the entire time.[65] Reading the Bill of Rights in a manner consistent with what Amar argued was its original meaning, Attorney General Speed and Benjamin Butler contrasted the "peace provisions" of the Fourth, Fifth, and Sixth Amendments with the Second and Third Amendments, which explicitly address war-related issues. Would fighting "armed rebels marching to attack the capital" deprive them of life, liberty, or property without due process of law, contrary to the Fifth Amendment? Or would searching and seizing the papers of and houses of persons in open rebellion, insurrection, and war against the government violate the Fourth Amendment?[66] That would be, well, "imbecile."

The veteran Butler taunted Black, who had been attorney general and secretary of state to the disgraced James Buchanan. Butler compared Black's contentions in *Milligan* to his holding for James Buchanan during the secession crisis that "there is no constitutional right in a State to go out of the Union, but that there is no power in the Constitution to coerce a State or her people, if she choose to go out."[67] In the face of a viciously racist refusal to accept black equality and black suffrage, Butler feared a return to the same "imbecility of administration" that characterized, in the popular Republican vernacular, James Buchanan, "the bachelor President."[68] Such was the contempt for the "copperhead" constitutionalism of Black and Buchanan among the committed radicals who fought for the Union alongside black troops. But Butler's arguments went well beyond mere expressions of contempt, and in *Ex parte Quirin,* the Supreme Court eventually endorsed Butler's contention that the Davis standard of applying the Bill of Rights to combatants was (mostly) unworkable.

In this light, it should be less surprising that dissent from *Milligan* began already with the concurring opinion. Chief Justice Salmon P. Chase argued that while the executive may not have had the power to try or sentence civilians in military courts, under its Article I war powers, Congress did have the power to authorize military commissions; it simply had not done so.

Chase and the concurring justices agreed that Milligan should be released or remanded for prosecution in civilian court.[69] Nevertheless, they pointed out that the Fifth Amendment included an exception for "cases arising in the land or naval forces, or in the Militia in actual service in time of war or public danger." The Civil War presented precisely such cases of domestic unrest "in which citizens conspiring or attempting the destruction or great injury of the national forces may be subjected by Congress to military trial and punishment." Chase stepped away from his earlier antislavery libertarianism and instead wielded the textbook rhetoric of republicanism: "Congress is but the agent of the nation, and does not the security of individuals against the abuse of this, as every other power, depend on the intelligence and virtue of the people, on their zeal for public and private liberty, upon official responsibility secured by law, and upon the frequency of elections, rather than upon doubtful constructions of legislative powers?"[70]

This was the basic pattern identified by Amar. The Chase opinion pointed out that the Bill of Rights had been co-crafted by Antifederalists concerned to preserve the power of state governments to protect republican liberty. "The states, most jealous of encroachments upon the liberties of the citizen, when proposing additional safeguards in the form of amendments, excluded specifically from their effect cases arising in the government of the land and naval forces."[71] For Chase and the concurring justices, the history of the amendments suggested that the exceptions of the Bill of Rights reflected concerns for the safety of republican institutions rather than for the integrity of the individual. The language here was of citizens in the plural, and such individual rights as there were in the Bill of Rights were a means to protect the collective right of self-government. Milligan was a threat to the republic, and in such cases, the health of the people was the highest law. War represented a potential public calamity not unlike famine, fire, or epidemic, and in the nineteenth century, private rights necessarily took a back seat while the safety of the people became the supreme law,[72] doubly so in a republic. Chase was able to perceive Milligan as a belligerent rather than a criminal, something Davis and Field refused to contemplate apart from the regular armies. As an (unlawful) belligerent, Milligan could be subject to trial and sentencing by military commission under the laws of war.

Narrowly squinting only at the constitutional text, Milligan's Democratic counsel, David Dudley Field, argued that the exception could only apply to members of the militia called to active service.[73] Field was as authentically liberal a figure as was to be found in the Civil War period. With the Thirteenth Amendment just passed, the American people had stated "the right of every human being to be free, except in punishment of a crime."[74] Field regularly espoused a belief in limited government out of a conviction that, far from a collective, communal good and the very expression of liberty by self-governing citizens, government itself was instead a threat to liberty conceived of in individual terms. Ahead of his time, therefore, as a constitutional and political thinker, Field saw majority rule as the problem well before the Fourteenth Amendment. For Field, energetic government posed a threat to individual liberty even when it was responsive to public opinion.[75]

But for Chase, it was agreed that the military exception in the Fifth Amendment applied as well to the other amendments in the Bill of Rights. With that, the Chase minority dismissed the libertarian use of the Bill of Rights proffered by Field and seemingly endorsed in Davis's majority opinion. According to Chase, the Bill of Rights provided for exceptions in cases of public emergency, especially military emergency, and Lincoln likely would have found Chase's reading of the Fifth Amendment congenial. His attorney general, James Speed, argued that the Fourth, Fifth, and Sixth Amendments were "peace provisions . . . silent amidst arms, and when the safety of the people becomes the supreme law."[76] Despite the way we now think about Bill of Rights protections, of the two views present in *Milligan*—Davis and Field's constitutional liberalism or the majoritarian republicanism of Chase and Lincoln—Chase and Lincoln's view was most consonant with nineteenth-century treatise writers.[77] Davis's views therefore, rather than Lincoln's, present the more difficult case for historical explanation.

In addition to the construction of the Fifth Amendment, Chase had Reconstruction in mind, and though this does nothing to disparage his constitutional reasoning, this almost certainly influenced his decision. By January 1866 it was apparent that white resistance to black freedom in the South meant that the army, using military commissions, would be essential to, in General Ulysses S. Grant's words, "protect the negro in his life, person and the few rights he has acquired." Grant suspended newspapers in the South and forwarded to Washington evidence of murders and assaults by whites on black people in the South.[78] In 1866, arguments over the limits of both congressional and military power, as well as over the definition of "peacetime," dominated political debates.[79] Coming at the end of a terrible year, one that saw massacres of African Americans in at least two major cities where open and functioning Southern courts provided slim consolation to blacks and white unionists, Chase's opinion addressed fears that the Davis opinion would be used to end any meaningful attempt by the US Army to secure black freedom in the South.

Less than a year after the opinions were handed down, these fears threatened to become real. When Democrats regained control in Maryland, their new state constitution took up the language of Davis's *Milligan* opinion, resolving "that the provisions of the Constitution of the United States, and of this State, apply, as well in time of war, as in time of peace."[80] In the midst of the army's war on Klan terror in November 1867, William McCardle, a Vicksburg, Mississippi, newspaper editor, threatened to publish the names of white Republican voters—if not a death sentence then something close to it. He also predicted the lynching of Major General E. O. C. Ord, the military commander for the district. Ord had him arrested, charging McCardle with several violations of the Military Reconstruction Act (recently passed by the Republican Congress over Johnson's veto), including disturbing the peace, inciting insurrection, disorder and violence, libel, and impeding reconstruction.[81]

Based on Davis's opinion in *Milligan*, McCardle's suit effectively challenged the entire basis of military reconstruction. In order to facilitate black enlistment in the army, Congress had recently expanded the jurisdiction of the federal courts to include granting the privilege of the writ of habeas corpus to "any person" restrained in violation of the US Constitution, treaties, or laws, also granting the Supreme Court appellate jurisdiction.[82] Former masters had been preventing the enlistment of (former) slaves into the US Army, and the act was intended to give ex-slaves a hearing to challenge *their* unlawful detentions. (This often-overlooked fact alone should caution anyone tempted to take uncritically the civil liberties pretensions, in liberal terms, of Democrats, or even of David Davis and David Dudley Field.)

Unfortunately, "any person" now also included McCardle. Though they were hardly functioning for black people or their white Republican allies, civilian courts were "open and unobstructed," and the president had proclaimed the war over. It remains unclear exactly how Davis himself would have voted had the case gone forward to be judged on its merits, but it was reported that Justices Clifford, Nelson, Grier, Davis, and (Stephen Johnson) Field had declined to affirm the constitutionality of military reconstruction.[83]

Fearing the Davis opinion in *Milligan* would be used in *McCardle* to inhibit the ability of the army to enforce meaningful black freedom in the South, Radical Republicans responded by stripping the Supreme Court of the very appellate jurisdiction over military commissions they had inadvertently granted only a year earlier. It would seem that Davis's opinion in *Milligan* had been cut off and that military commissions would continue.

Historians have conveniently identified the abolitionists as progenitors of rights-based constitutional and legal liberalism.[84] And indeed, as early as 1861, Radical Republican Lyman Trumbull argued that "the plea of military necessity was the plea of tyrants. I hold that under the Constitution the military is as much subject to the control of the civil power in war as in peace." But in fact, the abolitionist position aligned with the Chase opinion. Trumbull dismissed military necessity not on libertarian grounds but because military control was at best only temporary while, in his view a least, congressional lawmaking might be wielded to secure a more lasting reconstruction.[85] (As Michael Haggerty shows in chapter 8, prior to the war, Chase had denied that Congress had the power to enforce the Fugitive Slave Act of 1793.) No less than Lincoln and Davis, Radical Republicans, as Eric Foner notes, believed in a small-town world of sole proprietorship and self-government. The system of labor for wages was not the freedom of which congressional radicals dreamed. As it had for Lincoln, for the stalwart Grant, and for radicals prior to the Liberal Republican revolt in 1872, intimate and immediate self-government provided the "social basis" of republican representative institutions—institutions with sweeping plenary authority to create and preserve a well-regulated society. Out of concern to preserve and extend the gains made by African Americans during the war, radicals came to accept "the idea of a powerful national state guaranteeing blacks equal standing in the polity and equal opportunity in a free labor economy."[86] Nevertheless, radicals remained in the prevailing republican consensus that made sole proprietorship both the goal of political economy and the basis of republican citizenship.

This was equally true of other Republicans as well. As Benedict has argued, congressional reconstruction remained limited by fairly traditional constitutional ideas that precluded the creation of a permanent national state enforcing individual rights.[87] The rise of liberal rights-based constitutionalism paralleled the rise of a mass industrial society and permanent wage labor. In that new situation, participation in local government would decreasingly give self-governing citizens sufficient influence to secure their liberties. "Self-government" lost much of its meaning. A liberal state could not arise until judicially enforced constitutional protections were widely viewed as necessary. In 1866, that time was not yet.

For their part, Copperheads or Peace Democrats, and even War Democrats and conservative former Whigs, simply excluded blacks from participation while rejecting the proffered powerful national state on traditional republican grounds. Nevertheless, in *Milligan* they contributed essential DNA to the evolution of liberal constitutionalism and civil libertarianism in America by endorsing the shift to *individual* rights in *Milligan.* In turn, *Milligan* has helped cut us off from all memory of the positive freedom of John Quincy Adams's dictate that "freedom is power," for instance, or the republican understandings of government articulated by the Lincoln administration and by nearly everyone in the period with the possible exception of David Dudley Field.

As stated in the introduction, this raises troubling questions for liberal constitutionalism. Is it possible even for proper legal process to go viral and kill the creature of liberty itself? Is liberal constitutionalism even coherent? In *Milligan,* Davis all but accepted the Copperhead argument of convenience that the Bill of Rights should now protect individuals from the national state (though not black individuals from local governments). Certainly, Davis accepted the Emancipation Proclamation and the Thirteenth Amendment, but beyond that, he was now practically a Democrat. What does it tell us about the history of liberal constitutionalism in America that among the very inventors of the use of the US Constitution as the guardian, not of community or state rights, but of *individual rights,* were among the most extreme racists and race-baiters in an openly racist political party?

The pat answer, of course, is to say that the test of our commitments to civil liberties come when we are called to accord those rights to the most unsavory of characters.[88] But this does not take fair measure of the republican legal/constitutional order prior to *Milligan* and the Fourteenth Amendment. It is teleological because it assumes that modern liberal constitutionalism and its attendant rights-focused judicial supremacy were all along the latent goal of the Constitution, rather than the product of precisely these contingent historical developments. It assumes that Lincoln as well as radicals like Chase and Trumbull were inferior constitutional theorists rather than expert practitioners of a constitutional paradigm with its own integrity and one from which, at a very theoretical level, we might in fact be able to learn a thing or two.

In addition, it is not clear, to this critic at least, that the pat answer takes due account of what happened to African Americans for the next one hundred years and beyond.[89] Ask them whether a swift and severe example of the kind meted out by Butler in New Orleans or by Lincoln in the Sanborn-Wright case might better have been made of poor McCardle. As John Lupton shows in the next chapter, military officers risked suit for damages if they participated in military commission trials. In this legal universe, local common-law juries often had the final word rather than appellate justices applying the US Constitution as we now expect. Citing Davis's *Milligan* opinion, defendants in military commission trials now turned tables and sued their captors. After *Ex parte McCardle,* the use of commissions stopped, hamstringing the army's ability to protect blacks from terror.[90]

Lincoln did not seek permanent military rule. Nevertheless, Butler, the Lieber Code, and *Milligan* pose a profound and difficult set of questions: Is "imbecility of administration" the necessary price of civil liberty? When civil society descends into chaos and terror, does the Bill of Rights apply? Does the absence of the state really create liberty? And who pays the price when terror goes unprosecuted? Even as the Lincoln administration strove to restore normal local civilian rule, it knew through hard experience that military rule would be a necessary precondition. Hence, it turned its back on conciliation of the South in favor of international law, the Lieber Code, and "hard war."[91]

Three major positions regarding executive power emerged in *Ex parte Milligan*: Chase's plea for virtually unchecked congressional power; Davis's and Field's bid for full recognition of the Bill of Rights, in all times and all places, in peace as in war; and Lincoln's, for a vigorous executive under the commander-in-chief clause, but by virtue of that same clause subject to the laws of war including prohibitions against torture. As Benedict points out, one could plausibly argue that a synthesis of all three makes up current law. In *Quirin, Hamdan,* and *Boumediene* the Court has in part confirmed the habeas corpus requirements of *Milligan.* Noncombatant US citizens held anywhere are afforded a habeas corpus hearing and a civil trial in the United States. Beyond that, the Court seems to be adopting, ironically, Lincoln's position. Subject to the laws of war and the *concurrent* authority of Congress, military commissions may try unlawful combatants. Davis's position of rec-

Figure 9.3. "Halt!" by Thomas Nast, *Harper's Weekly,* October 17, 1874. The caption reads, "This is not the way 'to repress corruption and to initiate the Negroes into the ways of honest and orderly government.'" Justice is portrayed as a powerful female character wielding a double-edged sword engraved with the words "Constitution of the U.S." and "Law." Courtesy of the Library of Congress.

ognizing full Bill of Rights protections for individuals even under threat of terror and sabotage during wartime (albeit away from the actual armies) has been sustained only in part by the courts over a long course of history. But that part is not insignificant. Though Congress still has very important concurrent war powers, Chase's endorsement of sweeping congressional authority has been reigned in both by the courts and by the concurrent war powers of the president, particularly in emergencies, thus sustaining Lincoln's position. Finally, Lincoln's position that the laws of war govern in wartime still holds out a model for the vigorous prosecution of war without a descent into barbarity, even against a barbarous enemy. This outcome has less to do with original intent or textual meaning, though it takes some plausible root there. It is the outgrowth of historical experience. As the least naive position, it recognizes the reality of terrorism and the possible need for harsh measures up to and including the use of military commissions to secure domestic tranquility, but it also puts international law checks on the executive and admits of some Bill of Rights oversight. This combined position has been most credibly confirmed by hard-edged historical experience of war, both nationally and internationally, and by the moral and constitutional bearings of the nation in America's wars on terror.

NOTES

1. Spencer Ackerman, "Trump Administration Wants to Release US Citizen Enemy Combatant in Syria," *Daily Beast* (June 7, 2018).

2. Curtis A. Bradley, "The Story of *Ex parte Milligan*: Military Trials, Enemy Combatants, and Congressional Authorization," in Christopher H. Schroeder and Curtis A. Bradley, eds., *Presidential Power Stories* (New York: Foundation Press, 2009), 104.

3. *Ex parte Clement Vallandigham*, 68 US *Ex parte Vallandigham* 243–244 (1863).

4. Mark E. Neely Jr., *The Fate of Liberty: Abraham Lincoln and Civil Liberties* (New York: Oxford University Press, 1991), 68.

5. Though convicted under the doctrine of "military necessity," it is difficult to see how Vallandigham could have been classified as an unlawful combatant under the laws of war, as Milligan probably should have been. Bradley, "The Story of *Ex parte Milligan*," 105.

6. For an up-to-date tour of the literature see Robert O. Faith, "'This Despotic and Arbitrary Power': British Diplomacy and Resistance in the Habeas Corpus Controversy of the American Civil War" (PhD diss., University of Akron, 2018), 15–27.

Highlights include J. G. Randall, *Constitutional Problems under Lincoln* (New York: D. Appleton, 1926) and Daniel A. Farber, *Lincoln's Constitution* (Chicago: University of Chicago Press, 2003). For current libertarian counternarratives see Thomas J. DiLorenzo, *The Real Lincoln: A New Look at Abraham Lincoln, His Agenda, and an Unnecessary War* (Roseville, CA: Prima, 2002); Jeffrey Rogers Hummel, *Emancipating Slaves, Enslaving Free Men: A History of the American Civil War* (Chicago: Open Court, 1996); and Charles Adams, *When in the Course of Human Events: Arguing the Case for Southern Secession* (Lanham, MD: Rowman & Littlefield, 2000).

7. Herman Belz, "The Dictatorship Question Reconsidered," in Belz, *Abraham Lincoln, Constitutionalism, and Equal Rights in the Civil War Era* (New York: Fordham University Press, 1998), 28, 33, 43; Neely, *The Fate of Liberty*, 14.

8. Depending on how one reads him, Mark Neely may have moved in this direction in his more recent work. See Mark E. Neely Jr., *Lincoln and the Triumph of the Nation: Constitutional Conflict in the American Civil War* (Chapel Hill: University of North Carolina Press, 2011), 64–65, 109, 197. Wood Gray, *The Hidden Civil War: the Story of the Copperheads* (New York: Viking Press, 1942); John Yoo, "Lincoln and Habeas: Or Merryman and Milligan and McCardle," *Chapman Law Review* (2008): 505; John Yoo, "Merryman and Milligan (and McCardle)," *Journal of Supreme Court History* 34 (2009): 243–260.

9. David Ciepley, *Liberalism in the Shadow of Totalitarianism* (Cambridge, MA: Harvard University Press, 2006); James L. Huston, *Securing the Fruits of Labor: The American Concept of Wealth Distribution, 1765–1900* (Baton Rouge: Louisiana State University Press, 1998); Akhil Reed Amar, *The Bill of Rights: Creation and Reconstruction* (New Haven, CT: Yale University Press, 1998).

10. Thomas L. Krannawitter, *Vindicating Lincoln: Defending the Politics of Our Greatest President* (Lanham, MD: Rowman & Littlefield, 2010), 324–325, 332; Benjamin Kleinerman, *The Discretionary President: The Promise and Peril of Executive Power* (Lawrence: University Press of Kansas, 2009).

11. Roy P. Basler, ed., *The Collected Works of Abraham Lincoln*, 9 vols. (New Brunswick, NJ: Rutgers University Press, 1953), 4: 264.

12. John Fabian Witt, *Lincoln's Code: The Laws of War in American History* (New York: Free Press, 2012); Antonio F. Perez, "Lincoln's Legacy for American International Law," *Emory International Law Review* (2014): 167; Burrus M. Carnahan, *Act of Justice: Lincoln's Emancipation Proclamation and the Law of War* (Lexington: University Press of Kentucky, 2007); Burrus M. Carnahan, "Lincoln, Lieber, and the Laws of War: The Origins and Limits of the Principle of Military Necessity," *American Journal of International Law* 92 (1998): 213; Burrus M. Carnahan, *Lincoln on Trial: Southern Civilians and the Law of War* (Louisville: University Press of Kentucky, 2010).

13. John A. Marshall, *American Bastille*, 27th ed. (Philadelphia: T. W. Hartley, 1885).

14. Daniel Feller, "Libertarians in the Attic, Or a Tale of Two Narratives," *Re-*

views in American History, no. 2 (2004): 184; Jeffrey Rogers Hummel, *Emancipating Slaves, Enslaving Free Men: A History of the American Civil War* (Chicago: Open Court, 1996); DiLorenzo, *The Real Lincoln*; Charles Adams, *When in the Course of Human Events: Arguing the Case for Southern Secession* (Lanham, MD: Rowman & Littlefield, 2000).

15. William Alan Blair, *With Malice toward Some: Treason and Loyalty in the Civil War Era* (Chapel Hill: University of North Carolina Press, 2014), 160–162 passim.

16. Blair, *With Malice toward Some,* 160–190.

17. Mark E. Neely Jr., "'Seeking a Cause of Difficulty with the Government': Reconsidering of Speech and Judicial Conflict under Lincoln," in Phillip Shaw Paludan, ed., *Lincoln's Legacy: Ethics and Politics* (Urbana: University of Illinois Press, 2008), 48–66.

18. Two recent books address this seldom-asked question; Witt, *Lincoln's Code* and Blair, *With Malice toward Some.*

19. Jennifer L. Weber, *Copperheads: The Rise and Fall of Lincoln's Opponents in the North* (New York: Oxford University Press, 2006).

20. Gregory P. Downs, *After Appomattox: Military Occupation and the Ends of War* (Cambridge, MA: Harvard University Press, 2015), 4, 124, 206, 233, 237–238.

21. Robert H. Churchill, *To Shake Their Guns in the Tyrant's Face: Libertarian Political Violence and the Origins of the Militia Movement* (Ann Arbor: University of Michigan Press, 2009), 134–139.

22. *Ex parte Milligan,* 71 US, at 121, 127 (1866).

23. *Ex parte Milligan,* 107, 119–121.

24. Stephen G. Breyer, *The Court and the World: American Law and the New Global Realities* (New York: Knopf, 2015), 59–60, 64, 65, 80–81.

25. Quoted in Neely, *Fate of Liberty,* 175.

26. William J. Novak, *The People's Welfare: Law and Regulation in Nineteenth-Century America* (Chapel Hill: University of North Carolina Press, 1996), 10.

27. Michael Les Benedict, Personal Communication forwarded to Stewart Winger, March 14, 2018.

28. Neely, *Fate of Liberty,* 208.

29. In *Ex parte Merryman,* Chief Justice Taney did hold that Merryman's Sixth Amendment rights had been violated, but the case was not before the entire Supreme Court, and once again, it was Taney. See Jonathan W. White, *Abraham Lincoln and Treason in the Civil War: The Trials of John Merryman* (Baton Rouge: Louisiana State University Press, 2011), 31; *Ex parte Merryman,* 17 Fed. Cas. 144.

30. Jennifer K. Elsea, "Detention of American Citizens as Enemy Combatants," in Ralph D. McPhee, ed., *The Treatment of Prisoners: Legal, Moral, or Criminal?,* (New York: Nova Science Publishers, 2006) 8–9.

31. *Ex parte Milligan,* 85–87.

32. This entire analysis is taken from Neely, *Fate of Liberty,* 67.

33. See note 7 supra.

34. As noted in the introduction, if one goes to *Collected Works of Abraham Lincoln* online and executes a basic search of the term "public safety," one gets a clear indication that this is so.

35. Stacy Pratt McDermott, *The Jury in Lincoln's America* (Athens: Ohio University Press, 2012); Akhil Reed Amar, *The Bill of Rights: Creation and Reconstruction* (New Haven, CT: Yale University Press, 1998), chapter 5, "Juries."

36. There are 5,173 cases in the law practice of Abraham Lincoln, 388 of which were circuit court cases during the fourteen years when Davis was a circuit court judge, and 463 which were county or municipal court cases. Only six cases dealt with constitutional law, but all of them concerned the Illinois Constitution and none of them with its Bill of Rights. Because the cases were chosen merely because Lincoln or one of his partners were involved and because some record of the case survives, this represents a fair and significant sample of legal action at the level of Davis's Courts. (This query includes cases in which Davis was not presiding, and Davis presided over cases now missing from the archives due to fire or other mishap.) It is virtually certain Davis never fielded a US Bill of Rights question while on the Illinois Circuit bench and probably never an Illinois bill of rights question either. http://www.lawpracticeofabrahamlincoln.org/Search.aspx. In 1919, *Illinois Constitutions* Shephardized the bill of rights (Article XIII) of the 1848 constitution. Of the cases listed there, none of them came from Davis's circuit, though Abraham Lincoln was listed as counsel in *Ross v. Irving* 14 IL 171 (1852). Emil Joseph Verlie, *Illinois Constitutions* (Springfield: Trustees of the Illinois State Historical Library, 1919) 86–90.

37. John A. Lupton, "Basement Barrister: Abraham Lincoln's Practice before the United States Supreme Court," *Lincoln Herald* 101 (Summer 1999): 47–59.

38. Barry, "*Ex parte Milligan:* History and Historians," 357.

39. Neely, "'Seeking a Cause of Difficulty with the Government,'" 64 and passim. See also Joseph G. Gambone, "*Ex parte Milligan:* The Restoration of Judicial Prestige?" *Civil War History* 16, no. 3 (1970): 246.

40. Akhil Reed Amar, *The Bill of Rights: Creation and Reconstruction* (New Haven, CT: Yale University Press, 1998), 64–68.

41. Barry, "*Ex parte Milligan:* History and Historians," 357; Bradley, "The Story of *Ex parte Milligan*," 109.

42. Clinton Rossiter, *The Supreme Court and the Commander in Chief* (Ithaca, NY: Cornell University Press, 1976), 7.

43. That is, as originally conceived by Antifederalists. As Amar notes, Madison for his part *did* worry about majority tyranny, but his amendments protecting individual conscience against action by the states failed in the Senate, where those same states rejected it. As originally conceived in the Bill of Rights, "the people" was a collective noun that did not refer to individual rights.

44. Amar, *The Bill of Rights: Creation and Reconstruction*, xiii.

45. Amar, 80.

46. *Ex parte Clement Vallandigham*, 124, 119.

47. On Lincoln's intentions see Mark E. Neely Jr., "The Constitution and Civil Liberties Under Lincoln," in Eric Foner, ed., *Our Lincoln: New Perspectives on Lincoln and His World* (New York: W. W. Norton, 2008), 51–61.

48. Amar, *The Bill of Rights: Creation and Reconstruction,* chapter 4. Sometimes the Bill of Rights refers to "persons," unambiguously conceived as individuals.

49. Novak, *The People's Welfare.*

50. *Ex parte Milligan,* 21.

51. Witt, *Lincoln's Code,* 270.

52. *Ex parte Milligan,* 21 According to a search of Google Books, the phrase "unlawful combatant" appears for the first time in Douglas Owen, *Declaration of War: A Survey of the Position of Belligerents and Neutrals* (London: Stephens & Sons, 1889), 7. The Lincoln administration likely would have held al-Qaeda to be "uncivilized" rather than "unlawful" combatants.

53. Neely, *Fate of Liberty,* 14.

54. White, *Abraham Lincoln and Treason,* 119.

55. White, 8, 38, 88–89, 120–121.

56. Witt, *Lincoln's Code,* 266–267, 26.

57. Witt, 266–267, 26.

58. Witt, 312.

59. Neely, "Constitution and Civil Liberties under Lincoln," 51–61.

60. Basler, *Collected Works of Abraham Lincoln,* 8: 308.

61. Witt, *Lincoln's Code,* 258–259.

62. Blair, *With Malice toward Some.*

63. Mark E. Neely Jr., *Lincoln and the Democrats: The Politics of Opposition in the Civil War* (New York: Cambridge University Press, 2017), 187–198.

64. Witt, *Lincoln's Code,* 266.

65. *Ex parte Milligan,* 105.

66. *Ex parte Milligan,* 20.

67. *Ex parte Milligan,* 89.

68. Edward L. Ayers, *In the Presence of Mine Enemies: War in the Heart of America, 1859–1863* (New York: W. W. Norton, 2004), 143.

69. *Ex parte Milligan,* 137–142, 135.

70. *Ex parte Milligan,* 34, 139.

71. *Ex parte Milligan,* 137–388.

72. Novak, *The People's Welfare,* chapters 2 and 6.

73. *Ex parte Milligan,* 30.

74. David Dudley Field, *Speeches, Arguments, and Miscellaneous Papers of David Dudley Field* (New York: D. Appleton, 1884) I: 6.

75. Field, *Speeches, Arguments, and Miscellaneous Papers,* "River and Harbor Improvements by the Federal Government, Speech at the River and Harbor Convention in Chicago, July 6, 1846."

76. *Ex parte Milligan,* 20.

77. We will treat the late nineteenth-century treatise writers below. For the first seventy years of the nation's history on this point, see Louis Fisher, *Military Tribunals: Historical Patterns and Lessons* (Washington, DC: Congressional Research Service: Library of Congress,[2004]), 1–16.

78. Downs, *After Appomattox*, 120.

79. Michael Les Benedict, *A Compromise of Principle* (New York: W. W. Norton, 1974), chapters 7–10.

80. White, *Abraham Lincoln and Treason*, 111.

81. Swanberg, "*Ex parte McCardle* and the First Amendment during Reconstruction," 339; Downs, *After Appomattox*, 198.

82. Lee Epstein, *Contemplating Courts* (Washington, DC: CQ Press, 1995), 338.

83. Swanberg, "*Ex parte McCardle* and the First Amendment during Reconstruction," 346.

84. See Akhil Reed Amar, *The Bill of Rights: Creation and Reconstruction* (New Haven, CT: Yale University Press, 1998), 234–243, 379 n8.

85. Mark Grimsley, *The Hard Hand of War: Union Military Policy toward Southern Civilians, 1861–1865* (Cambridge: Cambridge University Press, 1995), 12.

86. Eric Foner, *Reconstruction: America's Unfinished Revolution, 1863–1877*, 1st ed. (New York: Harper & Row, 1988), 236–237.

87. Michael Les Benedict, "Preserving the Constitution: The Conservative Basis of Radical Construction," *Journal of American History* 61, no. 1 (1974): 65–90.

88. Wendy Swanberg, "*Ex parte McCardle* and the First Amendment during Reconstruction," in David B. Sachsman, ed., *A Press Divided: Newspaper Coverage of the Civil War* (New Brunswick, NJ: Transaction Publishers, 2014) 340–341.

89. Historians of civil liberties in the Civil War have often chastised the Lincoln administration, some gently and others more harshly, but rarely have they acknowledged the degree to which African-American civil liberties were even at stake in the Civil War. Several chapters in this volume attempt to correct this.

90. Downs, *After Appomattox*, 238.

91. Grimsley, *Hard Hand of War.*

Part Four

The Precedential Power of Milligan

CHAPTER 10

Ex Parte Milligan in the State Courts: Madison Y. Johnson's Vindication in Illinois

John A. Lupton

Ex parte Milligan has been called one of the "bulwarks of American liberty" in defending citizens against the encroachment of military authority and even the "heart of the difference between the United States of America and Nazi Germany or Communist Russia."[1] John P. Frank began a 1944 article on the case by noting that it "has become the fashion in recent years to criticize" the *Milligan* decision because it arose from "an obsolete day and an outmoded science of war."[2] Frank's article appeared during World War II, when the imprisonment of Japanese Americans resulted in a reassessment of presidential war powers. Mark E. Neely Jr. continued the "fashion" by declaring *Milligan* irrelevant, arguing that while written in "thunderously quotable language," the decision had "little practical effect."[3] Neely suggests that many constitutional scholars misinterpreted the case's legacy. Even though the decision supports personal liberties, according to Neely, the evidence shows that courts generally ignored *Milligan* when it mattered.[4]

The postwar Illinois case of *Johnson v. Jones* illustrates that *Milligan* was neither disregarded nor ignored in the states. In August 1862, US marshal J. Russell Jones arrested Madison Y. Johnson for disloyal activities. Imprisoned in Fort Lafayette in New York, then at Fort Delaware in Delaware, Johnson served a total of three and a half months before his release, with no charges ever brought against him. Johnson was one of at least fourteen thousand people the federal government imprisoned during the Civil War for opposition to the administration of President Abraham Lincoln.[5] After the war, Johnson sued Marshal Jones to recover damages for false imprisonment. Using the newly decided *Milligan* case, the Illinois Supreme Court heard and ruled on Johnson's attempt to gain vindication for his false imprisonment.

In the past, the topic of civil liberties during the Civil War was typically covered by the examination of the two bookend federal cases: the 1861 case *Ex parte Merryman* and the 1866 case *Ex parte Milligan.*[6] More recently, scholars have examined other federal cases that relate to the wartime activities of the Lincoln administration. Bruce Ragsdale adds to the discussion *In re McDonald, Ex parte Vallandigham,* and *Ex parte McCardle* as similar cases to *Milligan.*[7] Neely discouraged the examination of these notable cases and urged historians to look at many cases to obtain a "wide variety" of actions to discuss the larger subject of false imprisonment.[8]

In his later work, *Lincoln and the Triumph of the Nation,* Neely rightly points out that "constitutional historians are likely to overlook" legal conflicts that took place "not in the Supreme Court of the United States but in the lower courts of the states." Neely demonstrates, "The lower the judge, the higher his chances of encountering war issues in his courtroom."[9] Several state cases, indeed, better illustrate that government overreach with regard to military affairs was taken seriously by the courts, and demonstrate that far from being neglected, the *Milligan* decision was operative at the state level.

Milligan was not decided in a vacuum but rather was one link in a significant chain of personal liberty cases that occurred at the state level. A cursory examination of those state cases prior to *Milligan* and a deeper examination into the Illinois *Johnson* case after *Milligan* demonstrate the continuity of these types of cases and the overall importance of *Milligan.* Johnson's case is the best example of a state case that relied heavily on the then recently decided *Milligan* case, but it also affords an opportunity to observe the Illinois legal system at work during and after the Civil War in the context of state courts ruling on the overreach of presidential powers.

In re Kemp was one of the first cases that reached a state supreme court dealing with the writ of habeas corpus and "did much to shape early American civil liberties law."[10] Nicholas Kemp had been arrested in 1862 for leading a riot to prevent a draft in Wisconsin. The Wisconsin Supreme Court issued a writ of habeas corpus to release Kemp from Camp Randall, but General W. L. Elliott refused to turn over Kemp under General Orders No. 141 from President Abraham Lincoln.[11] In January 1863 the Wisconsin Supreme Court's opinion relied on US Supreme Court chief justice Roger B. Taney's ruling in *Merryman*—that the power to suspend the writ of habeas corpus was a legislative, not executive, responsibility. More importantly, however, the Wisconsin Supreme Court noted that "martial law may be necessary . . . where actual war exists, and yet not be necessary in other states. Wisconsin is not the theatre of war, but fortunately far removed from it. The civil authorities here maintain themselves. Justice is dispensed by the courts; the laws are administered without difficulty, and no necessity can exist for subjecting the citizen to the control of military power."[12] Ten months later, the New York Supreme Court reached a similar conclusion in *Jones v. Seward,* noting that the president cannot "extend martial law beyond the sphere of military operations."[13]

One month after *Jones,* the Indiana Supreme Court concurred in two separate cases, *Skeen v. Monkeimer* and *Griffin v. Wilcox.*[14] In *Skeen,* the court stated that "Indiana has never been in a condition to justify, according to any established principle of law, the superseding of the judicial by the military power, in the prosecution and punishment of crime."[15] The *Griffin* case stated this premise more directly. Joseph Griffin had been arrested for selling liquor to soldiers after Provost Marshal Frank Wilcox ordered the prohibition of liquor sales. After his release, Griffin sued Wilcox to recover damages for false imprisonment. The Marion County Court of Common Pleas ruled for Wilcox, and Griffin appealed to the Indiana Supreme Court. Following its logic in *Skeen,* the court overturned the lower court's judgment, noting that "martial law is exercised in our country . . . where no civil authority exists. But where the civil authority exists, the Constitution is imperative that it shall be paramount to the military." Later in the opinion, the court emphasized that point again, "in all parts of the country, where the Courts are open, and the civil power is not expelled by force, the Constitution and laws rule."[16]

The language in *Griffin* is very similar to *Milligan,* which occurred three years after *Griffin.* Even though Justice David Davis did not cite *Griffin,* it demonstrates that Davis's ruling in *Milligan* was not without precedent. Each of these state cases emphasized points made by Davis with respect to personal liberties and the overreach of the military. The Supreme Judicial Court of Massachusetts best summarized this tension between civil and military authorities in the 1864 case *Tyler v. Pomeroy.* Justice Horace Gray wrote that questions "of the lawfulness of acts done under color of military authority, in time of war, are among the most delicate and important that can come before a court of justice, whose duty it is equally to maintain the rightful powers of the government and to guard the subject against unlawful violence." Gray continued that when it becomes necessary to determine "the rights of parties in a judicial proceeding," acts done under color of military authority "must be treated in the same manner as any other question of law."[17]

Neely suggests that *Milligan* became irrelevant because it was written after the war and during peacetime, when "distinctions were clearer to the justices in 1866 than to the hard-pressed Lincoln administration between 1861 and 1865."[18] Justice Gray of Massachusetts would disagree. State courts recognized those distinctions during wartime and decided personal liberty cases in the same manner as *Milligan* after the war. State courts, where the great majority of cases nationwide occur, consistently agreed that while courts were open and where the military did not have a battleground presence, the laws in force could not be overruled by military law. State appellate court cases are not as well known as *Merryman* or *Milligan,* and Neely encourages further research in that area because "the judicial record of the Civil War has been underestimated."[19] In postwar Illinois, the case of Madison Y. Johnson continued the precedent set by other state courts during the war and by *Milligan* after the war. Johnson's lawsuit demonstrates the relevance of *Milligan* in the immediate postwar North. The case was never heard in a federal tribunal, giving local courts an opportunity to contribute to the civil liberties discussion.

Johnson's particular situation is not entirely unknown since Johnson himself wanted to tell his story to as many people as would listen. He was a frequent speaker at Democratic rallies after his release, and, not unlike Milligan and Vallandigham, he wore Lincoln's abuse of his civil liberties as a "badge of honor."[20] Springfield's Democratic newspaper, the *Illinois State Register,* reported after the war that nearly "every person in the state, and a large number in other localities, have heard of the atrocious treatment of Madison Y. Johnson, esq., at the hands of the secretary of war and his minions, during the late war."[21] Johnson contributed a chapter to John A. Marshall's anti-Lincoln book, *American Bastile* (1869), and in a local county history, he devoted five pages of his seven-page biography to his imprisonment.[22]

Historians of the Civil War era used Johnson's experience in their research. Frank L. Klement cited Johnson several times in his study of midwestern Copperheads, devoting several pages to Johnson's experience. Klement viewed Copperheads in a positive light as honest opponents of the

Figure 10.1. Madison Y. Johnson as he appeared in *American Bastile.*

Lincoln administration and suggested that Johnson's principal reason for taking his case to the Illinois Supreme Court was to obtain a favorable judgment from fellow Copperheads sitting on the Supreme Court.[23] Noted Lincoln and Illinois historian Paul Angle also authored an article on Johnson. Angle's article concerned Johnson's activities during the Civil War, devoting only a paragraph to Johnson's attempts at vindication through the legal system. Angle agreed with Klement in concluding that Johnson sincerely

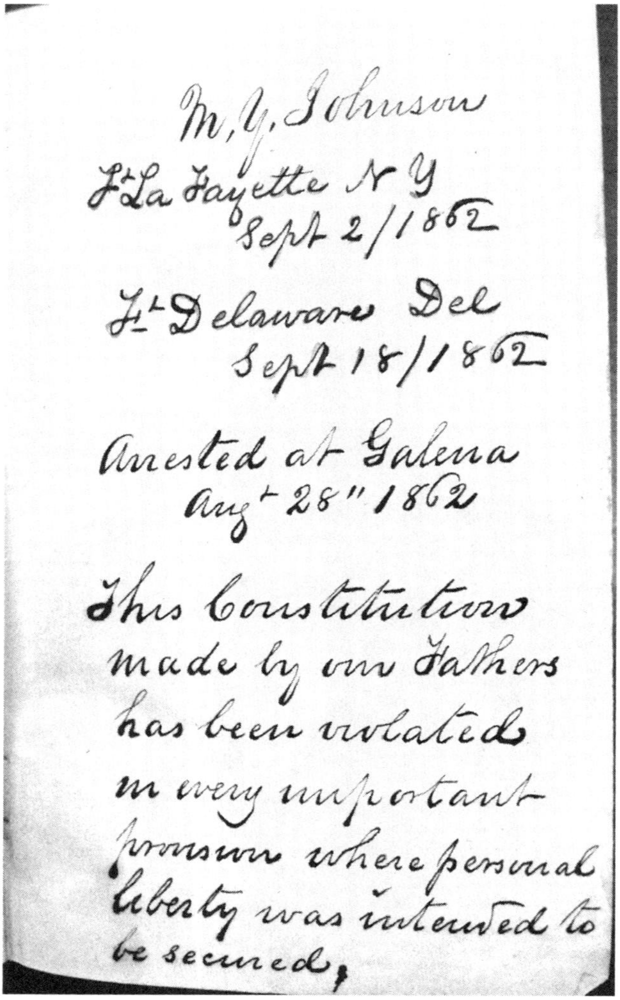

M. Y. Johnson
Ft La Fayette N Y
Sept 2/1862
Ft Delaware Del
Sept 18/1862
Arrested at Galena
Augt 28" 1862
This Constitution
made by our Fathers
has been violated
in every important
provision where personal
liberty was intended to
be secured,

Figure 10.2. The inside cover of Madison Y. Johnson's copy of the US Constitution. Courtesy of the Chicago History Museum.

believed in a strict construction of the Constitution, was not the threat that the government believed, and that "the world is better off for men of the Madison Y. Johnson stamp."[24] Gene Arnold authored a well-done but little-used master's thesis on Johnson's plight using Johnson's diary and papers housed at the Chicago History Museum.[25] Like Angle, Arnold focused on the treatment of Johnson's arrest and detainment, with the subsequent lawsuit merely a footnote to the story. In Arnold's otherwise excellent thesis, Johnson's lawsuit is relegated to an appendix.[26] Most recently, Stephen E. Towne mentions Johnson's arrest for "seditious speech and suspicious membership in the Knights of the Golden Circle."[27]

By focusing more on the lawsuit for damages and less on Johnson's arrest and detention, this study of Johnson's case demonstrates that the legal efforts to gain vindication are just as important as the story that leads up to the lawsuit. In his book written in the 1950s but published in 2015, Roger Severns notes that "arbitrary arrests and many instances of imprisonment without charge and without trial . . . found their way into the courts." Severns emphasized the influence of *Milligan* in that "the possibilities of successful legal action were strengthened by the decision . . . in the *Milligan* case in 1866."[28] Jonathan W. White argues that "scholars have overlooked the issue of damage suits for more than a generation" and that "it is a subject that demands attention."[29]

Madison Y. Johnson was born in Xenia, Ohio, in 1817. As a young boy, he and his family moved to Kentucky, where he grew to adulthood. He engaged in various business pursuits while studying law. He eventually obtained his law license and began working in Louisville, Kentucky. In 1841 he moved to Shawneetown, Illinois, practicing law there until 1844, when he moved to Galena.[30] Johnson immediately made a name for himself, engaging in Galena businesses, establishing a thriving law practice, and actively supporting the Whig Party. Despite living more than two hundred miles from Springfield, Johnson interacted with a fellow Whig lawyer named Abraham Lincoln on at least two occasions. Johnson and Lincoln both represented Levi Wilcoxon in the Illinois Supreme Court in 1846, and Johnson wrote to Lincoln in 1853 for assistance with a deposition. Johnson also worked with Stephen T. Logan in a case while Logan and Lincoln were legal partners.[31]

In addition to making close friends in Galena, he found himself embroiled in a rivalry with fellow Whig and Galena resident Elihu B. Washburne. In the early 1850s, Johnson allegedly defeated Washburne for the attention of Ann Wright, daughter of the superintendent of the Galena lead mines, and married her in 1854. Washburne had also expressed interest in purchasing a particular house in Galena, but Johnson bought the house instead. These actions resulted in a mutual dislike of one another. The Kansas-Nebraska Act in 1854 pushed Washburne, then a congressman, toward the soon-to-be-formed Republican Party, while Johnson became a man without a party. While he supported Abraham Lincoln—as an "old-line Whig"—in his 1858 Senate race against Stephen A. Douglas, Johnson did not support the Republican Party, feeling that it had become an abolitionist party. In the 1860 presidential election, Johnson supported John Bell and the Constitutional Union Party, serving as an elector, but he continued to call himself a former Whig even at the beginning of the Civil War.[32]

When war finally came, Johnson slowly moved toward the Democratic Party. At first he was not an outspoken critic of the administration, other than a public display of contempt for the presence of Union troops in Missouri. Johnson also took pride in his Southern heritage, claiming a familial relationship to Confederate General Joseph E. Johnston, but his words and actions did not indicate support for secession or the Confederacy. While Jo Daviess County was very Republican and the city of Galena had contributed a large number of soldiers and generals to the Union Army, there were a good number of Democrats, like General John A. Rawlins, Galena mayor Robert Brand, Johnson, and attorney David Sheean.[33] In 1862, newspapers regularly referred to Johnson as a Democrat, and Johnson was a very strong supporter of the Democratic-controlled constitutional convention in Illinois that year. Despite Johnson's mild antiwar criticisms, Washburne's friends and newspapers already branded him as a "traitor."[34]

The event that precipitated Johnson's arrest was not his outspokenness against the administration but simply his involvement in a lawsuit in Jo Daviess County. One of the first enlistments from Galena was a forty-year-old German named Nicholas Roth. He served for three months and then reenlisted for three years. During this second stint in the army, he was commissioned a lieutenant, serving until the Battle of Shiloh in the spring of 1862. He resigned from the service because of an ailment.[35] When he returned home in the summer of 1862, Galena was in the middle of significant recruiting to replenish the losses from Shiloh and to reach quotas without having to submit to the draft.[36]

That August, Secretary of War Edwin M. Stanton issued orders to arrest anyone who discouraged enlistments.[37] Stephen E. Towne suggests that draft dodging and Knights of the Golden Circle activity posed a valid threat to order.[38] Stanton's order gave broad powers to US marshals and other police forces to make arbitrary arrests.[39] Bradner Smith, another Galena resident, claimed that Roth had been telling his friends not to enlist. Smith submitted an affidavit to that effect, causing Jo Daviess County Sheriff Simeon Miner to arrest Roth for discouraging enlistments.[40] While Roth was in custody, Madison Johnson offered his legal services pro bono to Roth, requesting a writ of habeas corpus to free him. The state circuit court judge Benjamin Sheldon refused to issue the writ of habeas corpus, believing that Roth was guilty. The federal judge for the Northern District of Illinois, Thomas Drummond, also refused to assist, believing that suspending the writ of habeas corpus was illegal, but that military authorities would ignore his order. Roth, with Johnson as his lawyer, responded on August 12 with a trespass suit against Smith for false imprisonment, requesting $10,000 in damages.[41] Stanton's August 8 order came at the same time as Johnson becoming Roth's attorney, which heightened suspicion against Johnson. While Johnson did not discourage enlistments himself, he represented Roth, who had allegedly discouraged enlistments. From the government's perspective, this made Johnson a dangerous person and a valid threat to order.

Rather than fight the lawsuit in a court of law, Smith responded by sending an affidavit to the secretary of war, notifying Stanton of Johnson's "well known" and "notorious" "disloyalty to the government." He concluded by asking for relief from the lawsuit "in such a manner" as Stanton "would see fit."[42] Frank Klement suggested in *Copperheads in the Middle West* that the rising political strength of the Democrats in 1862 caused Republicans to arrest prominent Democrats.[43] Mark Neely and Jennifer Weber acknowledge that most arrests were made by Republicans against Democrats, but they disagreed with Klement's argument that arrests were politically motivated: Weber notes that the strong peace platform of many Democrats made them targets, but not because they were Democrats, whereas Neely claims the purpose of the arrests, at least in 1862, was to prevent draft resistance.[44] William A. Blair agrees that "it would be wrong to think of all targets of political arrests as victims," but in Johnson's case, he most likely was a victim.[45]

Klement frequently used Johnson as an example of political imprisonment, but Klement misinterpreted his situation. Supporting Neely's and Weber's assertions, Johnson's arrest was not a result of political intrigue but of an opposing client's attempt to extricate himself from a damages lawsuit. In this regard, Klement is correct in noting that Johnson probably was an honest opponent to the administration before his arrest. Johnson was not a political figure like Illinois congressman William J. Allen, who had been arrested about the same time. Ironically, Johnson became more political, more vociferous, and perhaps more dangerous after his arrest.[46]

Included with Smith's affidavit was a certification by the Jo Daviess County circuit clerk that Roth had brought a lawsuit against Smith, and that Johnson was Roth's attorney. On August 27, J. Russell Jones, the US marshal for the Northern District of Illinois, received a telegram from Judge Advocate Levi C. Turner containing an order from the secretary of war to arrest Johnson. Johnson's crime against the government was merely representing a client charged with disloyal activities, which apparently made Johnson guilty of disloyal activities in Stanton's eyes.

Johnson was in court the following day, representing a different client on a murder charge. Marshal Jones and two deputies entered court and notified Johnson of the arrest warrant. Illinois statutes prevented the federal officers from arresting Johnson while in court.[47] Johnson completed the trial at nine o'clock that evening, and upon leaving the courthouse was promptly taken into custody. He was transported to Chicago and met briefly with Judge Drummond, who told Johnson that he would issue a writ of habeas corpus. Johnson declined, instead wishing to defend his arrest on its merits.[48] Johnson was then transferred to Fort Lafayette in New York City harbor.[49]

A few weeks later, Judge Advocate Turner examined Johnson, asking him if he knew why he was arrested. Johnson replied that he did not. Turner then asked if he had been involved in a lawsuit with Nicholas Roth against Bradner Smith. Johnson replied that he had, but that he "had too much confidence in my Government to believe they would interfear and make the act of a lawyer in bringing a suit between two private individuals a cause for my arrest." Turner wanted, and Johnson provided, more information about the case, but Johnson was stunned, commenting that "that could not be the charge." Turner asked if he was a member of the Knights of the Golden Circle, and Johnson replied that he was not. Turner then asked if Johnson would take the loyalty oath. Johnson answered that he had taken the oath as an attorney but refused to do so in this instance because it implied wrongdoing.[50] The hearing ended, and Johnson remained imprisoned.[51]

Shortly after the hearing, Johnson was transferred to Fort Delaware, an island in the Delaware River.[52] He wrote several letters, including at least one to Secretary of War Stanton and two to President Lincoln, requesting information about why he was being detained.[53] None were answered. In another letter to a friend in Washington, DC, he worried about why an order for his discharge had not yet arrived. "I wish that you would look sharp &

see that it is sent soon," he instructed his friend. He also wondered whether his friend should visit the newly elected US senator from Illinois William A. Richardson to ask for assistance. "If I have to waite, for a general order, in the hurly burly of business, we are entirely overlooked, & it may be, weeks or months before the matter would be disposed of."[54] Johnson was given significant liberties at Fort Delaware, segregated from the Confederate prisoners and Union deserters, and put with other Northerners imprisoned for disloyal activities. Johnson said that "paradise" was open to him with "an Island of 80 acres to roam over."[55]

After some assistance from several of his Galena friends, Johnson finally obtained his release on December 13, 1862, upon taking a loyalty oath—perhaps several months of imprisonment had changed his mind.[56] His friend David Sheean, who had spent his entire imprisonment in Fort Lafayette, also gained release. The two traveled together back to Chicago and Galena and received a heroes' welcome. Both gave rousing anti-administration speeches in support of the Constitution and personal liberty, and in opposition to a war to free the slaves.[57] After regaining their freedom, both Johnson and Sheean received many invitations as speakers at Democratic rallies. Accepting nearly all of them, they denounced Lincoln's "usurpations," giving accounts of their lives as "prisoners of state" in the "Bastile."[58] His arrest and detention allowed him and Democrats in general to "depict themselves as champions of civil liberties."[59]

Johnson initially attempted to gain satisfaction through political means by requesting that Senator Richardson investigate the practice of false arrests. Johnson had earlier suggested that his friend contact Richardson, so the senator was more than likely aware of Johnson's plight. Richardson read on the floor of the Senate Johnson's petition that summarized Johnson's detention and attempts to discover the reason for his imprisonment. After debate, the senators concluded that Johnson "has by the law of the land, and he can ascertain whether he has or not, if he appeals to the judicial tribunals, and not to [the legislature]—a personal remedy against the person who illegally arrested him." In legal terms, a remedy is the "means employed to redress an injury."[60] Johnson's attempt to obtain a remedy through the legislature failed in the Republican body.[61]

In effect, the US Senate suggested that Johnson sue Jones. Aggrieved parties frequently turned to the legal system to recover damages against government officials for vindication. In the antebellum period, public officials could be sued for actions undertaken while in the public service.[62] In Abraham Lincoln's law practice, there were at least a dozen cases in which sheriffs or constables were sued for excessive force or false imprisonment in arresting individuals.[63] One of the first instances of a damage suit occurred against Secretary of War Simon Cameron after he had Pierce Butler arrested and detained in Fort Lafayette. Butler sued Cameron for false imprisonment in Pennsylvania. President Lincoln became involved in the lawsuit and told Secretary of State William H. Seward and Attorney General Edward Bates that Cameron acted under the president's orders, and that Cameron's actions were "necessary for the prompt suppression of the existing rebellion."[64] The case was eventually dropped, but Lincoln's role in the Butler case shows that he believed those acting on behalf of the government should be personally immune from lawsuits for false imprisonment.

As a successful and practicing Illinois lawyer, Johnson understood the legal system very well. He acted upon the advice of Congress to obtain vindication through the legal system, which was becoming a popular response of imprisoned, uncharged prisoners upon their release.[65] Marshal J. Russell Jones feared that Johnson would sue him for damages for simply performing his duties. On January 6, 1863, he wrote to his friend Elihu Washburne: "Johnson and Sheean are going to give me hell. Will not Congress pass a law to protect me?"[66] After his experience with the Pierce Butler case, even President Lincoln was concerned with civil lawsuits against government officials as potentially damaging the "public welfare as well as the safety of the individual officers of the government."[67] Congress's answer was the Indemnity Act of March 3, 1863, allowing officers in the service of the government who arrested citizens to use the president's orders as a defense in any lawsuit.[68] The act also called for state actions against officials performing their duties be transferred to the federal courts.[69] Kellee Green Blake offers one example of an Illinois case in the Tazewell County Circuit Court that was transferred to the federal court, and then dismissed.[70]

Some state courts resisted the change of jurisdiction from state to federal courts because the federal courts lacked jurisdiction. The language in the Indemnity Act to transfer cases originated in a similar 1815 law after the War of 1812, but a federal court in Massachusetts declared the law unconstitutional.[71] Harold Hyman noted that "some of these state judges, holding that they were competent to decide whether Congress could properly remove litigation involving national officer-defendants from state to national courts, pronounced the 1863 Habeas Corpus law unconstitutional."[72] In particular, the 1863 *Jones v. Seward* case in New York rejected Secretary of State William H. Seward's request to transfer the case from state to federal court. The court reasoned that the president's order to arrest a person not subject to military law was not warranted to give the federal courts jurisdiction. The case falls "within the jurisdiction of [the New York state] court."[73] Madison Johnson was most likely aware of this debate.

In August 1864, Johnson brought suit in the Jo Daviess County Circuit Court against Marshal Jones, deputy marshals John C. Hopkins and Oliver P. Hawkins, Elihu B. Washburne, and Bradner Smith for trespass for false imprisonment, requesting a total of $50,000 in damages.[74] According to an Illinois form book, a trespass was any offense against another person's body or property, and false imprisonment was one form of a trespass. Johnson sued the marshal and his two deputies because they were active participants in his detention, forcibly removing him from Illinois. Johnson included Washburne and Smith in the lawsuit because one who "counseled, advised, or procured the false imprisonment of another, is liable as a principal, although he did not participate actively in the commission of the act."[75] Johnson assumed that Washburne was behind his arrest and that Washburne used Smith to get to Johnson. After a year of attempting to summon all of the defendants, the case finally moved forward.[76]

The three marshals—Jones, Hawkins, and Hopkins—immediately requested and obtained permission to sever in pleading from co-defendants Washburne and Smith. Severance allowed for joint defendants to plea separately in order to rely upon certain defenses that other defendants could not use.[77] The marshals had a justifiable defense—the Indemnity Act—that did not apply to the congressman or to Smith. In a special plea filed in May 1865, Jones, not unexpectedly, relied on the Indemnity Act. He argued that he was under orders from President Lincoln, Secretary of War Stanton, and Judge Advocate Turner to arrest Johnson, and that Johnson's detention in Forts Lafayette and Delaware was out of his control.[78] In additional special pleas, Jones argued that Johnson was a member of the Knights of the Golden Circle, that he aided and abetted the rebellion, and that he participated in disloyal activities by discouraging enlistments.[79]

At the next term of court, in August 1865, Johnson filed demurrers to all of Jones's special pleas.[80] A demurrer is an objection in the common-law pleading process that does not dispute the truth of the allegation but argues that Jones's response was not sufficient in the law to continue the pleading process. If the court were to sustain the demurrer, then the pleas would be considered invalid and Jones would have to replead; if the court were to overrule the demurrer, then the pleas would be considered valid and Johnson would have to provide a suitable legal response to Jones's pleas.[81] Johnson stated his reasons for demurring: (1) because Jones's defense was vague, and Jones only offered his opinions, not proven facts; (2) there was no evidence to prove that Johnson was in the Knights of the Golden Circle; and (3) there was no war in northern Illinois, and thus no reason for Johnson to be detained. Moreover, Johnson argued that the indemnity law Jones used as a defense was unconstitutional, and that President Lincoln had usurped his powers as commander in chief and protector of the Constitution.[82]

In March 1866, Jo Daviess County Circuit Court judge Benjamin R. Sheldon overruled Johnson's demurrer. Jones was on firm ground in pleading that the Indemnity Act was a valid defense. Rather than continue the pleading process in the case, Johnson chose to stand by his demurrer. By refusing to continue the pleading process, Johnson defaulted in the case, and the court ruled in favor of Jones and the deputies. By standing by his demurrer, Johnson also provided a rationale for appealing his case to a higher-level court. A seasoned lawyer like Johnson certainly understood how the legal system worked and how to obtain a potential ruling from the highest court in Illinois. He also refused to prosecute further his case against the severed defendants Washburne and Smith, and the court ruled for them.[83]

Johnson immediately appealed the decision to overrule the demurrer to the Illinois Supreme Court. In the April 1867 term, the Illinois Supreme Court consisted of Justices Sidney Breese, Charles B. Lawrence, and Pinkney H. Walker. The political makeup of the justices is worth noting. Sidney Breese had been a strong Democrat since the 1830s and gained appointment to the Illinois Supreme Court in the Democratic court-packing legislation of 1841. A few years later, he won election to the US Senate. Upon his return to Illinois, he remained a Democrat, serving as speaker of the Illinois House of Representatives, then returning to the Supreme Court in 1857. Breese identified as a Peace Democrat during the Civil War. Charles B. Lawrence was a prominent Republican. Pinkney H. Walker identified himself as a Republican and was first appointed to the court by a Republican governor, but he was not active in politics. He won two popular elections to the Illinois Supreme Court in a judicial district that favored Democrats.[84]

Figure 10.3. ***From left*: Justices Charles Lawrence, Sidney Breese, and Pinkney Walker, who ruled in Madison Y. Johnson's case at the Illinois Supreme Court. Courtesy of the Abraham Lincoln Presidential Library and Museum.**

Frank Klement claimed that Johnson sought to take the appeal because he expected a favorable outcome from a sympathetic supreme court, but two of the three justices were Republicans.[85]

The three-justice court heard arguments from Johnson, who represented himself, and from Corydon Beckwith, a former Illinois Supreme Court justice who represented Jones and his deputies.[86] Johnson's argument before the court was a scathing attack on the Lincoln administration and offered only token attention to the points of the case. He stated that to "the errors assigned, we invite the attention of the court in passing."[87] Rather than concentrate on specific legal arguments, Johnson used the opportunity to criticize the deceased president and his "absolute, dictatorial, [and] imperial" policies. Johnson asked, "Can the President, because he happens to be President, do an act, that would be criminal, if done by a private individual, and escape the consequences?" He added that he had "not unnecessarily commented on the acts of the Executive; God knows, we would be willing to let him rest in his grave" but in speaking of "the President, I have intended to treat the officer with that respect due his exalted position. In speaking of the man, and his usurpations, I have intended to characterize them as they deserve."[88]

The arguments for Jones and the deputies stuck to the legal issues that they had made at the trial level. Since they won the case in Galena with these arguments, there was no reason to shift the focus to defending Lincoln's reputation. Beckwith argued that Johnson had been a member of the Knights of the Golden Circle and had discouraged enlistments, and that Jones was ordered by Lincoln to arrest Johnson to help suppress the rebellion.

At the April 1867 term of the Supreme Court, Justice Charles B. Lawrence gave the opinion for the unanimous court. Near the beginning of the opinion, Justice Lawrence asked, do the arguments of Jones and his deputies "justify the alleged trespass?" He quickly answered that they did not, clarifying that it "cannot be denied, that when [Johnson] was arrested without writ or warrant . . . , the letter and the spirit of . . . the Constitution were plainly violated."[89] Lawrence then examined the extent of wartime powers, using the *Prize Cases* to show that the "rebellion was more than an insurrection. It was a public war." The *Prize Cases* allowed the government to classify the Confederacy as a belligerent.[90] Jones's argument, however, did not classify Johnson as a belligerent, and therefore Jones could not make him a prisoner of war.

Following the logic of the *Prize Cases,* Lawrence also relied on the recently decided *Milligan* case from the US Supreme Court. Lawrence added that a "belligerent is a subject of the hostile power, and his character, in that regard, depends upon that of the community to which he belongs."[91] Lawrence used the same principles from previous state cases and from *Milligan* to argue that the declaration of martial law was unnecessary and extralegal in areas where the war was not raging. Since Johnson lived in northern Illinois, where the courts were open and where the actual war was nowhere to be found, he could not be considered a belligerent. To justify Johnson's arrest, Jones had to prove that he was a belligerent and in an area of open warfare. Jones failed to prove that.

The language Lawrence used is very similar to the language David Davis used in *Milligan* and in prior state supreme court cases. Justice Davis wrote that "martial rule can never exist where the courts are open and in the proper and uninterrupted exercise of their jurisdiction. It is also confined to the locality of actual war." Since Milligan lived in Indiana, where the courts were open and where the actual war was nowhere to be found, he could not be considered a belligerent. Lawrence added that of the two cases, *Johnson* and *Milligan, Johnson* was more decisive of the argument, since martial law had not been imposed when Johnson was arrested, but it had been when Milligan was arrested. The government could make a legitimate argument for Milligan's detention, but Jones could not make a legitimate argument for Johnson's.[92]

The court also rejected Jones's reliance on the Indemnity Act. Lawrence claimed that when one citizen of Illinois committed a trespass against another citizen of Illinois, the laws of Illinois offered a remedy, until Congress passed the Indemnity Act. Lawrence claimed that there "is nothing to be said in support of this legislation. With all our respect for congress, we must hold these acts beyond its constitutional authority." If not, Congress's power over people and property "is limited only by its own discretion, and constitutional government is merely a theory."[93] James G. Randall found that the Indemnity Act failed in its purpose of protecting marshals and other enforcement officers. Agents of the government who pleaded the Indemnity Act as a defense often found that many state court judges, like Lawrence, believed the act to be unconstitutional and that "no matter who issued the order, even the President, no legal protection was afforded."[94]

Lawrence also acknowledged the abuse of power of the Lincoln administration. He wrote that "we are not unconscious of the fact that the decision which we are obliged to make . . . attributes to our late lamented President the unlawful exercise of power, and therefore implies a certain degree of censure." While the court expressed its profound appreciation and "purity of motive" of Lincoln's actions to suppress the rebellion, it added that "neither our honor for his memory, nor our confidence in his honesty, can be permitted to sway our judgment here." Lawrence concluded that the questions presented "must be decided by us as questions of abstract law. If this plaintiff has been wrongfully restrained of his liberty, he has the right to call upon us so to declare, without fear, favor, or affection."[95]

Lawrence was unequivocally asserting the independence of the judicial branch in general. He excoriated the executive and legislative branches, claiming that both were attempting to assert their authority in areas beyond their enumerated powers. Lawrence argued that with the Indemnity Act, Congress attempted to assert judicial function in an ex post facto manner.[96] The Indemnity Act, passed in 1863, had no authority over an event from 1862, as only the "laws in force, at that time; and these are facts to be determined by judicial investigation, and facts which no Congress could change."[97] Lawrence was completely convinced of his argument but could have strengthened it further by citing several state cases, including *Skeen, Kemp,* and *Griffin,* which was the first case to declare the Indemnity Act illegal.[98]

The Illinois Supreme Court reversed and remanded the case back to Jo Daviess County for further proceedings with instructions that Jones's pleas were not a bar to the action, but that they could be used in mitigation of damages.[99] In a separate opinion, Justice Breese concurred with Lawrence's reasoning except for mitigating damages. Breese feared that a jury might "assess nominal damages for one of the greatest outrages ever perpetrated in a country claiming to be governed by a written constitution and having a code of laws." Breese conceded, however, that "pecuniary considerations" did not compel Johnson to bring this action, "but rather to vindicate that Constitution and laws so grossly violated in his person."[100]

The case returned to the Jo Daviess Circuit Court docket in March 1868. By consent of the parties, the court continued the case for several terms before Jones admitted defeat in May 1869 and "confessed the wrongful trespass and imprisonment," claiming that Johnson was "innocent of the violation of any law or of doing any act inimical to the government." In the agreement, Johnson echoed Breese's separate opinion in that the lawsuit was not brought to gain financial reward but merely for the "purpose of personal vindication of his character and conduct as a citizen." Johnson released all damages except for $1,000 to cover court costs.[101] Madison Johnson obtained his vindication.

Jones's newfound willingness to settle the case and prevent a new trial was probably due in part to the fact that newly elected president, Ulysses S. Grant, had just appointed him minister to Belgium, and he would not be able to continue his defense in the case from Europe. Even though Jones publicly admitted that Johnson's seizure was wrong, privately he believed that Johnson deserved to be imprisoned. Jones also continued to believe, also privately, that he was merely acting on the orders of his superiors, the secretary of war and the president, both of whom should have been responsible for Jones's actions.[102]

Johnson's case was not the only case to obtain vindication for the alleged victim. The US Circuit Court for the District of California heard John McCall's case against General Irvin McDowell, who had McCall arrested for celebrating the assassination of President Lincoln. McCall sued McDowell for false imprisonment and received a $635 judgment. US district judge Matthew Deady noted that "personal liberty . . . is the right of every citizen of the republic."[103] A few years after *Johnson,* Lambdin Milligan also obtained vindication in the federal court in the same manner as McCall, gaining a favorable judgment, albeit with only $5 in damages, against General Alvin Hovey, the army general who had Milligan arrested.[104]

Frank Klement called *Johnson* a "sequel" to *Milligan.*[105] After the Civil War, the Illinois Supreme Court played a major role in protecting civil liberties. The court agreed not only with Johnson in his lawsuit but also in several other cases in Illinois. David Sheean's case, heard at the same term as *Johnson,* resulted in the same judgment. The opinion stated that "this case is identical in principle with that of *Johnson v. Jones,* ante, and the judgment will be reversed for the reasons given in the opinion filed in that case."[106] One year later, another case that reached the Illinois Supreme Court against Marshal Jones also resulted in the same judgment. In the Court's opinion, Justice Breese noted that "this case is, in all its important elements, identical with that of *Madison Y. Johnson v. J. Russell Jones et al.,* decided at the April Term 1867, and we perceive nothing in the argument now submitted by the counsel of the defendants to induce us to re-examine the decision in that case. With the results there reached we are satisfied."[107]

The *Milligan* precedent resonated in the Illinois Supreme Court that in times of war—even during calamitous times as the Civil War—personal liberties were important, particularly in areas where the war was not raging. The "thunderously quotable language" was not simply lofty rhetoric but had practical meaning. Both *Milligan* and *Johnson* were the culmination of a series of cases in the state courts during the Civil War that emphasized the protection of personal liberties. *Milligan* established that same protection at the highest court in the United States. Its use in Illinois demonstrates that *Milligan* was not irrelevant and that it was part of a continuum stating that without constitutional protections to personal liberty, the republican experiment was a failure.

NOTES

1. Charles Warren, *The Supreme Court in United States History,* 2 vols. (Boston: Little, Brown, 1922), 2: 427; Henry Winthrop Ballantine, "Constitutional Limitations on the War Power," *California Law Review* 6 (1918): 138; Allan Nevins, "The Case of

the Copperhead Conspirator," in John A. Garraty, ed., *Quarrels That Have Shaped the Constitution* (New York: Harper & Row, 1964), 108.

2. John P. Frank, "*Ex parte Milligan* v. the Five Companies: Martial Law in Hawaii," *Columbia Law Review* 44 (1944): 639. Peter J. Barry adequately covers the changes over time in a concise manner of how authors have reacted to *Milligan* positively and negatively: Peter J. Barry, "*Ex parte Milligan:* History and Historians," *Indiana Magazine of History* 109 (2013): 359–375.

3. Mark E. Neely Jr., *The Fate of Liberty: Abraham Lincoln and Civil Liberties* (New York: Oxford University Press, 1991), 176; John Yoo, "Lincoln and Habeas: Of Merryman and Milligan and McCardle," *Chapman Law Review* 12 (2009): 507. Yoo particularly notes *Ex parte Quirin,* 317 US 1 (1942); *Korematsu v. United States,* 323 US 214 (1944); *Hamdi v. Rumsfeld,* 542 US 507 (2004); and *Hamdan v. Rumsfeld,* 548 US 557 (2006) as examples of the irrelevance of *Milligan.*

4. Neely, *The Fate of Liberty,* 183–184.

5. James G. Randall noted that the War Department counted 13,535 arrests, which did not include arrests prior to February 1862, when the War Department assumed control over arrests from the State Department. Randall added that the actual number of people arrested was far less than the exaggerated amount of 38,000 by Alexander Johnston, a Princeton historian, who wrote an article on habeas corpus in 1881: James G. Randall, *Constitutional Problems under Lincoln* (New York: D. Appleton, 1926), 152 n25. Mark Neely disregarded all of the numbers and attempted to frame the question differently. He then calculated varying governmental records, arriving at a figure of 13,298, but then added that many records are missing, and stated that the number of Northerners arbitrarily arrested was far more than the 13,535 that the War Department records: Neely, *The Fate of Liberty,* 115, 127–130.

6. *Ex parte Merryman,* 17 F. Cas. (Maryland) 144 (1861); *Ex parte Milligan,* 71 US (4 Wall.) 2 (1866); Bruce A. Ragsdale, *Ex parte Merryman and Debates on Civil Liberties during the Civil War* (Washington, DC: Federal Judicial Center, 2007); Philip S. Paludan, *The Presidency of Abraham Lincoln* (Lawrence: University Press of Kansas, 1994), 75–80.

7. *In re McDonald,* 16 F. Cas. (Missouri) 17 (1861); *Ex parte Vallandigham,* 68 US (1 Wall.) 243 (1863); *Ex parte McCardle,* 74 US (7 Wall.) 506 (1869); Ragsdale, *Ex parte Merryman and Debates on Civil Liberties,* 15–21.

8. Neely, *The Fate of Liberty,* 127. Two other books merit conversation and are worth examination to learn more about Lincoln's war powers in general and civil liberty views in particular. The first is Daniel Farber's *Lincoln's Constitution,* a more modern version of James G. Randall's *Constitutional Problems under Lincoln.* The second is Stuart Streichler's biography of Benjamin Curtis, who was known for his dissent in the *Dred Scott* case but a few years later claimed Lincoln exceeded his war powers authority. Daniel Farber, *Lincoln's Constitution* (Chicago: University of Chicago Press, 2003), 144–175; Stuart Streichler, *Justice Curtis in the Civil War Era* (Charlottesville: University of Virginia Press, 2005), 151–171.

9. Mark E. Neely Jr., *Lincoln and the Triumph of the Nation: Constitutional Con-*

flict in the American Civil War (Chapel Hill: University of North Carolina Press, 2011), 165.

10. *In re Kemp*, 16 Wis. 359 (1863); Joseph A. Ranney, "*Inter Arma Silent Leges:* Wisconsin Law in Wartime," *Wisconsin Lawyer* 82 (February 2009): 14.

11. General Orders No. 141 declared that anyone interfering with enlistments shall be arrested. Paludan, *The Presidency of Abraham Lincoln*, 191.

12. *In re Kemp*, 376–377.

13. *Jones v. Seward*, 3 Grant 431 (1863).

14. *Skeen v. Monkeimer*, 21 Ind. 1 (1863); *Griffin v. Wilcox*, 21 Ind. 370 (1863). See also Emma Lou Thornburgh, "Judge Perkins, the Indiana Supreme Court, and the Civil War," *Indiana Magazine of History* 60 (March 1964): 79–96.

15. *Skeen v. Monkeimer*, 3.

16. *Griffin v. Wilcox*, 378, 386.

17. *Tyler v. Pomeroy*, 8 Allen 480 (1864).

18. Neely, *Fate of Liberty*, 184.

19. Neely, *Lincoln and the Triumph of the Nation*, 198.

20. Jennifer Weber noted that paradoxically, arbitrary arrests "became something of a badge of honor for some dissidents." Jennifer L. Weber, *Copperheads: The Rise and Fall of Lincoln's Opponents in the North* (New York: Oxford University Press, 2006), 56.

21. "Retributive Justice," *Illinois State Register* (Springfield), April 9, 1870, 1, col. 2.

22. *Portrait and Biographical Album of Jo Daviess and Carroll Counties* (Chicago: Chapman Brothers, 1889), 205–211; John A. Marshall, *American Bastile: A History of the Illegal Arrests and Imprisonment of American Citizens during the Late Civil War* (Philadelphia: Thomas W. Hartley, 1869), 509–535. James G. Randall dismissed *American Bastile* as sensational and ahistorical, with its only purpose to denounce the government: Randall, *Constitutional Problems under Lincoln*, 150–151.

23. Frank L. Klement, *The Copperheads in the Middle West* (Chicago: University of Chicago Press, 1960), 19, 21–22, 50, 258–259.

24. Paul Angle, "Madison Y. Johnson: Copperhead?" *Chicago History* 6 (Spring 1963): 327–340.

25. Gene Arnold's thesis is by far the most extensive treatment of Johnson's life in general and in his detention and the circumstances surrounding it: Gene Edwin Arnold, "Without Due Process: Madison Y. Johnson and the Civil War" (master's thesis, DePaul University, 1967).

26. Arnold, "Without Due Process," 341–362.

27. Stephen E. Towne, *Surveillance and Spies in the Civil War: Exposing Confederate Conspiracies in America's Heartland* (Athens: Ohio University Press, 2014), 253.

28. Roger L. Severns, *Prairie Justice: A History of Illinois Court under French, English, and American Law* (Carbondale: Southern Illinois University Press, 2015), 190.

29. Jonathan W. White, *Abraham Lincoln and Treason in the Civil War: The Trials of John Merryman* (Baton Rouge: Louisiana State University Press, 2011), 120.

30. *Portrait and Biographical Album of Jo Daviess and Carroll Counties, Illinois*, 205; Arnold, "Without Due Process," 11–12.

31. *Wilcoxon v. Roby* (L02505), Johnson asked Lincoln to take deposition of Barret (N06021), and *Wight v. Kirkpatrick* (L01843), all in Martha L. Benner and Cullom Davis et al., eds., *The Law Practice of Abraham Lincoln: Complete Documentary Edition*, 2d ed. (Springfield: Illinois Historic Preservation Agency, 2009), http://www.lawpracticeofabrahamlincoln.org.

32. Arnold, "Without Due Process," 18, 43–44, 71, 87, 96.

33. Sheean had recently been licensed to practice law, having studied law with John A. Rawlins, who became General Ulysses S. Grant's assistant adjutant general and chief of staff. Sheean also was arrested for disloyal practices at the same time as Johnson, and his imprisonment and subsequent lawsuit followed the same path as Johnson's, but for the purposes of this study, Sheean's ordeal is noted mainly in passing. James Harrison Wilson, *The Life of John A. Rawlins* (New York: Neale Publishing , 1916), 102; Elmer Gertz, "Three Galena Generals," *Journal of the Illinois State Historical Society* 50 (Spring 1957): 24–35; John Y. Simon, ed., *The Papers of Ulysses S. Grant*, 31 vols. to date (Carbondale: Southern Illinois University Press, 1967–), 6: 220–221; Marshall, *American Bastile*, 451–462.

34. Arnold, "Without Due Process," 101, 113, 117. The word "traitor" became more synonymous with Northern Democrats than with Southern secessionists by the end of 1861. Jonathan W. White, "'To Aid Their Rebel Friends:' Politics and Treason in the Civil War North" (PhD diss., University of Maryland, 2008), 39; Robert E. Sterling, "Civil War Draft Resistance in Illinois," *Journal of the Illinois State Historical Society* 64 (Autumn 1971): 250.

35. Arnold, 138–139.

36. Sterling, "Civil War Draft Resistance in Illinois," 248–249.

37. Neely, *The Fate of Liberty*, 52–53. Neely referred to this order as the "lowest point for civil liberties in the North during the Civil War."

38. Towne, *Surveillance and Spies in the Civil War*, 252, 307.

39. William A. Blair, *With Malice toward Some: Treason and Loyalty in the Civil War Era* (Chapel Hill: University of North Carolina Press, 2014), 108.

40. Arnold, "Without Due Process," 145–148.

41. A similar set of circumstances followed David Sheean, who represented Bernard Donnelly, who was also arrested for discouraging enlistments and who also brought suit against his accusers, brothers Robert Harris and Daniel Harris, for false imprisonment for $10,000. Marshall, *American Bastile*, 451–462; Arnold, "Without Due Process," 144, 151, 154. Both Donnelly's and Roth's cases ended up at the Illinois Supreme Court with Sheean and Johnson representing them, respectively. *Donnelly v. Harris et al.*, 41 Ill. 127 (1866); *Roth v. Smith*, 41 Ill. 314 (1866); and *Roth v. Smith*, 54 Ill. 431 (1870). For a discussion on damage suits, see particularly, White, *Abraham Lincoln and Treason in the Civil War*, 90–95, 104–106.

42. Arnold, "Without Due Process," 152.

43. Klement, *Copperheads in the Middle West*, 23, 43, 108.

44. See particularly Neely, *The Fate of Liberty*, 61; Weber, *Copperheads*, 10.

45. Blair, *With Malice toward Some*, 120.

46. Blair, 160–161.

47. "Judges, counsellors, or attorneys, clerks, sheriffs and other officers of said courts, shall be privileged from arrest while attending courts." Attorneys and Counsellors at Law, *Revised Statutes of the State of Illinois* (1845), 74.

48. Diary, 31 August 1862, Madison Y. Johnson Papers, Chicago History Museum (hereafter cited as CHM), Chicago, IL.

49. For a description of Fort Lafayette see Marshall, *American Bastile*, 652–681.

50. In Illinois, as in most states, newly licensed attorneys take an oath to support the Constitution. *Revised Statutes of the State of Illinois* (1845), 73–74; Josiah Henry Benton, *The Lawyer's Official Oath and Office* (Boston: Boston Book Company, 1909). Many political prisoners refused to take the loyalty oath because it assumed guilt on the part of the suspected traitor. See generally Harold M. Hyman, *Era of the Oath: Northern Loyalty Tests during the Civil War and Reconstruction* (Philadelphia: University of Pennsylvania Press, 1954).

51. Diary, 9 September 1862, Johnson Papers, CHM.

52. For information on Fort Delaware in the Civil War see Dale Fetzer and Bruce Mowday, *Unlikely Allies: Fort Delaware's Prison Community in the Civil War* (Mechanicsburg, PA: Stackpole Books, 2000).

53. Madison Y. Johnson to Edwin M. Stanton, 20 October 1862; Madison Y. Johnson to Abraham Lincoln, 28 October 1862, both in Johnson Papers, CHM. In Johnson's letter to Lincoln, Johnson notes that a prior letter, not extant, dated September 7, 1862, had been sent and had not been answered.

54. Madison Y. Johnson to Darius Hunkins, 8 December 1862, eBay auction #231749801964 (sold November 18, 2015). In the letter Johnson expressed a desire to move out West when he was released from prison.

55. Diary, 18 September 1862, Johnson Papers, CHM.

56. Hyman, *Era of the Oath*, 34.

57. "Reception of M. Y. Johnson and D. Sheean, Esqs., at Galena, Illinois" (Galena, IL: Democrat Office, 1863), 5; Klement, *Copperheads in the Middle West*, 22.

58. Klement, 50.

59. Harold M. Hyman and William M. Wiecek, *Equal Justice under Law: Constitutional Development 1835–1875* (New York: Harper & Row, 1982), 237.

60. John Bouvier, *A Law Dictionary*, 2 vols. (Philadelphia: Childs & Peterson, 1857), 2: 442–445.

61. *The Congressional Globe*, February 2, 1863, 664–666; *Chicago Tribune*, February 7, 1863, 2. On December 1, 1862, when Richardson was a member of the US House of Representatives, he submitted a resolution to the president to inform the House who had been arrested from Illinois and why they were being detained. The House immediately defeated the proposed resolution. *Journal of the House of Representatives of the United States*, 37th Cong., 3rd Sess. (Washington, DC: Government Printing Office, 1863), 9–10.

62. Randall, "The Indemnity Act of 1863," 589–591.

63. See particularly *Schlenker et al. v. Risley* (L02485), *Liggett v. Frazier* (L01482), and *Haines v. Jones & Gaither* (L01258), all in Benner and Davis, *The Law Practice of Abraham Lincoln.* In two of the cases, *Liggett* and *Haines*, Lincoln represented the sheriff. The *Schlenker* case also was appealed to the Illinois Supreme Court, 4 Ill. 483 (1842).

64. James G. Randall, "The Indemnity Act of 1863: A Study in the Wartime Immunity of Governmental Officers," *Michigan Law Review* 20 (April 1922): 591–592; *The War of the Rebellion: A Compilation of the Official Records of the Union and Confederate Armies*, Series 2, Vol. 2 (Washington, DC: Government Printing Office, 1897), 505–509.

65. Klement, *Copperheads in the Middle West*, 254; Paludan, *The Presidency of Abraham Lincoln*, 191. John Merryman, of *Ex parte Merryman* fame, also brought a wrongful arrest case in the Maryland state court, but when the case moved to the federal court, Merryman did not prosecute the case. White, *Abraham Lincoln and Treason in the Civil War*, 92–93.

66. George R. Jones, *Joseph Russell Jones* (Chicago: George R. Jones, 1964), 25.

67. White, *Abraham Lincoln and Treason in the Civil War*, 91.

68. Randall, *Constitutional Problems under Lincoln*, 186–214, 428.

69. Harold M. Hyman, *A More Perfect Union: The Impact of the Civil War and Reconstruction on the Constitution* (New York: Knopf, 1973), 249–256.

70. Kellee Green Blake, "Aiding and Abetting: Disloyalty Prosecutions in the Federal Civil Courts of Southern Illinois, 1861–1866," *Illinois Historical Journal* 87 (Summer 1994): 103.

71. Randall, "The Indemnity Act of 1863," 612.

72. Hyman referenced the Indiana case *Griffin v. Wilcox* as one of his examples: Hyman, *A More Perfect Union*, 452.

73. *Jones v. Seward*, 3 Grant 431 (1863).

74. Abstract and Brief, *Johnson v. Jones et al.* (Galena, IL: Galena Democrat Press, 1868), 3.

75. Sabin D. Puterbaugh, *Puterbaugh's Common Law Pleading and Practice*, 6th ed. (Chicago: Callaghan, 1888), 541, 571.

76. The Jo Daviess County Circuit Court issued at least three summonses to the five defendants. Order, 13 March 1865, Circuit Court Record T, 216, Jo Daviess County Circuit Clerk's Office, Galena, IL.

77. Bouvier, *A Law Dictionary*, 2: 520.

78. Abstract and Brief, 5–6; Order, 27 May 1865, Circuit Court Record T, 287.

79. Abstract and Brief, 12–13, 22, 25.

80. Order, 28 August 1865, Circuit Court Record T, 318.

81. Bouvier, *A Law Dictionary*, 1: 402.

82. Abstract and Brief, 8–9, 16, 18, 24, 26.

83. Order, 16 March 1866; Order 19 March 1866, Circuit Court Record T, pp. 403, 414–15; *Galena Daily Gazette*, March 24, 1866, 2, col. 2.

84. David Kenney and Robert E. Hartley, *An Uncertain Tradition: US Senators from Illinois* (Carbondale: Southern Illinois University Press, 2003), 27–30. Robert P. Howard, *Illinois: A History of the Prairie State* (Grand Rapids, MI: Eerdmans, 1972), 363. *History of McDonough County, Illinois* (Springfield, IL: Continental History Company, 1885), 335–336.

85. Klement, *Copperheads in the Middle West*, 259.

86. Beckwith charged the government $3,000 for the defense of Jones in this case and in Sheean's cases. When the government found the amount to be excessive, Beckwith reduced his charge to $1,000. Simon, *The Papers of Ulysses S. Grant*, 17: 319–321.

87. Argument of Plaintiff, April Term 1866, *Johnson v. Jones et al.*, Arguments in the Supreme Court of Illinois, 1: 281.

88. Argument of Plaintiff, 1: 270, 277, 281, 286.

89. *Johnson v. Jones et al.*, 44 Ill. 142 (1867), 147.

90. 44 Ill. 142 at 149; *The Prize Cases*, 67 US (2 Black) 635 (1862); Kermit Hall, ed., *The Oxford Companion to the Supreme Court of the United States* (New York: Oxford University Press, 1992), 681.

91. *Johnson v. Jones et al.*, 151.

92. *Johnson v. Jones et al.*, 158.

93. *Johnson v. Jones et al.*, 163.

94. Randall, "The Indemnity Act of 1863," 599.

95. *Johnson v. Jones et al.*, 161.

96. Randall, "The Indemnity Act of 1863," 603.

97. *Johnson v. Jones et al.*, 161.

98. *Skeen v. Monkeimer*, 21 Ind. 1 (1863); *In re Kemp*, 16 Wis. 359 (1863); *Griffin v. Wilcox*, 21 Ind. 370 (1863).

99. White, *Abraham Lincoln and Treason in the Civil War*, 105–106.

100. *Johnson v. Jones et al.*, 166.

101. Order, 30 March 1868; Order, 25 May 1868; Order, 9 November 1868; Order, 27 March 1869; Order, 24 May 1869, all in Circuit Court Record U, 315, 336, 392, 522, 542–543, Jo Daviess County Circuit Clerk's Office, Galena, IL.

102. Jones, *Joseph Russell Jones*, 27.

103. *McCall v. McDowell*, 15 F. Cas (California), no. 8,673 (1867). Ragsdale, *Ex parte Merryman and Debates on Civil Liberties*, 539–540.

104. *Milligan v. Hovey*, 17 F. Cas. (Indiana), no. 9,605 (1871); White, *Abraham Lincoln and Treason in the Civil War*, 106; David E. Engdahl, "Intrinsic Limits of Congress' Power Regarding the Judicial Branch," *Brigham Young University Law Review* 75 (1999): 142.

105. Klement, *Copperheads in the Middle West*, 258.

106. *Sheean v. Jones et al.*, 44 Ill. 167 (1867).

107. *Carver v. Jones et al.* 45 Ill. 334 (1867). *Johnson v. Jones et al.* has been cited in support of civil liberty violations. In Illinois, see *Read v. Central Union Telephone Company*, 213 Ill. App. 246 (1919); *Gyenes v. People*, 9 Ill. Ct. Cl. 185 (1936); *Shelton v.*

Barry, 328 Ill. App. 497 (1946); and *People v. Shepherd*, 152 Ill.2d 489 (1992). In other jurisdictions, see *Clark v. Mitchell*, 64 Mo. 564 (1877); *Dunlap v. A.A. & G.T.R. Co.*, 50 Mich. 470 (1883); *In re Moyer*, 35 Colo. 159 (1904); *Ex Parte Orozco*, 201 F. Cas. (Texas) 106 (1912); *Herkey v. Agar Mfg. Co.*, 153 N.Y.S. 369 (1915); *Morton v. Sanders*, 178 Ky. 836 (1918), and *Lamont v. Haig*, 539 F. Supp. (South Dakota) 552 (1982).

CHAPTER 11

Ex Parte Milligan in Context and History: From Reconstruction to the War on Terror

MICHAEL LES BENEDICT

David Davis knew he had written a great opinion in *Ex parte Milligan,* one in which the nation's highest court had taken a firm stand in defense of American civil liberties. He hoped that it would not only establish a firm judicial precedent but recall the American people to their deepest commitments. He wanted it to resonate both in constitutional law and in constitutional politics—that is, in the way Americans took account of constitutional principles when making public policy. It is a great opinion, but it did not make the impact he wanted at the time, especially in the constitutional politics surrounding Reconstruction; nor has it provided the firm precedent he wanted in American constitutional law.

THE RECEPTION OF THE MILLIGAN *OPINION*

Davis expected universal praise for his opinion. It restated concerns both Republicans and Democrats had articulated about military commissions during the war, while implicitly reconfirming the broad powers Republicans had exercised to win the war. He had tried to separate the decision from the Reconstruction question: the case was "not a question of the power to proclaim martial law, when war exists in a community and the courts and civil authorities are overthrown," he had written.[1] He was stunned by the tidal wave of Republican invective that greeted it instead. "It is the old dogma of rigid construction as applied to the National Government and liberal construction as applied to the States," the usually moderate *New York Times* editorialized. "The Supreme court . . . throws the great weight of its influence into the scale of those who assailed the union and . . . impugned the constitutionality of nearly everything that was done to uphold it."[2] The more radical editor of the New York *Independent* called it "the most dangerous opinion ever produced" by the Supreme Court.[3] *Harper's Weekly* styled it "the new Dred Scott."[4]

Despite David Dudley Field's protestations, Milligan's Democratic lawyers had known that a decision in favor of their client would be a powerful weapon in the constitutional politics surrounding Reconstruction. They may have believed all ought to defer to Supreme Court interpretations of the Constitution, but they could not have expected it. That is why they published their full arguments rather than relying on the abbreviated versions published in the official report. Davis likewise addressed his opinion to the public as well as to the legal profession. All were proposing that the Court fulfill a role that it had rarely played before the war—a bulwark against the violation of individual rights by a democratic government. No doubt all hoped for the revival of judicial prestige that would be necessary to play such a role, and it is possible to see *Milligan* as a harbinger of a future when it would.[5]

But once again, critics denied that the Supreme Court's interpretations of the Constitution were binding on the people. "The opinion of the five judges is not law, and will not be so regarded," the *Independent* expostulated.[6] "The constitutional twaddle of Mr. Justice Davis will no more stand the fire of public opinion than the Dred Scott decision," predicted the *New York Herald*.[7] "These are all questions which the people of the United States have solemnly decided by the last appeal, and neither the Executive nor the Supreme Court will be allowed to reverse their decision," George William Curtis, the editor of *Harper's Weekly*, declared.[8] In Congress, the generally conservative Republican John A. Bingham warned, "If . . . the Court usurps power to decide political questions and defy a free people's will, it will only remain for a people, thus insulted and defied, to demonstrate that the servant is not above his lord."[9]

Davis clipped editorials from the *National Intelligencer* rebutting the criticisms. "There is nothing in the character or the conduct of any one of the five judges making the sweeping decision . . . to justify the suspicion even that they are influenced by political or personal considerations. They were professional lawyers of high repute. They have never been noted for partisanship, and since elevated to the bench they have not dabbled at all in politics."[10] Earlier, the editors had also written, "The anarchists who would destroy the public confidence in the Constitution and its Supreme Court

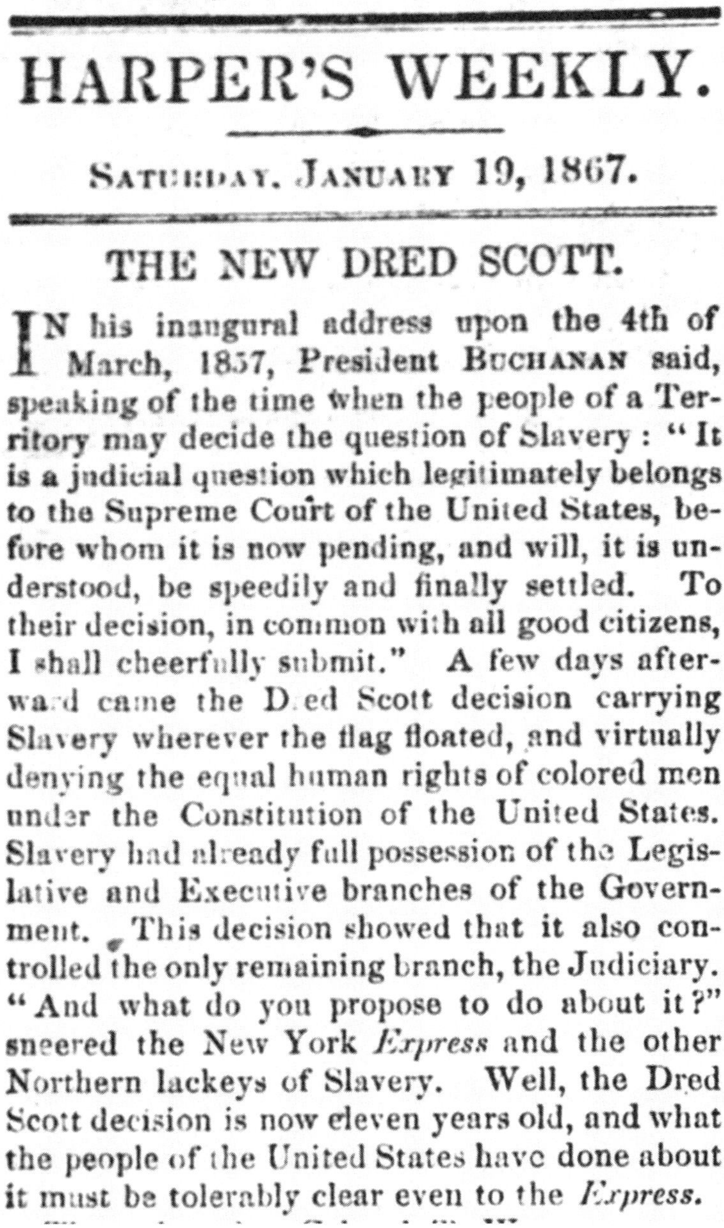

HARPER'S WEEKLY.

SATURDAY, JANUARY 19, 1867.

THE NEW DRED SCOTT.

IN his inaugural address upon the 4th of March, 1857, President BUCHANAN said, speaking of the time when the people of a Territory may decide the question of Slavery: "It is a judicial question which legitimately belongs to the Supreme Court of the United States, before whom it is now pending, and will, it is understood, be speedily and finally settled. To their decision, in common with all good citizens, I shall cheerfully submit." A few days afterward came the Dred Scott decision carrying Slavery wherever the flag floated, and virtually denying the equal human rights of colored men under the Constitution of the United States. Slavery had already full possession of the Legislative and Executive branches of the Government. This decision showed that it also controlled the only remaining branch, the Judiciary. "And what do you propose to do about it?" sneered the New York *Express* and the other Northern lackeys of Slavery. Well, the Dred Scott decision is now eleven years old, and what the people of the United States have done about it must be tolerably clear even to the *Express*.

Figure 11.1. Ten years after the Supreme Court handed down its infamous decision in the *Dred Scott* case (1857), *Harper's Weekly* denounced Justice David Davis's opinion in *Ex parte Milligan* as "The New Dred Scott." From *Harper's Weekly,* January 19, 1867.

are as dangerous, as the revolutionists" who tried to secede.[11] Yet the *Intelligencer* itself clearly was engaged in constitutional politics, day after day endorsing the *Milligan* decision, denouncing its critics, and urging Americans to defer to the Court's authority.

It was the breadth of the decision that was the problem. Moderate critics pointed to Chase's minority concurrence as having taken the correct approach. "There was not a particle of pretense that Congress had authorized the sitting of the Indiana military commission, yet a majority of the judges undertook to declare that Congress could not create such a tribunal," the editor of *The Nation* complained. "We most earnestly deprecate any weakening of popular confidence in this eminent court, as equivalent to an undermining of the people's faith in law itself," he said. Like Davis, he believed that faith "needs strengthening and upbuilding," especially in the wake of the war. But it could not be done by trying to settle fundamental questions through constitutional adjudication. The only way to deal with such questions is for the Court "to confine itself strictly to the matter in hand, to decide the precise points before it."[12] The case commentator in the newly established *American Law Review* would repeat the criticism. A unanimous decision on the facts at issue—that is, an opinion like Chase's—"would have commanded universal respect," he observed. Instead, Davis and the majority "seemed eager to go beyond the record . . . to lay down the principles on which they would decide other questions, not now before them, involving the gravest and highest powers of Congress."[13]

"The clamor has amazed me," Davis wrote a Bloomington friend. "Here is a decision in favor of human liberty, & yet it is denounced in nearly every Republican paper in the country."[14] By 1868 he would be complaining, "Both parties have run into extremes and middle men are crushed out." While traveling through the South for his wife's health, he was disgusted by African Americans and their Republican leaders. He could not abide the Democrats, whose leaders were Copperheads during the war, but he was as critical of the Republicans, who "are doing everything to keep up hate & . . . to degrade these Southern people."[15]

The experience rekindled his Whiggish skepticism about popular government. "The people are mad now, and, if they don't recover soon, civil liberty will be entirely gone," he worried. That in turn reconfirmed his conviction that the role of the Court should be essentially anti-majoritarian and libertarian. "Why . . . a written Constitution?" he expostulated to his brother-in-law. "Majorities don't need any. Our ancestors were not willing . . . to trust the virtue and intelligence of the people. They believed in the necessity of written, irrepealable guaranties to protect minorities against the aggressions of majorities." That meant the Court, not the people, must be the guardian of the Constitution. "Courts are made to interpret the will of the people, as manifested through laws & Constitutions. I did not suppose that it was their business to interpret that will as manifested by an election."[16] As he wrote his son, "The bar and the judicial mind of the country must settle its doctrines, & not the newspapers."[17]

MILLIGAN *AND RECONSTRUCTION*

Davis simply did not comprehend that in the interim between the announcement of the decision in April and the publication of the opinion in December, the context of the case had entirely changed. *Milligan* was no longer a civil liberties case; it had become a federalism case. The question was whether the federal government could project power in the South to protect the rights of freed people, Southern loyalists, and even its own soldiers. On April 2, 1866, President Johnson had proclaimed that peace had been restored in the South. As part of the Peace Proclamation he declared "standing armies, military occupation, martial law, military tribunals and the suspension of the privilege of the writ of habeas corpus dangerous to public liberty" and "contrary to the genius and spirit of our free institutions." None of them ought to be sanctioned "except in cases of actual necessity for repelling invasion or suppressing insurrection."[18] Even in the absence of a formal opinion, the Court's decision, coming a day later, seemed to confirm Johnson's reasoning.

The combination of the Peace Proclamation and the April *Milligan* decision sowed confusion among military commanders in the South, who were still under orders to protect freed people where they could not get protection and justice in Southern courts.[19] Johnson tried to end the confusion by banning military commissions wherever civil tribunals were available to try offenders.[20] But the Freedmen's Bureau Act, passed over the president's veto, made it the duty of the president to extend "military jurisdiction" to guarantee equal rights in any state not yet restored to representation in Congress.[21] From all over the South reports came to the top commander of the army, Ulysses S. Grant, and Secretary of War Stanton that commanders felt hamstrung to protect the former slaves. Local authorities were arresting US officers, soldiers, government employees, and veterans.[22] Grant issued an order instructing military commanders in the South to arrest anyone charged with crimes against military officers, government agents, citizens, and inhabitants of the United States wherever civil authorities failed to act and to hold them until "a proper judicial tribunal may be ready and willing to try them." The language implied trials by civilian courts rather than military commissions, but the order assumed the continued suspension of habeas corpus.[23] Although he did not countermand Grant's order, Johnson's Peace Proclamation implied that conditions no longer warranted suspension. Thus, matters had reached a crisis when the *Milligan* opinions finally appeared in December.

Davis's opinion echoed the language of Johnson's Peace Proclamation, and he should have foreseen that Republicans would conclude that he and the majority had gone beyond the facts of the case in order to draw into question Congress's power to continue military intervention in the South. Although he had acknowledged that it was necessary for the military to administer the law if civil war actually closed the civil courts, he had added that language calling it "a gross usurpation" if military government were continued after the courts reopened. "Martial law can never exist where the courts are open," he had written.[24] Davis would later complain that he had acknowledged the right to establish military tribunals during the war and had said nothing about Reconstruction.[25] But Republicans can be forgiven for having thought otherwise when ex-rebels celebrated "that the Supreme Court has come to the rescue of the Constitution," and "the future is lighted with signs of good cheer."[26] Or when Democrats at the party's annual Jackson Day dinner in Washington on January 8, with President Johnson in attendance, proposed a toast to "the Supreme Court of the United States: the great conservative power of the government; never more needed or better appreciated than now." Or when they chose Milligan's lawyer, Jeremiah S. Black, to respond.[27]

But Republicans were not about to let Court dicta determine their policy, nor concede the Court's power to decide so fundamental a political question as how to restore the Union. In March 1867 they passed the Reconstruction Act over Johnson's veto. The act divided the South into military districts and subjected the state governments reorganized under Johnson's guidance to military authority. It also explicitly authorized military commanders to institute military commissions to protect personal and property rights and suppress violence and disorder.[28] Republicans cited the *Milligan* opinion's dictum that the case did not involve Reconstruction. In fact, Senator John Sherman of Ohio, who managed the version of the bill that finally became law, said that its provision for military commissions fell squarely within the decision, pointing to Davis's acknowledgment that occupying forces could set them up in insurrectionary states.[29] Of course, this assumed that the Court would agree that the courts of the civil governments President Johnson had established did not count as functioning civil courts—quite an assumption. Democrats argued the opposite.[30]

Carrying out the Reconstruction Act, state and local commanders established hundreds of military tribunals. The justices might have agreed with the Democrats and ruled the military commissions unconstitutional, but we will never know. The process of establishing new state governments under the Reconstruction Act was completed in most of the states before they got the chance. Republicans made sure of that: when Southern opponents of Reconstruction challenged the right of a military commission to try a belligerent newspaper editor in Mississippi in *Ex parte McCardle*, argued in March 1868, Congress repealed the statute under which they brought the suit. To Democrats' dismay, the Supreme Court acquiesced.[31] By the time they got another case, *Ex parte Yerger*,[32] to the Supreme Court in 1869, the process was all but over. Rather than risk an adverse decision, the government simply turned the prisoner over to the new state authorities.[33]

Even though Congress explicitly authorized military commissions in the Reconstruction Act and even though hundreds if not thousands of cases were brought before them,[34] *Ex parte Milligan* had a powerful impact on Reconstruction and on the power of the federal government to project power generally. The justification for the Reconstruction Act was that the South was still held in the "grasp of war," despite President Johnson's peace proclamations.[35] As such, Southerners were subject to military government and the military commissions concomitant to it. This authority, Republicans argued, continued until each state was restored to normal relations in the Union and representation in Congress. That process ended with the restoration of Georgia in 1870. After that, according to *Ex parte Milligan*, the United States could not establish military commissions anywhere that the courts remained open in the South, no matter how biased judges and juries were against African Americans or that they were filled with Democratic judges who considered any active white Republican a carpetbagger or scalawag against whom resistance was justified.

In 1871 Congress empowered President Grant to take whatever measures necessary to suppress the Ku Klux Klan, including temporary suspension of the writ of habeas corpus, but it acquiesced in *Milligan* by not authorizing him to institute military tribunals to punish the offenders. They had to be tried in a civilian federal court, if tried at all.[36] The so-called Ku Klux Klan Act seemed to work at first. Federal judges were more likely to punish perpetrators of violence than state judges. Federal marshals could try to keep Klan sympathizers off juries, and the juries did convict. But the success was short-lived. An underfunded Justice Department, outgunned district attorneys, and federal judges determined to cabin national authority made it impossible to project federal power over the long haul. As a historian of the effort in South Carolina has put it, the government was obliged "to coax rather than coerce," to the dismay of soldiers on the ground.[37] The ironic consequence of a decision designed to shield civil liberty from federal intrusion was to make it practically impossible for the federal government to protect it. Never since has anyone proposed establishing military commissions to overcome the difficulty of enforcing federal laws on resistant localities.

MILLIGAN *IN HISTORY AND LAW SINCE RECONSTRUCTION*

Milligan has been recognized as a great case, mostly for Davis's eloquent dedication to constitutional liberty in time of war and crisis. Casebooks still quote it to contrast Davis's constitutionalism with Lincoln's supposed extra-constitutionalism.[38] It is often included among great cases of American constitutional history. Supreme Court justices call it "one of the great landmarks in this Court's history."[39] Chief Justice William H. Rehnquist called it the Court's "first important civil liberties decision."[40] Charles Warren devoted an entire chapter to the case—"since recognized by all men as the palladium of the rights of the individual"—in his seminal *The Supreme Court in United States History*.[41] That put it on a par with the Cherokee cases, *Dred Scott*, the *Slaughter-House Case*, and the *Legal Tender Cases*. (*Marbury v. Madison*, considered a preeminent case now, did not receive a whole chapter to itself.) It was included among the sixteen cases studied in John A. Garraty's classic *Quarrels That Have Shaped the Constitution.*[42] Writing in the wake of World War II and at the height of the Cold War, the chapter's author concluded, "The heart of this decision is the heart of the difference between the United States of America and Nazi Germany and the Soviet Union." It continues to be included in modern studies of great constitutional cases and in compilations of leading cases in American constitutional history.[43]

Political scientists and experts in military law have been more dubious. John W. Clampitt did not even mention *Milligan* in his entry on military commissions in the first *Cyclopaedia of Political Science,* which appeared in 1883, focusing instead on the rules developed in Halleck's *International Law* and his General Orders No. 1. "In construing different parts of the constitution together," Clampitt wrote, the idea that the Constitution mandates jury trials "must give way before the necessity for an efficient exercise of the war power which is vested in congress by that instrument."[44] Seven years later, pioneer political scientist John W. Burgess pronounced Chase's concurrence the correct analysis, dismissing Davis's majority opinion. If ever subjected to the stresses of war, Burgess wrote, "we may safely predict that it will necessarily be discarded."[45] On the eve of World War II, the great constitutional scholar Edward S. Corwin called Davis's opinion mere "fustian." The real precedent was Lincoln's actions, not the Supreme Court's opinion. To think the latter would trump the former in a real emergency "would be merely childish."[46]

These criticisms indicate the problem with Davis's opinion. By conflating martial law and military commissions, by failing to distinguish between speech and actual subversive activities, and by arguing at such a high theoretical plane, Davis had weakened its practical application. Attending only to Milligan's prosecution, he did not discuss the actual practice of military commissions during the war at all. As a modern analyst points out, there was an "unacknowledged inconsistency with widespread military practice during and immediately after the Civil War . . . , and it is unclear to what extent the Court meant to repudiate it."[47] Writing in 1991, historian Mark E. Neely Jr. went so far as to call *Milligan* "irrelevant."[48]

Did Davis really mean that *all* the prosecutions remote from the battlefields, where civil courts were open, had been unconstitutional and their convictions void? The "Blackstone of American military law," William Winthrop, apparently did not think so. Or if that was what Davis intended,

Winthrop clearly if implicitly rejected Davis's opinion. In his *Military Law,* published in 1886, he instead built upon Chase's distinction between martial law and military government. "A state of war may subsist though active hostilities are not prosecuted," he wrote. It may be continued "*in bello nondum cessante.*" In such a case, the president and his subordinates may establish military governments, with "extraordinary" powers, "subject only to the conditions and restrictions as the law of war . . . imposes on its exercise," Winthrop asserted. Regarding the scope of such government, he quoted the Supreme Court in an 1874 case referring to wartime governance in the South: "In such cases, the laws of war take the place of the Constitution and laws of the United States as applied in time of peace."[49]

But despite these challenges, *Milligan* remained influential. When a zealous US senator proposed during World War I that Congress authorize military commissions to punish anyone who endangered discipline, health, or operations of the armed forces, other senators and President Woodrow Wilson objected that the measure was unconstitutional. The legislation's sponsor withdrew it. In 1918 the attorney general opined that *Milligan* precluded a military trial of a German spy caught on American soil, an opinion quietly repudiated by his successor.[50] Still, Congress followed Winthrop's treatise rather than Davis's *Milligan* opinion when it authorized military commissions to try violations of the laws of war in revisions of the statutory Articles of War that governed the armed forces in 1916 and 1920.[51] State governors ignored the limitations *Milligan* suggested on the imposition of martial law when they suppressed strike-related violence or took drastic action to secure other policies.[52]

Writing from his perspective in the judge advocate general's office during World War II, legal scholar Charles Fairman looked at the state precedents and recent British experience to scout the notion that *Milligan* rendered unconstitutional Franklin Delano Roosevelt's order excluding people of Japanese ancestry from designated military areas. "Those agencies which are charged with the national defense surely must have authority to take on the spot some measures which in normal times would be ultra vires," he argued. He scoffed that while "college sophomores are taught that the Milligan case stands as a constitutional landmark," it did "not . . . meet the conditions of modern war."[53]

The Supreme Court seemed to agree in *Hirabayashi v. US* and *Korematsu v. US,* in which it carefully refrained from challenging a curfew on

Japanese in Hawaii and Roosevelt's executive order barring nearly 120,000 persons of Japanese descent from the West Coast. That order authorized their relocation to camps, possibly the greatest violation of civil liberties in American history.[54] The justices barely mentioned *Milligan* at all. In part, that was because the case did not involve the specific issue *Milligan* addressed. Congress specified that violations of Roosevelt's orders be tried in the civil courts.[55] None of the detainees was tried and sentenced by a military commission, nor were those who defied the order to move. But when the Court upheld the convictions of Gordon Hirabayashi, who had violated a curfew aimed solely at people of Japanese descent, and Fred Korematsu, who had refused to leave California, its course belied Davis's grandiloquent claim that the Constitution protected rights *equally* in war and peace. Justice Robert H. Jackson observed that in times of war it was "impractical and dangerous idealism" to expect that all military commands "conform to conventional tests of constitutionality." The justices should stay out of it, he wrote in dissent in *Korematsu,* neither trying futilely to prevent the action nor giving their legal imprimatur.[56]

Defending the *Korematsu* decision from Jackson's criticism, Justice Felix Frankfurter reflected the Court's disdain for Davis's oversimplification: "The provisions of the Constitution which confer on the Congress and the President powers to enable this country to wage war are as much part of the Constitution as provisions looking to a nation at peace. . . . The validity of action under the war power must be judged wholly in the context of war. That action is not to be stigmatized as lawless because like action in times of peace would be lawless."[57] *Milligan*'s narrow holding restricting military commissions had led Congress to enforce Roosevelt's executive order in civil courts rather than military commissions, but Davis's broader claim that all the provisions of the Constitution operated equally in war and peacetime was now clearly mere obiter dictum that could be disregarded.[58]

The case of *Ex parte Quirin* (1942)[59] narrowed the application of *Milligan* still further. Whereas the Japanese exclusion and relocation did not implicate military commissions, *Quirin* did. In that case Roosevelt had created a military commission to try eight German saboteurs caught in the United States. Their lawyers sought a writ of habeas corpus on the grounds that Congress had not authorized his action and that *Milligan* precluded the president from establishing a military commission on his own in an area remote from the theater of war where the ordinary courts were open. Again, the Court brushed the broader language of *Milligan* aside. That decision barred military trials of civilians, and it went no further. It was limited "to the facts before it." All that the *Milligan* Court held was "that Milligan, not being a part of or associated with the armed forces of the enemy, was a non-belligerent, not subject to the laws of war."[60] The saboteurs, in contrast, were under the orders of the enemy and engaged in belligerent actions out of uniform. They were what we now call unlawful combatants, and thus subject to military trial for their actions. The location of the trial, and the fact that the ordinary courts were open, had nothing to do with it. The Court distinguished *Milligan* on similar grounds when it sustained the military commissions that administered the trials of enemy leaders for war crimes[61] and tribunals that tried offenders outside the country.[62]

The courts had limited *Milligan*'s application to American citizens on American soil. Even there it had distinguished it away in the Japanese curfew and exclusion cases. Yet its great principle remained surprisingly resilient despite Frankfurter's jeremiad, Fairman's scorn, and the *Quirin* opinion. Although he concurred in the result in *Hirabayashi,* Justice Frank Murphy insisted, "It does not follow . . . that the broad guaranties of the Bill of Rights and other provisions of the Constitution protecting essential liberties are suspended by the mere existence of a state of war. It has been frequently stated and recognized by this Court that the war power, like the other great substantive powers of government, is subject to the limitations of the Constitution." *Milligan* was the first case he cited.[63] In *Ex parte Endo,* the Supreme Court held that the laws Congress passed to enforce Roosevelt's exclusion order did not authorize the government to detain a loyal citizen against her will.[64] The justices carefully distinguished the case from *Milligan;* it did not involve a military commission, they pointed out. But they interpreted Congress's intention in light of American commitments to civil liberty and writs of habeas corpus to secure it. Naturally, they cited Davis's opinion.[65]

In *Duncan v. Kahanomoku* the Court relied on *Milligan* in overturning military trials of civilians in Hawaii. The question was whether the Organic Act that established territorial government in Hawaii envisioned military commissions when it authorized the governor to turn his powers over to the military in case of lawlessness. The governor had done so after the attack on Pearl Harbor, and the military governor had replaced the civil courts with military tribunals. Congress could not have contemplated such a decision when it passed the Organic Act, the Court held. "Our system of government clearly is the antithesis of total military rule and the founders of this country are not likely to have contemplated complete military dominance within the limits of a Territory made part of this country and not recently taken from an enemy. They were opposed to governments that placed in the hands of one man the power to make, interpret and enforce the laws." Of course, the justices cited *Milligan* to sustain this proposition.[66] Justice Murphy was more explicit: "Tested by the *Milligan* rule, the military proceedings . . . plainly lacked constitutional sanction."[67]

Equally important, perhaps, the historical judgment of the Japanese relocation has been almost uniformly negative. The near universal conclusion is that it violated basic rights. The Court's failure to intervene has been roundly condemned. As early as June 1945 a leading law academic pronounced the decisions sustaining Japanese exclusion "a disaster."[68] As one of the leading American constitutional history textbooks observes, "no reputable scholar has defended the decisions" thereafter.[69] Congress has formally apologized and indemnified the victims.[70] And *Milligan* continued to be a touchstone for Court decisions sustaining civil liberties in succeeding decades.[71] It was and continues to be regularly included in essays on great Supreme Court cases and compilations of leading documents of American constitutional history.[72]

That brings us to the "War on Terror." From the beginning, the Bush administration insisted that the president had inherent power to hold unlawful combatants and subject them to trial by military commissions. It buttressed that claim by pointing to the resolution Congress passed after the terrorist attacks of September 11, 2001, authorizing the president to use "all necessary and appropriate force" against those responsible. Civil libertarians immediately protested the claim and the procedures that the government developed to carry it out. As military and constitutional historian Jonathan Lurie described post-9/11 developments, "The Ghost of *Milligan* Reappears Again."[73] *Milligan* once again became relevant to current constitutional law. It suddenly reappeared in constitutional law casebooks.[74] Essays and chapters on *Milligan* appeared in collections on legality during emergencies and timely histories of emergency powers.[75]

Much of the tortured dance among the George W. Bush administration, Congress, and the Supreme Court related to *Milligan*. One of the reasons that the Bush administration held prisoners at Guantanamo Bay in Cuba was its claim that neither *Milligan*'s specific holding nor its vaunted defense of constitutional liberty in time of war applied there. The Court rejected the arguments, even when the prisoners were foreign nationals, much less when they were citizens of the United States.[76] But the justices conceded that *if* the prisoners could be shown to be enemy combatants, the president had the right to detain them. They did so over a vigorous dissent by Justice Antonin Scalia, who insisted that *Milligan* applied to American citizen Yaser Esam Hamdi even if he *were* an enemy combatant (he had been captured fighting for the Taliban in Afghanistan). "If the law of war cannot be applied to citizens where courts are open, then Hamdi's imprisonment without criminal trial is no less unlawful than Milligan's trial by military tribunal," he opined.[77] *Milligan* has not proved decisive in the cases that have arisen out of 9/11. Yet, historian Jonathan Lurie has observed, "The shadows of *Milligan* . . . hover over them."[78]

Only the shadow, though. In the wake of World War II, the courts and experts in military law established a categorization of justifications for military commissions that cabined *Milligan* into a narrowly circumscribed place. Military commissions were an appropriate instrument of military government in occupied territories and on military bases. They were also appropriate to try enemies who had violated the laws of war, such as saboteurs, spies, fighters out of uniform, and those who had wantonly murdered civilians or captured prisoners. *Milligan* did not apply to these uses of military commissions, nor of course to courts-martial of those in uniform. *Milligan*'s holding was restricted to areas within United States jurisdiction placed under martial law (and as the Japanese exclusion and relocation showed, its specific strictures could be met while its spirit was violated).[79] The justices have applied these understandings in the cases that have arisen out of the military commission trials held at Guantanamo. In effect, the justices have considered Davis's opinion overbroad. The Court considers Civil War–era precedents "with caution" precisely because in *Milligan* neither military tribunals nor defendants were categorized according to later understandings.[80]

Nonetheless, the justices have proved reluctant to concede inherent presidential power to establish military commissions, even in categories where what they call *Milligan* Rules do not apply. Rather than conceding that presidents have such power, they have measured military commissions against the laws Congress has passed in authorizing them.[81] In doing so, they implicitly sustained Chase's reasoning in *Milligan*, rather than Davis's.

But if *Milligan*'s specific holding has been disregarded in the War on Terrorism cases, its general commitment to civil liberty in wartime has not. For foreign nationals, the justices have looked more toward international law. For American citizens, they look to the US Constitution. Even as it sustained Hamdi's detention at Guantanamo Bay, Justice Sandra Day O'Connor's opinion for the Court affirmed that "as critical as the Government's interest may be in detaining those who actually pose an immediate threat to the national security, . . . history and common sense teach us that an unchecked system of detention carries potential to become a means for oppression and abuse of others who do not present that sort of threat." For precedential support, she wrote "See *Ex parte Milligan*" and quoted one of Davis's telling observations: "[the founders] knew—the history of the world told them—the nation they were founding would be involved in war . . . and that unlimited power, wherever lodged at such a time, was especially hazardous to freemen."[82] Despite their appreciation of *Milligan*'s commitment to liberty, O'Connor and the majority of the justices opined that liberty must be balanced with national security, saying only that Hamdi must be given a due-process opportunity to challenge the facts justifying his detention. Justice Antonin Scalia went further. For him *Milligan* was dispositive. If Congress did not suspend the privilege of the writ of habeas corpus as the Constitution provided for, as a citizen Hamdi had the right to civil trial. "The reasoning and conclusion of *Milligan* logically cover the present case," he insisted. He scouted later judicial efforts to dilute its application.[83]

As a recent historiographer has observed, "The work of legal scholars and historians who have published on civil liberties in the post-9/11 period reveals how thoroughly the *Milligan* case has become woven into the historical fabric."[84] The Davis opinion continues to be a touchstone for those who are appalled by the disparity between the procedures of the civil courts and those accorded to War-on-Terror detainees held at Guantanamo,[85] or who worry about a potential system of detention on American soil.[86] Those defending long-term detentions and military trials dismiss *Milligan*'s relevance,[87] if they mention it at all.[88] More neutral observers recognize its relevance despite the limits of its authority.[89] *Milligan* is authoritative precedent only in a narrow set of circumstances, but Davis's paean to liberty still resonates. His opinion was the first in which the Supreme Court linked the Constitution to the great Anglo-American heritage of liberty. It was a harbinger of the way the Court would apply the Constitution to protect civil liberty in the twentieth century. In times of fear and anger, it still reminds Americans of the nation's deepest commitments.

NOTES

1. *Ex parte Milligan,* 68 US (4 Wall.) 2, at 126.

2. *New York. Times,* January 3, 1867, 4.

3. *The Independent* (New York), January 10, 1867, 4.

4. *Harper's Weekly,* January 19, 1867, 34. See Brooks Simpson, "*Ex parte Milligan,*" in Melvin Urofsky, ed., *The Public Debate over Controversial Supreme Court Decisions* (Washington, DC: CQ Press, 2006), 34–43.

5. Joseph G. Gambone, "*Ex parte Milligan:* The Restoration of Judicial Prestige?," *Civil War History* 3 (September 1970): 246–259. See generally Stanley I. Kutler, *Judicial Power and Reconstruction Politics* (Chicago: University of Chicago Press, 1968).

6. *The Independent,* January 10, 1867, 4.

7. *New York Daily Herald,* January 2, 1867, 4.

8. *Harper's Weekly,* January 19, 1867, 34.

9. *Congressional Globe,* 39th Cong., 2nd Sess., January 16, 1867, 502. Bingham was not directly addressing the *Milligan* opinion, however, but concerns that the Court would reject Congress's determination that it had the final authority to decide whether the Southern states had constitutional state governments after the war.

10. *Washington National Intelligencer,* December 31, 1866, 2.

11. *Washington National Intelligencer,* December 28, 1866, 2.

12. *The Nation,* January 10, 1867, 30.

13. "Summary of Events—Milligan's Case," *American Law Review* 1 (April 1867): 572.

14. Davis to John F. Henry, February 3, 1867, Davis Mss., Illinois State Historical Society (hereafter ISHS).

15. Davis to Julius Rockwell, April 22, 1868, Davis Mss., ISHS.

16. Davis to Rockwell, February 24, 1867, Davis Mss., Library of Congress.

17. Davis to George Perrin Davis, January 20, 1867, Davis Mss., ISHS.

18. Andrew Johnson, Proclamation of April 2, 1866, in James D. Richardson, ed., *A Compilation of the Messages and Papers of the Presidents* (New York: Bureau of National Literature, 1897), 8: 3627–3630 (quoted at 3629).

19. For a general description of the confusion over military authority in the South, and the consequences on the ground, see Gregory P. Downs, *After Appomattox: Military Occupation and the Ends of War* (Cambridge, MA: Harvard University Press, 2015), 137–155.

20. General Orders No. 26, May 1, 1866, in John Y. Simon, ed., *The Papers of Ulysses S. Grant,* vol. 16 (Carbondale: Southern Illinois University Press, 1988), 440.

21. *US Statutes at Large*, 14: 171 (July 2, 1866).

22. Benjamin P. Thomas and Harold M. Hyman, *Stanton: The Life and Times of Lincoln's Secretary of War* (New York: Knopf, 1962), 477–479, 490, 497–498; James E. Sefton, *The United States Army in Reconstruction, 1865–1877* (Baton Rouge: Louisiana State University Press, 1967), 74–85 and 86–106 passim; Robert J. Kaczorowski, *The Politics of Judicial Interpretation: The Federal Courts, Department of Justice, and Civil Rights, 1866–1876* (New York: Fordham University Press, 2004), 24–37. See especially the material associated with General Orders No. 44, in *The Papers of Ulysses S. Grant*, 15: 228–230; Lt. General Ulysses S. Grant to Maj. Gen. George H. Thomas, ibid., 230–231 and associated material at 231–232; Grant to Edwin M. Stanton, July 7, 1866, ibid., 233–234 and associated material at 234–236; Grant to Stanton, November 22, 1866, ibid., 389–392; Gen. Edward O. C. Ord to Grant, November 10, 1866, ibid., 399–402, esp. 400–401.

23. General Orders No. 44, July 6, 1866, Simon, ed., *Papers of Ulysses S. Grant*, 15: 228.

24. *Ex parte Milligan*, at 127.

25. Davis to Rockwell, February 24, 1867, Davis Mss., Library of Congress.

26. *Richmond Daily Enquirer*, December 27, 1866, quoted in Charles Warren, *The Supreme Court in United States History*, 3 vols. (Boston: Little, Brown, 1924), 3: 161.

27. *Washington National Intelligencer*, January 9, 1867, 2.

28. Reconstruction Act of 1867, *US Statutes at Large*, 14: 428 (March 2, 1867).

29. *Congressional Globe*, 39th Cong., 2nd Sess., February 16, 1867, 1462.

30. *Congressional Globe*, 39th Cong., 2nd Sess., appendix, 85 (February 7, 1867, Rep. Andrew J. Rogers), 1388 (February 15, 1867, Sen. Thomas A. Hendricks).

31. *Ex parte McCardle*, 74 US (7 Wall.) 596 (1868).

32. *Ex parte Yerger*, 75 US (8 Wall.) 85 (1869).

33. Kutler, *Judicial Power and Reconstruction Politics*, 100–108; Charles A. Fairman, *Reconstruction and Reunion, 1864–88: Part One* (New York: Macmillan, 1971), 433–514, 581–585.

34. For military commissions during Reconstruction see Detlev F. Vagts, "Military Commissions: The Forgotten Reconstruction Chapter," *American University International Law Review* 23, no. 2 (2008): 231–274. Historian Mark E. Neely Jr. counts 1,435 cases before military commissions between the end of the war and 1869. Some number of those brought in 1865 grew out of the war rather than Reconstruction, and it is not clear whether he includes cases brought in the courts administered by the Freedmen's Bureau, which may also inflate the total. Mark E. Neely Jr., *The Fate of Liberty: Abraham Lincoln and Civil Liberties* (New York: Oxford University Press, 1991), 176–177.

35. In *Texas v. White*, 74 US (7 Wall.) 700 (1869) the Supreme Court justified Reconstruction on the basis of the clause of the Constitution obligating the United States to guarantee republican forms of government to the states. However, that referred to the process for restoring civil government of the South. Republicans justified imposing martial law on the South on the ground that until new governments

were established, Southerners were still subject to military occupation. That was a particularly important basis after *Milligan* for justifying the provision of the Reconstruction Act authorizing military commissions. Republicans consistently made this argument when considering the Reconstruction Act, which began as a measure simply imposing martial law. See the debates in the *Congressional Globe,* 39th Cong., 2nd Sess., especially 1076 (February 7, 1867, Rep. Thaddeus Stevens and Rep. Augustus Brandegee), appendix 88 (February 7, 1867, Rep. Ebon Ingersoll), and 1099 (February 8, 1867, Rep. Samuel Shellabarger). *Texas v. White* notwithstanding, the original justification for Reconstruction had been the right of the conqueror to hold the conquered in the "grasp of war" until it agreed to appropriate terms of peace. See Michael Les Benedict, "Preserving the Constitution: The Conservative Basis of Radical Reconstruction," in Benedict, *Preserving the Constitution: Essays on Politics and the Constitution in the Reconstruction Era* (New York: Fordham University Press, 2006), 3–22.

36. Enforcement Act of 1871, *US Statutes at Large,* 17: 13–15 (April 20, 1871).

37. Richard Zuzcek, *State of Rebellion: Reconstruction in South Carolina* (Columbia: University of South Carolina Press, 1996), 121. For the government's inability to project power to protect rights through the ordinary courts, see Robert J. Kaczorowski, *The Politics of Judicial Interpretation: The Federal Courts, Department of Justice, and Civil Rights, 1866–1876* (New York: Fordham University Press, 2005); and Robert M. Goldman, *"A Free Ballot and a Fair Count": The Department of Justice and the Enforcement of Voting Rights in the South, 1877–1893* (New York: Garland, 1990). See also Charles Lane, *The Day Freedom Died: The Colfax Massacre, the Supreme Court, and the Betrayal of Reconstruction* (New York: Henry Holt, 2008); and George C. Rable, *But There Was No Peace: The Role of Violence in the Politics of Reconstruction* (Athens: University of Georgia Press, 1984).

38. For example, Gerald Gunther and Kathleen M. Sullivan, *Constitutional Law,* 17th ed. (New York: Foundation Press, 2010), 268–269.

39. Hugo Black, in *Reid v. Covert,* 354 US 1, at 30 (1957). Justice Antonin Scalia quotes Black's description of *Milligan* with approval in *Hamdi v. Rumsfeld,* 524 US 507, at 568 n1 (2004). Justice John Paul Stevens refers to "the seminal case of *Ex parte Milligan*" in *Hamdan v. Rumsfeld,* 548 US 557, at 591.

40. William H. Rehnquist, *Civil Liberty and the Civil War* (Washington, DC: National Legal Center for the Public Interest, 1996), 9.

41. Warren, *Supreme Court in United States History,* 2: 418–454, quoted at 432.

42. John A. Garraty, ed., *Quarrels That Have Shaped the Constitution* (New York: Harper & Row, 1964). It remained in the expanded edition published in 1987.

43. Christopher H. Schroeder and Curtis A. Bradley, eds., *Presidential Power Stories* (New York: Foundation Press, 2009); Richard J. Ellis, *Judging Executive Power: Sixteen Supreme Court Cases That Have Shaped the American Presidency* (Lanham, MD: Rowman & Littlefield, 2009); Kermit Hall and John J. Patrick, eds., *Equal Justice under Law: Supreme Court Cases That Shaped America* (New York: Oxford University Press, 2006); Gary L. Rose, *Shaping a Nation: Twenty-Five Supreme Court*

Cases That Changed the United States (Bethesda, MD: Academica Press, 2010); Melvin Urofsky, *Supreme Decisions: Great Constitutional Cases and Their Impact* (Boulder, CO: Westview Press, 2012); Melvin Urofsky and Paul Finkelman, *Documents of American Constitutional and Legal History*, 3d ed. (New York: Oxford University Press, 2007); PBS, The Supreme Court—Supreme Court History: The First Hundred Years—Landmark Case, http://www.pbs.org/wnet/supremecourt/antebellum/landmark_exparte.html.

44. John W. Clampitt, "Military Commissions," in John J. Lalor, ed., *Cyclopaedia of Political Science, Political Economy, and the Political History of the United States* (Chicago: Cary & Co., 1883), 2: 837–38.

45. John W. Burgess, *Political Science and Comparative Constitutional Law*, 2 vols. (Boston: Ginn & Co., 1893), 1: 250–252 (originally published 1890).

46. Edward S. Corwin, *The President: Office and Powers* (New York: New York University Press, 1940), 165–166.

47. Curtis A. Bradley, "The Story of *Ex parte Milligan*: Military Trials, Enemy Combatants, and Congressional Authorization," in Schroeder and Bradley, *Presidential Power Stories*, 93–94.

48. Neely, *Fate of Liberty*, 160.

49. William Winthrop, *Military Law* (Washington, DC: W. H. Morrison, 1886): 2: 18–21 (quoted material at 21). On Winthrop's influence see Joshua E. Kastenberg, *The Blackstone of Military Law: Colonel William Winthrop* (Latham, MD: Scarecrow Press, 2009).

50. Louis Fisher, *Military Tribunals and Presidential Power: American Revolution to the War on Terrorism* (Lawrence: University Press of Kansas, 2005), 86–89.

51. *US Statutes at Large*, 39: 619 (August 29, 1916), arts. 15, 38; ibid., 41: 787 (June 4, 1920), arts. 15, 81, 82.

52. Charles Fairman, "The Law of Martial Rule and the National Emergency," *Harvard Law Review* 55 (June 1942): 1273–1278.

53. Fairman, "The Law of Martial Rule and the National Emergency," 1254.

54. *Hirabayashi v. US*, 320 US 81 (1943); *Korematsu v. US*, 323 US 214 (1944). See Greg Robinson, *A Tragedy of Democracy: Japanese Confinement in America* (New York: Columbia University Press, 2009); Wendy Ng, *Japanese American Internment during World War II: A History and Reference Guide* (Westport, CT: Greenwood Press, 2002). The relocation was technically "voluntary," because those driven from their homes could have gone elsewhere. In reality the vast majority were interned in desert camps, which they could not leave until the Supreme Court decided otherwise in *Ex parte Endo*, 323 US 283 (1944).

55. *US Statutes at Large*, 56: 173 (March 21, 1942).

56. *Korematsu v. US*, at 244 (Jackson, dissenting). Even though Jackson dissented from the decision, he stressed the limits war placed on judicial authority to enforce the rule of law. He implied that he did not expect the president to change his order or modify its enforcement in light of a Court decision reversing Korematsu's conviction.

57. *Korematsu v. US*, at 224 (Frankfurter, concurring).

58. See Roger Daniels, *The Japanese American Cases: The Rule of Law in Time of War* (Lawrence: University Press of Kansas, 2013); Peter H. Irons, *Justice at* War (New York: Oxford University Press, 1983).

59. *Ex parte Quirin*, 317 US 1 (1942).

60. *Ex parte Quirin*, at 45.

61. *In re Yamashita*, 327 US 1 (1946).

62. *Johnson v. Eisentrager*, 339 US 763 (1950); *Madsen v. Kinsella*, 343 US 341 (1952). In a context similar to Reconstruction after the Civil War, military authorities held thousands of trials in occupied Germany, both of Germans accused of various crimes affecting American soldiers and of displaced persons accused of ordinary crimes, not trusting German courts to deal with them fairly. Vagts, "Military Commissions: A Concise History," 44–47.

63. *Hirabayashi v. US*, at 110 (Murphy, concurring).

64. *Ex parte Endo*, 323 US 283 (1944).

65. *Ex parte Endo*, 299.

66. *Duncan v. Kahanomoku*, 327 US 304 at 322 (1946).

67. *Duncan v. Kahanomoku*, 326 (Murphy, concurring).

68. *Eugene V. Rostow*, "The Japanese American Cases—A Disaster," *Yale Law Journal* 54 (June 1945): 489–533.

69. Melvin I. Urofsky and Paul Finkelman, *A March of Liberty: A Constitutional History of the United States*, 3d ed. (New York: Oxford University Press, 2011), 2: 822. For the judgment of other constitutional history textbooks, see Michael Les Benedict, *The Blessings of Liberty: A Concise History of the Constitution of the United States*, 3d ed. (Lanham, MD: Rowman & Littlefield, 2016), 314–315; Edgar J. McManus and Tara Helfman, *Liberty and Union: A Constitutional History of the United States* (New York: Routledge, 2014), 2: 166–169. For a possible recent exception, see constitutional scholar Mark Tushnet, "Defending *Korematsu*?: Reflections on Civil Liberties in Wartime," in Tushnet, ed., *The Constitution in Wartime: Beyond Alarmism and Complacency* (Durham, NC: Duke University Press, 2005), 124–140. The question mark in the title indicates the radicalism of the idea that *Korematsu* might be defensible.

70. Harry H. Kitano, *Japanese Americans: From Relocation to Redress* (Seattle: University of Washington Press,1991); Mitchell T. Maki et al., *Achieving the Impossible Dream: How Japanese Americans Obtained Redress* (Urbana: University of Illinois Press, 1999); Alice Yang Murray, *Historical Memories of the Japanese American Internment and the Struggle for Redress* (Stanford, CA: Stanford University Press, 2008).

71. See, for example, *Toth v. Quarles*, 350 US 11 (1955); and *Reid v. Covert*, 354 US 1 (1957).

72. For example, Nevins, "The Case of the Copperhead Conspirator," in Garraty, ed., *Quarrels That Have Shaped the Constitution*, 101–118. See the essays on *Milli-*

gan in Hall and Patrick, *The Pursuit of Justice under Law: Supreme Court Cases That Shaped America*; and Urofsky, *Supreme Decisions: Great Constitutional Cases and Their Impact*. In collections of documents and court opinions: Stanley I. Kutler, ed., *The Supreme Court and the Constitution: Readings in American Constitutional History* (New York: W. W. Norton, 1984); Rose, *Shaping a Nation: Twenty-Five Supreme Court Cases That Changed the United States*; Melvin I. Urofsky and Paul Finkelman, eds., *Documents of American Constitutional and Legal History*, 3d ed. (New York: Oxford University Press, 2008).

73. Jonathan Lurie, *The Supreme Court and Military Justice* (Los Angeles: Sage Reference/CQ Press, 2013), 171.

74. Among the leading constitutional law casebooks that added *Ex parte Milligan* to their table of cases after 9/11 were Paul Brest et al., *Processes of Constitutional Decision-Making: Cases and Materials*, 5th ed. (New York: Aspen Publishers, 2006); Daniel A. Farber et al., *Constitutional Law*, 3d ed. (St. Paul, MN: Thomson/West, 2003); Gerald Gunther and Kathleen M. Sullivan, *Constitutional Law*, 15th ed. (New York: Foundation Press, 2004); Geoffrey R. Stone et al., *Constitutional Law*, 5th ed. (New York: Aspen Publishers, 2005); and Ronald D. Rotunda, *Modern Constitutional Law*, 8th ed. (St. Paul, MN: Thomson/West, 2007).

75. For example, Bradley, "The Story of *Ex parte Milligan*: Military Trials, Enemy Combatants, and Congressional Authorization," 93–132; David Dyzenhaus, "The 'Organic Law' of *Ex parte Milligan*," in Austin Sarat, ed., *Sovereignty, Emergency, Legality* (New York: Cambridge University Press, 2010), 16–57; Chris Edelson, *Emergency Presidential Power: From the Drafting of the Constitution to the War on Terror* (Madison: University of Wisconsin Press, 2013), 50–62 (chapter 4: "Setting Limits on Wartime Presidential Power? The *Ex parte Milligan* Decision"); and Arthur H. Garrison, *Supreme Court Jurisprudence in Times of National Crisis, Terrorism, and War: A Historical Perspective* (Lanham, MD: Rowman & Littlefield, 2011), 69–77.

76. *Rasul v. Bush*, 542 US 466 (2004); *Hamdi v. Rumsfeld*, 542 US 507 (2004).

77. *Hamdi v. Rumsfeld*, at 567–568 (Scalia, dissenting).

78. Lurie, *The Supreme Court and Military Justice*, 171.

79. *Hamdan v. Rumsfeld*, 548 US 557, at 595–98 (2006).

80. *Hamdan v. Rumsfeld*, at 596 n27.

81. See, for example, *Hamdan v. Rumsfeld*, at 590–625.

82. *Hamdi v. Rumsfeld*, at 530–531.

83. *Hamdi v. Rumsfeld*, at 554–579 (Scalia, dissenting).

84. Peter J. Barry, "*Ex parte Milligan:* History and Historians," *Indiana Magazine of History* 109 (December 2013): 376.

85. See, for example, "The Law of War in the War on Terror," *Human Rights Watch* (online), December 22, 2003, https://www.hrw.org/news/2003/12/22/law-war-war-terror; Steven H. David, "*Ex parte Milligan* and the Detainees at Guantanamo Bay: A Legacy Lost," *Indiana Magazine of History* 109 (December 2013): 380–394.

86. Gene Healy, "The Imperial Presidency and the War on Terror," Cato Policy Report, March/April 2006, https://www.cato.org/policy-report/marchapril-2006/imperial-presidency-war-terror.

87. John Yoo, *Crisis and Command: A History of Executive Power from George Washington to George W. Bush* (New York: Kaplan, 2009), 234–235; Yoo, "Merryman and Milligan (and McCardle)," *Journal of Supreme Court History* 34 (November 2009): 243–290.

88. John Altenburg, "Military Commissions as the Forum to Prosecute Acts of Terrorism and Other Violations of the Law of War," in John Norton Moore and Robert F. Turner, eds., *Legal Issues in the Struggle against Terror* (Durham, NC: Carolina Academic Press, 2010), 35–64.

89. Lurie, *The Supreme Court and Military Justice*, 171–188.

CHAPTER 12

Ex Parte Milligan and the War on Terrorism: Testing the Constitutional Bedrock of a Civilian Criminal Trial

JONATHAN HAFETZ

The 150th anniversary of the Supreme Court's celebrated decision in *Ex parte Milligan* provides a valuable opportunity to reflect on the decision's relevance to current events and, in particular, to the US War on Terrorism. When Justice David Davis wrote his majority opinion in Bloomington, Illinois, the Civil War had ended. Yet, Davis issued one of the most sweeping decisions in the country's history regarding the primacy of civilian courts over military tribunals and the importance of the Constitution's jury trial safeguards during wartime.

In some ways, *Milligan* may be understood as an effort to restore constitutional limits after significant violations of civil liberties by the Lincoln administration in its quest to win the war, including widespread use of military commissions and the presidential suspension of the writ of habeas corpus, which Congress did not ratify until 1863.[1]

In *Milligan,* the majority held that Lambdin P. Milligan's trial by military commission violated the Constitution, and the Fifth and Sixth Amendments in particular, because the civilian courts were open and functioning.[2] The Court also ruled that Milligan could bring his challenge in federal court through habeas corpus because the provisions of the 1863 act suspending the writ did not cover him.[3] Chief Justice Salmon P. Chase, writing for four justices, concurred in the result but disagreed with Davis's constitutional analysis. Specifically, Chase maintained that Congress could authorize trials by military commissions during wartime, although he found it had not done so here. Chase reasoned that since the 1863 suspension act mandated the release of all military prisoners once a civil grand jury had met and failed to indict them, the act required Milligan's release once that period had expired.[4]

Thus, while the Supreme Court's ruling invalidating Milligan's military commission conviction and death sentence was unanimous, the Court narrowly divided on whether the Constitution categorically forbids military commissions during wartime outside areas of martial law if Congress supplies adequate authorization. This division—between categorical constitutional limitations and separation-of-powers objections over a lack of congressional approval—has played an important role in the evolving story of military commissions in the War on Terrorism.

Subsequent judicial decisions, particularly after World War II and during the War on Terrorism, have diluted *Milligan*'s prohibition on military jurisdiction over non–service members where the civilian courts are open and functioning. The most enduring legacy of Davis's opinion thus lies less in its broad and categorical holding than in its expression of a deeply rooted legal tradition that favors civilian criminal trials over military tribunals. It is that tradition—with its roots in a commitment to the fair-trial rights of the accused and to high professional standards among the bench and bar—that has served as the greatest bulwark against wider use of military commissions by the United States.

Even before the 9/11 attacks and the ensuing War on Terrorism, *Milligan* had been weakened by the Supreme Court's 1942 decision in *Ex parte Quirin*.[5] That case involved a group of eight German army saboteurs—including a US citizen[6]—who had traveled to the United States via submarine in military uniform on instructions from the German government, buried their military uniforms on arrival (four came ashore in Long Island, the other four in Florida), and snuck into the United States in civilian disguise to commit military sabotage.[7] The FBI apprehended the saboteurs after one of the men, George J. Dasch, had a change of heart and notified the FBI of the saboteurs' arrival and plans. The Justice Department initially planned to prosecute them in federal court.[8] President Franklin D. Roosevelt, however, insisted that a military commission instead try the saboteurs, even though the federal courts were open and functioning. Roosevelt issued an executive order hastily assembling a commission that met in Washington, DC, and commenced trial in July 1942.[9] One reason Roosevelt opted for a military commission was that, under then-applicable federal law, the defendants would likely have received sentences of only two or three years' imprisonment if convicted on federal conspiracy charges.[10] Roosevelt wanted the saboteurs executed and empowered the military commission to impose the death penalty.[11] Another reason Roosevelt chose a military commission is that he feared a public trial in civilian court might reveal embarrassing details surrounding the saboteurs' capture, including that the FBI foiled the plot only because Dasch had betrayed the other saboteurs and, even then, only because Dasch persisted in his betrayal after the FBI had initially rebuffed him.[12]

The military commission charged the saboteurs with violating the laws of war,[13] the branch of international law that applies during armed conflict. In the midst of the military commission trial, lawyers for the saboteurs challenged the commission's constitutionality in federal habeas corpus proceedings, claiming that under *Milligan* they had a right to trial by jury since the federal courts were open and functioning and the United States was not under martial law at the time. The Supreme Court, although adjourned for the summer, heard the saboteurs' legal challenge to the commission in a special session that began on July 29, 1942, and lasted into the next day.[14] On July 31 the Court denied the habeas petitions in a summary order and announced it would later file a full opinion addressing the merits.[15] The Court, however, did not issue its opinion until October 29, 1942, nearly three months later. By then, the commission had convicted all the saboteurs and sentenced them to death. Six had already been executed; President Roosevelt had commuted the sentences of the remaining two defendants based on assistance they had given to the FBI.[16] In the process of writing the opinion, several members of the Court raised legal concerns about the commission, including its failure to follow courts-martial procedure as required by the Articles of War, the predecessor to today's Uniform Code of Military Justice. Yet, death sentences had already been carried out, thus making it difficult for the Court to acknowledge these deficiencies or the division among its members. At the urging of Justice Felix Frankfurter, the Court issued a unanimous opinion by Justice Harlan Fiske Stone explaining its earlier ruling.[17] Of notable importance for later military commission cases, the *Quirin* Court found that at least one of the charges—that the German soldiers buried their military uniforms and surreptitiously entered the United States in civilian clothes—constituted a violation of the law of war that the Constitution allows to be tried by military commission. The Court emphasized, however, that its ruling should be limited to the facts, and it declined to define the "ultimate boundaries of the jurisdiction of military tribunals."[18]

History has not treated *Quirin* kindly. Several members of the Court have criticized the decision, including Justice Antonin Scalia, who said *Quirin* was not the Court's "finest hour."[19] Justice John Paul Stevens described the decision as the "high-water mark of military power to try enemy combatants for war crimes."[20] The Supreme Court, meanwhile, has continued to praise *Milligan* as "one the great landmarks in [its] history," citing it in a series of post–World War II decisions rejecting the exercise of court-martial jurisdiction over civilians.[21] Yet, *Quirin* remains good law. And *Quirin* modified *Milligan's* holding—or clarified it, depending on one's interpretation of *Milligan* itself. *Quirin,* in short, rejected the proposition that all individuals in the United States, including enemy belligerents accused of war crimes, must be tried by civilian courts, and cannot be tried by military commissions, as long as those civilian courts are open and functioning. *Quirin* instead acknowledged an exception to the constitutional rule articulated in *Milligan* by allowing for the establishment of military commissions to try enemy belligerents for offenses punishable by the law of war.[22] The Supreme Court subsequently upheld military commissions in other World War II–era cases such as *In re Yamashita*[23] and *Johnson v. Eisentrager* based on this reasoning.[24]

Quirin, however, did not resolve important questions surrounding the use of military commissions in a novel conflict like the War on Terrorism. In *Quirin,* the United States was fighting a war against an enemy nation, presumptively treated all captured enemy soldiers as combatants entitled to prisoner of war (POW) protections under international law, and alleged that the defendants had committed war crimes in violation of international law. These factors were important to the Court's decision. In the War on Terrorism, however, the United States is engaged in an armed conflict against terrorist organizations, not other nations; does not treat captured individuals as combatants entitled to POW protections under international law; and asserts military commission jurisdiction based on charges that, in many cases, do not constitute war crimes under international law.

As we consider *Milligan*'s legacy for military commissions today, it is worth considering a case that reflects the zenith of presidential war powers asserted in the first years of the George W. Bush administration and that occurred in close proximity to where Davis penned his *Milligan* opinion. That case began in December 2001 when FBI agents arrested Ali Saleh Kahlah al-Marri at his home in Peoria, Illinois. The government suspected that al-Marri, who had traveled to the United States from Qatar on a student visa on September 10, 2001, was an al-Qaeda sleeper agent who was plotting terrorist acts against the United States. As explained below, al-Marri's case, with its questioning of traditional assumptions about the nature of the battlefield during wartime and its direct military incursion on civilian criminal process, provides a clear illustration of *Milligan* in modern dress.

After detaining al-Marri as a material witness in the 9/11 investigation, federal officials charged him with credit card fraud and making false statements to the FBI. In June 2003, just weeks before his scheduled trial on those charges, and on the eve of a hearing on al-Marri's motion to suppress the evidence against him as the fruit of an unlawful search, President Bush issued a one-page order declaring al-Marri an "enemy combatant" and directing his transfer to military custody.[25] The Defense Department took custody of al-Marri and held him in a naval brig in Charleston, South Carolina, for the next five-and-one-half years, without charge and often in extremely harsh conditions of confinement. For the first sixteen months of his military detention, al-Marri was held *incommunicado* and denied all access to the courts. During that time, the government subjected al-Marri to highly coercive interrogation methods, including prolonged isolation and extreme sensory deprivation.[26] Al-Marri was the second—and, at time of writing, remains the last—person arrested in the United States to be declared an enemy combatant and held in military custody. The first person treated in this manner, Jose Padilla, a US citizen arrested by the FBI at Chicago's O'Hare International Airport in May 2002, was detained by the military as an enemy combatant based on an order by the president. The United States held Padilla as an enemy combatant in the Charleston naval brig until November 2005, when it charged him with federal crimes and sought his transfer to civilian custody to face criminal prosecution, while Padilla's challenge to his military detention was pending in the US Supreme Court.[27] The Court ultimately dismissed Padilla's challenge as moot,[28] and Padilla was prosecuted and convicted in federal court on terrorism-related charges.[29]

Like Padilla, al-Marri challenged the lawfulness of his military detention by habeas corpus.[30] This legal challenge lasted for more than five years, ending only after the US government returned al-Marri to civilian custody to face criminal charges after the Supreme Court had agreed to hear his case.

The *al-Marri* case produced the most extensive discussions of *Milligan* in judicial opinions in the post-9/11 era, as judges grappled with *Milligan*'s meaning and relevance to the threats the country faces in an age of global terrorism. While the case involved indefinite military detention rather than military prosecution, *al-Marri* squarely raised questions about *Milligan*'s application to the War on Terrorism. Most fundamentally, *al-Marri* raised the question whether the president could, by declaring an individual a member of an enemy terrorist organization during wartime, subject him to military custody, thus depriving him of the constitutional right to a trial in civilian court, *even if* he was not a member of an enemy state's armed forces, had never taken up arms on a battlefield, and was arrested in the United States. While the government did not charge al-Marri before a military commission, if it could detain al-Marri militarily as an enemy combatant, it could also presumably subject him to trial before a properly constituted military commission for war crimes.

Although al-Marri was not a US citizen, the United States had claimed the same detention power with respect to US citizens in *Padilla,* and the same constitutional protections asserted in opposition to this detention power—including those contained in the Fifth and Sixth Amendments to the Constitution—applied to all persons within the United States. Further, the Supreme Court had clarified not only in *Quirin* but also more recently in *Hamdi v. Rumsfeld*[31] that US citizenship itself does not preclude the assertion of military jurisdiction over enemy combatants. Thus, if al-Marri could be held by the military as an enemy combatant based on his suspected involvement with al-Qaeda or associated terrorist organizations, so too could US citizens arrested in the United States. Indeed, *al-Marri* presented a starker test of *Milligan*'s durability than *Padilla* because the government did not allege that al-Marri was ever on a battlefield during wartime, let alone that he took up arms there. By contrast, the government alleged that Padilla had fought alongside enemy forces against the United States in Afghanistan during the war there before coming to the United States to engage in acts of terrorism on behalf of al-Qaeda.[32]

Al-Marri's primary contention was that Congress had not authorized the president to engage in the military detention of individuals in the United States when it enacted the 2001 Authorization for Use of Military Force (AUMF),[33] which authorizes the use of military force against the nations, persons, or organizations responsible for the 9/11 attacks. The legality of al-Marri's military detention turned in good part on whether *Milligan* or *Quirin* controlled. These cases not only provided the backdrop for judicial interpretations of the AUMF's scope but also bore directly on al-Marri's alternative claim that Congress could not, consistent with the Constitution, authorize the indefinite military detention of suspected terrorists arrested in the United States when the federal courts were open and functioning, absent a valid suspension of habeas corpus.

From the US government's perspective, *al-Marri* represented a straightforward application of *Quirin* to the War on Terrorism. In 1942 the enemy was Germany; today, the United States argued, the enemy is al-Qaeda and associated terrorist groups. Like the German saboteurs in *Quirin*, al-Marri had entered the United States in civilian dress (albeit lawfully under a valid nonimmigrant student visa), with the intention of committing hostile and war-like acts. It made no difference, the government argued, that al-Marri was not captured on a battlefield or that the federal courts remained open and available to prosecute him under federal criminal statutes. Al-Marri, the government insisted, could still be subjected to military custody, including to indefinite military detention and, presumably, to trial before a military commission for war crimes.

Al-Marri maintained that *Quirin* did not control because the Nazi saboteurs there were all members of the German army acting under the direction of the German government and, therefore, clearly had the status of combatants under international law. While the saboteurs accordingly had combatant immunity for legitimate acts of warfare, such as attacking US soldiers or military targets, they could nonetheless be prosecuted for acts punishable as violations of the law of war. In *Quirin*, the Court found that the saboteurs had committed a war crime under international law when they buried their uniforms and secretly crossed military lines to enter the United States while heavily armed.[34]

Al-Marri, however, was not a member of or affiliated with any state's armed forces. He therefore retained the status of a civilian under international law, a critical point for the constitutional analysis under *Milligan*. (Like Milligan, but unlike the saboteurs in *Quirin*, al-Marri would in today's parlance be deemed an unprivileged belligerent.) As a civilian captured outside the battlefield and where the courts were open and functioning, al-Marri could not be subjected to military authority. He could neither be tried in a military commission nor be detained indefinitely without charge absent a valid suspension of habeas corpus (and there was no claim the writ had been suspended).

Lower court judges reached conflicting resolutions to these competing arguments based, in good part, on their different understandings of *Milligan.* A divided panel of the US Court of Appeals for the Fourth Circuit initially invalidated al-Marri's continued military detention, ruling that he had to be charged with an offense in civilian court or released. As Judge Diana Gribbon Motz of the US Court of Appeals for the Fourth Circuit explained, *Milligan* continues to stand for the proposition that even those individuals who commit "enormous crimes" during wartime on behalf of "secret" enemy organizations bent on overthrowing the government must, under the Constitution, be tried in a civilian court, as long as those courts are open and functioning. *Quirin,* she said, represents a narrow exception to this constitutional rule, permitting the exercise of military jurisdiction over individuals in the United States only in the case of combatants, defined by tradition and international law as members of an enemy government's armed forces.[35]

But the full Fourth Circuit, which reheard the case en banc, disagreed. It held in a closely divided opinion that al-Marri could be subject to indefinite military detention based on the government's allegations that he came to the United States to engage in terrorist activities on behalf of al-Qaeda, an organization with which the United States is at war. (The Fourth Circuit also concluded that al-Marri must receive adequate procedural due process to challenge those allegations, which, it said, he had not been afforded.[36]) The separate opinions upholding the exercise of military jurisdiction over alleged enemy combatants agreed that *Quirin,* not *Milligan,* controlled. *Quirin,* these judges said, permitted the exercise of military jurisdiction over alleged members of an enemy force even if they are arrested in the United States, even if they never took up arms on a battlefield, and even if the civilian courts are available. These judges rejected any distinction for purposes of the constitutional analysis between membership in a terrorist organization like al-Qaeda and the military arm of an enemy government like Germany during World War II.[37]

In December 2008 the US Supreme Court granted certiorari and agreed to hear al-Marri's case.[38] The next month, President Barack Obama was inaugurated. Though Obama did not disavow the use of military detention against members of al Qaeda and affiliated groups, he promptly issued executive orders banning torture and other abusive interrogation practices[39] and directing the closure of the detention center at the US naval base in Guantanamo.[40] In February 2009, prior to the Supreme Court hearing al-Marri's case, the Obama administration returned al-Marri to civilian custody to face federal charges for providing material support for terrorism.[41] The Supreme Court subsequently vacated the lower court's judgment and remanded with instructions to dismiss the habeas case as moot.[42] Al-Marri would ultimately plead guilty to one count of providing material support for terrorism in exchange for a reduced sentence.[43] The United States returned al-Marri to Qatar upon completion of his federal sentence in January 2015.[44]

Al-Marri's case thus failed to resolve the critical question of whether the president may exercise military detention authority against members of al-Qaeda or associated terrorist groups arrested in the United States. Notably, the Bush administration—likely in recognition of the controversial nature of this practice—did not place another terrorism suspect arrested in the United States in military custody after designating al-Marri an enemy combatant in June 2003. And while the Obama administration did not deny that it had legal authority to exercise such exceptional detention power, it said that placing individuals seized in the United States in military custody contradicted America's values and traditions and refused to engage in the practice. "Our military does not patrol our streets or enforce our laws—nor should it," remarked former CIA director John O. Brennan.[45] The US government has, to date, prosecuted all domestic terrorism suspects since al-Marri in federal court.

Yet, virtually each time an act of terrorism is attempted or committed in the United States—from the failed car bombing in New York City's Times Square to the deadly marathon bombing in Boston—conservative politicians and pundits renew their calls for labeling the suspects "enemy combatants" and subjecting them to military custody rather than prosecuting them in civilian court.[46] They claim—falsely—that prosecuting terrorism suspects in federal court weakens the country's security by affording suspects constitutional rights. The election of Donald Trump, who has endorsed sending new terrorism suspects, including US citizens, to Guantanamo, has sparked concerns about the revived use of military measures against terrorism suspects, although to date these concerns have not been realized.[47] In sum, while *Milligan* continues to provide a powerful counterweight against domestic military detention and prosecution, it remains vulnerable to broad assertions of executive war powers.

Milligan has also had an important impact on military commissions, the tribunals established by President Bush at Guantanamo. In November 2001, President Bush issued an executive order creating military commissions to try suspected terrorists of war crimes.[48] A primary purpose of the order was to evade the constitutional protections provided to defendants in the federal criminal justice system as well as those fair-trial protections afforded to defendants in courts-martial, whose procedures were deemed inapplicable to military commissions. The United States has detained more than 780 prisoners at Guantanamo since January 2002, and it has attempted to prosecute a small number of those prisoners in military commissions. These military detentions and prosecutions have prompted numerous legal challenges and led to landmark decisions on the scope of presidential war powers and the guarantees of habeas corpus.[49]

In 2006, in *Hamdan v. Rumsfeld*,[50] the Supreme Court invalidated the commissions initially established under Bush's November 2001 order, concluding that they exceeded congressional authority and violated the international law limitations that Congress had placed on military commissions—namely, the requirement under Common Article 3 of the 1949 Geneva Conventions that prisoners be tried only by "a regularly constituted court, affording all the judicial guarantees which are recognized as indispensible by civilized peoples."[51] The *Hamdan* Court found support for its decision in *Milligan*, which it labeled "the seminal case," although the Court relied more on Chase's reasoning in *Milligan* than Davis's. The Court did not categorically bar military commissions under the Constitution when the civilian courts were open and functioning, as they had been throughout the post-9/11 period. Rather, it ruled that Congress had failed to provide the requisite authorization for military commissions. Such authorization, the Court said, is necessary to satisfy separation-of-powers requirements, at least absent evidence of what Chief Justice Chase described in *Milligan* as "a controlling necessity."[52]

In the Military Commissions Act of 2006 (2006 MCA),[53] enacted four months after *Hamdan*, Congress supplied the legislative authorization the Supreme Court had said was lacking. Congress codified a list of crimes triable by military commission and provided procedures for conducting such trials. Some of those crimes, such as intentionally attacking civilians, are recognized as war crimes under international law, but others, such as conspiracy and material support for terrorism (MST), are not.[54]

Passage of the 2006 MCA revived military commissions, but their flaws remained manifest, including their continued use of coerced evidence. Obama's election in 2008 raised hopes that he would end this experiment based on his critiques of military commissions during the campaign and his promise to close the detention center at Guantanamo.[55] Obama, however, instead sought to salvage the commissions by reforming them. At the administration's urging, Congress enacted the Military Commissions Act of 2009 (2009 MCA).[56] The 2009 MCA strengthened the commissions' procedures, including by tightening restrictions on the use of hearsay and prohibiting evidence gained by torture and other abuse. But it maintained the same list of offenses triable by military commission, including offenses such as conspiracy and MST that are not punishable as war crimes under international law and that have historically been prosecuted in federal court.[57] Indeed, MST remains by far the most commonly prosecuted terrorism-related offense in federal court because it allows for "preventive" prosecutions based on various types of support given by an individual to a terrorist organization and does not require the commission of a terrorist act.[58] The continued inclusion of these offenses within military commission jurisdiction threatens to entrench commissions as an alternative forum for counterterrorism prosecutions—one more favorable to the government and less protective of the fair-trial rights of defendants. Further, the MCA applies exclusively to noncitizens, thus raising serious questions based on constitutional guarantees of equal protection of the law.[59]

The Supreme Court has not addressed the legality of military commissions since its 2006 decision in *Hamdan*. However, the US Court of Appeals for the DC Circuit has issued multiple decisions addressing statutory and constitutional challenges to the continued use of military commissions in the War on Terrorism.

In 2012, in *Hamdan v. United States* ("*Hamdan II*"),[60] the DC Circuit invalidated the defendant's military commission conviction for MST. *Hamdan II* involved the post-2006 military commission prosecution of Salim Hamdan, who had formerly served as Osama bin Laden's personal driver but whom the government had never connected to the 9/11 attacks or any other terrorism plot. Hamdan had already been returned to Yemen after completion of his sentence, but he sought to overturn his conviction. (The military commission had sentenced Hamdan to six years but given him credit for the five-and-a-half years he had previously spent in US custody at Guantanamo and at the Bagram Air Base in Afghanistan.[61]) The DC Circuit held that retroactively applying the 2006 MCA to prosecute Hamdan for pre-2006 conduct that did not constitute a war crime under international law would raise ex post facto concerns under the Constitution because, prior to 2006, Congress had authorized military commission jurisdiction only over offenses punishable by statute or by the international law of war.[62]

In 2014, in *United States v. Al Bahlul*,[63] the DC Circuit, sitting en banc, considered a similar ex post facto challenge brought by the defendant, Ali Hamza Ahmad Suliman Al Bahlul. In 2008 a military commission had convicted Al Bahlul of conspiracy for serving as an al-Qaeda propagandist and sentenced him to life imprisonment.[64] As in *Hamdan II*, the commission had never linked Al Bahlul to a specific terrorism plot or act. In a fractured opinion, the DC Circuit rejected Al Bahlul's ex post facto challenge. The precedential value of the court's ruling, however, was limited because it decided the case under a deferential "plain error" standard of review due to Al Bahlul's failure to raise his ex post facto challenge before the commission.[65]

In October 2016 the DC Circuit, again sitting en banc, addressed Al Bahlul's remaining legal challenges, including his claim that conspiracy does not constitute a war crime under international law and therefore must be prosecuted exclusively in federal court under Articles I and III of the Constitution.[66] This challenge required the court to confront the interplay between *Milligan* and *Quirin* in determining the constitutional limits on military jurisdiction. Several judges believed that *Milligan* limits military commission jurisdiction to situations where the civilian courts are unavailable and that *Quirin* provides only a narrow exception for offenses committed by enemy belligerents that are punishable as war crimes under international law. These judges concluded that conspiracy as a stand-alone offense—that is, conspiracy as an unlawful agreement, and not as a mode of liability in the commission of another substantive crime—does not meet this requirement, citing precedents of international criminal tribunals dating to Nuremberg.[67] They therefore would have precluded the exercise of military commission jurisdiction over conspiracy and other offenses that are not punishable under international law, at least absent a claim of controlling necessity.

But a narrow majority of the DC Circuit judges disagreed. They acknowledged that conspiracy is not a war crime punishable under international law but accepted the government's argument that commissions may also prosecute domestic war crimes. Specifically, the DC Circuit held that Congress could empower military commissions to prosecute conspiracy because US military commissions had historically prosecuted this offense. The court thus refused to confine *Quirin*—and its carve-out for law-of-war commissions from *Milligan*'s default rule of civilian court prosecution—to offenses punishable under international law. While the court did not decide whether Congress could authorize military jurisdiction more broadly over crimes not historically prosecuted by military commissions, such as cyberattacks by enemy forces, it did not foreclose more expansive use of military commissions to include such offenses.[68] In October 2017 the US Supreme Court denied Al Bahlul's petition for certiorari challenging the DC Circuit's ruling.

In total, federal courts have convicted more than five hundred individuals on terrorism-related charges since 9/11. Federal court prosecutions, moreover, afford defendants the full protections of the Constitution and are widely regarded as effective, lawful, and legitimate. By contrast, military commissions have still failed to produce accountability or justice by any metric, despite the passage of more than fifteen years since President Bush's November 2001 executive order creating them and after repeated attempts at reform. Military commissions have convicted only eight individuals; three of those convictions have been overturned completely and one overturned partially.[69] Further, the most important terrorism case in US history—that of alleged 9/11 mastermind Khalid Sheikh Mohammed (KSM) and his co-conspirators—continues to languish in pretrial proceedings before a military commission at Guantanamo. It is virtually certain that had KSM and his co-conspirators been prosecuted in federal court—as the Obama administration attempted to do in 2009 before abandoning the plan in the face of a political backlash[70]—they would have been tried, convicted, and sentenced years ago.

Milligan continues to be important to the unfolding story of military commissions in the War on Terrorism, but its full impact still remains to be determined. The broadest reading of *Milligan* based on Justice Davis's opinion—that military tribunals cannot be used when federal courts are open and functioning—no longer holds sway. Yet, *Milligan* continues to have bite in limiting the sweep of military commission jurisdiction. In particular, it provides support for cabining this jurisdiction to offenses that constitute punishable crimes under international law, as was the case in *Quirin,* but as is not the case in *Al Bahlul* and several other military commission prosecutions of Guantanamo detainees. *Milligan,* and Chief Justice Chase's concurring opinion in particular, also reinforces the need for Congress to authorize clearly any assertion of military jurisdiction, even where permitted under the Constitution, based on separation-of-powers principles.

Milligan's most enduring legacy, however, lies less in its formal status as legal precedent than in its reflection of a long and deeply rooted tradition of prioritizing civilian courts over military tribunals. The War on Terrorism broke sharply with that tradition, with deleterious consequences. It opened the door to torture and other abuses, undermined the nation's reputation, and weakened the government's ability to fight terrorism. If the War on Terrorism showed this tradition's vulnerability, it also underscored its resilience and wisdom. Put simply, the United States would have been in a much better place now—both from the standpoint of its security and its fidelity to constitutional principles—had it heeded Judge Davis's advice and avoided this ill-fated experimentation with jerry-rigged military justice.

Justice Davis's words thus ring as true today as they did when he penned them 150 years ago: "The Constitution of the United States is a law for rulers and people, equally in war and in peace, and covers with the shield of its protection all classes of men, at all times and under all circumstances. No doctrine involving more pernicious consequences was ever invented by the wit of man than that any of its provisions can be suspended during any of the great exigencies of government."

Those words not only underscore the imperative of protecting constitutional rights under leaders who openly assail them, whether that be President Bush after 9/11 or President Trump today. They also suggest why it is critical to maintain constitutional boundaries even under leaders more sensitive to constitutional norms, whether that be President Lincoln during the Civil War or President Obama, who modified but nevertheless defended and continued using military commissions during his administration despite their clear flaws. Absent such boundaries, to paraphrase another Supreme Court justice's warning nearly a century after *Milligan,* the availability of military tribunals will "lie about like a loaded weapon ready for the hand of any authority that can bring forward a claim of urgent need."[71]

NOTES

1. *An Act Relating to Habeas Corpus, and Regulating Judicial Proceedings in Certain Cases,* act of March 3, 1863, in 12 Stat. 755.

2. *Ex parte Milligan,* 71 US (4 Wall.) at 121–122.

3. Although the first section of the act empowered the president to suspend the writ anywhere in the country, the second and third sections limited that authority for non-prisoner-of-war detainees held in states where the federal courts continued to operate, and provided that such detainees should be discharged if a grand jury did not indict them in a timely fashion. See Habeas Corpus Act of 1863. Since Milligan had been arrested in Indiana (where the federal courts remained open) and a grand jury had failed to indict him, the Court concluded that the writ had not been suspended as to him. *Ex parte Milligan,* 71 US (4 Wall.) at 108, 115–116.

4. *Ex parte Milligan,* 71 US (4 Wall.) at 133–136 (Chase, C. J., concurring).

5. *Ex parte Quirin,* 317 US 1 (1942).

6. While the United States disputed that one of the saboteurs (Herbert Hans Haupt) was a US citizen, the Court found it unnecessary to resolve that issue and treated him as a US citizen for purposes of its decision. *Ex parte Milligan,* at 20.

7. *Ex parte Milligan,* at 21–22.

8. David J. Danelski, "The Saboteurs' Case," *Journal of Supreme Court History* 21 (July 1996): 61, 64–65.

9. Appointment of Military Commission, 7 Fed. Reg. 5103 (July 7, 1942); Danelski, "Saboteurs' Case," 67–68, 71.

10. Louis Fisher, *Nazi Saboteurs on Trial: A Military Tribunal and American Law* (Lawrence: University Press of Kansas, 2003), 47–48.

11. Danelski, "Saboteurs' Case," 65–66.

12. Fisher, *Nazi Saboteurs on Trial,* 46, 54.

13. *Ex parte Quirin,* at 18–19.

14. Danelski, "Saboteurs' Case," 71.

15. *Ex parte Quirin,* at 1, 5–6.

16. Danelski, "Saboteurs' Case," 71; Pierce O'Donnell, *In Time of War: Hitler's Terrorist Attack on America* (New York: New Press, 2005), 248–249.

17. Michal R. Belknap, "Frankfurter and the Nazi Saboteurs," *Supreme Court Historical Society Year Book* (1982): 66, 68.

18. *Ex parte Quirin,* at 45–46.

19. *Hamdi v. Rumsfeld,* 542 US 507, 569 (2004) (Scalia, J. dissenting).

20. *Hamdan v. Rumsfeld,* 548 US 557, 597 (2006) (Stevens, J., concurring).

21. *Reid v. Covert,* 354 US 1, 30 (1957).

22. Stephen I. Vladeck, "Military Courts and Article III," *Georgetown Law Journal* 100 (2015): 933, 957–958.

23. *In re Yamashita,* 327 US 1 (1946).

24. *Johnson v. Eisentrager,* 339 US 763 (1950).

25. Memorandum, the White House to the Secretary of Defense and the At-

torney General, June 23, 2003, http://news.findlaw.com/cnn/docs/almarri/almarri62303exord.pdf.

26. Jane Mayer, "The Hard Cases: Will Obama Institute a New Kind of Preventive Detention for Terrorism Suspects," *New Yorker*, February 23, 2009, http://www.newyorker.com/magazine/2009/02/23/the-hard-cases.

27. Linda Greenhouse, "Justices Let US Transfer Padilla to Civilian Custody," *New York Times*, January 5, 2006.

28. *Padilla v. Hanft*, 547 US 1062 (2006).

29. Peter Whoriskey, "Jury Convicts Jose Padilla of Terror Charges," *Washington Post*, August 17, 2007.

30. I served as al-Marri's lead counsel in his habeas corpus challenge to his military detention.

31. *Hamdi v. Rumsfeld*, 542 US at 519.

32. *Padilla v. Hanft*, 423 F.3d 386, 389–390, 391–392 (4th Cir. 2005).

33. Pub. L. No. 107–40, 115 Stat. 224 (2001).

34. *Ex parte Quirin*, 317 US at 21–22, 30–31 and n7.

35. *Al-Marri v. Wright*, 487 F.3d 160, 182–183, 186–187 (4th Cir. 2007).

36. *Al-Marri v. Pucciarelli*, 534 F.3d 213, 216 (4th Cir. 2008) (en banc).

37. *Al-Marri v. Pucciarelli*, 259–261 (Traxler, J., concurring in the judgment), 309 (Wilkinson, J., concurring in part, dissenting in part).

38. *Al-Marri v. Pucciarelli*, 555 US 1066 (2008).

39. Executive Order No. 13,491, 74 Fed. Reg. 4893 (January 27, 2009).

40. Executive Order No. 13,492, 74 Fed. Reg. 4897 (January 27, 2009).

41. Carrie Johnson, "Terrorism Suspect Headed to US Court," *Washington Post*, February 28, 2009.

42. *Al-Marri v. Spagone*, 555 US 1220 (2009).

43. John Schwartz, "Plea Deal Reached with Agent for Al-Qaeda," *New York Times*, April 30, 2009.

44. Andy Kravetz, "Former West Peoria Enemy Combatant Ali al-Marri Released from Prison Early, Deported from US," *Peoria Journal Star*, January 17, 2015.

45. The White House, Office of the Press Secretary, Remarks of John O. Brennan, "Strengthening Our Security by Adhering to Our Values and Laws," September 16, 2011, https://obamawhitehouse.archives.gov.

46. Opinion, "Should the Boston Bombing Suspect Be Tried as an Enemy Combatant?" *US News & World Report*, April 2, 2013, https://www.usnews.com; Peter Baker, "A Renewed Debate Over Suspect Rights," *New York Times*, May 4, 2010, http://www.nytimes.com/2010/05/05/nyregion/05arrest.html.

47. Laura Jarrett, "Can Trump Send American Citizens to Guantanamo Bay," CNN.com, December 3, 2016, http://www.cnn.com/2016/12/03/politics/trump-guantanamo-bay/.

48. Military Order of November 13, 2001, Detention, Treatment and Trial of Certain Non-Citizens in the War against Terrorism, 66 Fed. Reg. 57,833 (November 16, 2001).

49. For Supreme Court decisions addressing the indefinite military detention of enemy combatants, see *Boumediene v. Bush*, 553 US 723 (2008), and *Rasul v. Bush*, 542 US 466 (2004).

50. *Hamdan v. Rumsfeld*, 548 US 557 (2006).

51. Convention for the Amelioration of the Condition of the Wounded and Sick in Armed Forces in the Field, Article 3, August 12, 1949, 6 UST 3114, 75 UNTS 31; Convention for the Amelioration of the Condition of the Wounded, Sick, and Shipwrecked Members of Armed Forces at Sea, Article 3, August 12, 1949, 6 UST 3217, 75 UNTS 85; Convention Relative to the Treatment of Prisoners of War, Article 3, August 12, 1949, 6 UST 3316, 75 UNTS 135; Convention Relative to the Protection of Civilian Persons in Time of War, Article 3, August 12, 1949, 6 UST 3516, 75 UNTS 287 ("Common Article 3").

52. *Hamdan v. Rumsfeld*, 548 US at 591–593, 611–613; at 636 (Breyer, J., concurring). The original quotation of Chase comes from *Ex parte Milligan*, at 139–140.

53. Military Commissions Act of 2006, Pub. L. No. 109–366, 120 Stat. 2600.

54. David Glazier, "Destined for an Epic Fail: The Problematic Guantanamo Military Commissions," *Ohio State Law Journal* 75 (2014): 903, 950–951.

55. Gary A. Isaac, "The Wrong Person: How Barack Obama Abandoned Habeas Corpus," in Jonathan Hafetz, ed., *Obama's Guantánamo: Stories from an Enduring Prison* (New York: NYU Press, 2016), 27.

56. Military Commissions Act of 2009, Pub. L. No. 111–184, ch. 47A, sec. 1802, 123 Stat. 2574 (codified at 10 USC ch. 47A [2012]).

57. Jonathan Hafetz, "Policing the Line: International Law, Article III, and the Constitutional Limits of Military Jurisdiction," *Wisconsin Law Review* (2014): 681, 700.

58. 18 USC § 2339A, § 2339B; Faiza Patel and Adrienne Tierney, "The Reasons Why Dylann Roof Wasn't Charged with Terrorism," *Just Security*, July 30, 2015, https://www.justsecurity.org.

59. Neal Katyal, "Equality in the War on Terror," *Stanford Law Review* 59 (2007): 1365, 1379–1381.

60. *Hamdan v. United States*, 696 F.3d 1238 (DC Cir. 2012) ("*Hamdan II*").

61. William Glaberson, "Bin Laden Driver Sentenced to Short Term," *New York Times*, August 7, 2008.

62. *Hamdan II*, 696 F.3d, at 1248–1253.

63. *Al Bahlul v. United States*, 767 F.3d 1 (DC Cir. 2014) (en banc) ("*Al Bahlul I*").

64. Press Release, US Department of Defense, Detainee Sentenced to Life in Prison, November 3, 2008, http://www.defense.gov/releases/release.aspx?releaseid=12331.

65. *Al Bahlul I*, 767 F.3d, at 8–11.

66. *Al Bahlul v. United States*, 840 F.3d 757 (DC Cir. 2016) (en banc) ("*Al Bahlul II*").

67. *Al Bahlul II*, 840 F.3d, at 812–816 (Rogers, J., dissenting).

68. *Al Bahlul II*, 758, 763–764, 770–771.

69. Human Rights First, "Myth v. Fact: Trying Terror Suspects in Federal Court,"

February 2018), http://www.humanrightsfirst.org/resource/myth-v-fact-trying-terror-suspects-federal-courts.

70. Charlie Savage, "In Reversal, Military Trials for 9/11 Cases," *New York Times*, April 4, 2011.

71. *Korematsu v. United States*, 323 US 214, 246 (1944) (Jackson, J., dissenting).

Contributors

Michael Les Benedict is professor of history emeritus at Ohio State University and visiting scholar at the Ohio State University Moritz College of Law. He is an authority on Anglo-American constitutional and legal history, the history of civil rights and liberties, the federal system, and the Civil War and Reconstruction. His books *The Impeachment and Trial of Andrew Johnson* (1973) and *A Compromise of Principle: Congressional Republicans and Reconstruction, 1863–1869* (1975) have long been standard reading for students of the Civil War and Reconstruction. He published a collection of essays as *Preserving the Constitution: Essays on Politics and the Constitution in the Reconstruction Era* (2006) and is the author of the American constitutional history textbook *The Blessings of Liberty* (3d ed., 2016) and a companion, *Sources in American Constitutional History* (2nd ed., 2017). He prepared the American Historical Association's bicentennial essay on the history of American civil liberty, *Civil Rights and Civil Liberties* (1987), and coedited *The History of Ohio Law* (2004). Benedict has published more than fifty essays on American constitutional history and the history of Reconstruction in leading American history and law journals, as well as in books of essays. He is currently writing a book on Salmon P. Chase and constitutional politics during the Civil War era.

Laura F. Edwards is the Peabody Family Professor of History at Duke University. She has published four books: *A Legal History of the Civil War and Reconstruction: A Nation of Rights* (2015), *The People and Their Peace: Legal Culture and the Transformation of Inequality in the Post-Revolutionary South* (2009), *Scarlett Doesn't Live Here Anymore: Southern Women in the Civil War Era* (2000), and *Gendered Strife and Confusion: The Political Culture of Reconstruction* (1997). *The People and Their Peace* won the Charles Sydnor Prize for the best book on Southern history by the Southern Historical Association and the Littleton-Griswold Prize for the best book on American law and society by the American Historical Association. She is currently working on a new book project, *Only the Clothes on Her Back: Textiles, Law, and Commerce in the Nineteenth-Century United States.*

A. James Fuller is professor of history at the University of Indianapolis. An award-winning teacher and scholar, he is primarily a biographer with a focus on the Civil War era and American political history. His recent work has contributed to a revival of midwestern history, as he has written about the origins of the midwestern regional identity and has offered interpretations of political leadership in the development of that identity. Among Fuller's many publications are six books, including *Chaplain to the Confederacy: Basil Manly and Baptist Life in the Old South* (2000), *The Election of 1860 Reconsidered* (2013), and *Oliver P. Morton and the Politics of the Civil War and Reconstruction* (2017). His current projects are a biography of Richard Yates, the Civil War governor and Reconstruction senator of Illinois; a book entitled *Morton, Marshall, McNutt, and Mitch: Four Governors Who Shaped Indiana and the Midwest;* and *Man-Devil in the Midwest,* a coauthored study of a midwestern serial killer in the 1870s.

Jonathan Hafetz is professor of law at Seton Hall University School of Law. He is the author of the award-winning book *Habeas Corpus after 9/11: Confronting America's New Global Detention System* (2011), *Punishing Atrocities through a Fair Trial: International Criminal Law from Nuremberg to the Age of Global Terrorism* (2018), and numerous scholarly articles on constitutional law, federal courts, and international human rights. Prior to joining Seton Hall, Hafetz was a senior attorney at the American Civil Liberties Union and at NYU's Brennan Center for Justice; he has litigated numerous constitutional law cases throughout the federal courts, including *Al-Marri v. Spagone,* 555 US 1220 (2009), *Boumediene v. Bush,* 553 US 723 (2008), *Munaf v. Geren,* 553 US 674 (2008), *Rasul v. Rumsfeld,* 542 US 466 (2004), *Doe v. Mattis* (DC Cir. 2018), *Meshal v. Higgenbotham,* 804 F.3d 417 (DC Cir. 2015), *Salahi v. Obama,* 625 F.3d 740 (DC Cir. 2010), and *Jawad v. Obama* (DDC 2009). He has authored or coauthored more than thirty amicus curiae briefs for the US Supreme Court and federal courts of appeals.

Michael Haggerty is a PhD candidate in the Department of History at the University of California, Davis. He received his BA in history from the College of Wooster and his MA in American history from Miami University (Ohio). He has been the recipient of numerous fellowships, including the Russell J. and Dorothy S. Bilinski Educational Foundation Dissertation Writing Fellowship at the University of California, Davis, and the Leo J.

Hershkowitz Fellowship at the New York Historical Society. His current research examines urban incarceration and the politics of slavery in antebellum New York.

Brian Matthew Jordan is an assistant professor of history at Sam Houston State University and the author of *Marching Home: Union Veterans and Their Unending Civil War* (2015), a finalist for the 2016 Pulitzer Prize in History. He received his MA, MPhil, and PhD in history from Yale University, where his dissertation earned the George Washington Egleston Prize (for best US history dissertation at Yale) and the John Addison Porter Prize, one of Yale's highest honors. He is at work on a life of Benjamin Butler, and his coedited volume, *The War Went On: Reconsidering the Lives of Civil War Veterns*, is forthcoming with Louisiana State University Press.

John A. Lupton is executive director of the Illinois Supreme Court Historic Preservation Commission. He has been with the commission since 2009. From 1991 to 2009 he worked with the Papers of Abraham Lincoln to make Lincoln's legal papers available to the public in two separate award-winning publications: *The Law Practice of Abraham Lincoln: Complete Documentary Edition* and *The Papers of Abraham Lincoln: Legal Documents and Cases.* Lupton received his BA in history from Southern Illinois University Carbondale and MA in history from the University of Illinois Springfield. He has written numerous articles and chapters on Lincoln's law practice and Illinois legal history and is editor of *Prairie Justice: A History of Illinois Courts under French, English, and American Law* (2015) and *Adjudicating Illinois: Justices of the Illinois Supreme Court* (2018).

Christopher Phillips is the John and Dorothy Hermanies Professor of American History and University Distinguished Professor in the Arts, Humanities, and Social Sciences at the University of Cincinnati. He is the author or editor of seven books, most recently *The Rivers Ran Backward: The Civil War and the Remaking of the American Middle Border* (2016), which received a number of awards and recognitions, including the 2017 Tom Watson Brown Prize for the best published book on the Civil War from the Society of Civil War Historians; the 2018 Distinguished Book Award from the Society of Military Historians; the 2017 Jon Gjerde Book Prize, the Midwestern History Association's top award given for a book on midwestern regional history; the 2017 Distinguished Book Award by the Ohio Academy of History; and the 2017 Missouri History Book Award from the State Historical Society of Missouri. It was named a "best book" of 2016 by *Civil War Monitor*, a Choice Outstanding Academic Title for 2017, and was a finalist for the 2017 Ohioana Book Award for Non-Fiction.

Mark S. Schantz is professor of history at Birmingham-Southern College and the author of *Piety in Providence: Class Dimensions of Religious Experience in Antebellum Rhode Island* (2000) and *Awaiting the Heavenly Country: The Civil War and America's Culture of Death* (2008). He appeared as a consultant and on-screen in the Ric Burns documentary for the PBS American Experience series *Death and the Civil War* (2012). More recently he contributed an essay, "Death and the Gettysburg Address," for Sean Conant, ed., *The Gettysburg Address: Perspectives on Lincoln's Greatest Speech* (2015). He is currently working on a book manuscript on the murder of Lt. Alanson L. Sanborn by Dr. David M. Wright in Norfolk, Virginia, on July 11, 1863.

Stephen E. Towne is university archivist at Indiana University–Purdue University Indianapolis. He is the author or editor of several books, including *Surveillance and Spies in the Civil War: Exposing Confederate Conspiracies in America's Heartland* (2015). He is also author of the award-winning article "The Persistent Nullifier: The Life of Civil War Conspirator Lambdin P. Milligan" (2013).

Jonathan W. White is associate professor of American studies at Christopher Newport University and is the author or editor of ten books, including *Abraham Lincoln and Treason in the Civil War: The Trials of John Merryman* (2011) and *Emancipation, the Union Army, and the Reelection of Abraham Lincoln* (2014), which was a finalist for both the Lincoln Prize and Jefferson Davis Prize, a "best book" in *Civil War Monitor*, and the winner of the Abraham Lincoln Institute's 2015 book prize. He has published more than one hundred articles, essays, and reviews and is the winner of the 2005 John T. Hubbell Prize for the best article in *Civil War History*, the 2010 Hay-Nicolay Dissertation Prize, and the 2012 Thomas Jefferson Prize for his *Guide to Research in Federal Judicial History* (2010). He is chairman of the board of the Abraham Lincoln Institute, vice chair of the Lincoln Forum, and serves on the boards of the Abraham Lincoln Association and the John

L. Nau III Center for Civil War History at the University of Virginia. He also serves on the Fords Theatre Advisory Council. Other recent books include *Midnight in America: Darkness, Sleep, and Dreams during the Civil War* (2017), which was selected as a "best book" by *Civil War Monitor* and *"Our Little* Monitor*": The Greatest Invention of the Civil War* (2018), which he coauthored with Anna Gibson Holloway. In 2019 he won the State Council of Higher Education in Virginia's Outstanding Faculty Award, the highest honor given to college professors by the Commonwealth of Virginia.

Stewart L. Winger is associate professor of history at Illinois State University, Normal. After earning his BA from the University of Chicago in 1985 and studying for two years at the Freie University in Berlin, he returned to Chicago for his MA (1993) and his PhD (1998) in history of culture, where he won the Hay-Nicolay Dissertation Prize. His first book, *Lincoln, Religion, and Romantic Cultural Politics* (2002), won the 2004 Barondess/Lincoln Prize. He has written articles and reviews on Abraham Lincoln, American religion, and American law and has received several teaching awards in the Department of History at Illinois State University. In 2013 Winger was the recipient of a National Endowment for the Humanities (NEH) Fellowship for research on Abraham Lincoln, public power, and the expansion of the market economy, 1835–1877. He is currently working on a book coming out of that project entitled *The Fostering Hand of Government: Lincoln and Internal Improvements.* He also serves on the board of directors of the Abraham Lincoln Association.

Index

Numbers in italics represent pages with figures.